ADMINISTRATION _
ORGANIZATION OF WAR IN
THIRTEENTH-CENTURY ENGLAND

The essays brought together in this volume examine the conduct of war by the Angevin kings of England during the long thirteenth century (1189–1307). Drawing upon a wide range of unpublished administrative records that have been largely ignored by previous scholarship, David S. Bachrach offers new insights into the military technology of the period, including the types of artillery and missile weapons produced by the royal government. The studies in this volume also highlight the administrative sophistication of the Angevin kings in military affairs, showing how they produced and maintained huge arsenals, mobilized vast quantities of supplies for their armies in the field, and provided for the pastoral care of their men. Bachrach also challenges the knight-centric focus of much of the scholarship on this period, demonstrating that the militarization of the English population penetrated to men in the lower social and economic strata, who volunteered in large numbers for military service, and even made careers as professional soldiers.

David S. Bachrach, Professor of Medieval History at the University of New Hampshire, USA, is a specialist in the military, administrative, and governmental history of the English and German kingdoms during the Middle Ages. He has published numerous articles and books, including *Warfare in Medieval Europe c. 400–c. 1453* (2016), *Warfare in Tenth-Century Germany* (2012), and *Religion and the Conduct of War c. 300–1215* (2003).

ADMINISTRATION AND ORGANIZATION OF WAR IN THIRTEENTH-CENTURY ENGLAND

David S. Bachrach

VARIORUM COLLECTED STUDIES

Routledge
Taylor & Francis Group

LONDON AND NEW YORK

First published 2020 by Routledge

2 Park Square, Milton Park, Abingdon, Oxon OX14 4RN
605 Third Avenue, New York, NY 10017

Routledge is an imprint of the Taylor & Francis Group, an informa business

First issued in paperback 2022

Publisher's Note

The publisher has gone to great lengths to ensure the quality of this reprint
but points out that some imperfections in the original copies may be apparent.

British Library Cataloguing-in-Publication Data
A catalogue record for this book is available from the British Library

Library of Congress Cataloging-in-Publication Data
A catalog record has been requested for this book

ISBN: 978-0-367-40761-2 (hbk)
ISBN: 978-1-03-233672-5 (pbk)
DOI: 10.4324/9780367808938

Typeset in *Times*
by Deanta Global Publishing Services, Chennai, India

VARIORUM COLLECTED STUDIES SERIES CS1088

THIS BOOK IS DEDICATED TO MICHAEL
PRESTWICH WITH GRATITUDE

CONTENTS

TABLES

PREFACE

This volume brings together sixteen essays published in the period 2003–2015 that are focused collectively on the conduct of war by the kings of England from the reign of Richard I (1189–1199) through that of his great-nephew Edward I (1272–1307). The studies are divided into three parts: (1) Military technology and engineering, (2) Military logistics, and (3) Military organization.

Three of the articles in the first part seek to resolve long-standing historiographical debates regarding the types of artillery and crossbows that were available in the thirteenth and early fourteenth century. These essays draw upon large numbers of administrative documents, including many unpublished texts, in contrast to the work of earlier scholars that depended almost exclusively on historical narratives and images drawn from manuscripts and stone reliefs. Whereas the authors and artists who produced these latter sources had little, if any, direct knowledge or understanding of military technology, the royal clerks and administrators who produced administrative documents were intimately involved in all aspects of weapons production. As a consequence, these administrative texts provide crucial insights regarding the nature of the military technologies that previously escaped the notice of scholars. The other two essays in Part 1, which similarly draw upon administrative documents, illuminate the careers of the men, who were employed by the royal government to produce artillery and crossbows. Both of these studies are prosopographical in nature, meaning that these provide a collective biography of the individual engineers and craftsmen. This collective approach makes it possible to extrapolate information about the members of the group as a whole that cannot be learned from the examination of just one individual.

The seven essays in the second part also draw largely on administrative documents to illuminate the breadth and sophistication of the logistical operations of the English royal government during the long thirteenth century. The first two essays in this part describe the auditing procedures put in place by the government to keep track of arms and equipment produced and purchased by the crown. These auditing procedures were intended both to prevent fraud and malfeasance, and to provide information to the king's planners so that they could prepare for military operations. The third essay focuses directly on the organization of transportation resources for the army to ensure that supplies would reach troops in the field. Concomitantly, the fourth essay examines the work of royal officials in the requisitioning of supplies for the army, and considers the impact of large-scale compulsory purchases of grain and animals on local markets. The fifth and sixth essays consider, in turn, the administrative systems developed by the royal government to undertake the large-scale production of crossbow quarrels and crossbows. The final essay in Part 2 offers an examination of the work of the royal clerk and administrator, Peter of Dunwich, whose career illuminates many aspects of the work done by Edward I's military bureaucrats. This study also highlights the need for further research to gain a clearer understanding of the background and careers of Peter's fellow administrators.

Part 3 is divided into two parts, which consider, in turn, the role of religion in the conduct of war, and the deployment of militia forces by the royal government for military campaigns. The first essay in this part examines the efforts made by Edward I to ensure that soldiers, both in the field and in garrisons, had access to pastoral care, with a particular emphasis on the employment of chaplains who spoke the language of the soldiers for whom they were responsible. The second essay considers Edward I's use of the English church to deliver royal propaganda throughout his realm, and to mobilize the entire population to participate in religious rites and ceremonies on behalf of the army in the field. The next essay in this part draws comparisons between the urban military forces, including both naval resources and land-based troops, which were available to the kings of England and of Germany from the mid thirteenth to the early fourteenth century. The final study in Part 3 focuses on the men, denoted in administrative documents as *centenarii*, who played a central role in the command structure of shire levies that operated in Wales and Scotland during the reign of Edward I, and eventually emerged as a cadre of professional officers.

All of the essays in this volume are revised, in many cases substantially. The footnotes in each study have been harmonized so that the format is consistent across the entire collection. I also have added additional citations, both to research that has appeared in the time since the original study was published, and to scholarly works that I missed in the first iteration. The individual essays in the collection also now have cross-references to each other in the notes.

The greater changes, however, appear in the text of the individual studies. Many of the earlier articles in this volume included a lengthy discussion of the sources that are available for the examination of the thirteenth and early fourteenth century. These in-text treatments of the sources have been removed in all but the first essay in the collection, and replaced with more streamlined references to sources in the notes. I also have edited all of the studies for stylistic purposes, largely to improve poorly worded or unclear passages.

More importantly, the content of the individual studies has been updated to take account of changes in my own views, and also to bring to bear the considerable additional information that I have uncovered in my research in the National Archives at Kew. For example, I am now convinced, based upon my own research and that by Thom Richardson and Michael Prestwich, that the *springaldus* was a two-armed, torsion, spear-casting engine, whereas in 2006, I was under the impression that this weapon was a type of tension-powered artillery. In addition, the examination of many hundreds of additional unpublished documents has allowed me to refine and also expand upon my conclusions regarding the production of military equipment by the royal government, as well as to gain a deeper understanding regarding elements of royal military organization. For example, in the period since the publication of my study of military religion during the reign of Edward I, I have been able to identify a significant number of chaplains who served in the military units that were recruited in Wales for service in Scotland. In a similar vein, I have been able to identify the service of military chaplains in a large number of fortifications maintained by the English in Scotland. Additional research also has allowed me to provide a more detailed discussion of the careers of individual *centenarii*.

The process of revising the essays in this volume for republication has been exceptionally rewarding. I did much of the research for the earliest of these studies while I was in graduate school at the University of Notre Dame in the late 1990s. Re-reading this work has given me an opportunity to experience again the original thrill of discovery, but now with the benefit of greater knowledge and perspective. In several of the earlier articles, I referred in the notes to studies that I intended to write. In some cases, I followed through, and those subsequent efforts appear in this volume. In other cases, however, I lost track of my original intentions and did not write a promised essay. In sum, after re-reading and revising these sixteen studies, the abiding conclusion for me is that although I have been able to contribute to the understanding of English military history in this period, much work remains to be done.

I offer my profound thanks to Michael Greenwood and the staff at Taylor & Francis for this opportunity. I also want to thank Michael Prestwich, whose pioneering work, particularly in the use of administrative documents, has been an essential guide for my examination of the military history of this period. But more importantly, Michael was exceptionally generous to me as a young scholar, offering invaluable help and insights, and still continues in this generous spirit to the present day. This volume, therefore, is dedicated to him.

David S. Bachrach

Part 1

MILITARY TECHNOLOGY AND ENGINEERING

1

THE ROYAL CROSSBOW MAKERS OF ENGLAND, 1204–1272

Spurred on, at least in part, by King Richard I's interest in crossbows during his reign (1189–1199), these weapons were quickly adopted as the dominant missile weapon used by English soldiers, particularly those serving in garrisons.[1] This period of dominance, which began in the late twelfth century, continued throughout most of the thirteenth. Indeed, crossbows continued to play an important role in the defense of royal fortresses even during the reign of King Edward I (1273–1307), who is credited by many scholars with having introduced the longbow into military use on a large scale.[2]

Richard's immediate successors, John and Henry III, directed considerable resources to ensuring the continued availability of crossbow men in their armies, not only employing numerous soldiers armed with these weapons but also lavishing exceptionally generous salaries and perquisites on the specialist craftsmen who were willing to take up positions in the royal service as crossbow makers. Indeed, these artisans were among the best paid and supported of all royal servants throughout the period 1204–1272. However, despite the exceptional

---

1 Concerning King Richard's appreciation of the military value of the crossbow, see Jim Bradbury, *The Medieval Archer* (New York, 1985), 76. Richard's contemporary, William the Breton, went so far as to claim that the English king actually introduced the weapon to France. On this point, see *Oeuvres de Rigord et de Guillaume le Breton*, 2 vols, ed. Henry-François Delaborde (Paris, 1885), II: 147, *Philippidos*, bk 5, lines 580–581, "*utique Francigenis baliste primitus usum tradidit*". King John similarly employed crossbowmen, particularly foreign mercenaries, within his own household. For example, an entry in the *missae* rolls for 9 December 1209 notes that wages were paid to eighteen mounted crossbowmen who had arrived from Poitou. *Rotuli* [*de Liberate ac de Misis et Praestitis regnante Johanne*], ed. T. D. Hardy (London, 1844), hereafter *Rotuli*, 142.

2 On the question of the supersession of the crossbow by the longbow, see John E. Morris, *The Welsh Wars of Edward I* (1901, repr. New York, 1969), 100; Bradbury, *Medieval Archer*, 76; Claude Gaier, "Quand l'arbalète était une nouveauté: reflections sur son rôle militaire du Xe au XIIe siècle", *Le moyen âge* 99 (1993), 201–229, here 228–229; and Michael Prestwich, *Armies and Warfare in the Middle Ages: The English Experience* (New Haven, 1996), 131. After the Welsh war of 1282–1284, King Edward I decided to establish a permanent military presence in Wales through the construction of a series of mutually supporting fortifications. The majority of the men garrisoned in these castles were crossbowmen. See National Archives C77/5.

importance accorded to crossbow makers by King John and Henry III, these men have received virtually no scholarly attention. This article, therefore, is intended to illuminate a glaring lacuna in both the administrative and military history of thirteenth-century England.

Sources

The great majority of the evidence available for the study of the royal office of crossbow maker can be found in the financial and administrative records of the royal government. The documents maintained in the great series of close rolls and liberate rolls deal with such matters as the employment, pay, supply, and transfer of royal agents and officials.[3] The liberate records receive their name from the command *liberate*, which means "pay" and appears at the beginning of the text immediately following the salutation.[4] These documents were issued by the Chancery to the treasurers and chamberlains of the Exchequer. It was normal administrative procedure that the latter were not permitted to disburse money from the treasury without the written permission of the king. The documents in the close rolls similarly were issued by the Chancery. However, rather than being characterized by the use of particular formulae, these records were grouped together because they had been sealed or closed when sent out. In terms of their content, the liberate rolls were largely a subset of the close rolls from the origin of the latter in 1204 until the two sets were permanently separated in 1226 during the tenth year of King Henry III's reign. During the first six years of John's reign (1199–1204), the liberate documents were maintained separately, and many of these documents have survived.[5]

A third set of Chancery documents were included in the patent rolls that, in contrast to the close rolls, were issued open or unsealed. In addition to dealing with many matters concerning high policy, these documents also include ordinary financial and administrative records and correspondence with important individuals and royal officials, such as the sheriffs and castle constables. The patent rolls survive for the entire reigns of John and Henry III. The records of the liberate, close, and patent rolls are supplemented in John's reign by the *missae* accounts which deal with the king's daily expenses as well as by the "*praestita* roll" which records the money advanced by the royal government to individuals, largely for the payment of military expenses. All of these government records overlap to

---

3   In addition to those discussed in note 1, the basic published works are *Rotuli Litterarum Clausarum in Turri Londonensi Asservati 1204–1227*, ed. T. D. Hardy, 2 vols (1833–1834) = *CR I* and *CR II* (1204–1227); *The Close Rolls 1227–1272* (London, 1892–1938) = *CR*; *The Calendar of Liberate Rolls 1226–1272* (London, 1916–1964) = *CLR*; and *The Calendar of Patent Rolls 1216–1272* (London, 1891– 1913) = *CPR*.

4   For a useful introduction to the development of the liberate rolls, see *Rotuli*, iii–xv.

5   These documents, along with the *missae* accounts for the eleventh year of John's reign and the *praestita* rolls for the twelfth year of John's reign, were published by Hardy in *Rotuli*.

a certain extent so that it is possible, for example, to find pay records for some crossbow makers within the close, liberate, and patent rolls. In addition to these records produced by royal clerks of the central administration, it is also possible to make use of the various pipe rolls which record the expenditures made by royal officers at the local level, particularly the sheriffs, on behalf of the government. By contrast, there is virtually no information in contemporary narrative sources concerning the office of the crossbow maker, or the artisans who held this office. In addition, I have found no references to crossbow makers or their office in contemporary legal records such as the *curia regis* rolls.[6]

Origins of the office

Despite King Richard's extensive deployment of soldiers armed with crossbows in his campaigns on the continent and in the eastern Mediterranean during the Third Crusade (1190–1192), there is no indication in the surviving sources that he established a domestic industry to produce these weapons. Similarly, surviving records from the early years of John's reign make no references to crossbow production in England. In fact, documents from John's government indicate that Italy, particularly Genoa, provided a substantial number of the crossbows used by English soldiers during the early thirteenth century, and one might draw the inference that this was the case during the late twelfth century as well. For example, on 30 January 1204, the treasurer of the Exchequer received orders to pay 4 marks to John of Genoa for the crossbows (*balistae*) that he had transported from Genoa to England.[7] The next year, on 25 June 1205, Peter of Genoa was authorized by the royal government to receive the money that he was owed for transporting 100 *balistae* from Northampton to London.[8] The Exchequer received orders on 18 January 1207 to pay another Genoese, named Benedict, 20 marks for the crossbows that had been purchased from him and further 40 marks as a gift from the king (*de dono nostro*).[9] This pattern of purchasing crossbows from Genoa also can be seen in Henry III's reign. On 22 February 1228, a merchant named Anselm of Genoa was authorized to receive 300 marks for the crossbows he had sold to the royal government.[10]

It would appear, however, that sometime during the early years of his reign, King John decided to establish a domestic source for crossbows that could supplement supplies from abroad. The first surviving evidence for the production of crossbows by royal servants in England comes from an order issued on 29 January 1204 to the constable of Windsor Castle instructing him to pay the wages of a man

---

6   *Curia Regis Rolls* (London, 1922–).
7   *Rotuli*, 78-79.
8   *CR I*, 39. The possibility that *balista* here refers to a catapult is obviated by the quantity involved.
9   Ibid., 76.
10   CLR (1226–1240), 71.

named Gerald for his work as a royal *balistarius* and to provide him with the gut and horn necessary for making crossbows (*ad balistas faciendas*).[11] It is notable that these materials were used in the construction of composite weapons, that is those in which the bow was made of layered levels of horn, glue, and wood. Consequently, it would appear not only that the origin of crossbow production in England should be dated to very early 1204 or perhaps the second half of 1203, but also that from the very beginning the craftsmen were producing the most complex types of weapons.

Nature of their work

Artisans employed by the royal government as crossbow makers received a variety of designations over the course of the thirteenth century that reflected the nature of the weapons that they produced. The first "official" terminology that royal clerks used to describe the men responsible for the production and repair of the king's crossbows was simply *balistarius*, which is the same word used for designating soldiers armed with crossbows. As noted in the preceding paragraph, the first surviving document to use this term was issued on 29 January 1204 on behalf of Gerald, called *balistarius*.[12] The initial impetus to describe the royal crossbow makers as *balistarii* may have come from the normal practice that the soldiers who were equipped with these weapons were called *balistarii* in contemporary Latin sources, including royal financial and administrative records.[13] Economy of language may well have suggested the expansion of the meaning of the term to include newly employed royal artisans. However, it may also be the case that some of the first men employed by the crown to build, and especially to repair crossbows, originally served among the ranks of the soldiers equipped with these weapons. In this latter circumstance, it would have seemed natural to the royal clerks to continue to designate the soldiers-turned-artisans with the traditional term.

There is some indication in the sources, however, that royal clerks found that the use of the term *balistarius* for both soldiers and crossbow makers had the potential to cause confusion. Several documents survive from late 1222 and early 1223 that describe the duties of the crossbow makers rather than calling them *balistarii*. For example, on 9 October 1222, orders were issued to the royal treasurer and royal chamberlains instructing them to deliver 10 s. each to Master Guillotus and Philip Conversus who are described as "making crossbows in our Tower of

---

11 *Rotuli*, 79.
12 *Rotuli*, 79.
13 Perhaps the single most famous use of the term *balistarius* to describe soldiers armed with this weapon comes from canon 29 of the Second Lateran Council issued in 1139. Here, the council declared that the art (*ars*) of crossbowmen (*balistariorum*) was hateful to God and could not be practiced against Christians. See *Conciliorum oecumenicorum decreta*, 3rd edn (Bologna, 1973), 203.

London at our order".[14] Similarly, on 12 February 1223, orders were again sent to the Exchequer ordering that Guillotus and Philip be paid for making the king's crossbows.[15] As had been the case the previous autumn, this document did not describe either man as a *balistarius*. However, this innovation in Chancery practice was terminated sometime in the mid-1220s as the last surviving document that describes the duty of the king's crossbow makers rather than terming them *balistarii* was issued on 27 May 1224.[16]

By the mid-1240s, however, the term *balistarius* would appear to have fallen out of favor and been almost completely replaced by *atilliator balistarum regis* or occasionally *atilliator noster*. The first surviving document using this term was issued on 29 July 1246 to the constable of the Tower of London requiring him to take possession of fifty-two crossbows that had been purchased from the estate of William Marshal, the former earl of Pembroke.[17] The constable was ordered to send Hugh the Picard, described as the *atilliator earundem balistarum*, to ensure that all of the weapons were in working order, and to repair them if they were not.[18] Royal clerks serving Henry III apparently decided that *atilliator* was, in fact, a better term than *balistarius*, and it remained the dominant usage in royal documents not only throughout the remainder of Henry's reign, but also throughout the reign of Edward I as well.[19] The only exceptions to this general pattern were the occasional reappearance of the word *balistarius*, and an experiment in 1263 with the word *factor* in place of *atilliator* of the king's crossbows.[20]

The term *atilliator* may have been suggested to the royal clerks by the fact that the crossbow maker's equipment was called his *atillia* in the government records. This word could mean either to make or to repair in thirteenth-century Latin usage and might therefore have seemed appropriate for artisans who, as we shall see below, were engaged both in the production and the repair of crossbows. In addition, any residual confusion deriving from the double meaning of *balistarius* as both a soldier and a craftsman could be avoided through the use of *atilliator*.

---

14 *CR I*, 511–512, "*facienti balistas nostras in Turri nostra Lond' per preceptum nostrum*".
15 Ibid., 535.
16 Ibid., 601.
17 Ibid., 446.
18 Ibid.
19 For the use of the term *atilliator* by Edward I's clerks to describe the crossbow makers stationed at the fortresses of Caernarvon, Bere, Harlech, Conway, and Criccieth in 1284, see National Archives C77/5.
20 The only crossbow maker designated as a *factor* was Conrad, who appears in two documents issued on 23 May and 28 November 1263 as the *factor balistarum de cornu*. See *CR (1261–1264)*, 233 and 323. However, even Conrad was usually described as an *atilliator*.

Duties of the crossbow maker

Throughout the period 1204–1272, crossbow makers working for the royal government were engaged in three distinct but complementary tasks. Their first and primary occupation was to produce crossbows to equip soldiers employed by the royal government, both in England and in Gascony. The second duty of the royal crossbow makers was to repair weapons that had been damaged or had been allowed to fall into disrepair through the negligence of their keepers. The final duty of the royal crossbow makers was to oversee and help assure the proper maintenance of stocks of crossbows stored in royal arsenals throughout the kingdom.

The basic task of the royal *atilliator balistae* was to build crossbows, as is indicated by the scores of references in the surviving sources to this duty. For example, on 9 October 1222, during Henry III's minority, the royal treasurer and the chamberlains were ordered to provide 2 marks to Master Guillotus and 10 s. to Philip Conversus (the Convert) for making crossbows (*facienti balistas nostras*) in the Tower of London for the king.[21] In another instance, an order issued on 8 August 1225 required a royal forester named Haschulf de Athelakeston to send all of the deer antlers (*perchias de cerco*) that were discovered in his forest to Philip so that the latter could use them for making nuts for crossbows.[22] Later in King Henry's reign, on 22 June 1259, the constable of Windsor Castle was ordered to provide the *atilliator balistarum regis*, with all of the materials that he needed *ad balistas faciendas*.[23] To add one final example, on 27 February 1266, John Waleran and John de la Lind, the guardians of the city of London, were ordered to provide Conrad, called in this document *balistarius regis*, with £12 for supplies so that he could make the king's crossbows.[24]

In addition to building the weapons, crossbow makers also were assigned the task of repairing them when they were broken or had fallen into disrepair. On 22 March 1206, King John issued an order to the barons of the Exchequer authorizing them to repay Peter de Stokes, the royal seneschal, for the money he had given to Peter, called *balistarius*. The latter had been paid for the expenses he had incurred in securing the tools and other supplies (*utensilia et alia necessaria*) necessary for repairing the king's crossbows (*ad balistas nostras attornandas*).[25] In an example from Henry III's reign, on 14 May 1236, a letter was issued to Hugh Giffard, constable of the Tower of London, in which he was informed that three men, John of Valence, Guillotus, and Philip Conversus, would be arriving to repair (*reparare*) the crossbows kept in the royal magazine. John was authorized

---

21 *CR I*, 511–512.
22 *CR II*, 50.
23 *CR (1256–1259)*, 398.
24 *CR (1264–1268)*, 174.
25 *CR I*, 70. The word *attornare* was commonly used in place of *adornare*, that is "to see to" or "to repair".

to view all of the weapons in order to ascertain what was wrong with them, and was given specific instructions to inspect the cords to see if they required repairs.[26]

Although building and repairing *balistae* appear to have been the most common duties assigned to the king's crossbow makers, these men also were responsible for overseeing the transportation of crossbows from one depot to another and for helping to assure the quality of weapons purchased from foreign makers.[27] These duties were clearly consistent with the general responsibility of royal crossbow makers to secure a reliable stockpile of weapons for the king's military forces. Furthermore, the decision by royal officials to have crossbow makers engaged in tasks outside their workshops indicates a great deal of trust in the expertise of these artisans with respect to all aspects of these weapons.

For example, Peter Sarazcenus, who was responsible during John's reign for making and repairing crossbows in castles throughout southern England, also was charged with overseeing the transportation of a large number of weapons from one royal depot to another. For example, on 25 June 1205, King John ordered Reginald de Cornhill, the sheriff of Kent, to provide Peter and another man called Peter of Genoa with enough money to enable them to bring 100 crossbows from Northampton to London.[28] Another example of this practice took place during the autumn of 1229 when Henry III was planning an expedition to Brittany that was to embark from Portsmouth on 13 October 1229.[29] In preparing for this campaign, royal officials sent orders throughout the kingdom summoning men and supplies to assemble at the port. Within the compass of this general mobilization, Henry son of Aucher, the constable of the Tower of London, received instructions on 11 October 1229 to send thirty-one crossbows from his magazine to Portsmouth for the king's use.[30] Two of the royal crossbow makers serving at that time in the Tower of London, named William and Robert, were entrusted not only with the task of bringing the weapons to the royal fleet, but also of going oversees with the king to help maintain them.[31] Royal officers similarly decided to use a crossbow maker to transport weapons in the summer of 1241.[32] In this case, King Henry ordered the constable of the Tower of London to transport twenty crossbows without delay to Richard Marshal. The man chosen to supervise the delivery of these

26 *CR (1234–1237)*, 265, "*ad incordandum et reparandum eas que incordatione et alia emendatione indigent*".
27 For example, on 25 June 1205, Peter Balistarius accompanied Peter of Genoa while the latter transported 100 crossbows that the latter had imported from Italy. See *CR I*, 39.
28 Ibid.
29 On this point, see F. M. Powicke, *King Henry III and the Lord Edward: The Community of the Realm in the Thirteenth Century*, 2 vols (Oxford, 1947), I: 179–181.
30 *CR (1227–1231)*, 217.
31 Ibid.
32 *CR (1237–1242)*, 315.

weapons was James of Toulouse, *balistarius regis*, one of the crossbow makers then serving in the Tower of London.[33]

Eventually, the royal government formalized this supervisory function and created a new position to be held by one of the king's crossbow makers. Thus, on 21 June 1253, Thomas de Sancto Sepulchro, who had been hired the previous year to serve as a crossbow maker at the Tower of London, was appointed to oversee all production of crossbows for the royal government throughout the kingdom.[34] Thomas was reappointed to this position at least once more on 16 May 1258.[35]

Locus operandi

During King John's reign, at least some, and perhaps all crossbow makers led a peripatetic existence moving from workshop to workshop throughout southern and central England to build and repair weapons used by royal troops. The most important of the crossbow makers in this period, as gauged from various records, is Peter Sarazcenus, who appears in twenty-two documents in the period 1204–1215. From April 1204 until February 1208, Peter served at no fewer than five royal fortresses, that is Salisbury, Nottingham, Northampton, Marlborough, and Gloucester.[36] Peter generally remained in residence at a particular fortress for many months at a time. Thus, for example, he worked at Salisbury from May 1204 until October of the same year.[37] In the next year, Peter spent most of the spring at Nottingham where he built and repaired crossbows from 14 March until at least 2 June.[38] From March 1206 until January 1207, Peter was employed at the workshop in Northampton.[39]

Several of Peter's contemporaries, although they do not appear as frequently as he did in the royal records, can also be seen to have served the king in a peripatetic manner. Roger, called *balistarius*, first appears in the surviving royal accounts on 4 August 1204 when King John ordered the sheriff of Kent to provide transportation (*carragium*) to Roger so that he could move his tools (*utensilia sua*) to Nottingham.[40] Eight weeks later, however, on 30 September 1204, the sheriff of Wiltshire received royal orders to pay Roger for his work and to repay him for

---

33 Ibid.

34 For Thomas' appointment as chief inspector of crossbows and crossbow production, see *CPR (1247–1258)*, 200. For Thomas' original appointment at the Tower of London, see *CLR (1251–1260)*, 48.

35 *CPR (1247–1258)*, 630.

36 The first surviving reference to Peter Sarazcenus appears on 30 April 1204 when an order was issued to Hugh Neville requiring that he pay the crossbow maker his wages and provide him with a suit of clothing. See *Rotuli*, 94.

37 *CR I*, 9 and 10.

38 Ibid., 23 and 35.

39 Ibid.,70 and 76.

40 Ibid., 4.

the money he had spent on supplies.[41] By 14 March 1205, Roger was back in Nottingham with Peter and another crossbow maker named Hamo, each of whom was to receive 15 s. from the sheriff of Nottingham to purchase clothing for themselves.[42] Roger appears three further times in the royal administrative record on 2 June 1205, 14 February 1208, and 9 December 1209.[43] In the first case, Roger along with Peter, and three other crossbow makers, Benedict the Moor (Maurus), Robert, and Nicholas, were to receive their wages from Robert Oldbridge, the sheriff of Nottingham. In 1208, Roger again appears alongside Benedict, Robert, and Nicholas at Nottingham, where all four men were to be paid by the constable.[44] To add one final example, a document from the *missae* accounts notes that Roger received 25 s. for transporting crossbows and supplies to and from the royal fortress a Nottingham.[45]

Indeed, if there was any single castle that served as a primary center for the production and repair of crossbows during the first decade of the thirteenth century, it was Nottingham. Although Peter Balistarius, about whom we have the most information, spent only a small fraction of his time there (approximately four of the forty-six months for which we have good information), his contemporary crossbow makers are recorded to have served more frequently at Nottingham than in any other royal castle.

The English civil war, the invasion by Prince Louis of France (1216–1217), and the following period of administrative reorganization during the early years of Henry III's minority led to a substantial disruption in government activity. As a consequence, very little administrative material survives from the period 1216–1222. However, when we begin to have significant numbers of documents available again in the summer of 1222, it is clear that the royal crossbow makers were firmly established in permanent workshops. For example, aside from a brief trip to Corfe Castle on the south coast in June 1222 to repair the crossbows stored there and to set up a new center of production, a crossbow maker named Guillotus appears fourteen times in the royal record between 1222 and 1226 carrying out his duties at the Tower of London.[46] In the same period, Philip Conversus appears seventeen times carrying out his duties at the Tower of London.[47] In neither case does the crossbow maker appear serving at any other fortress. A similar pattern of stability can be identified in the case of Peter, called *balistarius*, who was established at Corfe Castle. Peter is recorded carrying out his duties in the workshop there nine times between 23 September 1225 and 1 May 1230.[48] As was the case

---

41 Ibid., 9.
42 Ibid., 23.
43 *CR I*, 35 and 102; and *Rotuli*, 121.
44 *CR I*, 102.
45 *Rotuli*, 101.
46 *CR I*, 508, 511–512, 524, 535, 541, 557, 591, 601; *CR II*, 9, 22, 44, 88, 115, 140.
47 *CR I*, 506, 511–512, 524, 535, 541, 544, 557; *CR II*, 8, 22, 44, 50, 68, 88, 115, 140.
48 *CR II*, 63 and 142; and CLR (1226–1240), 2, 31, 80, 111, 156, and 182.

for Guillotus and Philip, there is no indication that Peter traveled to other centers to build crossbows.

In addition to having crossbow makers carry out their duties in fixed locations, during the first half of the 1220s the royal government would also appear to have decided to concentrate most crossbow production in workshops at the Tower of London. As we saw earlier, Guillotus and Philip Conversus were both fully established at the Tower by 1222. The latter had originally been stationed at Nottingham, as is clear from pay authorizations issued on 19 July 1222 and 19 August 1222.[49] These two men were joined in London in late 1224 or early 1225 by Roger. He first appears in the royal record on 18 October 1224 in an order sent to Archbishop Walter Gray of York in which the king insisted that Master Roger be sent to the Tower of London along with all of his tools.[50] A second order making the same demand was issued on 20 October 1224.[51] By 9 January 1225, Roger was firmly ensconced in his new workshop at the Tower of London as is indicated by an order to the treasurers to advance him two marks toward his pay.[52] On the same day, the clerks sent a reminder to Archbishop Walter Gray to have the remainder of Roger's tools and property at Knaresborough Castle transported without delay to the Tower of London where Roger was now working.[53] A crossbow maker named William joined the growing staff at the Tower of London no later than 4 March 1225 when he was authorized to receive a set of clothing (*una roba*) consisting of a tunic and a green overtunic costing 26 d.[54]

The heavy concentration of crossbow makers at the Tower of London continued throughout Henry III's reign. Guillotus, Philip, Roger, and William were joined in 1228 by two additional crossbow makers, William the *novus balistarius* and Robert, although the latter only served for a short time before disappearing from the royal record. The first surviving account concerning William the new crossbow maker is an order issued on 13 March 1228 noting that he was to receive his wages.[55] Robert, also called *novus balistarius*, is listed among the crossbow makers serving at the Tower who were to receive their wages there on 10 October 1229.[56] However, as discussed, Robert along with William *novus balistarius* was detailed to oversee the transport of crossbows to the king's fleet at Portsmouth for the invasion of Brittany in March 1228. William, it would appear, returned to

---

49 *CR II*, 506. A document issued on 6 May 1223 to the barons of the Exchequer authorizing them to credit the sheriff of Nottingham for expenses he incurred sending Philip and his tools to the Tower of London makes clear that Philip Conversus was, in fact, Philip de Nottingham. See *CR I*, 544.
50 *CR I*, 620.
51 Ibid.
52 *CR II*, 13, "*Liberate de thesaurio nostro Rogero balistario duas marcas ad liberaciones suas*".
53 Ibid., "*Mandamus vobis quod utensilia Magistri Rogeri balistarii et res suas alias que remanserunt apud Cnaresburg sine dilacione cariari faciatis usque ad Turrem Lond' ubi idem Rogerus moraturus est per preceptum nostrum*".
54 *CR II*, 22.
55 *CLR (1226–1240)*, 74.
56 *CLR (1226–1240)*, 147.

the Tower when this expedition was postponed as he is noted in subsequent pay records alongside the other crossbow makers.[57] Robert, however, does not appear at the Tower again, and it may be thought that he stayed at Portsmouth.

The Chancery documents in the period 1231–1236 have many gaps, and it is difficult to draw firm conclusions about where crossbow production was concentrated. The relatively slim surviving evidence indicates that the Tower of London continued to house workshops for the production of crossbows during the first half of the decade but that it may have suffered a brief eclipse sometime before 1236. Both Guillotus and Philip Conversus appear in pay records issued in 1232 and in 1233 as crossbow makers in the Tower.[58] However, a three-year gap follows during which we have no information concerning crossbow production. It is only on 14 May 1236 that we again have confirmation of the employment of crossbow makers at the Tower of London. On this date, a letter was issued to the constable of the Tower to admit Philip and Guillotus, under the direction of another crossbow maker named John of Valence, to the fortress for the purpose of examining, and, if necessary, repairing the weapons that were stored there.[59]

The text of this order to the constable indicates that both Philip and Guillotus had been gone from the Tower for some time before May 1236.[60] In addition, there is some suggestion that all production may have ceased at the Tower sometime before this date. The king's letter to the constable emphasized that the latter was to assign a suitable place to the artisans in which to carry out their duties.[61] If the royal workshops were still in service during the spring of 1236, it does not seem likely that it would have been necessary to find yet more space to carry out repair operations. Indeed, the fact that the weapons in the arsenal at the Tower had fallen into such a state of neglect that it was necessary to send three artisans to repair them suggests that no one there had been looking after the crossbows for some time.

After 1236, royal officials again concentrated the production of crossbows at the Tower of London. Philip Conversus continued in residence there until at least April 1242.[62] He was joined at the Tower on 9 March 1239 by James of Toulouse.[63] On this date, Richard de Grey, constable of the Tower of London, was ordered to admit the new crossbow maker and to pay his wages as long

---

57 Ibid., 182 and 184.
58 Ibid., 191 and 203.
59 *CR (1234–1237)*, 265.
60 The letter to the constable orders him to admit Philip and Guillotus so that they could carry out their duties. The need to issue such an order strongly indicates that there was a break in the continuity of their service at this royal center.
61 Ibid., "*assignantes eidem in eidem turri locum competentem ad operationes suas faciendas*".
62 *CLR (1240–1245)*, 122 contains the last surviving reference to the wages paid to this crossbow maker.
63 *CLR (1226–1240)*, 370.

as he remained in royal service.[64] During his tenure at the Tower of London, James served alongside both Philip Conversus and Hugh the Picard, whose duties are noted earlier.[65] It would appear that James served for more than a decade at the Tower before he was replaced by Thomas de Sancto Sepulchro on 17 May 1252.[66] As already indicated, Thomas was promoted the next year to serve as the king's chief overseer of crossbow production and maintenance, which required him to travel around the kingdom. However, his main residence continued to be at the Tower of London, where he maintained a workshop until at least 11 November 1272 when he received authorization to draw 20 s. for the purchase of sinews, cords, and other materials necessary for the production and repairs of crossbows there.[67]

During the final two decades of King Henry's reign, crossbow production continued to be concentrated at the Tower of London although at least one other workshop also was established at Windsor Castle. Thomas de Sancto Sepulchro was joined at the main production center in the Tower in 1255 by Henry the German (le Tyeys). Henry first appears on 7 November of that year in the royal record when he was authorized to receive his pay as *atilliator balistarum regis* at the Tower.[68] Thomas and Henry were joined by another German named Conrad in 1261. On 6 August of this year, Conrad was authorized to receive a suit of clothing (*una roba*) from Richard Ewell and Hugh de Turi, officers serving the king's Wardrobe.[69] For a period in 1263 and 1264, Conrad was assigned to work at Windsor Castle. On 28 November, royal officers were ordered to transport Conrad's equipment from the Tower to Windsor so that he could carry out his duties there just as the king had ordered.[70] However, Conrad was back at the Tower of London no later than 11 January 1264 when he as well as Thomas and Henry were authorized to receive their clothing allowance from the Wardrobe for their work there.[71] During his entire period of service at both the Tower and at Windsor, Conrad also employed three assistants who aided in the production and repairs of the composite crossbows in which he specialized.[72]

---

64 Ibid.
65 Ibid.
66 On this date, an order was issued to the constable of the Tower to admit Thomas de Sancto Sepulchro to work as a crossbow maker there. The order specifically notes that Thomas was meant as a replacement for James. See *CLR (1251–1260)*, 48.
67 *CLR (1267–1272)*, 238.
68 *CLR (1251–1260)*, 251.
69 *CR (1259–1261)*, 418.
70 *CR (1261–1264)*, 323, "*ad officium suum ibidem exercendum prout rex ei injunxit*".
71 *CR (1264–1268)*, 12–13.
72 The pay records for Conrad all note that the wages paid to him were also meant for his three assistants. Thus, for example, the record for 28 November 1263 notes that Drogo de Barentin, the constable of Windsor Castle, was to provide 12 d. a day to Conrad "*pro stipendiis suis et trium servientum suorum*". See *CR (1261–1264)*, 324. Similar records survive in *CLR (1260–1267)*, 66, 68, 166, and 185; *CLR (1267–1272)*, 90, 147, 173; and *CPR (1258–1266)*, 173.

While the Tower of London clearly maintained a dominant position as a center of crossbow production after 1222, Windsor Castle became an important secondary location. As was noted earlier, Conrad and his staff took up quarters at Windsor for about a year in 1263 and 1264. Long before this, however, the castle at Windsor had a permanent crossbow maker of its own. Henry, the *atilliator balistarum regis*, first appears in the royal accounts on 12 May 1248 when Godfrey de Liston, constable of Windsor Castle, was ordered to pay him his wages and to secure a sufficient supply of wood and other materials necessary for him to carry out his duties.[73] Indeed, Henry may have been in service as early as 13 February 1247 when the constable of Windsor was ordered to pay an unnamed *atilliator* 5 d. daily. Henry remained in royal service from 1247 until the very end of King Henry's reign and was subsequently employed by King Edward I's government.[74]

Rates of pay

The rates of pay for crossbow makers during the reigns of John and Henry III varied greatly both among contemporaries and over time. During the initial development of domestic crossbow production, John's government employed no fewer than seven artisans, and of these we have pay records for six. The highest paid of these workers was Peter Sarazcenus, who is also the man about whom we have the most surviving evidence. At least eleven surviving documents record payments to Peter, of which seven report his daily wage rate between 19 May 1204 and 18 February 1208.[75] On six of these occasions, including the two dates noted here, Peter was authorized to receive a basic wage of 9 d. per day. The only exception to this standard rate was on 21 September 1205 when Hugh de Neville was ordered by the king to provide Peter with wages of 6 d. a day for repairing the king's crossbows at Marlborough Castle.[76] In this case, however, it was not simply Peter who was to receive wages, but his wife and his son as well.[77]

Gerald, Roger, Nicholas, Robert, and Benedict Maurus, the five other crossbow makers for whom we have evidence of daily pay rates, would appear to have earned substantially less than Peter. In a letter to the sheriff of Wiltshire issued on 19 May 1204, King John instructed his official to pay Roger for his service at

---

73 *CLR (1245–1251)*, 180.
74 *CR (1272–1279)*, 26. At the very end of his term of service in 1272 Henry moved to Gloucester Castle for what may have been his retirement.
75 The six documents noting specific rates of pay can be found in *CR I*, 3, 9, 50, 70, 76, 102; *Rotuli*, 94.
76 *CR I*, 50.
77 Ibid., "*Mandamus vobis faciatis habere Petro balistario quandam domum in castro nostro de Marle' ad operandum balistas et ei et uxori et garcioni suo faciatis habere vi. d. qualibet ad liberacionem*".

Salisbury Castle at the rate of 6 d. a day.[78] Later that year on 30 September, the sheriff received new instructions that Roger was to receive 7 d. per day for his work.[79] However, by 14 February 1208, Roger was again receiving only 6 d., now at Nottingham Castle.[80] Gerald, the first crossbow maker to appear in the surviving royal record, received a lower rate of remuneration than Roger. On 29 January 1204, the constable of Windsor Castle was instructed to pay him his wages at the rate of 4.5 d. per day.[81] Nicholas, Robert, and Benedict were also authorized to be paid at the lower rate of 4.5 d. for their work at Nottingham Castle in a document issued on 14 February 1208.[82]

The discussion of these daily rates of pay is, to a certain extent, misleading, however, because although the amount of money received by any individual crossbow maker may have been calculated at this rate, these artisans were neither paid on a daily basis nor were their incomes determined by the absolute number of days on which they actually worked. For example, when on 19 May 1204 King John ordered the sheriff of Wiltshire to pay Peter for his service at Nottingham, he noted that these wages were to be paid for the entire period from the third Sunday after Easter (16 May) until Peter actually left his service at the castle.[83] Thus, Peter was paid for feast and fast days as well as every Sunday although there is no indication that he was expected to violate canon law by working on these days. In another case, on 2 June 1205, the king ordered the barons of the Exchequer to credit the sheriff of Nottingham for the wages he had paid to Peter, Roger, Benedict Maurus, Robert, and Nicholas for as long as they were in the castle there.[84] Once again, these five artisans were paid as salaried employees rather than as daily laborers although their pay was calculated according to a daily rate.

The next period for which we have surviving records of pay rates, as opposed to documents that note the payment of a particular sum of money to a crossbow maker, is the second half of the 1220s during the early years of King Henry III's personal rule. Of the six men known to have served at the Tower of London during this half decade, we can identify the pay rates for five. The sixth, Guillotus, appears in numerous records between 1222 and 1230, frequently as the recipient of cash payments, but his basic daily wage rate is never enunciated.[85] By contrast, Roger appears in fourteen separate documents in the liberate rolls between

---

78 *Rotuli*, 101.
79 *CR I*, 9.
80 Ibid., 102.
81 *Rotuli*, 79.
82 *CR I*, 102.
83 Ibid., 3, "*Inveni Petro balistario nostro liberaciones suas a die Dominica tercia post Pascha ... quam diu moram fecerit in castro nostro de Sarr*".
84 Ibid., 35.
85 Concerning cash payments to Guillotus, see *CR I*, 511–512, 524, 535, 541, 557, 591, 601; *CR II*, 44, 88, 115, 140.

6 November 1226 and 12 July 1230 when his rate of pay is firmly established at 12 d. per day.[86] Although not quite as numerous, we have similar documents for William, Philip Conversus, William called *novus balistarius*, and Robert.[87] All of these artisans were paid a standard rate of 7.5 d.

As was true of their predecessors during King John's reign, the crossbow makers working at the Tower during the late 1220s received a *de facto* salary even if their wages were determined on a daily scale. For example, an order issued on 22 November 1226 required that Roger, William, and Philip Conversus be paid their wages for the forty-eight day period between St. Leonard's day (6 November) until Christmas Eve including both the saints' days and the feast day.[88] Roger, who received 12 d. (= 1 s.) per day, was to receive 48 s., while William and Philip, who each earned 7.5 d., were to receive 30 s. In another case, on 8 February 1228, Roger, William, and Philip were authorized to receive their wages for 146 days for their service at the Tower from the day after All Saints 1227 (1 November) until Easter day 1228 (26 March).[89] Again, Roger received 1 s. for each of these 146 days, while William and Philip received 7.5 d. Thus, it is clear that the crossbow makers were to be paid for each of the days in question whether they were Sundays, fast days, or feast days, a situation more reminiscent of a regular salary than of a daily wage rate.

The structure of the wages received by the crossbow makers during the early years of Henry III's majority clearly resemble those paid to their predecessors during the first decade of the century. Not only were the men paid as if they received a salary, the government continued to maintain significant variation in the rates of pay. Roger, who may have been the chief crossbow maker, received 60 percent more money than any of the other crossbow makers about whom we have information. However, it is also quite clear that the entire pay structure was increased dramatically sometime between 1208 and 1226. Roger received a third more than the highest paid artisan working during the earlier period. The difference is even greater at the lower end of the spectrum. The four crossbow makers earning 7.5 d. per day in the late 1220s received almost 75 percent more than their counterparts two decades before.

The wages received by these crossbow makers are even more impressive when considered within the wider context of the remuneration received by the upper strata of royal servants in this period. For example, the crossbow makers clearly outstripped their fellow artisans both in their daily rates of pay and in paid holidays. Master masons employed to work on Bristol Castle in the early 1220s received a maximum of 4 d., that is barely half of that received by most of the crossbow

---

86 *CLR (1226–1240)*, 4, 5, 15, 24, 39, 43–44, 67, 80, 93, 111, 130, 147, 182, 184.

87 Most of these men appear in the same records. See, for example, *CLR (1226–1240)*, 4, 5, 25, 24, 43–44, 67, 80, 93, 111, 130, 147, 182, and 184.

88 *CLR (1226–1240)*, 5.

89 Ibid., 67.

makers and only a third of Roger's daily rate.[90] In addition, this maximum rate for masons was reduced during the winter months when shorter days limited the amount of work that could be done. As a result, the wages of the masons at Bristol dipped as low as 2.5 d., or only a third of that earned by the crossbow makers.[91] The common laborers at the building sites received even lower daily rates of pay ranging from 1.5 to 2 d.[92] Furthermore, as contrasted with the crossbow makers, neither the master masons nor the common laborers were paid for holidays or fast days so that their annual incomes were reduced even further.[93]

Masons and other artisans experienced significant increases in their wages over the course of the thirteenth century. For example, smiths, carpenters, miners, and masons employed by Edward I in his Scottish campaigns during the 1290s and early fourteenth century could earn as much as 4 d., while masters could earn as much as 6 d.[94] It is noteworthy, however, that even these higher rates of pay failed to match the wages earned by crossbow makers employed during the 1220s.

Very few pay records for crossbow makers survive from mid-1230 until the spring of 1236, and none of these notes the actual pay rates of the artisans. It is not until 14 May 1236, when King Henry ordered Hugh Giffard, the constable of the Tower of London, to pay three crossbow makers that we again have evidence for daily wages.[95] Two of the men noted in this document, Philip Conversus and Guillotus, made regular appearances in the royal financial records throughout the 1220s and even appeared on a few occasions during the first years of the 1230s.[96] In the Chancery document issued on 14 May 1236, both Philip and Guillotus were to receive 4.5 d. for their services "*ad operationes suas faciendas*".[97] John of Valence, the third man involved in the repair and construction of crossbows at the Tower, was to be paid 7.5 d. per day for his wages.[98]

On the basis of the evidence in this document, which is one of the single longest and most detailed texts issued by the royal Chancery dealing specifically with the production and repair of crossbows, it would appear that wage rates for crossbow makers dropped precipitously between 1230 and 1236, the period for which we do not have surviving records. Philip Conversus saw his daily wage go from 7 d. to 4.5 d. daily, a drop of more than 90 s. per year. To put this in perspective, priests

---

90 Concerning the wages of the master masons at Winchester Castle, see *Building Accounts of King Henry III*, ed. Howard M. Colvin (Oxford, 1971), 10.

91 Ibid., 11.

92 Ibid., 12.

93 Ibid., 11.

94 A. Z. Freeman, "Wall-Breakers and River-Bridgers: Military Engineers in the Scottish Wars of Edward I", *Journal of British Studies* 10 (1971), 1–16, here, 2.

95 *CR (1234–1237)*, 265.

96 Both Philip and Guillotus appear in records issued on 23 November 1232 and 1 March 1233 when they were authorized to receive part of their wages from the constable of the Tower of London. See *CLR (1226–1240)*, 191 and 203.

97 *CR (1234–1237)*, 265.

98 Ibid.

serving in the royal chapels in this period at royal residences such as Windsor generally earned 50 s. a year.[99] It is also quite clear from the text of a document issued on 14 May that John of Valence was in command of the crossbow operations at the Tower with responsibility for the entire project of assuring the reliability of the entire stockpile of weapons in the king's most important arsenal. Roger, who appears to have been the chief, or at least the *primus inter pares* among the crossbow makers at the Tower during the late 1220s, earned not less than 12 d. By contrast, John of Valence was to be paid only 7.5 d. This was the same wage-rate earned by the second tier of crossbow makers during 1220s and represents a decline of more than 150 s. a year from the rate that had been achieved by Roger.

There is no obvious explanation for the apparent decline in wages between 1230 and 1236. However, as noted earlier, it would appear that sometime between the last surviving record for the pay of Philip and Guillotus issued on 1 March 1233 and 14 May 1236 crossbow production at the Tower ceased. If this, in fact, happened, it might be an indication that the government's desire for the weapons and consequently its desire to pay high wages had diminished to a certain degree.

Indeed, pay records surviving from the final thirty-six years of King Henry's reign indicate that only a few crossbow makers achieved the rates of pay provided to their predecessors during the second half of the 1220s, and that the higher wage levels during the later era were only achieved gradually. For his part, Philip Conversus continued in royal service at the Tower at least until the spring of 1242, when a royal order issued on 25 April of that year authorized him to receive his pay of 4.5 d. until Michaelmas (29 September). There is no indication that he ever again achieved his previous rate of pay. Nevertheless, Philip's daily wage of 4.5 d. was near the lower end of the scale for crossbow makers during the 1240s and 1250s. James of Toulouse, who was appointed to join Philip at the Tower on 9 March 1239, initially was authorized to receive only 5 d. per day, or about 10 percent more than Philip.[100] No later than 4 May 1246, however, James was earning 7.5 d. per day, which was the same rate as the majority of the crossbow makers serving at the Tower during the period 1225–1230. Henry, the *atilliator balistarum* who was employed by the royal government at Windsor Castle, was not so fortunate. In 1248, when Godfrey de Liston was ordered to pay the new artisan, Henry was authorized to receive 5 d.[101] He was still

---

99 This point is made by N. J. G. Pounds, *The Medieval Castle in England and Wales: A Social and Political History* (Cambridge, 1990), 245. Parish priests, in general, were supposed to receive 60 s. a year. This view was enunciated in episcopal statutes by many English bishops including William Raleigh of Winchester (1247), Peter Quinel of Exeter (1287), and Bishop Gilbert of Chichester (1289). See *Councils and Synods with other Documents Relating to the English Church AD 1205–1313*, 2 vols, ed. F. M. Powicke and C. R. Cheney (Oxford, 1964), I: 406; and II: 1026 and 1084. There are no surviving documents from the 1220s that note Guillotus' daily wage rate. However, it would have been out of the ordinary for him to have received less than 7.5 d. per day, because every other crossbow maker employed at the Tower during his tenure there earned at least that much. Thus, his wage of 4.5 d. in 1236 very likely also represented a significant decline.

100 *CLR (1226–1240)*, 370.

101 *CLR (1245–1251)*, 180.

earning the same wage twenty-five years later when the sheriff of Gloucester was ordered to pay him his wages on 6 August 1273.[102] Even less fortunate was Henry the German, who served as a crossbow maker at the Tower during the second half of the 1250s and the early 1260s. When Henry first appears in the royal record on 7 November 1255, he was authorized to receive 4.5 d. per day.[103] However, by 9 January 1256 Henry appears to have received a pay cut, because on this date his daily wage was reduced to 4 d.[104]

In contrast to Henry the German, however, several other crossbow makers serving during the 1250s and 1260s were paid rates comparable with those provided to artisans during the late 1220s. In August 1246, Hugh the Picard, discussed previously, was authorized to receive 7.5 d. daily for as long as he remained in royal service.[105] About six years later, Thomas de Sancto Sepulchro, who was appointed on 17 May 1252 to replace James of Toulouse at the Tower, earned a starting wage of 7.5 d. per day.[106] Just one year later, on 21 June 1253, Thomas was appointed to serve as the chief inspector and officer in charge of all crossbow production for the royal government throughout the kingdom.[107] In his new role, Thomas was charged with inspecting the facilities for building and repairing crossbows anywhere in the kingdom and was authorized to call on the aid of sheriffs and constables throughout England to help in fulfilling his duty.[108] In accordance with his new duties, on 21 July 1253 Thomas received a pay increase of 1.5 d. so that his daily wage rose to 9 d.[109] Thomas was still receiving this rate of pay on 20 June 1266, that last date for which we have surviving pay evidence for him.[110]

Conrad, who first appears in the royal pay records on 6 August 1261, worked alongside both Thomas and Henry the German.[111] The earliest surviving document that records Conrad's daily wages was issued on 10 November 1261.[112] This text and eight more surviving documents issued between 1261 and 1270 make it clear that he and his staff of three assistants (*pro stipendiis suis et trium servientium suorum*) were to receive a daily wage of 12 d.[113]

---

102 *CR (1272–1279)*, 26.
103 *CLR (1251–1260)*, 251.
104 Ibid., 328.
105 *CLR (1245–1251)*, 73.
106 *CLR(1251–1260)*, 48.
107 *CPR (1247–1258)*, 200.
108 Ibid. This order was repeated and is preserved in a letter patent issued on 16 May 1258. See *CPR (1247–1258)*, 630.
109 *CLR (1251–1260)*, 148.
110 *CLR (1220–1267)*, 219.
111 *CR (1264–1268)*, 12–13.
112 *CLR (1260–1267)*, 66.
113 See *CR (1261–1264)*, 324. For the remainder of Conrad's pay records that deal with his daily wage rate, see *CLR (1260–1267)*, 66, 68, 166, 185; *CLR (1267–1272)*, 90, 147, and 173; *CPR (1258–1266)*, 173.

In considering the wage rates of Thomas and Conrad it should be noted that although both men were very well paid for their work as crossbow makers, they were never as well compensated as Roger had been in the period 1225–1230. Despite the fact that in 1253 Thomas achieved the highest office available to a crossbow maker, he never earned more than 9 d., or three-quarters of Roger's salary. In this context it should be emphasized that there is no evidence Roger ever held a rank equivalent to chief inspector of all crossbow production. For his part, Conrad received 12 d. but was required to use some part of the money to pay his three assistants. So, even if he only paid them each 1.5 d., which was the standard wage rate for unskilled labor, he only earned about two-thirds of Roger's salary.[114]

In considering wage rates for crossbow makers throughout the period 1204–1272, it would appear that over time the government formulated three separate policies regarding the remuneration of these important royal servants. Wages would seem to have risen between 1204 and 1230, and then to have fallen between 1230 and 1236. Finally, in the period after 1236, the government would appear to have established a two-tier system of wages that took into account both the high rates employed during the first three decades of the century and the lower rates established during the fourth decade. It should be stressed, however, that even the lowest paid of the King Henry's crossbow makers in the period after 1236 earned as much as master craftsmen in other fields, while the highest paid *balistarii* and *atilliatores* were among the best compensated of all royal servants throughout the entire thirteenth century.

Perquisites

In addition to receiving wages that were substantially higher than those earned by virtually any other group of royal servants, crossbow makers employed by John and Henry III benefited from a wide range of perquisites that added substantially to their real income. The most frequent and consistent benefit enjoyed by crossbow makers throughout the period 1204–1272 was the grant of clothing or a clothing allowance. During John's reign, when crossbow production was distributed through many royal fortresses in southern and central England, the official directly responsible for providing clothing was frequently the local constable or sheriff. Thus, for example, on 14 March 1205, King John ordered the sheriff of Nottingham to provide suits of clothing to Peter, Roger, and Hamo, the king's crossbow makers, who at this time were based at Nottingham Castle, or to provide each of them with 15 s. to purchase clothing.[115] To put this amount in perspective, 15 s. amounted to the daily wages of a common laborer for 90 to

---

114 *Building Accounts of King Henry III*, 12.
115 *CR I*, 23, "*Precipimus tibi quod facias habere Magistro Petro et Magistero Rogero et Hamoni balistariis nostris morantibus in castro nostro Nottingham robas de dono nostro vel cuilibet eorum xv s. ad robas emendas*".

120 days. In another order, issued on 16 August 1207, we learn that the sheriff of Nottingham had already provided two sets of clothing to the crossbow makers serving in his fortress.[116] The Exchequer was ordered to issue money to the sheriff to cover the expense involved in this grant.[117]

In addition to such generous gifts made directly to the artisans, the royal government also provided clothing and clothing allowances to the families of the crossbow makers. For example, on 4 October 1204 King John ordered the sheriff of Wiltshire to provide two green tunics to the wives of Benedict the Moor and Master Peter who, at that time, were residing in the royal castle in Salisbury.[118] In another order, on 22 March 1206, the barons of the Exchequer were authorized to issue 30 s. to Master Peter to provide clothing for his wife as well as for the other expenses he had incurred in purchasing the tools and other materials necessary for the repair of the king's crossbows.[119] In one final example, on 5 December 1207, the constable of Marlborough Castle was ordered to provide Peter and his wife with two sets of clothing worth 30 s.[120] This grant of clothing was worth just about an entire year's salary for a common laborer.

The practice of providing clothing to the wives of crossbow makers appears to have ended following John's reign, as no records issued by Henry III's government note grants of this type. The artisans themselves, however, continued to benefit from generous royal gifts. For example, on 4 March 1225, the sheriff of London was ordered to provide William with a set of clothing (*una roba*) consisting of a tunic (*tunica*) and a green overcoat (*supertunica de viridi*) with a wool lining (*cum furura agnina*) worth a total of 26 d.[121] Later that year on 11 December 1225, Guillotus, Philip Conversus, and Roger each was authorized to receive 1 mark, that is 13 s. 4 d., from the treasurer for the purpose of buying clothing (*robae*).[122] The order indicates, however, that these grants were intended as supplements to rather than as a regular element of the crossbow makers' salaries. This is a reasonable inference from the emphasis in the text that the money was a gift (*de dono nostro*) from the king.[123]

The surviving documents from the middle and late years of Henry III's reign indicate that crossbow makers continued to receive clothing allowances and gifts of clothing. For example, on 22 October 1259, Richard Ewell and Hugh of the Tower, two of the purchasing agents employed by the royal Wardrobe (*emptores garderobe*), were issued an order to provide Thomas the crossbow maker with a

---

116 *CR I*, 90.
117 Ibid.
118 Ibid., 10.
119 Ibid., 70.
120 Ibid., 97.
121 *CR II*, 22.
122 Ibid., 88.
123 Ibid.

suit of clothing (*una roba*).[124] As was true in earlier grants, the text of the royal document makes it clear that this clothing allowance was made by the gift of the king (*de dono regis*) and was not part of Thomas's normal wages. A similar order was issued on 13 August 1260 to the same purchasing agents informing them that Henry, *atilliator balistarum regis*, was to receive *unam robam*.[125] In this case too, Henry like Thomas was to receive his clothing *de dono regis*.[126] A text dated 13 December 1265 makes explicit that crossbow makers could expect to receive gifts of this type on a regular basis.[127] Here, Hugh and a new royal purchasing agent named Robert of Lynton were ordered to provide Henry with *unam robam* just as he was earlier accustomed to receiving it (*sicut eam prius habere consuevit*).[128]

Conditions of service

As discussed earlier, crossbow makers working during John's reign tended to be peripatetic, while those employed by Henry tended to remain in one location. Furthermore, after 1225, most crossbow production was concentrated at the Tower of London. The one constant throughout the period 1204–1272 is that crossbow makers carried out most of their duties in workshops located in royal castles. To make this point somewhat differently, the crossbow makers were not independent masters who carried out contract work for the government in their own workshops. Instead, they were very clearly direct employees of the crown working on government premises. By contrast, many masons, carpenters, and other artisans who worked for the government were employed on a temporary basis on a particular project until it was finished.

The extent to which these artisans were employees rather than independent contractors is underscored by the fact that the government paid for the materials used to repair and build crossbows. Crossbow makers did not purchase their own wood, glue, horn, and other materials and then add the costs of these goods into the final products that they then sold to the king. Instead, the royal government worked out three separate methods for ensuring both that their artisans had sufficient materials to carry out their duties, and that the payment for these materials ultimately came from the Exchequer.

The first method entailed having royal household officials send materials directly to a workshop for the use of the artisans employed there. For example, on 11 May 1212, King John sent a letter to Engelhard de Cigoné, constable of Porchester, informing him that sixty wooden bow staves (*baculi*) used in the making of crossbows (*ad balistas faciendas*) were being sent to the castle. Engelhard

---

124 *CR (1256–1259)*, 453.
125 *CR (1259–1261)*, 100–101.
126 Ibid.
127 *CR (1264–1268)*, 72.
128 Ibid.

was commanded to ensure that those experienced in the construction (*ad operandum*) of wooden crossbows received these materials.[129]

The second method of obtaining supplies was to have the constable or sheriff, who was charged with overseeing a particular royal crossbow workshop, purchase the materials himself. For example, on 8 August 1225 an order was issued to the constable of the Tower of London to acquire lumber and have it delivered to Philip Conversus so that he could make stocks (*telariae*) for the royal crossbows (*balistas nostras*).[130] In another case, on 10 May 1228 the constable at the Tower was issued orders to have wood cut in the royal park at Havering that would be used to make crossbow stocks.[131] The constable was further ordered to have this lumber transported to the Tower and delivered to Philip Conversus.[132]

The third method of obtaining needed materials was to have the crossbow makers themselves order what they needed directly from the suppliers. During John's reign and during the early years of Henry III's tenure, the crossbow makers tended to pay money out of their own pockets and subsequently receive reimbursement from the constable or sheriff of the castle or shire in which they worked, or directly from the Exchequer. For example, on 30 September 1204, King John issued a letter to the sheriff of Wiltshire in which the latter was required to reimburse Peter and Roger for the money that they had spent on thread, rope, gut, and glue.[133] The letter went on to say that the money spent by the sheriff on repaying Peter and Roger would be credited to him during his audit at the Exchequer.[134]

It would appear, however, that by the mid-1220s, when crossbow makers bought supplies directly they no longer were required to use their own funds. Thus, instead of having the artisans make purchases with their own resources and later seek reimbursement, officers serving in the royal household authorized direct payments to the crossbow makers in advance of their purchases. The earliest surviving example of this new procurement system, that I have found, appears in a document issued on 29 October 1226. In this case, the king ordered the Exchequer to provide Peter, *balistarius regis*, with 2 marks to purchase keys and stirrups, as well as gut and cork for the repair of the king's crossbows located at Corfe.[135] Crossbow makers continued to be supplied with coin to purchase supply directly throughout the remainder of Henry III's reign, as was the case on 27 February 1266, when the king issued orders to John Waleran and John de la Lind, described as the *custodes civitatis Londonensis*, to deliver £12 from the city's revenues to

---

129 *CR II*, 118.
130 Ibid., 50.
131 *CR (1227–1231)*, 49, "*ad telarias faciendas ad balistas regis*".
132 Ibid., "*Mandatum est Henrico filio Aucheri ... cariari usque ad Turrim et London' liberandum Phillip Converso balistario regis*".
133 *CR I*, 9, "*facias eis habere id quod ... ponent in filo et cordis balistarum nostrarum et in nervis et visco*".
134 Ibid., "*et computabitur tibi ad scaccarum*".
135 *CLR (1226–1240)*, 2.

Conrad, *balistarius regis*, so that he could purchase the gut and rope necessary for making the king's crossbows.[136]

Curiously, despite the fact that they worked in royal workshops in royal castles and had all of their supplies paid for by the government, many of the crossbow makers would appear to have owned their own tools and to have taken them from place to place rather than using tools provided for them in each workshop. For example, on 4 August 1204 John sent orders to the sheriff of Kent ordering him to pay Roger 20 s., and to provide him with transportation (*carragium*) to move his tools (*utenilia sua*) and some lumber to the royal castle at Nottingham.[137] Similarly, on 14 February 1208, the king issued orders to the sheriff of Northampton requiring that he have Master Peter's equipment and tools (*harnasium et utensilis*) moved to Gloucester.[138]

We can see the same *modus operandi* during the early years of Henry III's reign when crossbow makers at the Tower of London and elsewhere also appear to have owned their own tools rather than using implements provided by the government. Thus, on 6 May 1223 orders were issued to the barons of the Exchequer requiring that they credit 10 s. to the sheriff of Nottingham against his farm for the money that he had issued at royal order (*per preceptum nostrum*) to Philip.[139] The money was intended to reimburse Philip for the expenses that he had incurred moving himself and his tools to the Tower of London to take up royal service (*servicium nostrum*) there.[140] When Roger joined the staff at the Tower of London in the autumn of 1224 he also required assistance in moving, as is made clear in a royal letter issued on 18 October of that year to Archbishop Walter Gray of York.[141] The king ordered Archbishop Walter to send Roger to London, and to cover the expenses involved in moving both the crossbow maker and his tools.[142] As was true in the case of the sheriff of Nottingham, the king's letter to the prelate concluded by adding that these expenses would be credited to the archbishop's account at the Exchequer.

Crossbow makers continued to own and use their own equipment throughout the later decades of Henry III's reign. For example, on 28 November 1263 orders were issued to Hugh Despenser to ensure that Conrad, described here as the *factor* of the king's composite crossbows, did not face any difficulties in moving from the Tower of London to a new establishment at Windsor Castle.[143] According to

---

136 *CR (1264–1268)*, 174.
137 *CR I*, 4.
138 Ibid., 102.
139 *CR II*, 544.
140 Ibid., "*ad expensas suas ad eundem cum utensilibus suis apud Turri London in servicium nostrum*".
141 *CR II*, 626.
142 Ibid., "*Mandamus vobis ... mittatis nobis usque ad Turri London' Magistrum Rogerum balistarum cum omnibus utensilibus suis et ei in veniendo expensas suas inveniatis*".
143 *CR (1261–1264)*, 323.

the letter, Hugh had to undertake the disposition and transportation of Conrad's *atillium* as well as all of the other materials (*alia necessaria*) so that the artisan could exercise his office (*officium suum ibidem exercendum*) just as the king had ordered him to do (*prout rex ei injunxit*).[144]

Length of service

In addition to the loss, noted previously, of very large numbers of documents produced in the years 1208–1212, 1216–1222, and 1233–1236, it is clear that many of the records concerned with the various aspects of crossbow production issued in other years also have been lost. As a consequence, it is usually impossible to identify both the starting and ending dates for the employment of a particular crossbow maker. We find most of these artisans when they are already in royal employ, and they usually disappear from royal records without any surviving reference to their retirement or death. Of the twenty-eight artisans who can be identified as being involved in either crossbow production or repair during the reigns of John and Henry III, we have relatively certain information regarding the exact number of years served for only one. Eight men appear in only one document each and therefore shed light no light on terms of service. The remaining nineteen artisans who appear in two or more documents can provide some guide to how long crossbow makers served the crown. With regard to this latter group it must be emphasized, however, that the available figures represent only a minimum term of service.

The man about whom we have the best information is James of Toulouse. He first appears in the royal record on 9 March 1239 when an order was issued to Richard de Gray, constable of the Tower, to admit James to the royal fortress so that he could make crossbows there.[145] It is likely that the letter sent to Richard de Gray represents the original order posting James to the Tower.[146] James last appears in the royal record on 17 May 1252 in an order issued to the Exchequer that deals with the pay of Thomas de Sancto Sepulchro who is identified as James' replacement.[147] This document does not note explicitly when or why James left the king's service. However, his departure was almost certainly very recent because the officer in charge considered it proper to provide James' name to the royal clerks in order to help them to place Thomas in the proper context. Consequently, it does not seem unreasonable to place the end of James' service sometime in the spring of 1252, giving him a total career at the Tower of thirteen years.

---

144 Ibid.

145 *CLR (1226–1240)*, 370.

146 If James had already been in royal service at the Tower, there would have been no need to authorize his admittance. In addition, given the centralization of crossbow production at the Tower that had taken place over the course of the early 1220s, it is unlikely that James had worked elsewhere in the years before 1239.

147 *CLR (1251–1260)*, 48.

On the basis of the surviving information from the period 1204 to 1272 it would appear that James' term of service was of middling length during Henry III's reign but on the long end of what might be expected during John's reign. Of the seven men who can be identified as crossbow makers during the period 1204–1216, five appear in two or more documents. Robert and Nicholas first appear on 2 June 1205 and are last mentioned on 14 February 1208.[148] Roger first appears on 4 August 1204 and is last mentioned in a government record issued in July 1209.[149] Benedict the Moor first appears on 2 June 1205 and is last mentioned on 16 April 1215 when King John wrote to Engelhard de Cigoné to have him release the crossbow maker from prison and to leave him in peace.[150] Unfortunately, there is no indication in the sources when these four men were actually first employed or when they finally left royal service. It is possible only to say that at a minimum they worked for the king for terms ranging from thirty-two months to eleven years.

By contrast, we know considerably more about Peter Sarazcenus' tenure. He is first mentioned in a surviving royal document on 19 May 1204 when orders were issued to the sheriff of Wiltshire to pay Peter for his service at Salisbury Castle.[151] Because Peter was clearly already in royal service by the time he appears in the royal document, the date of his first appointment cannot be determined. However, as was noted earlier, he is unlikely to have worked for the king as a crossbow maker much before 1204. Peter continued to produce and repair crossbows for John for at least a decade after his first appearance in the royal record. As late as 20 January 1214, the constable of Bristol Castle was ordered to provide Peter and his wife with their clothing allowance.[152] The last surviving record dealing with Peter was issued on 14 August 1215 and suggests that he left royal service about this time.[153] According to the text, a royal officer named Philip de Albino was supposed to deliver a mill (*molendinus*) located near Stapleton to Peter. The letter notes that this property had been granted to the crossbow maker by the king.[154] It is not made explicit in the text of King John's order to Philip de Albino whether the crossbow maker would actually take possession of the mill and run it himself, or simply receive the proceeds from it. In either case, however, it seems clear that the king had decided to provide a secure retirement for a valuable servant, and

---

148 *CR I*, 35 and 102.
149 Ibid., 3; *Rotuli*, 121. In the second text, Roger is authorized to receive 25 s. for the expenses he incurred in moving his tools and supplies from the royal fortress at Nottingham. Given his apparent continued service as a crossbow maker, it is likely that Roger continued in his duties for at least some time after July of this year.
150 *CR I*, 4 and *CPR (1201–1216)*, 133.
151 *CR I*, 3.
152 Ibid., 160.
153 Ibid., 225.
154 Ibid.

that Peter's last year of service can therefore be dated to 1215, for a total of about eleven years in royal service.

In comparison with their predecessors, the crossbow makers who worked for Henry III appear to have had longer careers. As we saw previously, James of Toulouse served King Henry for about thirteen years as a crossbow maker based at the Tower of London. This term of service was exceeded by at least five other artisans who worked for the king: Guillotus (fourteen years), William Cheval (nineteen years), Philip Conversus (twenty years), Thomas de Sancto Sepulchro (twenty years), and Henry (twenty-five years).[155] Two other men, Henry the German and Conrad, each served for at least nine years.[156] On the shorter end of the spectrum, three men, Roger, William, and Peter, appear in the records for six, five, and five years respectively.[157] Three other crossbow makers, William, called *novus balistarius*, Conrad de Turre, and Hugh the Picard, can only be certainly identified to have worked for the royal government for two years, for seven months, and for five months, respectively.[158] It is not possible to determine how long five other artisans, Galfridus, Boniface, Semaine, Robert, and Nicholas worked, since each of them appear in only one document.[159]

It must be emphasized again, however, that all of the terms of service noted here, other than James of Toulouse' tenure, represent *minima*. We have neither the initial appointments to royal service, nor the final service dates for most of these artisans. Furthermore, the substantial losses of royal records for the periods 1216–1222 and 1230–1236 make it impossible to determine when many of the men noted here actually entered and left the king's service.

Even given these substantial lacunae in the surviving records, it nevertheless seems fair to conclude that crossbow makers enjoyed long tenures in their positions and had the opportunity to gain substantial expertise through experience. No fewer than eleven of the twenty men known to have built and repaired crossbows for Henry III served for at least five years. Of these, eight served for between nine

---

155 The first and last dates on which these men appear in royal documents can be found in *CR I*, 503 and *CR (1234–1237)*, 265; *CR I*, 538; *CLR (1240–1245)*, 116; *CR I*, 506, and *CLR (1240–1245)*, 122; *CLR (1251–1260)*, 48;*CLR (1267–1272)*, 238; *CLR (1245–1251)*, 180; *CR (1272–1279)*, 26 respectively.

156 The first and last dates on which these men appear in the royal documents can be found in *CLR (1251–1260)*, 251; *CR (1264–1268)*, 12–13;*CR (1259–1261)*, 418; *CLR (1267–1272)*, 173 respectively.

157 The first documents in which these men appear can be found in *CR I*, 620, *CR II*, 12, and *CR II*, 58. Roger and William last appear in the royal record on 12 July 1230 in *CLR (1226–1240)*, 184. Peter last appears on 1 May 1230 in *CLR (1226–1240)*, 182.

158 The first and last records in which these three men appear can be found in *CLR (1226–1240)*, 93 and 184; *CR I*, 506 and 535; and *CR (1242–1247)*, 446 and *CLR (1245–1251)*, 92 respectively.

159 Robert appears in two documents issued on 10 October and 13 October 1229, so that it is not possible to determine how much longer he served than the four days noted here. See *CLR (1226–1240)*, 147 and *CR (1227–1231)*, 217. The remaining four crossbow makers can be found in *CR I*, 160; ibid., 503; ibid., 524; *CLR (1240–1245)*, 7 respectively.

and twenty-five years. Crossbow makers serving under King John's would also appear to have worked for at least several years at their crafts even if their terms of service were substantially shorter than those of their successors in the later thirteenth century. Within this context, it should be noted that there does not appear to have been any overlap in personnel between the reigns of John and Henry III.

Conclusion

At some point early in his reign, certainly no later than 1203, King John's government determined that it was necessary to supplement the purchases of crossbows from abroad, particularly from Genoa, with domestic production. To this end, John's government recruited crossbow makers to serve the crown directly as royal servants and provided them with workshops in several royal castles in southern and central England, including Nottingham, Salisbury, Marlborough, Northampton, and Gloucester. Rarely exceeding half a dozen in number at any one time, these artisans nevertheless played an exceptionally important role in the English military organization, as is indicated by the consistent and detailed support and attention that they received from the royal government. Crossbow makers were among the highest paid of any royal servants throughout the thirteenth century, far outstripping their fellow artisans in both wages and perquisites. Many of them had very long careers, stretching in some cases for more than two decades—a feat that was remarkable in a period when the royal government tended to pursue short-term expedients in place of sustained policies. Finally, they produced, repaired, and oversaw the maintenance of the dominant missile weapons used by the English army in this period. In considering the entire corpus of evidence concerning these men it is difficult to escape the conclusion that the crossbow makers were among the more important royal servants under John and Henry III. Furthermore, their long terms of service, the standardization of their pay, and royal control over the purchase of supplies, as well as their places of employment, all point to a high degree of institutionalization. The royal clerks used the term *officium* to describe the duties of the king's crossbow makers, and it would seem reasonable to describe the *atilliator balistae* as the holder of a royal office.

2

CROSSBOWS FOR THE KING

The crossbow during the reigns of John and Henry III of England

By the second half of the twelfth century, and throughout the thirteenth, the crossbow was the dominant handheld missile weapon in most of Western Europe, particularly in the context of siege operations and warfare at sea.[1] The armies of the Angevin Empire, including England, were no exception to this general rule. Soldiers armed with crossbows appear in royal records from early in the reign of King Henry II (1154–1189).[2] Military service by men armed with crossbows was so common by the end of Henry II's reign that the contemporary legal writer known as Glanville used the obligation of a landowner to provide a *balistarius*, that is a crossbowman, for campaign duty as an example in his model writ of right.[3] Nevertheless, despite the frequency with which crossbows were used by soldiers in royal pay during the reign of Henry II, it is son Richard I (1189–1199), who was credited by contemporaries and by modern scholars alike with having inaugurated the widespread deployment of this weapon among his troops.[4] William the Breton, Richard's contemporary and a biographer of King Philip II of France (1190–1223), even claimed that the English king "was the first to bring the

1   On this point see, Eric Christiansen, *The Northern Crusades: The Baltic and Catholic Frontier, 1100–1525* (Minneapolis, MN, 1980), 88; Philippe Contamine, *War in the Middle Ages*, trans. Michael Jones (Oxford, 1984, repr. 1994), 71, originally published as *La guerre au moyen âge* (Paris, 1980); David C. Nicolle, *Arms and Armour of the Crusading Era 1050–1350*, 2 vols (White Plains, NY, 1988), 297; Christopher Marshall, *Warfare in the Latin East, 1192–1291* (Cambridge, 1992), 151; Matthew Strickland, *War and Chivalry: The Conduct and Perception of War in England and Normandy 1066–1217* (Cambridge, 1996), 72; and Andrew Ayton, "Arms, Armour, and Horses", in *Medieval Warfare A History*, ed. Maurice Keen (Oxford, 1999), 186–209, here 205.
2   *The Great Roll of the Pipe for the Eighth Year of the Reign of King Henry the Second AD 1159–1160* (London, 1885), 53, "*et in liberationibus viii arbalastariis viii l. et xvi s*".
3   *The Treatise on the Laws and Customs of the Realm of England Commonly Called Glanville*, ed. and trans., G. D. G. Hall (Oxford, 1993), 137.
4   Ferdinand Lot, *L'Art militaire et les armées au moyen âge en Europe et dans le Proche Orient*, 2 vols (Paris, 1946), I: 313; Maurice Powicke, *The Loss of Normandy 1189–1204: Studies in the History of the Angevin Empire*, 2nd edn. (Manchester, 1960, repr. 1999), 224; Jim Bradbury, *The Medieval Archer* (New York, 1985), 77; and Contamine, *War in the Middle Ages*, 72.

use of the crossbow to the French".[5] Richard's thirteenth-century successors John (1199–1216) and Henry III (1216–1272) continued the practice of employing noteworthy numbers of crossbowmen, particularly for service in garrisons both home and abroad.[6] Edward I, for his part, employed substantially larger numbers of men armed with crossbows than was the case under his father or grandfather despite gaining renown for introducing the long bow to English forces on a massive scale.[7]

However, despite the enormously important role played by *balistae* in the English military arsenal during the thirteenth century, very little is known about the weapons actually used by soldiers in royal pay during this period. Questions of particular importance include: What types of materials were used in the construction of crossbows? What means were used to span them? How many different types of crossbows, from a technological perspective, were in service at any one time? In large part, these lacunae in current knowledge are the result of the disinclination of medieval chroniclers and other writers to distinguish among the various handheld weapons that they called *balistae*. Contemporaries writing in Latin used this term to designate weapons ranging from spear-casting field artillery to a variety of handheld arms.[8] Scholars investigating English armaments have not conducted a thorough investigation of handheld weapons denoted in the

---

5   *Oeuvres de Rigord et de Guillaume le Breton*, ed. Henry-François Delaborde (Paris, 1885), II: 147; and William the Breton, *Philippidos* (reproduced in Delaborde), bk 5, lines 580–581, "utique Francigenis baliste primitus usum tradidit".

6   On the general use of crossbows in England during the thirteenth century, see Contamine, *War in the Middle Ages*, 89; and for their use in garrisons, specifically, see R. Allen Brown, *English Castles* (London, 1954, repr. 1970), 188.

7   John E. Morris, *The Welsh Wars of Edward I* (London, 1901, repr. New York, 1969), 87–92, notes the exceptional importance of crossbowmen, particularly Gascon mercenaries, in King Edward I's service during his Welsh campaigns of 1277, 1282–1284, and 1294. Michael Prestwich, *War, Politics and Finance under Edward I* (Totowa, NJ, 1972), 108, also discusses the importance of crossbows under Edward I. It is notable, in addition, that Edward employed very large numbers of men armed with crossbows in his Scottish campaigns, with over a 1,000 crossbowmen serving at any one time, on several occasions. See, for example, the pay records for crossbowmen in National Archives E101/6/5; E101/6/35; E101/7/2; E101/7/8; E101/7/10; E101/8/20; E101/9/1; E101/9/9; E101/9/14; E101/9/16; E101/9/18; E101/10/5; E101/11/1; E101/12/10; E101/12/17; E101/12/20; E101/13/16; E101/13/34.

8   On the use of the term *balista* to describe artillery, see Ralph Payne-Gallwey, *The Crossbow* (London, 1903, repr. 1958), 301–308; and Kelly DeVries, *Medieval Military Technology* (Peterborough, 1992), 132. For criticisms regarding the generalizations drawn about artillery builders and artillery types based on a limited treatment of the available sources, see David S. Bachrach, "The Royal Arms Makers of England 1199–1216: A Prosopographical Survey", *Medieval Prosopography* 25 (2004, appeared 2008), 48–74; and idem, "English Artillery 1189–1307: The Implications of Terminology", *The English Historical Review* 121.494 (2006), 1408–1430, both of which are also in this volume.

thirteenth century by the term *balista*, and have been content to translate the word as "crossbow".[9]

This study sheds light on the obscure history of the technology of crossbows used by forces in the employ of the English royal government, by identifying the material construction of crossbows, the technology used to span crossbows, and the periods in which new technologies were introduced. This essay also considers the relative rates at which the various types of crossbow were put into service by the royal government in the period 1204–1272. These seven decades saw the first regular production of crossbows under royal control in England, beginning in 1204, as King John sought alternatives to crossbows imported from abroad, particularly from Genoa.[10] The reigns of John and Henry III also coincided with the all of the major developments in crossbow technology that determined the types of weapons that were available until the introduction of the steel bow in the fourteenth century. Both wooden and composite crossbows were being produced in England no later than 1204.[11] In addition, hand-drawn and mechanically drawn crossbows were available in England no later than 1213.[12] Finally, the government during the reigns of John and Henry III produced a very large number of administrative documents dealing with military matters, including the production, purchase, repair, and distribution of *balistae*,

---

9 See Prestwich, *War, Politics and Finance*, 74, 106, 111–112; and H. J. Hewitt, *The Organization of War under Henry III 1338–1362* (New York, 1966), 63–73. Even in cases where some effort has been made to draw a distinction among crossbows on the basis of their material construction, little attention has been paid to the means by which they were spanned. See, for example, Morris, *Welsh Wars*, 92, who argues that the majority of the *balistae* used by English forces in Wales were made of wood, but does not distinguish among the various types of mechanisms used to span either the composite or wood weapons. Similarly, Michael Prestwich, *Armies and Warfare in the Middle Ages: The English Experience* (New Haven, CT, 1996), 129 notes the presence of different types of crossbows used in England, i.e., one-foot and two-foot, but does not consider their relative frequency, or how often they were built of wood or composite materials.

10 Concerning the importation of crossbows from Genoa and the origins of the crossbow industry in England, see David S. Bachrach, "The Origins of the Crossbow Industry in England", *Journal of Medieval Military History* 2 (2003), 73–87.

11 In regard to the introduction of the composite bow, see Payne-Gallwey, *Crossbow*, 62; Kalervo Huuri, *Zur Geschichte des mittelalterlichen Geschützwesens aus orientalischen Quellen* (Helsinki, 1941), 46; and DeVries, *Medieval Military Technology*, 41. The first evidence for the production of these weapons in England is an order for a crossbow maker (*balistarius*) named Gerald to receive his wages for making crossbows (*balistas faciendas*). The constable of Windsor Castle, who was responsible for paying Gerald, was also instructed to provide him with the gut (*nervos*) and horn (*cornu*) necessary for the construction of composite weapons. See *Rotuli de Liberate ac de Misis et Praestitis regnante Johanne*, ed. T. Duffy Hardy (London, 1844), 79, hereafter *Rotuli*.

12 There is considerable controversy among scholars about the types of mechanical devices used to span crossbows and when they were introduced. This question is discussed in more detail in this chapter.

which permit a detailed examination of the types of weapons actually used soldiers in royal service.[13]

Materials used in crossbow construction

It is generally agreed by scholars that the techniques used for making composite bows entered Europe in the wake of the First Crusade.[14] These weapons were produced by gluing sinew and horn either in alternating thin layers with wood or around a solid wooden core.[15] These composite bows were superior to their wooden counterparts because they stored more potential energy per square inch of surface area, and therefore provided more power with a smaller bow.[16] Composite bows also maintained their form, and consequently their ability to store potential energy, for a longer period than wooden bows of the same size.[17] One major disadvantage of the composite bow as compared to its solid wood counterpart was its susceptibility to the degrading effects of a damp climate, a problem of particular importance in northern Europe.[18]

It was once thought that the obvious advantages of the composite technology led to the complete replacement of older wooden crossbows in the thirteenth century.[19] However, it is clear from a very large number of administrative documents that soldiers in royal service made extensive use of wood crossbows, described either as *balistae de fusto* or *balistae ligneae*, throughout the reigns of both John

---

13　The sources available for the study of crossbows are discussed in the first study in this collection. In addition to the published Pipe Rolls from the reigns of King John and King Henry III, the collections of published documents used in this article are listed here: *Rotuli Litterarum Clausarum in Turri Londonensi Asservati 1204–1227*, ed. Thomas D. Hardy, 2 vols. (1833–1834), hereafter *CR I* and *CR II*; *Rotuli de Liberate ac de Misis et Praestitis regnante Johanne*, ed. Thomas D. Hardy (London, 1844), hereafter *Rotuli*; *The Close Rolls 1227–1272* (London, 1892–1938), hereafter *CR*; *The Calendar of Liberate Rolls 1226–1272* (London, 1916–1964), hereafter, *CLR*; and *The Calendar of Patent Rolls 1216–1272* (London, 1891–1913), hereafter *CPR*.

14　On this point, see Payne-Gallwey, *Crossbow*, 62; and Bradbury, *Medieval Archer*, 146–147.

15　For a brief technical discussion of the construction of composite bows in Western Europe, see Vernand Foley, George Palmer, and Werner Soedel, "The Crossbow", *Scientific American* (January 1985), 104–110. For a more detailed examination of the construction of composite bows, primarily in Central Asia, see Christopher A. Bergman and Edward McEwen, "Sinew-Reinforced Composite Bows: Technology, Function, and Social Implications", in *Projectile Technology*, ed. Heidi Knecht (New York, 1997), 143–160.

16　On this point, see Foley, Palmer, and Soedel, "Crossbow", 106–107; and Bergman and McEwen, "Composite Bows", 144–146.

17　See Huuri, *Geschichte des mittelalterliche Geschützwesens*, 5; and Bergman and McEwen, "Composite Bows", 151.

18　Huuri, *Geschichte des mittelalterliche Geschützwesens*, 5.

19　Payne-Gallwey, *Crossbow*, 62, argues that because of its advantages over the wooden bow, the composite bow replaced the older version no later than the 1180s. However, Morris, *Welsh Wars*, 92, insists that most of the crossbows utilized by King Edward I's forces in Wales during the late thirteenth century were made of wood. Contamine, *War in the Middle Ages*, 72, notes that French soldiers also continued to use wooden crossbows during the later thirteenth century.

and Henry III, and indeed, through the reign of Edward I (1272–1307) as well.[20] For example, on 8 May 1205, King John issued a letter instructing two royal officers, William Cornhill and Peter Terrington, to provide Walter de L'Isle with three wooden *balistae* and a thousand well-feathered quarrels.[21] A writ issued by King Henry III on 23 September 1228 required the mayor and sheriff of London to take possession of fifteen *balistae de fusto*, which had been stored at the magazine in the Tower of London. Once they had possession of these wooden crossbows, the mayor and sheriff were to have them delivered to the royal castle at Shrewsbury for storage in the magazine there.[22] A writ of liberate issued by the Chancery to the Exchequer on 10 October 1229 records that Henry, the constable of the Tower of London, was to be reimbursed for expenses incurred in the repair of 100 wooden crossbows, and for the purchase of another 100 wooden crossbows, that were to be stored at the Tower.[23] In another writ issued on 14 May 1249, the king ordered that John, the former royal administrator of the bishopric of Durham, was to receive 44 s. for the costs he incurred in transporting forty wooden crossbows from Northampton to Nottingham.[24] In yet another order, issued on 2 October 1252, the constable of Windsor Castle was required by the king to provide twenty *balistae ligneae* from the stores maintained at this magazine to Elyas de Rabayn, the sheriff of Somerset and Dorset. The latter was required subsequently to transport the weapons to Corfe Castle for the use of its garrison.[25]

Composite bows also constituted an important part of the arsenal of the English royal army throughout the period under investigation here. In 1204, a crossbow maker named Gerald was employed by King John at Windsor to build composite crossbows. A writ of liberate issued on 29 January of this year required the constable at Windsor to provide Gerald with glue, sinews, and horn, which he required for his work.[26] In June 1213, King John sent a letter to Engelhard de Cigoné, one of the royal officials who oversaw the production of crossbows, confirming that a shipment of thirty-five composite weapons and 20,000 quarrels had been delivered safely to the royal arsenal at Porcester by Engelhard's men. The king added that it was now Engelhard's responsibility to see to it that his men were paid for their work.[27] On 20 March 1237, Henry III ordered the constable of the Tower of London to transfer thirty-five *balistae de cornu* to Bertram de

---

20 In this context, see David S. Bachrach, "Crossbows for the King Part II: The Crossbow during the Reign of Edward I of England 1272–1307)", *Technology and Culture* 47.1 (2006), 81–90, and in this volume.

21 *CR I*, 31.

22 *CLR 1226–1240*, 98.

23 Ibid, 147.

24 *CLR 1245–1251*, 234.

25 *CR 1251–1253*, 163.

26 *Rotuli*, 79, "*Rex etc. constabulario Windelsour', salutem. Praecipimus tibi quod facias habere Gir' Balistario liberationes suas, scilicet, in die iiii. d. et oble, et praeteria facias habere husce, et nervos, et cornu ad balistas faciendas*".

27 *CR I*, 144.

Criol, the constable of Dover Castle, for use by the garrison there.[28] Henry issued a similar order to his constable at the Tower on 24 April 1242 requiring him to hand over forty *balistae de cornu* being stored there to Peter Chaceporc, the keeper of the king's Wardrobe.[29] Many of these composite weapons were being produced in royal workshops, with at least two crossbow makers in Henry III's reign, Guillotus and Conrad, specializing in the production of composite arms.[30]

The production of these composite crossbows required that the government procure large quantities of supplies that were specific to this technology, as contrasted with materials that were needed for wooden bows. As seen already, the crossbow builder Gerald received horn (*cornus*) for his work at Windsor Castle. Also of considerable importance was the purchase by government officials of glue, particularly glue made from fish bones, which was used to bind strips of horn and wood that together formed a composite bow. For example, in March 1225, Henry III issued an order to the sheriff of London to provide the enormous sum of £50 to the crossbow maker Guillotus, then working at the Tower of London, for the purchase of a particular type of fish glue (*glu de pisce*) called *huse*.[31] The king's letter specifies that the glue was to be used *ad balistas nostras faciendas*.[32]

Types of crossbows in use

In addition to differentiating among weapons on the basis of the material from which they were constructed, that is between wooden and composite bows, royal administrative officials also classified crossbows according to the method used to span them. During the thirteenth century, this task could be accomplished in one of two ways: through the application of direct human strength, and through the use of a mechanical device that transferred human energy more efficiently to the task at hand. Crossbows that were spanned manually were described in the sources as *balistae ad pedem*, *balistae ad duos pedes*, or occasionally as *balistae ad estrivos*. The first two terms refer to the size of the stirrup at the bank of the bow into which the man equipped with this weapon placed his foot or feet while spanning it. *Estrivos* simply means stirrup. Bows utilizing a mechanical devise to transfer human energy were denoted, usually, as *balistae ad turnum*.

28 *CR 1234–1237*, 424.
29 *CR 1237–1242*, 415.
30 In an order issued on 12 February 1223, Guillotus is described as "*magister facienti balistas nostras corneas*". See *CR I*, 535. Conrad, also described as the king's maker of composite bows (*factor balistarum regis de cornu*), employed a team of three assistants to help in his work. See *CR 1261–1264*, 324.
31 *CR II*, 22.
32 Ibid. Other notable purchase of glue for crossbow production can be seen in *CR I*, 9; *CR II*, 28; *CLR 1226–1240*, 5, 444; *CLR 1251–1260*, 406; *CLR 1260–1267*, 92, 186, 211, 255; *CLR 1267–1272*, 109.

Balistae ad unum pedem

When an archer equipped with a "one-foot" bow wished to draw the firing cord into position, he placed his foot into the stirrup, then bent over and hooked the cord to his belt using a special hook called a *crocus*.[33] He then stood up, drawing the firing cord into position using the strength of his leg and back muscles until it was locked into place by the nut.[34]

Balistae equipped with a stirrup fitted for one foot were used throughout the reigns of John and Henry III and were constructed from both wood and composite materials. For example, a lot of thirty-five composite bows shipped to Porcester during the late spring of 1213, discussed previously, included twenty-five that were described as *balistae ad estrivos*.[35] Conversely, on 22 January 1214, King John ordered his chancellor to purchase six wooden *balistae ad unum pedem* and have them shipped to Colchester to be stored in the royal magazine there.[36] When we turn to Henry III's reign, on 4 March 1233, Stephen de Segrave, the royal justiciar and constable of the Tower of London, was ordered by the king to release six *balistae ligneae ad unum pedem* from the royal magazine under his command and to transfer these weapons to Peter de Rivallis, then serving as the keeper of the Cinque Ports. Peter was then supposed to transport the crossbows to the fortress of Carmarthen in Wales for the use of the garrison there.[37] Royal officials dealt with a much larger shipment of crossbows on 28 July 1245 when Peter de Plessetis, serving as constable of the Tower of London, received an order to issue thirty *balistae ad unum pedem* to Richard Marshal. The order stipulated that one-half of these *balistae* were to be *de cornu*, permitting the inference that the other fifteen weapons were to be of wood.[38] Almost exactly one year later, on 29 July 1246, Peter de Plessetis received instructions to take possession of thirteen *balistae ad unum pedem de cornu* that had been purchased by royal agents from the executors of William Marshal, the recently deceased earl of Pembroke and father of Richard Marshal.[39] To add one final example, on 21 November 1265, Hugh, the constable of the Tower of London, was commanded to release three composite *balistae ad unum pedem* to Lord Edward, the king's eldest son, as well as two buckets of quarrels suited to these weapons.[40]

---

33   For images of the hook used in this manner, see Nicolle, *Arms and Armour* I: 327, 329, and 492.
34   One of the most famous images of a crossbowman spanning his bow in this manner comes from a miniature in the Luttrell Psalter, London, British Library ADD MS 42130 (completed before 1340). The image is reproduced by Claude Gaier, "Quand l'arbalète était une nouveauté: réflections sur son rôle militaire du Xe au XIIIe siècle", *Le moyen âge* 99 (1993), 201–229, here 220.
35   *CR I*, 144.
36   Ibid., 184.
37   *CR 1231–1234*, 198.
38   *CR 1242–1247*, 332.
39   Ibid., 446.
40   *CR 1264–1268*, 149, "*tres boketos quarellorum de quibus ... duo ad unum pedem*".

Surviving government documents dealing with *balistae ad unum pedem* indicate that composite and wooden crossbows were used in roughly equal numbers. Of the sixteen documents that I have found that describe the material from which crossbows of this type were constructed, eight include orders for wooden bows, and nine include orders for composite bows (one document lists both types). The number of bows listed specifically as wooden or composite *balistae ad unum pedem* also are roughly similar, with eighty-one of the former and ninety of the latter.[41] It should be emphasized that these relatively small numbers of weapons do not represent all of the *balistae ad unum pedem* recorded in the surviving government records during the period 1204–1272, but rather only those which royal clerks explicitly noted were made of wood or composite materials.[42]

Balistae ad duos pedes

Scholars working on medieval illustrations of crossbows have been unable to identify depictions of *balistae ad duos pedes*. There is general agreement among scholars, however, that this type of crossbow was a more powerful version of the standard muscle-drawn one-foot bow and, therefore, the two-foot bow required more muscle power to span. The major differences between the two types of crossbow was that the *balistae ad duos pedes* came with a stirrup that was large enough to accommodate both of the archer's feet.[43] The *balistae ad duos pedes*, like their less powerful counterparts, were produced throughout the first seven decades of the thirteenth century using both wood and composite materials. On 6 May 1215, for example, King John sent a letter to Engeldhard de Cigoné to release *duas balistas de cornu ad duos pedes* to the famous earl William Marshal.[44] In Henry III's reign, an order from the Chancery to the constable of the Tower of London on 17 December 1233 instructed him to provide ten *balistae ad duos pedes* to Henry de Trubleville or the latter's agent. Five of these weapons were to be *ligneae* and five were to be *corneae*.[45] Similarly, on 20 March 1237, Hugh Giffard, the constable

---

41   For wooden *balistae ad unum pedem*, see *CR I*, 184; *CR 1231–1234*, 198; *CR 1234–1237*, 258, 265; *CR 1242–1247*, 332; *CR 1251–1253*, 163; *CR 1259–1261*, 356; *CLR 1226–1240*, 98. For composite bows of this type, see *CR I*, 144 and 156; *CR 1234–1237*, 424; *CR 1237–1242*, 325; *CR 1242–1247*, 332, 446; *CR 1264–1268*, 149; *Rotuli*, 540; *CLR 1226–1240*, 98.

42   The government records also make frequent reference to *balistae ad unum pedem* without providing specific information concerning the materials from which they were constructed. For example, *CR 1237–1241*, 364, originally issued on 20 August 1241, required the sheriff of Hereford to release ten *balistae ad pedem* to Master Jacob of Toulouse, but did not specify whether these were to be wooden or composite bows.

43   Gaier, "Quand l'arbalète était un nouveauté", 221. Concerning the size of the stirrup in the *balistae ad duos pedes*, see Josef Alm, *European Crossbows: A Survey*, trans. H. Bartlett Wells (London, 1994), 22. This work was originally published under the title "Europeisk Armbrust: Ein Översikt", in *Vaaben-Historisk Aarbogen* (1947), 107–255.

44   *CR I*, 199.

45   *CR 1231–1234*, 358.

of the Tower of London, was ordered to provide fifteen *balistae ad duos pedes* to Bertram de Criol, then constable of Dover Castle. The letter from Henry III specified that the crossbows were to be released from the stores of composite weapons, that is *de balistis regis de cornu*, which were kept at the Tower.[46] The specificity of the request permits the inference that the magazine also was being used at this time to store wooden crossbows of the two-foot model. In a contrasting situation, Richard Coleworth, the constable of Windsor Castle, was ordered on 11 March 1261 to provide five *balistae ad duos pedes* to Robert Waleran, the constable of Marlborough Castle, so that the latter could equip his fortress for defense. On this occasion, the royal order specified that the weapons were to be drawn from the stores of the wooden crossbows, that is *de balistis regis de ligneo*, which also permits the inference that composite weapons of this time were being stored there as well.[47]

In contrast to the relative parity in the numbers of wooden and composite *balistae ad unum pedem*, there would appear to have been significantly greater numbers of composite two-foot crossbows than their wooden counterparts. Of the twenty-one documents that I have been able to identify that indicate the material from which two-foot crossbows were produced, sixteen refer to those *de cornu*, and eight refer to wooden weapons (three of these documents refer to both types).[48] In addition, more than twice as many composite bows (105) of the two-foot type are reported than wooden bows of the same model (forty-two). Again, it should be noted that relatively few records actually indicate both the type and composition of the *balistae ad duos pedes*, and so the numbers provided here are only a small fraction of those in use by royal troops.

Balistae ad turnum

By 1213, royal administrative records begin to include numerous references to *balistae ad turnum*, which are contrasted explicitly with *balistae ad pedem*. In the letter, discussed previously, sent by King John to Engelhard to Cigoné, the thirty-five composite bows are divided into three groups: twenty-four *balistae de cornu estrivos*, six *balistae de cornu ad duos pedes*, and four *balistae de cornu ad turnas* (sic).[49] Similarly, in the letter, also discussed already, sent to Hugh Giffard in March 1237, the thirty-five crossbows included fifteen *balistae ad duos pedes*,

---

46   *CR 1234–1237*, 424.
47   *CR 1259–1261*, 356.
48   For wooden *balistae ad duos pedes*, see *CR I*, 184; *CR 1231–1234*, 198, 358, 391, 476; *CR 1242–1247*, 332; *CR 1251–1253*, 163; *CR 1259–1261*, 356. Composite bows of this type are mentioned in *CR I*, 144, 145, 199, 226; *CR 1233–1234*, 198, 358; *CR 1234–1237*, 258, 424; *CR 1237–1242*, 415; *CR 1242–1247*, 446; *CR 1254–1256*, 221; *CR 1259–1261*, 502; *CR 1264–1268*, 149; *CLR 1226–1240*, 98; *Rotuli*, 540.
49   *CR I*, 144. It should be noted that the royal clerks occasionally used feminine endings on normally masculine nouns, such as *turnus*, as in the case noted here.

ten *balistae ad unum pedem*, and ten *balistae ad turnum*. In addition, the order specified that two of the *balistae ad turnum* were to be of the largest type, that is *de quibus due balistae sunt maxime*, which suggests that even within types of crossbows there may have been a range of sizes.[50] Six year later, on 23 April 1242, Bertram de Criol, who was still serving as constable of Dover Castle, received orders from the king to deliver forty composite bows to the royal chamberlain, Peter Chaceporc. This lot of weapons was to be composed of both *balistae ad turnum* and *balistae ad duos pedes*.[51] In one final example, in July 1246 Peter de Plessetis, the newly appointed constable of the Tower of London, was ordered to receive and store four types of crossbows: thirteen *balistae de cornu ad duos pedes*, thirteen *balistae de cornu ad unum pedem*, four *balistae ad turnum*, and nine *balistae ad turnum de cornu*.[52]

But what did this description of the *balistae ad turnum* actually mean? Prima facie, the contrast between the *ad pedem* and the *ad turnum* suggests a difference in the means by which the weapons were spanned, that is in the way in which a soldier drew the firing cord of the *balista* into position so that it could be locked in place and made ready to shoot. Two texts dealing with the logistical administration underpinning the deployment of large pieces of artillery shed light on this point. On 14 October 1225, Henry III issued orders to the barons of the Exchequer to credit the account of the sheriff of Bedford for the expenses that he had incurred for transporting a large amount of war materiél from his shire back to its home magazine at the Tower of London. Among the supplies returned to the capital were "two circles of iron used in the *turnus* for mangonels".[53] The *mangonelli* were stone-throwing engines that were based on the torsion principle, so that the rotating arm had to be drawn back against a fibrous material, which provided the kinetic energy to drive the rotating arm forward.[54] The second document is a letter issued on 20 October 1261 to William la Zusche, then serving as a constable at Rochester Castle, which informed him that Henry le Tyeys, a royal crossbow maker, would be arriving to join the garrison there. The letter added that Henry would be bringing certain supplies with him, including two *balistae*, ninety quarrels, and a *turnus*. According to the letter, this *turnus* was to be used in spanning the great *balistae*, that is *ad majores balistas tendendas*.[55] This letter appears to

---

50 *CR 1234–1237*, 424. Alm, *European Crossbows*, 22–23 argues that all *balistae ad turnum* were necessarily very large weapons, but this seems unlikely given the distinctions drawn by royal clerks between *balistae* that were *maxime* and those that were not.

51 *CR 1237–1242*, 415.

52 *CR 1242–1247*, 446.

53 *CR II*, 265, "*in duobus circulis ferri ad turnos mangonellos*". Also see the discussion of this document in the essay "English Artillery 1189–1307: The Implications of Terminology", in this volume.

54 In the original version of this essay, I incorrectly identified the *mangonellus* as a spear-casting engine, which was like a large *balista*.

55 *CR 1259–1261*, 449.

have been referring to large stationary spear casters that were stationed on the walls at Rochester Castle. In both cases, at Bedford and Rochester, the *turnus* clearly was a device for bringing the engine into firing position. Neither the *mangonellus* nor the large *balistae* could be spanned by muscle power alone in the manner of small handheld crossbows. When attached to crossbows, therefore, the *turnus* appears to have been a similar, albeit smaller version, of the device used on large-scale artillery pieces. It served the same purpose of facilitating the spanning of a crossbow and lessening the amount of pure muscle power needed to use this weapon.

As was true of muscle-drawn crossbows, the *balistae ad turnum* were constructed both from solid wood and from composite materials. However, it appears that the composite bows of this type were much more common than their wooden counterparts. I have found only three documents that treat *balistae ad turnum* constructed of wood, comprising a total of eight weapons.[56] By contrast, I have been able to identify nine separate document dealing with *balistae ad turnum de cornu*, which refer to sixty-nine individual weapons.[57] It seems likely that the *balistae de cornu* among the most powerful of the hand held bows resulted from the greater ability of the composite weapons to store potential energy, a factor which made it possible for them to be smaller than their wooden counterparts without sacrificing power.[58]

But what kind of spanning device was the *turnus*? Using a phrase that does not seem to appear in the relevant sources, Payne-Gallwey described *balistarii turnii* as men equipped with a belt-hook and a pulley device that, in conjunction with a stirrup on the back of the bow, could be used to span very powerful hand held weapons.[59] He was motivated to speculate about the hook and pulley, despite the lack of references to a design of this type in the sources, because he did not wish to consider the *turnus* as a crank. He argued that because there are no examples of a crossbow equipped with a crank surviving from earlier than the late fourteenth century, it was not likely that such bows existed earlier.[60]

Leaving the problem of the crank to the side for a moment, if Payne-Gallwey were correct that the *turnus* of the crossbow should be understood as a pulley and that this pulley was intended to be used in conjunction with a stirrup, one might reasonably expect to find descriptions of weapons equipped with both. However, the opposite is the case. As discussed already, royal clerks consistently

---

56 *CR I*, 196; *CR 1234–1237*, 265; *CR 1242–1247*, 446.
57 *CR I*, 144, 145, 558; *CR 1234–1237*, 424; *CR 1237–1242*, 415; *CR 1242–1247*, 446; *CR 1251–1253*, 163, 431; *CR 1259–1261*, 449.
58 On this point, see Alm, *European Crossbow*, 15; as well as Foley, Palmer, and Soedel, "Crossbow", 106–107; and Bergman and McEwen, "Composite Bows", 144–146.
59 Payne-Gallwey, *Crossbow*, 73, does not provide a citation for this term, nor is the accompanying image taken from a medieval text. Rather, it is Payne-Gallwey's own invention. In my own investigation of the relevant administrative documents, I have not found references to *balistarii turnii*.
60 Payne-Gallwey, *Crossbow*, 81–83.

distinguished between *balistae ad pedem*, that is those equipped with a stirrup, and the *balistae ad turnum*, because they were different types of weapons. Given the absence of any evidence for a pulley and stirrup combination—indeed the clear differentiation between weapons with stirrups and those with a *turnus*—it would appear that Payne-Gallwey's hypothetical model must be discarded.

On the question of the crank, Payne-Gallwey's rejection of this device on thirteenth-century weapons largely has been accepted by scholars. Lynn T. White, who made a special study of the use of the crank in the Middle Ages, placed the introduction of the cranked crossbow in the West in the early fifteenth century. He argued that no secure evidence survived for the crossbow crank before about 1405 when Konrad Keyser produced his *Bellifortis*, which included images of five different types of cranks in use on *balistae*.[61] More recently, Claude Gaier has argued that the *arablete a tour* (the French term for the *balista ad turnum*) was equipped with a pulley affixed to a double crank.[62] However, this position has not found general acceptance from scholars.[63]

The most plausible explanation for the type of device described by royal clerks as a *turnus* would seem to be that suggested by Kalervo Huuri. He argues that the phrase *ad turnum* or *de torno*, when used in conjunction with a crossbow, is a winch. This winch would have made it possible for a man equipped with a crossbow to span a more powerful weapon than could be manipulated using muscle power and a stirrup.[64] Huuri's view is consistent with that of J.-F. Finó in his study of crossbows used by French forces during the thirteenth century.[65]

One final point which should be made concerning the *turnus* is its relatively early introduction into England. As discussed previously, the first surviving evidence for the production of *balistae ad turnum* in England dates from 1213. By contrast, crossbows equipped with mechanical spanning devices do not appear to have been available elsewhere in the Christian West, including in France, much before 1240.[66] In fact, one of the earliest known references to the use of the *turnus* in a Christian source outside of England comes from the island of Majorca in 1232, shortly after its conquest from the Muslims by King James I of Aragon (1213–1276). In this case, a charter issued by Peter of Portugal, then serving as the Aragonese governor of Majorca, required that the town of Palma maintain

---

61 Lynn T. White Jr., *Medieval Technology and Social Change*, (Oxford, 1963), 111.
62 Gaier, "Quand l'arbalète était une nouveauté", 221. Gaier bases his view on a study of a military treatise composed for Saladin c. 1190. This latter text was studied in detail by Claude Cahen, "Un traité d'armurerie composé pour Saladin", *Bulletin d'études orientales de l'institut français de Damas*, 12 (1947–1948), 103–163, here 132, and 151–154.
63 On this point, see De Vries, *Medieval Military Technology*, 42.
64 Huuri, *Geschichte des mittelalterlichen Geschützwesens*, 46.
65 J.-F. Finó, *Forteresses de la France médiévale: Construction-Attaque-Défense* 3rd edn. (Paris, 1977), 151.
66 Huuri, *Geschichte des mittelalterlichen Geschützwesens*, 46.

stationary artillery, including *balistae de torno*, that is large spear casting engines equipped with mechanical spanning devices.[67]

It does not seem to be a coincidence that an island just captured from the Muslims would provide some of the first evidence for the use of a mechanical spanning device. A treatise composed for Saladin c. 1190 refers to such a mechanical device for crossbows, although scholars have not agreed on the identity of this device as a crank or a winch.[68] Muslim control of Majorca up to 1232 may have facilitated the transfer of advanced military technology to the island before its conquest by the Aragonese. Despite its slow introduction into Europe, generally, it would appear that the superiority of the mechanically spanned Muslim weapon came to the attention of royal officials in England at an earlier date, perhaps through the agency of returning veterans of King Richard's crusade to the East.

When King John decided to invest in the development of a domestic crossbow industry early in the thirteenth century, his government recruited at least two men to serve as crossbow makers, who very likely came from the eastern Mediterranean. Peter, called the Saracen (Sarazcenus), first appears in royal records on 30 April 1204.[69] Peter's exceptionally high status both among the king's crossbow makers and in the broader society is indicated by his daily wage rate of 9 d.[70] This amounted to more than twice the pay of contemporary craftsmen in other fields.[71] In addition, Peter and his wife were both given very generous perquisites, including gifts of clothing from the king, amounting in some cases to 30 s.[72] To put this sum into perspective, the average daily laborer would require half a year or more to earn this amount of money.[73] Peter quickly was joined by

---

67 *Glassarium mediae et infimae Latinitatis*, ed. Carolus Dufresne Domino du Cange (Paris, 1840), VIIII: 132, under *tornus*. The word *turnus* is commonly spelled *tornus* in medieval Latin sources.

68 For the basic study of this treatise, see Cahen, "Un traité", 103–163. The controversy regarding the nature of this spanning device is best exemplified in Gaier, "Quand l'arbelèt ètait un nouveauté", 221; and Finó, *Forteresses de la France médiévale*, 151. Lynn White, "The Crusades and the Technological Thrust of the West", in *War, Technology, and Society in the Middle East*, ed. V. J. Parry and M. E. Yapp (London, 1975), 97–112, here 101, argues that Frankish crossbows were superior to their Muslim counterparts during the late twelfth century. He based this conclusion on philological evidence in which he traced Byzantine and Turkish words for crossbow back to an original Latin term. White was aware of the treatise on arms, noted in this chapter, and observed that the Muslims used several different types of crossbow during the twelfth century. White does not appear to have been aware, however, that the mechanical method for spanning crossbows, which is discussed in the Muslim arms treatise, remained unknown in most of the West outside of England for a generation after 1190, when the treatise was composed for Saladin.

69 *Rotuli*, 94.

70 Ibid.

71 Concerning the wages of the master masons during the thirteenth century, see *Building Accounts of King Henry III*, ed. Howard M. Colvin (Oxford, 1971), 9–13; and A. Z. Freeman, "Wall-Breakers and River-Bridgers: Military Engineers in the Scottish Wars of Edward I", *Journal of British Studies* 10 (1971), 1–16, here, 2.

72 *CR I*, 97.

73 See Colvin, *Building Accounts of King Henry III*, 12.

another easterner named Benedict, with the byname "the Moor" (Maurus), who first appears in the royal record on 4 October 1204.[74] Given the presence of these two men among the earliest crossbow makers employed by the English government, it seems likely that one or both of them brought the *turnus* technology from the East or otherwise facilitated its introduction into England.

Relative numbers of weapons in use

As discussed in the preceding paragraphs, the surviving records that detail both the material composition and the means of spanning *balistae* in use by English forces during the period 1204–1272 indicate that composite weapons were more common than their wooden counterparts. However, the relative difference in the number of composite and wooden crossbows was not consistent across all types. Rather, the royal government appears to have decided that it was preferable to use composite materials for the more powerful two-foot and *ad turnum* bows. By contrast, a much higher percent of the less powerful one-foot bows were constructed of wood.

When we consider the total number of documents that refer to the means by which *balistae* were spanned, including those that do not provide information about the material from which they were constructed, this larger corpus of information can reveal the relative proportion of each type in use.[75] In the course of a systematic examination of the administrative records for the reigns of John and Henry III, I have found references to 232, 162, and 106 *balistae ad unum pedem*, *ad duos pedes*, and *ad turnum* types, respectively. These numbers do not include references to the many hundreds of weapons that royal clerks described simply as *balistae* without any other identifying characteristics.

The relative frequency of the various types of crossbows in the administrative records suggests that *balistae ad unum* were the most common in use, followed by the *balistae ad duos pedes*, with the *balistae ad turnum* the least common. As a general rule, the less powerful and less expensive crossbows were more common than their more powerful and more expensive counterparts. It should be noted these findings are consistent with the purchasing habits of the French royal government during the later thirteenth century. For example, in 1295 the crossbow makers of Toulouse provided King Philip IV (1285–1314) with 506 *balistae ad unum pedem* and only sixty-one *balistae ad duos pedes*. No mention is made in this contract to *balistae ad turnum*.[76]

---

74 *CR I*, 4.

75 Documents dealing with the type but not the material composition of the *balistae ad unum pedem* can be found in *CR 1237–1242*, 315, 364; *CR 1256–1259*, 25; *CLR 1251–1260*, 387, 390. For *balistae ad duos pedes*, see *CR 1227–1231*, 312; *CR 1237–1242*, 425; *CR 1242–1247*, 5; *CLR 1251–1260*, 387, 390; *CPR 1258–1266*, 632. For *balistae ad turnum* see *CR 1237–1242*, 315, 364, 425.

76 Philippe Wolff, "Achats d'armes pour Philippe le Bel dans la Règion Toulousaine", *Annales du Midi* 51 (1948–1949), 84–91.

These findings also are supported by royal administrative documents dealing with the production and transportation of crossbow quarrels. In general, the millions of quarrels produced and purchased by the royal government are described in Chancery records only as *quarellae*. However, in those cases when particular types of quarrels are identified, the ammunition for *balistae ad unum pedem* appear to have predominated. For example, an order issued on 13 March 1261 by Henry III to the constable of St. Briavels Castle to transport 10,000 quarrels to Marlborough Castle stated that 2,000 of these projectiles were to be suitable for use with *balistae ad duos pedes* and 8,000 for *balistae ad unum pedem.*[77] Similarly, an order to the bailiffs of Colchester issued on 9 June 1267 stated that the king required 10,000 quarrels for *balistae ad duos pedes*, and 20,000 quarrels for *balistae ad unum pedem.*[78] Even more striking is an order issued three months earlier to the bailiffs of the city of London, who were commanded to produce 50,000 quarrels, of which 5,000 were for two-foot bows, and 45,000 were for one-foot bows.[79]

Conclusion

The English royal government in the period 1204–1272 used at least six varieties of hand held *balistae* in magazines and garrisoned fortifications for use by royal troops. These ranged from the least powerful and expensive wooden *balistae ad unum pedem* to the most powerful *balistae ad turnum de cornu*. Overall, the government appears to have produced and purchased more composite weapons than wooden weapons, with the highest percentage of composite *balistae* among the most powerful weapons. However, it also seems that the government purchased and produced more of the one-foot crossbows than either of the more powerful two-foot or mechanically spanned models. These findings indicate that royal logistics officers did not have a one-size-fits-all mentality, but rather devoted considerable attention to purchasing and producing a range of crossbow models that served a variety of needs. Finally, it would appear that royal officials actively sought out technology from foreign sources, going so far as to recruit men from the eastern Mediterranean in order to bring the *turnus* to England a generation before it was introduced in other regions of the Christian West.

---

77 *CLR 1260–1267*, 25.
78 Ibid., 276.
79 Ibid., 264.

3

THE ROYAL ARMS MAKERS OF ENGLAND, 1199–1216

A prosopographical survey

The English royal government produced very large quantities of arms, principally siege artillery, crossbows, and ammunition for both, throughout the thirteenth century.[1] Several of the specialists who worked for King John (1199–1216), Henry III (1216–1272), and Edward I (1272–1307), have benefited from scholarly attention.[2] There has been no systematic effort, however, to consider the cadre of royal arms makers as a group. This lacuna in scholarly efforts has had negative consequences both for our understanding of the importance of the royal arms industry as a whole, and for the identification by scholars of individual arms makers. In the first instance, the focus on prominent individuals has obscured the overall administrative and financial commitment of the royal government to the production of arms. We know a great deal, for instance, about the royal engineer Bertram, employed by Edward I, to design both siege engines and royal fortifications.[3] By contrast, comparatively little information has been developed concerning the enormous investments made by the royal government in the construction of siege engines, and the master carpenters and engineers who built them.[4]

The second major problem that has resulted from a focus on a few individuals and the lack of consideration of the cadre of arms makers as a group is the significant confusion about who actually produced weapons for the royal government

---

1   The production of this equipment is considered in many of the studies included in this volume.
2   See, for example, A. J. Taylor, "Master Bertram, Ingeniator Regis", in *Studies in Medieval History Presented to R. Allen Brown* (Woodbridge, 1989), 289–315; and Alf Webb, "John Malemort—King's Quarreler: The King's 'Great Arsenal'", St. Briavels and the Royal Forest of Dean", *Society of Archer Antiquaries* 31 (1988), 40–46.
3   Taylor, "Master Bertram", passim; and Michael Prestwich, *Plantagenet England 1225–1360* (Oxford, 2005), 152.
4   However, now see Michael Prestwich, "The Trebuchets of the Tower", in *The Medieval Way of War: Studies in Military History in Honor of Bernard S. Bachrach*, ed. Gregory Halfond (Farnham, 2015), 283–294; as well as David S. Bachrach, "English Artillery 1189–1307: The Implications of Terminology", *The English Historical Review* 121.494 (2006), 1408–1430; and idem, "The Military Administration of England: The Royal Artillery (1216–1272)", *Journal of Military History* 26 (2004), 1083–1104, which are included in this volume.

and under what conditions. As specialists in English administrative history are well aware, the tendency of royal clerks to use the same term or phrase to describe two distinct offices or actions can lead to problems of interpretation when a text is viewed in isolation. A noteworthy example of this type of confusion can be found in Maurice Powicke's often cited discussion of royal engineers in *The Loss of Normandy 1189–1204*.[5] Here Powicke argues that royal clerks working for King Richard and King John regularly used the word *balista* as a generic term for siege artillery, including both spear-casting and stone-throwing machines. Powicke also observes that soldiers, who were armed with crossbows, were denoted in the sources as *balistarii*.[6] Given his assumption that the term *balistarius* was also used to describe the engineers who constructed siege engines, Powicke concluded that it is difficult to determine from a single text whether an individual was a crossbow-bearing soldier or an engineer who built siege engines called *balistae*.[7]

At first glance, Powicke's observation would seem to be a reasonable conclusion based on the important problem of the terminology used by English clerks in the period 1199–1216. In this case, however, Powicke's focus on a very few men described in the sources, particularly the royal engineer named Urric who worked for both King Richard and John, and his lack of consideration of the all of the information from the administrative sources that dealt with royal arms makers in this period, led him astray. In most cases, royal clerks used the terms *mangonelli* and petrariae to denote stone-throwing engines. The term *balista* was reserved, in the context of artillery, for spear casting engines, and not as Powicke asserted, as a generic term for artillery.[8] The term *balista* was used most often, however, to denote the six different types of crossbows that were deployed by English forces in the early thirteenth century.[9]

Secondly, the men who built siege engines for the royal government during the reigns of Richard and John were not denoted by royal clerks as *balistarii* in administrative documents.[10] When the names of these specialists in the construction of siege engines are accompanied by descriptive appellations, they are denoted either as engineers (*ingeniatores*) or as carpenters, often master carpenters (*magister*

---

5 Maurice Powicke, *The Loss of Normandy 1189–1204: Studies in the History of the Angevin Empire* 2nd edn (Manchester, 1960, repr. 1999), 224.

6 Ibid., 224–225.

7 Ibid.

8 See the observations on this point by R. Rogers, *Latin Siege Warfare in the Twelfth Century* (Oxford, 1992), 254–273; and Bachrach, "English Artillery", passim.

9 See David S. Bachrach, "Crossbows for the King: The Crossbow During the Reigns of John and Henry III of England", in *Technology and Culture* 45.1 (2004), 102–119, and in this volume.

10 I draw this conclusion on the basis of an exhaustive examination of the all of the administrative documents surviving from the reign of King John, including Pipe Rolls, *liberate* rolls, close rolls, patent rolls, accounts of the Norman Exchequer, and the daily expenses of the royal household. In no case in which it is possible to identify the men associated with the production of artillery to royal clerks ever use the term *balistarius* to describe these individuals.

carpentarius).[11] Powicke was correct to point out the confusion that could result from the use of the term *balistarius* by royal clerks. However, this confusion was not between the builders of artillery and soldiers armed with crossbows but rather between soldiers armed with crossbows and the men who built crossbows for the crown.[12]

A similar problem of confusion can arise from the use by royal clerks of the terms *ingeniator* and *carpentarius*, which appear in administrative documents describing a variety of specialists working for the crown on projects ranging from water mills to fortresses, as well as for the builders siege engines.[13] This same broad matrix of activities can be seen for those artisans denoted by royal clerks as *fabri*, which served as a generic term for smith, but also was used to designate specialists in the production of iron heads for crossbow bolts and the iron fittings on siege engines. The only solution to the potentially confusing terminological ambiguity is to consider all of the surviving documents produced by the royal government to ascertain on the basis of context which skilled professional fulfilled which specialized function.[14]

---

11 A full list of the references in the surviving administrative documents to each of these specialists in arms production is provided in the register at the end of this chapter. It should be noted that other terms, including *trebuchetarius*, also came into use by administrative clerks during Henry III's reign, particularly for the officer named Jordan.

12 Concerning the terms used by royal clerks to designate crossbow makers over the course of the thirteenth century, see David S. Bachrach, "The Royal Crossbow Makers of England, 1204–1272", *Nottingham Medieval Studies* 47 (2003), 168–197, and in this volume.

13 A good example of an engineer who worked on both siege engines and royal building projects, including castle towers, was a man named Gerard. He appears regularly in administrative documents from Henry III's reign. See, for example, *Close Rolls 1242–1247* (London, 1916, repr. 1970), 69, 200, and 283.

14 A typical example of the type of confusion that can result from a limited sampling of the available information is the identification by Powicke, *Loss of Normandy*, 224 of Urric *balistarius* with Urric *ingeniator*. There is no evidence in any of the surviving sources that any arms maker who specialized in the construction of siege engines was ever described by royal clerks as a *balistarius* on the basis of this occupation. There is also no evidence that a specialist in the construction of siege engines ever built crossbows and would ever have been considered a *balistarius* by royal clerks. It is, therefore, almost certainly the case that the Urric *balistarius* either was a soldier who was armed with a crossbow or was a specialist in the construction of crossbows. It is far more likely, however, that this Urric was a soldier rather than a craftsman because there were far more of the former than the latter throughout the late twelfth and early thirteenth century. In addition, there is no information in the surviving sources that would indicate a man named Urric ever was involved in the production of crossbows. Similar confusion reigns in Powicke's identification (225) of Lupillus *balistarius* as an artillery engineer. The surviving sources clearly indicate that Lupillus was an officer in command of a company of crossbowmen. All of the sources that refer to him describe Lupillus as the commander of a royal fortress, and none of these sources give any indication that he had anything to do with the production of any weapon of any type. See *Rotuli literrarum patentium in Turri Londinensi asservati 1201–1216*, ed. Thomas D. Hardy (London, 1835), hereafter *Rotuli*, 25, 116, and 195.

Arms production in John's reign

This study is focused on the reign of King John for three reasons. First, although it is clear from surviving documents that siege engines as well as ammunition for siege engines and crossbows were produced by the royal government during the reigns of Henry II (1154–1189) and Richard, it is only from John's reign that a sufficient corpus of information survives to develop a collective biography of the arms builders employed by the royal government.[15] Secondly, beginning with John's reign, as contrasted with the rule of Henry II or Richard I, we see the development of a large-scale crossbow industry under royal control.[16] Before the loss of Normandy and many other crown possessions in France, the royal government imported large numbers of crossbows from abroad, mainly from Italy and particularly Genoa. However, in 1204, the royal government began to employ a cadre crossbow makers in England, thereby substantially increasing the total number of arms makers in royal pay.[17]

Finally, a study ending John's reign in 1216 is suggested by the disruption in both royal administration and arms production caused by the civil war and French invasion of that year. The surviving administrative documents for the period 1216–1220 are lacunose. When we again have sufficient information from administrative documents to draw conclusions about royal arms production in 1221, it is clear that there had been substantial changes in personnel and in administrative structures. All of John's crossbow builders and several of the specialists in the construction of artillery had disappeared from the sources and been replaced by new men. By 1221, the organization of crossbow production also had been altered substantially.[18] Finally, a much greater corpus of information survives from Henry III's reign concerning the production of ammunition for both crossbows and siege engines than does for the reign of his father. For these reasons, it seems prudent to leave a prosopographical examination of Henry III's arms makers, including specialists in the production of ammunition, to a later study that can take full account of this long reign and concomitant vast corpus of administrative sources.

---

15 The sources used in this study are *Rotuli*, seen above, as well as *Rotuli Litterarum Clausarum in Turri Londonensi Asservati 1204–1227*, ed. Thomas D. Hardy, 2 vols (1833–1834), hereafter *CR I* and *CR II*; The *misae* accounts and *praestita* rolls, which are recorded in *Rotuli de Liberate ac de Misis et Praestitis regnante Johanne*, ed. Thomas D. Hardy (London, 1844), hereafter *Rot. de Lib*; *Rotuli Normannie in Turri asservati Johanne et Henrico Quinto Anglie Regibus*, ed. Thomas D. Hardy (London, 1835), hereafter *Rot. Norm;* and individual Pipe Rolls, which are cited individually in this chapter.

16 See David S. Bachrach, "The Origins of the English Crossbow Industry", *Journal of Medieval History* 2 (2003), 73–87.

17 Bachrach, "Royal Crossbow Makers", 170–171.

18 Ibid., 176–181.

Artillery builders

Although local magnates occasionally besieged their neighbors' strongholds in thirteenth-century England, the overwhelming consumer of siege artillery of all types was the royal government. As a result, King John, following in the footsteps of his father and brother, found it prudent to maintain a cadre of specialists who could oversee the production and repair of artillery on a continuing basis, both during peacetime and in periods of intense military conflict. It was by no means the case, as some scholars have suggested, that building artillery was simply an *ad hoc* process carried out at sieges in the heat of a conflict.[19] Rather, King John routinely ordered the construction and repair of siege artillery even during periods of calm and had these weapons stored at depots or magazines throughout the kingdom.[20]

Wages

Specific information about the wages paid by the royal government to its employees, as contrasted with the grant of a specific sum of money, is relatively rare. It is, nevertheless, possible to identify the daily wages of nine of the ten men who oversaw the construction of the king's siege engines between 1199 and 1216. Daily wages ranged from a low of 6 d. earned by four men—Baldwin, Hugh de Barentin, Laurence de Sancto Agnino, and Robert—to a high of 9 d. earned by three specialists named Burnellus, Nicholas de Andelys, and Thomas.[21] Two other artillery builders, named Drogo of Dieppe and Ralph, earned 7.5 d. and 7 d. per day, respectively.[22] It is somewhat ironic that the wage rate of the artillery engineer from John's reign, who has received the most attention from scholars, namely Urric, is not recorded in the surviving administrative records.[23]

In most cases, these daily wage rates only can be identified on the basis of a single reference in the surviving sources, and it is therefore not possible to determine whether we are seeing the high point or low point in any individual's career. In addition, the scarcity of data points makes it impossible to ascertain whether

---

19 See, for example, John France, *Western Warfare in the Age of Crusades 1000–1300* (London, 1990), 124–125.

20 Regarding the administration of artillery, including its storage, see Bachrach, "Military Administration", passim.

21 For the wages of all of these men see *Pipe Roll 17 John*, ed. R. A. Brown (London, 1964), 13; and National Archives E372/66 6r. In the case of Thomas, Burnellus, and Robert, their wage rates can be dated back to the reign of King John on the basis of a writ issued on 19 February 1221 to Sheriff Philip Mark of Nottingham, instructing him to pay these three men the same wages that they were accustomed to receive *tempore domini J rex patris nostri*. See *CR I*, 449. The actual rates of pay earned by these specialists are known from the Pipe Roll E372/66 6r.

22 *The Great Roll of the Pipe for the Thirteenth Year of the Reign of King John Michaelmas 1211*, ed. Doris M. Stenton (London, 1953), 84; and *CR I*, 191.

23 For the scholarly discussion of Urric, see the register at the end of this chapter.

there were any overall patterns in the rate of wages paid to this cadre of arms makers in the period 1199–1216. What is clear, however, is that even the lowest paid specialists in the construction of siege artillery received much higher rates of compensation than most other royal personnel. By contrast with the 6 d. earned by Laurence de Sancto Agnino, for example, the typical royal chaplains during John's reign earned about 2 d. a day.[24] Porters and watchmen, who obviously required less training than chaplains, earned half this amount.[25]

When contrasted with other craftsmen, the specialists in the construction of siege artillery were among the better compensated officers working for the royal government. Some master carpenters in the early thirteenth century earned as much as 6 d. per day, but the majority received substantially less than this, and received wages of just 2–3 d. per day.[26] Similar rates of compensation appear to have been the norm for miners and masons, with masters sometimes earning as much as 6 d. per day, while their subordinates earned, at most, just half this amount.[27] Thus, the lowest paid artillery builders were compensated at the same rate as the highest paid carpenters, miners, and masons. The only group that earned consistently higher wages than specialists in artillery construction were mounted soldiers, who could earn from 6 d. to 15 d. a day, depending on how much equipment and how many horses they brought to the host.[28]

In addition to high rates of pay, it is clear that least one of the specialists in artillery construction, namely Urric, received both estates and a pension from King John. On 2 June 1201, John issued a writ to a royal officer named Geoffrey, who had responsibility for overseeing a portion of the royal lands near Lincoln, ordering that properties that formerly belonged to a man named Henry of Essex be transferred to Urric.[29] The writ noted that Urric currently was in royal service and that the king required him to build engines. As a consequence, Geoffrey not only was to ensure the transfer of the property to Urric, but also was to guard it along with all of its appurtenances until Urric's duties permitted him to go there himself to take formal possession.[30] Urric held additional estates from the king at Sutton near Gloucester. Following Urric's death in 1216, William Marshal, who was acting as regent in King Henry III's name, ordered Engelhard de Cigoné, then serving as sheriff of Gloucester, to transfer this estate to Gilbert Basset.[31] Evidence for Urric's pension comes from the roll of imprests for 1210, which record two

24 Paul Latimer, "Wages in Late Twelfth and Early Thirteenth-Century England", *Haskins Society Journal* 9 (1997), 185–205, here 188–190.
25 Ibid., 192–193. During the early years of Henry III's reign, however, these wage rates doubled (193).
26 Latimer, "Wages", 196.
27 Ibid., 197.
28 Ibid., 200–202.
29 *Rotuli*, 14.
30 Ibid.
31 *CR I*, 294.

payments of 40 s. and 26 s. 8 d. to the royal engineer.[32] Taken together, these two sums were greater than the yearly salary of a royal chaplain.

Conditions of service

The high rates of pay and, in Urric's case, the perquisites as well, provided by the royal government to these specialists in artillery construction are understandable both in light of their skills and because they served not as individual craftsmen, but rather as team leaders. In a typical example of this practice, Drogo of Dieppe traveled to Marlborough Castle in 1208 to oversee the construction of a battery of siege engines described the royal clerks as *mangonelli* and *petrariae*, which were torsion-powered and traction engines, respectively.[33] The clerks working at the Exchequer recorded that the sheriff of Wiltshire spent in excess of £12 to provide iron and other materials needed for the construction of the siege engines at Marlborough, which were being built by Drogo and his *socii*.[34]

In a similar case, a royal writ issued on 24 August 1212 to Philip Mark, the sheriff of Nottinghamshire, informed this official that two master carpenters named Ralph and Nicholas had been ordered to travel to the town of Nottingham to build two smaller engines of the *petrariae* type, denoted in the sources as "Turkish" in construction.[35] Philip Mark was instructed to receive both the master carpenters and their *socii* at Nottingham Castle and to ensure the provision of the supplies that were necessary for their work. The Pipe Roll for 1214 confirms that Ralph and Nicholas de Andelys along with their *socii* completed the construction of the two engines at a total cost to the royal government of just over £38.[36]

In one final example, the engineer Urric also is identified in royal administrative documents as leading a team of workers in the construction of artillery. In 1194, during Richard's reign, Urric was given responsibility not only for building engines but also for purchasing supplies, the cost of which was to be reimbursed by the royal government. The 1194 Pipe Roll for London and Middlesex records that a payment in excess of 70 s. had been made to Urric to reimburse him for the purchase of two cartloads of rope that were used to build engines at Nottingham.[37] In a writ issued six years later, on 30 May 1200, to the provost of Chinon, in the Touraine, the recently elevated King John makes clear that Urric still held a position of command in the overall royal efforts to build siege engines. In this case,

---

32 *Rotuli*, 190 and 215.
33 *The Great Roll of the Pipe for the Tenth Year of the Reign of King John Michaelmas 1208*, ed. Doris M. Stenton (London, 1947), 201–202.
34 Ibid.
35 *CR I*, 122.
36 *The Great Roll of the Pipe for the Sixteenth Year of the Reign of King John Michaelmas 1214*, ed. Patricia M. Barnes (London, 1962), 156.
37 *The Great Roll of the Pipe for the Sixth Year of the Reign of Richard the First Michaelmas 1194*, ed. Doris M. Stenton (London, 1928), 176.

Urric was operating with a team of four *socii*, who were aiding him in the building of both *petrariae* and *mangonelli*. The provost of Chinon was commanded to provide everything required by Urric, his four men, and their six horses until the king arrived to take charge of the operations there in person.[38]

In addition to higher pay and superior status enjoyed by specialists in the construction of siege engines, it seems clear that many of them also benefited from long terms of employment in royal service. Indeed, in several cases the artillery engineers continued to work for the crown after the king who had hired them had died. Urric, for example, was already an important figure in 1194 under Richard and stayed on in active service under John until at least 1201, as discussed earlier. Moreover, he continued to receive gifts and maintained the possession of estates from the royal government for another fifteen years. The fragmentary nature of the surviving documents does not make it possible to determine whether Urric worked for the crown during this entire period, but it seems likely that he was available if the king needed him.

At least five other artillery builders began their careers under John and continued to work for the royal government during Henry III's reign. Nicholas de Andelys first appears in the surviving records as an artillery specialists in August 1212.[39] On this occasion, as discussed earlier, Philip was paired with Ralph as a leader of a team of artillery builders dispatched to Nottingham Castle. The last surviving reference to Nicholas is from 28 November 1236, when a writ issued by the Chancery to the Exchequer instructed the latter to pay him his wages.[40] Hugh de Barentin was one of five artillery specialists employed in 1216 by the military commander Brian de L'Isle to build two *petrariae* and three "Turkish" *mangonelli* at Knaresborough Castle.[41] Hugh last appears in the surviving sources in 1230 as the recipient of 30 s. 5 d. from Galfridus de Hatfeld, who was serving as the royal administrator of Canterbury at that time.[42]

As discussed, three other artillery engineers—Burnellus, Robert, and Thomas—can be identified as having worked for King John on the basis of a writ issued by Henry III's regents to Sheriff Philip Mark on 19 February 1221.[43] The three men were to be paid at the same rate that they were accustomed to earn during the reign of King John.[44] All three of these artillery builders subsequently had long careers under Henry III. Robert worked until at last 1228, and Thomas did not leave royal service before 1229.[45] Burnellus last appears in the surviving royal records on 4

---

38   *Rotuli Norm.*, 24.
39   *CR I*, 122.
40   *Calendar of Liberate Rolls 1226–1240* (London, 1916), 247.
41   Ibid.
42   National Archives E372/75 1r.
43   *CR II*, 449.
44   Ibid.
45   *Liberate Rolls 1226–1240*, 82 and 121.

May 1242 in a routine writ of *liberate* to the Exchequer authorizing the payment of his wages, which indicates that he was still actively in service at that time.[46]

In addition to specialists who stayed in royal service after the previous king had died, two other artillery builders can be seen to have worked for John over a period of years. Drogo of Dieppe first appears in the royal administrative documents on 9 March 1207. On this occasion, John issued a writ to the Exchequer authorizing officials there to provide Drogo with £3 so that he could purchase supplies that he required for the construction of the king's engines.[47] The last time that Drogo appears in royal records is in the Pipe Roll account for 1211.[48] The first surviving record of Ralph's service as a royal artillery builder was alongside Nicholas de Andelys at Nottingham Castle in August 1212.[49] Ralph's last appearance is in 1215.[50] The minimum length of service for these two specialists, therefore, was four years and three years, respectively. Two other artillery builders, Baldwin and Laurence de Sancto Agnino, appear only one time each in the surviving records, and it is therefore not possible to give a minimum figure for their terms of service.[51] Taken as a group, the length of service of the specialists in building artillery ranges from a minimum of three to a minimum of twenty-six years, with the majority having served the crown for more than a decade.

Origins of the artillery builders

Taking into account their high pay, high status, and longevity in royal service, the artillery builders serving King John can be characterized as having possessed a distinctive and prized collection of skills both as craftsmen and as administrators. It is therefore natural to consider the origins of these men and ask where they may have gained the knowledge necessary to build the king's engines. On the basis of his admittedly narrow reading of the sources, Powicke concluded that the *balistarii*, whom he thought included both crossbow-armed soldiers and artillery engineers, largely were "foreign born."[52] A careful reading of all of the pertinent administrative documents would seem to confirm Powicke's view, at least as it regards birth in England, proper. To take one of the most obvious examples, Drogo consistently is described in the sources as coming from Dieppe, a town in Normandy (department of Seine-Maritime). The fact that the royal clerks habitually used a place name as a byname for a royal officer is not conclusive

---

46 *Calendar of Patent Rolls 1232–1247* (London, 1906), 286. All of the references to the service of Burnellus, Robert, and Thomas during the reign of Henry III can be found in the register at the end of this chapter.

47 *CR I*, 82.

48 *Pipe Roll 13 John*, 84.

49 *CR I*, 122.

50 For a full list of references to Ralph's career, see the register at the end of the chapter.

51 *Pipe Roll 17 John*, 13.

52 Powicke, *Loss of Normandy*, 224–225 does not define what he means by foreign, but from the context of the passage, it appears that he is referring to regions outside of England.

evidence that this individual came from that place. But it is noteworthy that the royal clerks did not call him "Drogo Deppa" but rather "Drogo *de* Deppa". The inclusion of the preposition "de" is important in this context because specialists in onomastics have concluded that in the late twelfth and early thirteenth century, the use of "de" in English administrative records indicates an individual's place of origin just as the loss of the "de" is an indication of the fossilization of the place name.[53] Similar considerations also apply in the cases of Hugh de Barentin, Nicholas de Andelys, and Laurence de Sancto Agnino. Barentin (department of Seine-Maritime) and Andelys (department of Eure), along with Dieppe, all are located in Normandy, which was lost by John in 1204. I have not been able to identify the location of the potential home of Laurence de Sancto Agnino.

It is rather more difficult to draw conclusions about the origins of the remaining artillery engineers just noted. Nevertheless, several factors indicate a continental as opposed to an English origin for at least some if not all of these men. First, none of them has an Anglo-Saxon name. This is important for identifying their origins because when they were named, likely during the last quarter or third of the twelfth century, it was still the norm for most children of Anglo-Saxon origin born below the elite level to be given Anglo-Saxon rather than continental names.[54] Admittedly, because we do not know the interests, hopes and aspirations of the individuals involved, it would be imprudent to draw a conclusion about a particular case from general naming patterns. However, it is noteworthy to find *no* Anglo-Saxon names among a group of men born c. 1160–1180 to families of middling to lower social status if, in fact, these men were born in England.

The hypothesis that at least some of these artillery builders were of continental as opposed to Anglo-Saxon origin is strengthened further when we consider that they bear names that were relatively uncommon in England, in some cases well into the thirteenth century. Several of the men, namely Nicholas, Laurence, and Thomas, bore saints' names that were popular on the continent but not in England at this time. The names of Italian, French, and even New Testament saints entered the lay, English *Namengut* only very slowly over the course of the twelfth and thirteenth century. The most striking example of the slow penetration into England of saints' names common on the continent is Peter, prince of the apostles, which remained exceptionally rare among laymen almost to the end of the thirteenth century in some regions.[55]

---

53 See, for example, Gillian Fellows Jensen, "The Surnames of the Tenants of the Bishop of Lincoln in Nine English Counties c. 1225", in *Binamen och slècktnamen: Avgrèansning och Ursprung*, ed. Thorsten Andersson (Uppsala, 1975), 39–65, here 47.

54 David A. Postles, "Nomina villanorum et burgensium: Oxfordshire Bynames before c. 1250", in *Oxoniensia* 54 (1989), 319–325, here 320–321, argues for the strong survival of insular names into the late twelfth century. Postles reiterates this view in "Cultures of Peasant Naming in Twelfth Century England", *Medieval Prosopography* 18 (1997), 24–54, here 39.

55 P. M. Stell, "Forenames in Thirteenth- and Fourteenth-Century Yorkshire: A Study Based on a Biographical Database Generated by a Computer", *Medieval Prosopography* 20 (1999), 95–128.

The second category of names found among the king's artillery builders, which include Baldwin, Drogo, Hugh, Ralph, and Robert, belong to what specialists in onomastic studies refer to as the West Germanic group.[56] These names, although uncommon in twelfth-century England, were very common in Normandy, Flanders, and northern and western France, that is the areas on the continent either ruled by the Angevin kings of England or that were allied to them.[57]

The onomastic trends in both England and the continent indicate that Powicke was correct to suggest that many, if not most, of the men who built King John's artillery came from outside of England. It would seem relatively certain that some of these specialists, particularly Drogo, Nicholas, and Hugh, came from Normandy. The others, particularly Ralph, Robert, and Baldwin, may also have come from Normandy or surrounding regions, but this cannot be demonstrated on the basis of the surviving evidence. The remaining builders of the king's siege engines, including Laurence, Urric, Burnellus, and Thomas, bore names that were not widely used in England during the late twelfth and early thirteenth century, but without further information, it is not possible to draw any firm conclusions about their national or ethnic origins.

Crossbow builders: Wages and perquisites

In the wake of the disasters of 1202 and 1203, King John's government found it necessary to replace the importation of crossbows from abroad with the establishment of a domestic crossbow industry under royal control.[58] By 1216, no fewer than ten specialists in crossbow production worked in royal workshops. Despite the relatively taciturn nature of the sources, discussed previously, regarding the daily wages of royal arms makers, it is possible to identify the daily wage of eight of the ten crossbow makers employed by the royal government during King John's reign. The highest paid of these arms builders was a man named Peter the Saracen, who earned 9 d. a day.[59] The second highest paid builder was a man named Roger of Genoa, who earned either 6 d. or 7 d. a day. The rate changed

---

56 Postles, "Cultures", 30.
57 Numerous studies treat the onomastic patterns in the lands that border on the English Channel. See, for example, Monique Mestayer, "Prénoms et hypocoristique duaisiens de 1225 á 1270", *Bulletin philologique et historique (jusqu'à 1610) du comité des travaux historiques et scientifiques* (1977), 179–189; and François Neveux, "Le système anthroponymique en Normandie d'après le cartulaire du chapitre de Bayeux XIe-XIII siècles", in *Genèse medieval de l'anthroponymie moderne* (Tours, 1997), 127–139. For the West Germanic names of the men who came to England with William the Conqueror in 1066 and in the wake of the conquest, see *Domesday Names: An Index of Latin Personal and Place Names in Domesday Book*, ed. K. S. B. Keat-Rohan and David E. Thornton (Woodbridge, 1997).
58 Bachrach, "Origins", 170–171.
59 *CR I*, 3, 9. 50, 70. 76, 102.

several times over the course of his career.[60] The six remaining crossbow makers for whom we have evidence of daily wages—Adam, Benedict the Moor, Gerard, Nicholas, Reginald, and Robert—all earned 4.5 d. per day.[61]

These rates of pay were certainly very favorable when compared to other royal employees, such as chaplains and porters, discussed already. The wages of the crossbow makers also were generous when compared to the 2–3 d. earned by craftsmen such as carpenters, smiths, and miners below the master class.[62] In comparison, however, to master craftsmen and to their fellow arms builders, who constructed siege engines, the wages of most of John's crossbow makers are less generous. Only one, Peter the Saracen, was paid at the 9 d. per day scale enjoyed by the upper tier of siege engine builders. The only other crossbow maker whose wages equaled the lower ranks of these men was Roger of Genoa, whose 6–7 d. per day place him at the same level as master carpenters and other master craftsmen.

One of the reasons why Peter the Saracen and Roger of Genoa may have been paid at rates higher than the other crossbow makers was that they, like several of the artillery builders already discussed, were in charge of teams of craftsmen. The Pipe Roll for 1207 makes clear, for example, that the sheriff of Nottinghamshire had paid almost £30 for the wages of Roger of Genoa and his three *socii*, to construct crossbows.[63] Similarly, the Pipe Roll for 1211 records that Engelhard de Cigoné spent just over £3 to purchase suits of clothing for Peter the Saracen, his wife, and two of his *socii*.[64]

While the discussion of the daily wage rates for crossbow makers permits us to make helpful comparisons with artillery engineers and other specialists employed by the royal government, it is important to understand that in contrast to many other royal employees, the crossbow makers earned yearly salaries rather than daily wages. Thus, whereas artillery builders were paid only for the days on which they worked, crossbow makers were paid their daily wage rate both on days when they worked and on days when they did not.[65] By contrast, there is no comparable evidence that artillery builders were paid as *de facto* salaried employees. This difference in the pay structure between crossbow makers and artillery builders may explain the higher daily wage rates of the latter.

---

60 Ibid., 9, 102; and *Rotuli*, 101.
61 For their wages see *The Great Roll of the Pipe for the Seventh Year of the Reign of King John Michaelmas 1205*, ed. Sidney Smith (London, 1941), 101; and *CR I*, 3, 79. 102.
62 Latimer, "Wages", 193–204.
63 *The Great Roll of the Pipe for the Ninth Year of the Reign of King John Michaelmas 1207*, ed. A. Mary Kirkus (London, 1946), 116.
64 *Pipe Roll 13 John*, 176.
65 The structure of crossbow makers' pay as salaries is discussed in detail in David S. Bachrach, "The Royal Crossbow Makers of England, 1204–1272", *Nottingham Medieval Studies* 47 (2003), 168–197, and in this volume.

The comparatively lower daily rate earned by the crossbow makers as compared with the king's artillery builders also does not take into account the fact that the former would appear to have benefited on a regular basis from grants of royal gifts, while that does not seem to have been true of the latter, with the notable exception of Urric, discussed previously. As a consequence, the "real wages" of the crossbow makers very likely was considerably higher than the nominal wages would seem to indicate. The most common of the perquisites received by the crossbow makers was the periodic grant of either clothing, or of donatives that were designated for the purchase of clothing by the beneficiary. On 14 March 1205, for example, the royal government issued a writ to Sheriff Philip Mark of Nottinghamshire requiring him either to provide each of the crossbow makers working there—Peter, Roger, and Hamo—with a suit of clothing or with 15 s. each, so that they could purchase clothing on their own.[66] To put this sum into perspective, 15 s. equaled twenty days' pay for Peter and probably about forty days' pay for Hamo.

In addition to making grants of clothing and money to the crossbow makers themselves, the royal government also provide perquisites to their families. On 4 October 1204, for example, King John ordered the sheriff of Wiltshire to provide two green tunics to the wives of Benedict the Moor and Peter the Saracen who, at that time, were residing in the royal castle at Salisbury.[67] The Pipe Roll account for 1204 confirms that the sheriff of Wiltshire spent just over 12 s. to acquire these tunics.[68] Although specialists in the production of ammunition are not the focus of this study, it is clear that they too benefited alongside their colleagues in the royal crossbow workshops from royal largesse. The Pipe Roll account for 1211 records that the sheriff of Gloucestershire received credit at the Exchequer for having purchased clothing for Peter the Saracen, a fletcher working with him named Philip, both of their wives, and Philip's son.[69] It may be the case that Philip and Philip's son were among the *socii* of Peter the Saracen, discussed previously.

In addition to gifts of clothing, King John's government also made much more substantial grants to highly valued officers. It is in this context that we should understand a writ issued on 14 August 1215 to a royal official named Philip de Albino.[70] Philip was required to transfer possession of a mill located near the town of Stapleton to the crossbow maker Peter the Saracen. It would certainly appear that Peter, like the artillery builder Urric, had earned the king's gratitude and his favor.

---

66 Ibid, 23.
67 Ibid., 90
68 *Pipe Roll 6 John*, 248.
69 *Pipe Roll 13 John*, 171.
70 *CR I*, 225.

Conditions of service

Of the ten men who can be identified as crossbow makers working for the royal government in England during John's reign, six are mentioned in two or more documents, making it possible to determine at least the minimum period that they worked for the crown. Roger of Genoa, who would appear already to have been in John's service before the beginning of large-scale crossbow production, is mentioned in the Pipe Roll account for 1202 as the recipient of more than £3 paid by the sheriff of Kent for work on crossbows.[71] Roger was still actively engaged in royal service in 1215, when he is identified in the Pipe Roll for that year working at Knaresborough Castle, then under the command of Brian de L'Isle.[72]

Nicholas, Reginald, Benedict the Moor, and Peter the Saracen all first appear in the royal administrative records in the summer of 1204.[73] Nicholas was active in the king's service until at least 1215, when he worked alongside Roger of Genoa building crossbows at Knaresborough Castle.[74] The last reference to Benedict the Moor is from April 1215, when King John sent a writ to Engelhard de Cigoné, the sheriff of Gloucestershire, ordering him to release Benedict from prison.[75] It is not clear how long Benedict had been in prison at this time; however, the last reference to him building crossbows dates to February 1208.[76] As mentioned previously, Peter the Saracen received a mill from the king in 1215, and this may mark his retirement from royal service. The last surviving reference to Peter actually building crossbows is in a writ issued on 20 January 1214, when the constable of Bristol Castle was commanded to provide clothing for Peter and his wife.[77] The crossbow maker named Robert, who is first mentioned in the Pipe Roll account for 1205, last appears in 1208.[78] Reginald, who would seem to have worked for the royal government for the shortest period, does not appear in royal administrative records after 1205.[79]

Like the artillery builders already discussed, it would appear that the king's crossbow makers benefited from long terms of service to the government. Half of the men for whom we have two or more data points worked for at least a decade. Two others worked at least three and four years, respectively. As was also true of the artillery builders, however, the lacunose nature of the surviving sources makes it impossible to develop firm figures for the complete length of the tenures of the king's crossbow makers. These texts do not mention when of any of these

---

71 *The Great Roll of the Pipe for the Fourth Year of the Reign of King John Michaelmas 1202*, ed. Doris M. Stenton (London, 1937), 202.
72 *Pipe Roll 17 John*, 13.
73 *CR I*, 3.
74 *Pipe Roll 17 John*, 13.
75 *CR I*, 133.
76 Ibid., 102.
77 Ibid., 160.
78 *Pipe Roll 7 John*, 39 and *CR I*, 102.
79 The last reference to Roger's work is in *Pipe Roll 7 John*, 39.

men were first employed, and there is also no firm indication when any of them left the king's service. Consequently, all of these terms of service must be seen as *minima*. Nevertheless, it does seem safe to conclude, on the basis of the surviving documents, that in contrast to the artillery builders, there was a complete break in continuity between the personnel employed by King John and those employed by Henry III's regency government to build the king's crossbows.

Families and backgrounds

The documents discussing the perquisites granted to the king's crossbow makers also make not infrequent references to the families of some of these men. The wives of Peter the Saracen and Benedict the Moor appear several times each over the course of John's reign as recipients of royal donatives of clothing and money.[80] A writ issued on 21 September 1205 to Hugh Neville, then serving as constable of Marlborough Castle, indicates that Peter the Saracen also had a son traveling with him in the course of his duties.[81] Roger of Genoa and Galfrid also can be identified as having wives either working with them or traveling with them on the basis of royal gifts of clothing.[82] Given that we can only see these wives, and in one case a child, of the king's crossbow makers because they were recipients of specific royal grants, it seems reasonable to conclude that others of the king's crossbow makers also were married. It is also worthy of note that two of the crossbow makers, Nicholas and Reginald, are identified by royal clerks as brothers.[83]

Origins

In considering the origins of the royal crossbow makers in the early thirteenth century, it must be kept in mind that before King John established production centers in England for crossbows in 1203–1204, the royal government had purchased most of its weapons from abroad, and particularly from the city of Genoa.[84] By contrast, there is no evidence that the royal government purchased crossbows produced within England, itself.[85] One would not, therefore, expect to find Englishmen among the earliest crossbow makers in the king's service.

As was the case with the artillery builders, previously discussed, it is helpful to begin with the names of the crossbow makers in the king's employ to see if these give a clue about their origins. The first point to make in this context is that like the artillery builders, not a single one of the king's crossbow makers had an Anglo-Saxon name. The lack of Anglo-Saxon names is not, in itself, proof that

---

80   *Pipe Roll 6 John*, 248; *Pipe Roll 12 John*, 83; *CR I*, 10, 35, 70, 92, 166.
81   *CR I*, 50.
82   *Pipe Roll 17 John*, 13 and *CR I*, 166.
83   *CR I*, 9.
84   See the discussion of this point in Bachrach, "Origins", 81–83.
85   Ibid.

the crossbow makers were born outside of England. Nevertheless, as discussed, the complete absence of such names among a group of men born into the middling to lower ranks of English society in the third quarter of the twelfth century would be unusual.[86]

The second point to be made about the names of these crossbow makers is that they also are drawn from the West Germanic *Namengut*, from continental saints' names, and from the Old Testament. These categories of names, as discussed, were adopted very slowly into the lower and middle ranks of English society, but were comparatively common in Normandy, the west of France, and also in southern Italy, which had a strong Norman presence, dating back to the mid-eleventh century.[87]

Within this overall historical and onomastic framework, certain of the crossbow makers stand out as more obviously foreign both to England and to the English possessions on the continent in Normandy and the west of France. The first of these is Roger of Genoa. As was true of the artillery builders Drogo, Nicholas, Hugh, and Laurence, discussed here, the royal clerks used the preposition "de" when discussing Roger, indicating that Roger was from Genoa and not simply someone with an ancestor from this city.[88] In light of the fact that John's government had purchased large numbers of crossbows from Genoa, it does not seem unreasonable that the king would seek to employ a specialist from this center of production when attempting to establish his own crossbow workshops. Indeed, the fact that Roger's employment began in 1202, two years before the major influx of crossbow makers in 1204, suggests that the royal government was relying on Roger's expertise in order to make decisions about the best way to set up major workshops in England.

Two other men, whose names suggest an origin outside of King John's realms, either in England or on the continent, are Peter the Saracen and Benedict the Moor. It is possible, of course, that royal clerks simply recorded bynames acquired by Englishmen who had served, for example, in King Richard's crusade in the early 1190s. However, the combination of peculiar bynames with the continental saints' names Peter and Benedict, both of which were exceptionally rare among laymen in England during the late twelfth century, would seem to argue against their having been born on the island.[89]

---

86 Postles, "Culture", 39.
87 L. R. Ménager, "Pesanteur et l'étiologie de la colonization normande en Italie", and idem, "Inventaire des familles normandes et franques émigrées en Italie méridionale et en Sicilie (XIe-XIIe siècles)", both published in *Fonti e Studi de Corpus Membranarum Italicarum* 9 (1975), 89–215 and 260–340. These articles were reprinted in *Hommes et Institutions de l'Italie Normande* (London, 1981).
88 Jensen, "Surnames", 47.
89 The rarity of continental saints names in England up through the mid- to late thirteenth century is discussed by Stell, "Forenames", passim.

But the question remains whether Peter and Benedict were born in the West, perhaps in Normandy or southern Italy, or in the East. In order to address this problem, it is necessary to step back from the onomastic argument and return to the historical context in which these men were employed. First, it must be recalled that during the last quarter of the twelfth century, Muslims in the Levant achieved a level of technical superiority over Latin Christians in the production of crossbows. In particular, craftsmen working for Saladin (c. 1180) developed a mechanical means of spanning a crossbow using a winch, which made it possible for an individual soldier to use a heavier and more powerful crossbow while exerting less physical effort than previously had been required for a weaker bow.[90] There is no written record that discusses whether King Richard, who had a well-known interest in crossbows, or his military advisors became aware of this technical innovation.[91] It is a fact, however, that the winch-powered spanning device was being used in the construction of crossbows in England during John's reign, a generation before comparable weapons can be found elsewhere in Western Europe.[92] The knowledge for building these spanning devices had to come to England from the Middle East in some way. Given the absence of other plausible explanations, two crossbow makers with training in Muslim lands would seem to be a reasonable transmission vector. The fact that Peter the Saracen was also the most highly paid and most honored of John's crossbow makers indicates that he was viewed by this king as an exceptionally able artisan.[93]

As was true with respect to several of the artillery builders discussed, the origins of the remaining seven crossbow makers, namely Adam, Galfridus (Geoffrey), Girard, Hamo, Nicholas, Reginald, and Robert, cannot be ascertained definitively on the basis of the information recorded in the royal administrative records. However, the combination of onomastic evidence and the historical reality of the need by King John to establish *de novo* crossbow workshops to produce weapons for the crown does suggest that at least some of these men were recruited from outside of England.

Conclusion

As is frequently the case when a group is subjected to a prosopographical analysis, this examination of the royal arms makers during the reign of King John permits certain broader generalizations than were possible from earlier focused examinations of one or two individuals. First, it is clear that Urric, who has benefited from

---

90 For a full discussion of this question see Bachrach, "Crossbows for the King", 117.
91 Regarding Richard's fame as a devotee of crossbows, see the observations by William the Breton, *Philippidos* bk 5, lines 580–581 in *Oeuvres de Rigord et de Guillaume le Breton*, 2 vols, ed. Henry-François Delaborde (Paris, 1885), II: 147; and the commentary by Jim Bradbury, *The Medieval Archer* (Woodbridge, 1985), 76.
92 Bachrach, "Crossbows for the King, 117.
93 See the discussion by Bachrach, "Royal Crossbow Makers", 181–182.

the most scholarly attention of any of John's arms makers, was not typical in his receipt of royal largesse. John did value his arms producers. However, he usually demonstrated his appreciation of their service through high wages and, in the case of the crossbow builders, a combination of good wages and valuable perquisites, rather than through the grant of estates. The one exception to this pattern is the grant of a mill to Peter the Saracen in 1215. The second point to be emphasized is that many of the king's artillery and crossbow builders served the crown for long periods. This tendency is especially striking among the artillery builders, many of whom remained in royal service even after the death of the king who originally had employed them. Third, many and perhaps most of the king's arms builders were recruited from outside of England, despite the fact that the majority of their work was carried out in England, especially after 1204.

Finally, it is important to turn our attention from the arms builders, themselves, to the implications of their service for our understanding of English royal administration more generally. King John employed no fewer than twenty professional arms builders *whose names we know*. Many of these men were the supervisors of teams of assistants who may well have doubled the actual number of arms producers in royal service. This number of specialists in the construction of artillery and crossbows is indicative of production on a large scale, with the necessity for a concomitantly large administrative apparatus to facilitate their continued productivity. There can be no question of *ad hoc* or haphazard efforts here. Rather, we are observing in these arms makers the human face of a long term administrative effort by the royal government to produce large numbers of weapons for use by the king's troops.

Register of arms makers during the reign of King John

Artillery builders

BALDWIN likely was born on the continent, perhaps in Flanders, during the third quarter of the twelfth century. He earned 6 d. a day for his work building the king's artillery. Unfortunately, Baldwin appears in only one surviving document, and therefore it is not possible to determine his length of service or his family status.

Sources: *Pipe Roll 17 John*, 13.

BURNELLUS likely was born during the final quarter of the twelfth century. He probably was not born in England, but his place of origin remains obscure. Burnellus served under both King John and King Henry III for at least twenty-six years (1216–1242). He earned a daily wage rate of 9 d. There is no information in the surviving sources concerning his family status.

Sources: *Liberate Rolls 1226–1240*, 42, 135, 136, 137; *Patent Rolls 1232–1247*, 286; *CR I*, 449, 527; *CR II*, 44; *The Great Roll of the Pipe for the Fifth Year of the Reign of King Henry III Michaelmas 1221* (London, 1990), 74; National Archives E372/66 6r.

DROGO OF DIEPPE likely was born in the town of Dieppe in the modern department of Seine-Maritime in Normandy, probably during the third quarter of the
twelfth century. Drogo worked as a master artillery builder for King John from at
least 1207–1211, although this timeframe must be seen as a minimum. The surviving records do not provide any information about Drogo's family.

Sources: *Pipe Roll 10 John*, 201–202; *Pipe Roll 13 John*, 84; *CR I*, 82, 87, 108.

HUGH DE BARENTIN likely was born in the town of Barentin in the modern department of Seine-Maritime in Normandy during the third quarter of the
twelfth century. He worked for both King John and King Henry III as an artillery builder for at least fourteen years (1216–1230), and in 1221 at least, he
earned a daily wage of 6 d. The surviving records do not provide any information about his family.

Sources: *Pipe Roll 17 John*, 13; *Liberate Rolls 1226–1240*, 41, 79, 81, 82; *CR II*,
44; National Archives E372/75 1r.

LAURENCE DE SANCTO AGNINO likely was born during the final quarter of
the twelfth century in the town of Saint Agninus (Lamb) although it is not clear
where this town is located. Laurence appears in only a single surviving royal
document. In 1216, he earned 6 d. a day for his work as a royal artillery builder.
The sources do not provide information his family.

Sources: *Pipe Roll 17 John*, 13.

NICHOLAS DE ANDELYS likely was born in the town of Andelys in the modern
department of Eure in Normandy during the final quarter of the twelfth century.
He served under both King John and Henry III from at least 1212–1236, and
received a daily wage of 9 d. The surviving sources do not provide information
about his family.

Sources: *Pipe Roll 16 John*, 156; *Pipe Roll 17 John*, 13; *CR I*, 122, 267, 473; *CR
II*, 198; *Close Rolls 1227–1231*, 531; *Close Rolls 1231–1234*, 200, 352; *Liberate
Rolls 1226–1240*, 41 (2), 47, 48, 51, 79, 81, 82, 110, 121, 129, 138, 169, 184, 247.

RALPH likely was born in the second half of the twelfth century, He was probably born on the continent, perhaps in Normandy. Ralph worked as a master carpenter and artillery builder for King John for at least three years (1212–1215)
and earned a daily wage of 7 d. The surviving sources do not provide information
about his family,

Sources: *Pipe Roll 16 John*, 156; *CR I*, 122, 191.

ROBERT likely was born in the last quarter of the twelfth century, probably in
Normandy. He worked as an artillery builder for both King John and Henry III for
at least twelve years (1216–1228) and in 1221 earned a daily wage rate of 6 d. The
surviving sources do not provide information about his family.

Sources: *Liberate Rolls 1226–1240*, 41, 79, 81, 82; *CR I*, 449, 527, 621; *CR II*, 44; *Pipe Roll 5 John*, 74; National Archives E372/66 6r.

THOMAS likely was born during the final quarter of the twelfth century. He worked as an artillery builder for both King John and King Henry III for at least thirteen years (1216–1229) and earned a daily wage rate of 9 d. The surviving sources do not provide information about his family.

Sources: *CR I*, 449, 455, 527; *CR II*, 44, 198; *Liberate Rolls 1226–1240*, 41, 47, 48, 79, 81, 82, 110, 121; *Pipe Roll 5 John*, 74; National Archives E372/66 6r.

URRIC likely was born in the mid twelfth century on the continent, perhaps in Normandy. He served as a master artillery builder under both King Richard and King John for at least seven years (1194–1201), although probably for much longer. His daily wage rate is not known, but Urric did receive both estates and a pension from the royal government. Urric died in 1216. The surviving sources do not provide information about Urric's family.

Sources: *Pipe Roll 6 Richard*, 176; *Rotuli Norm.*, 24; *Rotuli*, 14, 190, 215; *CR I*, 293, 294

Scholarly Literature: Powicke, *Loss of Normandy*, 224; *The History of the King's Works: Volume I The Middle Ages*, ed. R. Allen Brown, H. M. Colvin, and A. J. Taylor (London, 1963), 59–61; Michael Prestwich, *Armies and Warfare in the Middle Ages: The English Experience* (New Haven, CT, 1996), 285; France, *Western Warfare*, 2 and 125.

Crossbow makers

ADAM likely was born during the second half, and perhaps during the final quarter of the twelfth century. He may have come from the continent in a region that owed allegiance to the king of England, but this is not certain. He served as a crossbow maker under King John and earned a daily wage of 4.5 d. The surviving sources do not include information about his family.

Sources: *Pipe Roll 7 John*, 101.

BENEDICT THE MOOR likely was born in the Levant during the second half of the twelfth century. He was recruited by the royal government to come to England to help in the development of a domestic crossbow industry and remained in King John's service for at least four years (1204–1208). Benedict last appears in the royal records in 1215 when King John ordered his release from custody. Benedict was married although we do not know the name of his wife. Both Benedict and his wife received regular donatives of cash and clothing from the royal government that supplemented his pay of 4.5 d. per day.

Sources: *Pipe Roll 6 John*, 248; *Rotuli*, 133; *CR I*, 3, 9, 10, 35, 102.

GALFRIDUS likely was born during the last quarter of the twelfth century but the place of his birth is not known. He built crossbows for King John but the surviving sources do not provide information about his wages or his term of service. The surviving sources also do not include information about his family.

Sources: *CR I*, 160.

GIRARD likely was born during the final quarter of the twelfth century, but the place of his birth is not known. He built crossbows for King John but the surviving sources do not permit any conclusions about his wages or his term of service. The surviving sources do not include information about his family.

Sources: *Rotuli*, 79.

HAMO likely was born during the final quarter of the twelfth century. It seems unlikely that he was born in England, and he may have come from the continent. Hamo benefited from royal donatives of clothing that supplemented his daily wage of 4.5 d. that he earned for building crossbows for King John. The surviving sources do not include information about his family.

Sources: *CR I*, 23.

NICHOLAS likely was born on the continent during the second half of the twelfth century. He worked for at least eleven years as a crossbow maker for King John (1204–1215) during which time he earned a wage of 4.5 d. per day. The surviving sources indicate that Nicholas' brother Reginald (see his entry in this register) also served as a royal crossbow maker under King John.

Sources: *Pipe Roll 6 John*, 248; *Pipe Roll 16 John*, 67; *Pipe Roll 17 John*, 13; *CR I*, 3, 9, 35, 64, 102, 150.

PETER THE SARACEN likely was born in the Levant during the second half of the twelfth century. He served as King John's master crossbow maker for at least a decade (1204–1214) before potentially retiring in 1215. In addition to a daily wage of 9 d., Peter the Saracen benefited from frequent royal donatives in cash and clothing. Peter also received a mill from the king in 1215. We know that Peter was married and had least one son, although the names of his family members were not recorded in the surviving administrative records.

Sources: *Pipe Roll 6 John*, 248; *Pipe Roll 7 John*, 39, 112, 255, 256; *Pipe Roll 9 John*, 114; *Pipe Roll 10 John*, 172; *The Great Roll of the Pipe for the Twelfth Year of the Reign of King John Michaelmas 1211*, ed. Doris M. Stenton (London, 1953), 111; *Pipe Roll 13 John*, 83, 171, 176; *The Great Roll of the Pipe for the Fourteenth Year of the Year of the Reign of King John Michaelmas 1213*, ed. Patricia M. Barnes (London, 1955), 146; *Rotuli*, 94, 102; *CR I*, 2, 10, 23, 35 (2), 39, 47, 50, 70, 76 (2), 92, 97, 102 (2), 160, 225.

Scholarly Literature: Ralph Payne-Gallwey, *The Crossbow: Mediaeval and Modern, Military and Sporting: Its Construction, History and Management with a Treatise on Balista and Catapult of the Ancients and an Appendix on the Catapult, Balista and Turkish Bow*, 2nd edn (London, 1903, repr. 1958), 62; David Nicolle, *Medieval Warfare Source Book Volume I: Warfare in Western Christendom* (London, 1995), 291; and Prestwich, *Armies and Warfare*, 129.

REGINALD likely was born on the continent during the second half of the twelfth century. He served as a royal crossbow maker alongside his brother Nicholas (see previously in this register) for at least one year (1204–1205). Reginald earned a daily wage of 4.5 d.

Sources: *Pipe Roll 6 John*, 213; *Pipe Roll 7 John*, 39; *CR I*, 3, 9.

ROBERT likely was born on the continent during the second half of the twelfth century. He served King John as a crossbow maker for at least three years (1205–1208) and earned a daily wage of 4.5 d. The surviving sources do not include information about his family.

Sources: *Pipe Roll 7 John*, 39; *CR I*, 35, 64, 102.

ROGER OF GENOA likely was born in Genoa during the second half of the twelfth century. Roger was invited to England no later than 1202 to help develop a domestic crossbow industry and remained in King John's service for at least thirteen years (1202–1215). Roger's daily wage of 6–7 d. was supplemented by royal donatives of cash and clothing. We know that Roger was married, but the surviving sources do not record the name of his wife.

Sources: *The Great Roll of the Pipe for the Third Year of the Reign of King John Michaelmas 1201*, ed. Doris M. Stenton (London, 1936), 202; *Pipe Roll 6 John*, 213, 248; *Pipe Roll 9 John*, 116; *Pipe Roll 16 John*, 67; *Rotuli*, 100, 101, 121, 123; *CR I*, 4, 23, 35, 64, 102.

Secondary Literature: Powicke, *The Loss of Normandy*, 225.

Crossbow bolt makers

DENIS THE FLETCHER

Sources: *The Great Roll of the Pipe for the First Year of King John Michaelmas 1199*, ed. Doris M. Stenton (London, 1933), 132

PHILIP THE FLETCHER had a wife and son, although the surviving sources do not record their names.

Sources: *Pipe Roll 13 John*, 171.

THOMAS THE FLETCHER

Sources: *CR I*, 2.

4

CROSSBOWS FOR THE KING, PART 2

The crossbow during the reign of Edward I of England (1272–1307)

Throughout the thirteenth century, the English government maintained a significant military administrative system dedicated to acquiring arms and ammunition
for soldiers serving in the king's armies.[1] Among the most important of these
weapons during the course of the long thirteenth century were crossbows. These
arms were produced in government manufacturing facilities and purchased from
private arms makers in very large numbers, likely reaching the many thousands of
individual units.[2] When judged in terms of government expenditures, the military
importance of the crossbow increased dramatically following Edward I's accession to the throne in 1272.[3] In comparison to the relatively few, brief, and small-
scale military conflicts of his father and grandfather Henry III and John, Edward I
waged large-scale and lengthy wars throughout almost his entire reign. His government regularly mobilized many tens of thousands of soldiers for service, particularly for wars of conquest in Wales and Scotland, and equipped very large
numbers of these men with crossbows.[4] Soldiers armed with crossbows served in
the field, and acted as marines on the hundreds of ships and barges used by the
English to transport supplies along the coasts and rivers of Wales and Scotland, as
well as in the English Channel. In addition, large numbers of soldiers armed with

1   Concerning this administrative system, see David S. Bachrach, "The Military Administration of
     England (1216–1272): The Royal Artillery", *Journal of Military History* 68 (2004), 1083–1104;
     and idem, "Military Planning in Thirteenth-Century England", *Nottingham Medieval Studies* 49
     (2005), 42–63. Both of these essays are included in this volume.
2   See David S. Bachrach, "The Origins of the Crossbow Industry", *Journal of Medieval Military
     History* 2 (2003), 73–87; and idem, "The Royal Crossbow Makers of England, 1204–1272", *Not-
     tingham Medieval Studies* 47 (2003), 168–197, which is also included in this volume.
3   Many hundreds of surviving documents refer to the purchase and production of crossbows and
     quarrels during Edward I's reign, showing a marked increase over the already large number of
     documents dealing with these matters in during the reigns of Henry III and John. It should be
     emphasized, however, that despite the evidence for many thousands of crossbows and millions
     of quarrels in the surviving administrative documents, these records represent only a fraction of
     those that once were produced by the royal government.
4   On Edward I's military resources and manpower, see Michael Prestwich, *War, Politics and Finance
     under Edward I* (Totowa, NJ, 1972).

crossbows guarded the numerous fortifications that were established by Edward I's government to secure English conquests in the west and north.[5]

When Edward I began his reign, the English government had its choice of six major types of crossbows with which to equip the now much larger number of soldiers serving as crossbowmen.[6] These crossbows, differentiated by their material composition and means of spanning, were in service throughout Henry III's reign (1216–1272), as they had been through most of John's reign as well (1199–1216). From a technological perspective, although continuing to experiment with improvements on the margins of crossbow technology, Edward I's government equipped the majority of the soldiers in royal service with the most basic crossbows available. From a cultural perspective (here to be understood in terms of the economy), the decision of the English government to deploy large numbers of weapons that were technologically inferior to others that were available was done in the hope of saving considerable sums of money. This was of great importance because Edward's frequent and extensive wars required the deployment of ever larger numbers of crossbows and ammunition, all of which had to be purchased by the government.[7]

Technological development

The surviving evidence suggests that craftsmen working for the royal government during Edward I's reign did not develop fundamentally new types of crossbows with respect to either their material composition or to the means by which they

---

5   The two largest collection of unpublished administrative documents for the reign of Edward I held by the National Archives (formerly known as the Public Record Office) are the liberate rolls (series number C62) and the Pipe Rolls (series number E372). In addition, the archives hold thousands of original documents produced by the bureaus of the Chancery and Exchequer and are catalogued under "C" and "E", respectively. Hundreds of these documents record the pay and recruitment of crossbowmen to serve the king as well as the mobilization of crossbowmen from the city militias of Carlisle, Bristol, London, and Oxford. See, for example, National Archives C47/22/4 #38; C62/56 9r; C62/64 4r; E101/5/19 #15; E101/5/27; E372/121 11v; E372/132 1v.

6   See David S. Bachrach, "Crossbows for the King: The Development of the Crossbow during the Reigns of King John and Henry III of England", *Technology and Culture* 45 (2004), 101–119, and included in this volume.

7   The basic sources for understanding crossbow technology and material resources of the government during Edward I's reign are the documents produced by the royal government, itself. For information on the types of crossbows used during Edward I's reign, the primary series of published calendars of documents are *Calendar of Close Rolls 1272–1307* (London, 1900–1908) and *Calendar of Patent Rolls 1272–1307* (London, 1893–1901). Surviving narrative sources provide an enormous amount of information about large scale political and military affairs, but are silent regarding military technology, particularly of crossbows. On this point, see Jim Bradbury, *The Medieval Archer* (New York, 1985), 76; and Peter Dinzelbacher, "Quellenprobleme bei der Erforschung hochmittelalterliche Bewaffnung", *Mediaevistik* 2 (1989), 43–79, here 61–64. Similarly, artistic representations of crossbows from this period provide little information about the material from which they were constructed, and only limited and often confusing information about the means used to span them (Dinzelbacher, 46–61).

were spanned. The royal government continued to deploy "one-foot", "two-foot", and winched (*turnus*) crossbows, which were constructed of wood and composite materials. However, the major development under Edward was the introduction and deployment on a large scale of a winch that could be removed from one crossbow and attached to another. The earliest surviving description of this detachable winch, called variously a *turnus* and a *vica* in Latin, actually appeared in a document issued during the latter part of Henry III's reign.[8] A letter sent in 1261 by the Chancery to William la Zusche, the constable of Rochester Castle, informed him that the crossbow maker Henry the German would be arriving soon with a winch (*turnus*) used to span larger-sized (*majorae*) *balistae*.[9] The next surviving reference to this type of winch comes from a document issued in 1273, at the beginning of Edward I's reign. An inventory of Welsh castles conducted in March of that year found that the armory at Drosselan contained two *balistae de turno*, and one *turnus pro eisdem*.[10] This document clearly reveals that there were two crossbows that utilized a winch, alongside a single winch that was to be used with both of them.

Despite the dearth of references to removable winches during the period 1261 to 1273, it seems clear that these devices were used to at least some extent from the last decade of Henry III's reign to the accession of Edward I. The officers who conducted the inventory at Drosselan Castle, William Brebelshute and Thomas Roshale, were experience royal officials with considerable backgrounds in military affairs. This was particularly true of Roshale who, after conducting the inventory, would serve as commander (*constabularius*) of Drosselan.[11] Both men were quite capable of identifying the usual types of weapons that they were cataloging. If Brebelshute and Roshale had considered the replaceable *turnus* to be a new or unusual piece of equipment, the normal administrative procedure would have been for them to make note of this fact. This they did not do.[12]

---

8   There is no term in the administrative vocabulary used by the royal clerks for a specialist in the production of winches, namely no *turnarius* or *viciarius*. It therefore seems likely that the men who built the high quality *balistae ad turnum/de vice* were also responsible for constructing the removable winches deployed by the royal government.

9   These *balistae majorae* may have been light artillery rather than crossbows or simply larger sized handheld weapons. See *Close Rolls of the Reign of Henry III* 14 vols (London,1902–1938), here *CR 1259–1261*, 449.

10   National Archives E213/118.

11   Ibid.

12   When new types of artillery were introduced by the royal government, clerks, and other royal officials routinely made clear in their accounts and reports that they were dealing with hitherto unknown types of weapons. For example, when the counterweight engine called the *blida* began to be deployed by the government during the first half of the 1240s, the clerks recording their presence added the note that the engine "is termed" (*vocatur*) *blida*, to emphasize that they were dealing with a new type of artillery. See, for example, National Archives C62/15, and *CR 1242–1247*, 21. After the initial years of deployment, however, royal officials no longer used the expression *ut vocatur* when discussing the *blida*. See, for example, *Calendar of Liberate Rolls 1245–1261* (London, 1937), 141 and 369.

Separate winches for *balistae ad turnum* appear quite frequently throughout the surviving documents from Edward I's reign. In some instances, such as an inventory of the armory at Berwick on Tweed, which was conducted in 1298, these removable winches were denoted as *turnus*, or *tours* in documents written in French.[13] In another case, the sheriffs of London, Thomas of Suffolk and Adam Fulham, purchased four *turni* to serve the twelve *balistae ad turnum* that they had in storage.[14] In other cases, however, royal clerks used the term *vica/viz* to denote the removable winches. An inventory conducted in 1304 by Richard de Bremesgrave, the royal official in command of the depot at Berwick, lists six *balistae ad tour* and two *vicae* to be used with them.[15] These removable winches were of considerable value to the English government because they made it possible to deploy the powerful *balistae ad turnum* without providing each with its own costly winch.[16]

The development of the new winch affected the ways in which royal clerks recorded information about crossbows because they now had to distinguish between new winches, which could be used on crossbows that traditionally had been spanned using muscle power alone, and the winches that were designed specifically for heavier crossbows. For example, in a list of arms shipped to Berwick Castle, a royal clerk recorded that there were three *vicae ad balistas de vice tendendas* (that is, three winches used to span crossbows of the winched type).[17] Having replaceable mechanical devices for spanning crossbows was very appealing for royal officials, and new types of winches appear to have been adopted during the latter part of Edward I's reign. These devices made it possible to use replaceable *turni* on even the least powerful and least expensive one-foot crossbows, which normally were spanned by hand. An inventory of supplies shipped to Gascony in 1297, for example, lists eight *turni ad tendendum balistarum unius pedis,* or winches for spanning one-foot crossbows.[18]

---

13   National Archives E101/7/1 #7.
14   National Archives C62/75 1r.
15   National Archives E101/10/19/. While the fact that the *balista ad turnum* could be spanned with a device called a *turnus* as well as with a device called a *vica* does not necessarily mean that the two terms refer to the same device, there is no evidence that the terms refer to different devices. There is, by contrast, considerable evidence that clerks sometimes used two different terms to designate the same item, e.g. large stone-throwing engines could be called both an *ingenium* and a *blida*. See the discussion on this point by David S. Bachrach, "English Artillery 1189–1307: The Implications of Terminology", *The English Historical Review* 121.494 (2006), 1408–1430, and in this volume.
16   Although surviving administrative documents do not refer specifically to the costs of winches, it is likely that the difference in cost between *balistae ad unum pedem* and *balistae ad duos pedes,* on the one hand, and the winched crossbows on the other was due largely to the cost of the winch.
17   National Archives E372/145 2v.
18   National Archives E101/699/28.

As the information developed regarding the *turnus/vica* indicates, even though Edward I's craftsmen did not develop entirely new types of crossbows, they did continue to improve the weapons used by royal troops. In constructing a winch that could be detached from one crossbow and used on another, they may well have been inspired by the replaceable winches on tension-powered artillery (the large *balista*), which were available no later than the final decade of Henry III's reign. The first phase of development of the *turnus* permitted the deployment of a removable winch for use on the powerful frames of the *balistae ad turnum*, that traditionally were spanned by mechanical means. In the second phase, royal craftsmen were able to produce a removable winch that could be used on the relatively weaker and less expensive crossbows of the one-foot type, traditionally spanned by muscle power alone.

Relative numbers of crossbows deployed during Edward I's reign

During the reign of Henry III, the royal government deployed roughly equal numbers of wooden and composite bows, with perhaps a slightly larger number of the latter.[19] Henry III's government also appears to have acquired relatively more one-foot weapons than either the two-foot or winched crossbows, so that out of every 100 crossbows deployed by the crown, approximately forty-seven were of the one-foot variety, thirty-two were of the two-foot variety, and twenty-one were of the winched type.[20] As will be discussed in more detail in this chapter, we see a very different distribution of types in use under Edward I, with one-foot crossbows predominating to a much greater degree. This change in the distribution among the three types of crossbows suggests that the royal government made a conscious decision to emphasize the production of the lighter, weaker, and less expensive one-foot model.

It should be emphasized that the discussion of the relative numbers of crossbows deployed by the royal government is based on surviving administrative documents, which represent just a fraction of those originally produced. Consequently, the numbers of crossbows discussed here almost certainly also represent just a fraction of those that were produced for use by royal troops during Edward I's reign. However, because there is no reason to conclude that the surviving documents dealing with any particular type of crossbow were preserved at a greater or lesser rate than those dealing with other types of crossbows, it may be postulated that the texts discussed here are representative of the full corpus of information originally committed to writing by royal officials.

19 Bachrach, "Crossbows for the King", 109–113, and 117.
20 Ibid., 118.

Types of crossbows in use

A thorough examination of the published and unpublished administrative documents from Edward I's reign reveals thirty-six separate documents that refer to the means by which crossbows were spanned.[21] Together, these documents record 773 one-foot, 325 two-foot, and 123 winched crossbows, which represent 63 percent, 26 percent, and 10 percent of the total, respectively. On the basis of these data, it appears that Edward I's government made an effort to produce relatively more of the less powerful and less expensive types of crossbow than was the case during Henry III's reign.

The percentages for the types of crossbows deployed by Edward I's government also generally reflect the numbers of crossbow quarrels identified in the surviving administrative documents as being designed for use with a particular type of crossbow. The twenty-four surviving texts that I have identified as referring to a specific type of quarrel refer to the deployment of 824,000 quarrels for one-foot crossbows, 336,000 quarrels for two-foot crossbows, and 43,000 quarrels for crossbows equipped with a winch. These represent 68 percent, 28 percent, and 4 percent of the total, respectively.[22] The percentages of quarrels for the one-foot and two-foot bows are similar to those for the relative appearance of the crossbows, themselves. By contrast, the percentage of quarrels designated for use in winched crossbows is significantly smaller than the relative appearance of the winched crossbows in the surviving records. If it is possible to draw a connection between the quantities of ammunition purchased by the royal government for a particular type of weapon and the perception by royal officials of the usefulness of these weapons, then it seems clear that Edward I's military planners foresaw much more action for the one-foot, and to a lesser extent, two-foot *balistae*, than for their winched counterparts.

One important reason why Edward I's government may have deployed a higher percentage of the one-foot crossbows than was the case during the reign of Henry III may have been the low cost of these weapons. These least powerful crossbows could be purchased for as little as 18 d., the equivalent of four and a half days' wages for a crossbowman.[23] By contrast, a two-foot crossbow was more than twice as expensive costing 4 s., and crossbow with a winch could cost as much

---

21 *Patent Rolls 1272–1281*, 419; *Calendar of Various Chancery Rolls: Supplementary Close Rolls, Welsh Rolls, Scutage Rolls. Preserved in the Public Record Office 1277–1326* (London, 1912), 317; *Close Rolls 1279–1288*, 502; National Archives C47/2/1; C47/2/2 #96; C47/22/2 #57; C47/22/5 #24; C47/22/9 #70; C47/10/3 # 2; C62/50 8r; C62/64 14; C62/66 5r; C62/74 5r; C62/75 8r; C62/77 4r; E101/3/23; E101/5/19 #15; E101/6/20/14; E101/7/1 #5 and #7; E101/7/6; E101/7/10; E101/8/6; E101/8/17; E101/10/19; E101/12/3; E101/12/20; E101/351/9 E101/486/20; E101/699/28; E159/72; E213/118; E372/133 29r; E272/143 33v; E372/145 2v; E372/145 14v.

22 *Close Rolls 1272–1279*, 372; *Close Rolls 1279–1288*, 308; *Close Rolls 1288–1296*, 303; National Archives C47/2/2 #96; C47/22/2 #57; C47/22/9 #70; C62/54 2r; C62/64 1r; C62/66 5r; C62/73 4r and 5r; C62/74 5r; C62/75 8r; C62/76 1r; E101/5/19 #15; E101/6/20; E101/16/20/14; E101/7/1 #7; E101/10/19; E101/12/20; E159/72; E213/118.

23 For this price, see National Archives C47/22/2.

as 10 s. or about seven times more than the least expensive wooden bows with a one-foot stirrup.[24] Moreover, the ammunition for the lighter crossbows was also less expensive than the quarrels produced for their more powerful counterparts. In 1278, a thousand quarrels for *balistae ad unum pedem* could be purchased for just 13 s. 4 d., whereas a thousand quarrels for two-foot crossbows cost 20 s.[25] By 1302, the price for both types of ammunition had increased significantly, but the quarrels for one-foot *balistae* were still comparative much less expensive, at 20 s. per thousand compared with 40 s. per thousand for *quarellae ad duos pedes*.[26] I have not been able to find comparable information regarding quarrels designed for use in *balistae ad turnum*.

Material construction

Royal clerks and officers rarely noted the materials from which crossbows were constructed. I have been able to find, however, fifteen documents from the reign of Edward I that collectively record a total of 697 *balistae ligneae* and 211 *balistae de cornu* (roughly 77 percent wooden and 23 percent composite weapons). These numbers reveal a change from the reign of Henry III, when slightly more than half of the crossbows produced and acquired by the royal government were composite in construction.[27]

The priority given to wooden crossbows under King Edward I, despite the relative superiority in power of composite weapons of equal size, may be explained by the very substantial increase in the offensive military activity during his reign, which required that far larger numbers of troops be equipped with crossbows for campaigns in Gascony, Wales, Flanders, and Scotland.[28] First, it seems likely that composite weapons were more expensive than their wooden counterparts of the same size and method of spanning. Although there is little information in the surviving sources about the comparative prices of wooden and composite crossbows during Edward I's reign, it is clear that the latter required a wider range of materials to construct, and that these materials included expensive shaped bone or horn and large quantities of glue.[29] In addition, the building of composite bows required the services of a crossbow maker (*attiliator*), who specialized in these types of weapons, such as the German immigrant named Conrad who worked for

---

24 Ibid.
25 National Archives C62/54 2r.
26 National Archives C47/22/2 #57.
27 Bachrach, "Crossbows for the King", 112–113.
28 Concerning the greater potential energy of composite as contrasted with wooden crossbows, see Vernand Foley, George Palmer, and Werner Soedel, "The Crossbow", *Scientific American* (January, 1985), 104–110, here 106–107; and Christopher A. Bergman and Edward McEwen, "Sinew-Reinforced Composite Bows and Composite Bows: Technology, Function and Social Implications", in *Projectile Technology*, ed. Heidi Knecht (New York, 1997), 143–160, here 151.
29 See, for example, National Archive C62/51 5r; E101/8/6.

both Edward I and his father Henry III between 1261 and 1278.[30] When equipping thousands of soldiers with crossbows, the royal government certainly had to take such costs into account. Indeed, as discussed earlier, this attention to cost almost certainly goes far toward explaining the predominance of the relatively inexpensive one-foot crossbows.

A second probable reason for the decision by the royal government to deploy far more wooden crossbows than their composite counterparts is that if the latter were not carefully stored and tended, which was frequently not possible on campaigns in the field, they were more susceptible to damage from the damp climate of the British Isles.[31] It should be emphasized here that the far larger numbers of men armed with crossbows were deployed in the field by Edward, and in service on ships and barges, than had been the case under his father.[32]

Inventories of royal arms depots and magazines make regular mention of the condition of the crossbows stored there, including the numbers and types that were in poor repair.[33] It is almost certainly the case that the royal officials in charge of purchasing and producing crossbows for use by marines and soldiers knew that wooden weapons, although less powerful, were more likely to function for longer periods of time and to require less frequent replacement than their composite counterparts. When supplying thousands of crossbowmen with their weapons, the reliability and durability of those arms must have been of considerable importance to Edward's logistics officers.

Because most crossbows deployed by the royal government were constructed of wood and were of the one-foot type, it is reasonable to expect that the largest single subset of crossbows listed in surviving administrative records would be one-foot wooden weapons. This is, in fact, the case. Seven documents survive that record both the crossbows' type and the material from which they were constructed. If we take the total number of crossbows listed in these documents, we find 228, 30, and 1, respectively, for the wooden one-foot, two-foot, and winched crossbows, and 19, 126, and 3 for the equivalent composite weapons.[34] This information suggests that composite materials were reserved for the more powerful weapons. The major problem with the information from the surviving administrative documents is that only four crossbows with a winch are described specifically

---

30 See Bachrach, "The Royal Crossbow Makers of England", 187; and National Archives E372/122 1v.

31 See Kalevero Huuri, *Zur Geschichte des mittelalterlichen Geschützwesens aus orientalischen Quellen* (Helsinki, 1941), 5.

32 Although it is not possible to provide exact numbers for the forces deployed by Henry III and Edward I, it is likely that the order of magnitude of Henry's troops never exceeded 10,000 at one time, while Edward I deployed in excess of 25,000 men on several occasions and may have planned to mobilize more than twice as many on occasion as well. See Prestwich, *War, Politics and Finance*, 92–93.

33 See, for example, National Archives E101/486/20, where the 1306 inventory of Beaumarais Castle notes that thirty-four *balistae* were in poor repair (*debiles*).

34 National Archives C62/64 14; E101/3/23; E101/486/20; E213/118; E372/127 2v; #272/143 33v.

as wooden or composite. In all likelihood, most *balistae ad turnum* were composite weapons. This was certainly the case during Henry III's reign.[35]

Conclusion

Faced by the need to rapidly equip very large numbers of soldiers with crossbows,
the government of Edward I made substantial changes in the arms-procurement
policies of his predecessor. Instead of deploying roughly equal numbers of wooden
and composite weapons, Edward's government decided to invest its resources
in obtaining far more of the less expensive wooden arms. This same pattern is
observable in the decision to increase the percentage of the least expensive one-
foot crossbows rather than the more powerful but more expensive two-foot and
winched crossbows. It is likely that the decisions made by Edward I's military
planners were guided by two factors. The first of these was cost. The second
was the relative durability of wooden weapons as contrasted with composite
crossbows in the damp climate of northern Europe, particularly under the rough
conditions of the operating in the field.

At the same time that the government instituted cost-saving measures with
respect to the production and purchase of crossbows, royal craftsmen also made
two key improvements in the technology of the crossbow that dovetailed with
these fiscal efforts. First, they developed the removable winch for use on the powerful *balistae ad turnum*, which made it possible to use a single winch on several
crossbows rather than providing each weapon with its own winch. Secondly, they
developed a removable winch that could be used on one-foot crossbows, thereby
improving the efficiency the most common weapon type in the royal arsenal. It
was now possible for a larger number of men, particularly those who were physically weak or awkward, to span these weapons. Because Edward's government
required far larger numbers of men to serve in the army than had been the case in
previous decades, it is likely that a larger number, even if not a larger percentage,
of these conscripted fighting men were physically weaker than had been the case
during the reign of Henry III.

In sum, the information developed here about the development of crossbow
technology and the deployment of crossbows during the reign of Edward I indicates that the royal government had a sophisticated understanding of the interplay
between technology and finance. Rather than blindly following the policies of his
predecessor, Edward I and his advisors considered the relative advantages and
disadvantages of the technologies available to them in light of the new political
and military conditions, and then they made decisions that had extensive financial implications. In addition, the king's logistics officers took advantage of, and
perhaps even encouraged, technological developments that supported the government's policy decisions.

---

35   See Bachrach "Crossbows for the King", (Part 1), 113–115.

5

ENGLISH ARTILLERY, 1189–1307

The implications of terminology

It has come to be accepted as a commonplace by medieval military historians that sieges were the dominant form of warfare throughout the Middle Ages. Battles in the open field were comparatively rare, especially those involving large armies, and as a result medieval rulers routinely devoted extensive human and material resources both to defending and capturing fortresses and fortified cities.[1] One of the most distinctive aspects of siege warfare was the deployment of various types of artillery used by medieval soldiers to crush town and castle walls, wreak havoc on their defenders, and devastate their material assets within the defensive works. However, despite the prominence of artillery in both contemporary sources and in works of modern scholars, there remains much confusion about the types of machines in use. The burden of this study is to shed some light on this confused state of affairs by drawing on a range of heretofore underutilized sources to examine the types of artillery that were built and deployed by the royal government of England during the period 1189–1307.

Specialists in the history of military technology long have recognized that it is exceptionally difficult to identify the types of artillery used by medieval armies on the basis of descriptions found in narrative sources, most of which were written by clerics, or even from images produced by manuscript illustrators.[2] In particular,

---

1 The observation by J. B. Gillingham, "Richard I and the Science of War in the Middle Ages", in *War and Government in the Middle Ages*, ed. J. B. Gillingham and J. C. Holt (Woodbridge, 1984), 78–91, that King Richard engaged in a battle-avoiding rather than a battle-seeking strategy over the course of his career is generally applicable to the kings of England from the mid-twelfth to the early fourteenth century. Concerning the general point that sieges dominated medieval warfare, see Jim Bradbury, *The Medieval Siege* (Woodbridge, 1992); Peter Purton, *A History of the Early Medieval Siege: c. 450–1220* (Woodbridge, 2009); and idem, *A History of the Late Medieval Siege, 1200–1500* (Woodbridge, 2010).

2 Randal Rogers, *Latin Siege Warfare in the Twelfth Century* (Oxford, 1992), 251–273, provides an invaluable introduction to the problems inherent in identifying artillery types on the basis of discussions in narrative texts and manuscript illustrations. In particular, Rogers (254–260) notes the dispute between G. Kohler, *Die Entwicklung des Kriegswesens und der Kriegführung in der Ritterzeit von Mitte des 11. Jahrhunderts bis zun den Hussitenkriegen*, 3 vols (Breslau, 1886–1890), III: 154 and 159; and R. Schneider, *Die Artillerie des Mittelalters* (Berlin, 1910),

specialists have noted two significant problems that caused the authors of medieval narrative sources as well as contemporary artists to provide vague and even
inaccurate descriptions of artillery. First, the authors and artists were frequently
ill-informed about the technical aspects of the engines, even if they were familiar
with the fact that these engines were used in sieges.[3] Secondly, medieval authors,
in particular, frequently allowed their knowledge of Roman and late antique texts
to influence their descriptions of contemporary events, so that even if they were
familiar with specific aspects of contemporary artillery, these authors nevertheless did not provide accurate descriptions of these engines.[4]

Despite these difficulties, however, scholars have relied almost entirely on
these two types of sources, namely narrative descriptions and manuscript images,
to draw conclusions about the types of artillery that were employed by medieval
armies.[5] This approach can be explained, at least in part, for the period before
1200 by the relative dearth of documents that could shed light on the types of
artillery that were constructed by medieval governments. In the period after 1200,
however, the numbers of surviving administrative documents dealing with the
production, storage, transportation, repair, and use of artillery grows exponen-
tially. This is particularly true in England where the government produced hundreds of thousands of documents over the course of the thirteenth century, many
tens of thousands of which survive.

By and large, however, specialists in medieval military technology either
have ignored the existence of these documents or dismissed them wholesale as

---

60–61, concerning the survival of torsion artillery as contrasted with lever artillery into the Middle Ages. Relying on the same body of narrative sources, Kohler and Schneider came to diametri-
cally opposed conclusions, with Kohler arguing that medieval armies continued to use torsion
engines into the twelfth century and Schneider concluding that engines employing the lever were
introduced in the ninth century and took the place of torsion artillery. See also the recent survey
of the literature in Paul E. Chevedden, Zvi Shiller, Samuel R. Gilbert, and Donald J. Kagay, "The
Traction Trebuchet: A Triumph of Four Civilizations", *Viator* 31 (2000), 433–486, at 433–436.;
and William Sayers, "The Name of the Siege Engine Trebuchet: Etymology and History in Medieval France and Britain", *Journal of Medieval Military History* 8 (2010), 189–196. Peter Dinzelbacher, "Quellenprobleme bei der Erforschung hochmittelalterlicher Bewaffnung", *Mediaevistik*
2 (1989), 43–79, at 46–61, emphasizes the particular problems inherent in using contemporary
images of weapons to draw conclusions about their construction.

3   On this point, see Dinzelbacher, "Quellenprobleme"; and Bradbury, *Medieval Siege*, 251.

4   On this point, see Rogers, *Siege Warfare*, 251.

5   In this regard see, for example, Kohler, *Entwicklung*; Schneider, *Artillerie*; Kalervo Huuri, *Zur
Geschichte des mittelalterlichen Geschutzwesens aus orientalischen Quellen* (Helsinki, 1941);
J.-F. Fino, "Machines de Jet médiévales", *Gladius* 10 (1972), 25–43; idem *Forteresses de la
France médiévales: Construction-Attaque-Défense*, 3rd edn (Paris, 1977), 150–158; Donald R.
Hill, "Trebuchets", *Viator* 4 (1973), 99–115; David C. Nicolle, *Arms and Armour of the Crusad-
ing Era 1050–1350* (New York, 1988); Kelly DeVries, *Medieval Military Technology* (Peterbor-
ough, 1992) as well as in the second revised edition (Toronto, 2012); Bradbury, *Medieval Siege*,
particularly 250–255; Emilie Amt, "Besieging Bedford: Military Logistics in 1224", *Journal of
Medieval Military History* 1 (2002), 101–124; and Michael S. Fulton, *Artillery in the Era of the
Crusades* (Leiden, 2018).

incapable of shedding light on the many questions surround the types of artillery employed by medieval governments.[6] This tendency is particularly unfortunate because the surviving administrative documents, as contrasted with the narrative texts noted earlier, were produced either by royal officers intimately familiar with the construction of various types of artillery or by royal clerks who copied and redacted documents produced by these officers. Administrative records, therefore, can be understood as the work product of experts in contemporary artillery production.[7] In contrast to traditional scholarly practice, therefore, *this* study brings to bear a vast corpus of surviving administrative documents, both published and unpublished, to discuss the types of artillery constructed and deployed by the royal government of England during the long century between the accession of King Richard I and the death of Edward I.[8]

Although there is still some controversy on this point, most specialists now agree that by the thirteenth century, engineers had available three different means for propelling projectiles. These were torsion, tension, and lever-action.[9]

1. Torsion engines provided lift to their projectiles through the transformation of potential energy stored in twisted fibrous material, ranging from gut to

---

6 Even Michael Prestwich, the leading specialist in thirteenth-century English military and administrative history, was hesitant in his earlier works to identify artillery types on the basis of administrative documents, and relied largely on narrative accounts. See, for example, Michael Prestwich, *Armies and Warfare in the Middle Ages: The English Experience* (Yale, 1996), 288. However, in his more recent work Prestwich has drawn upon documentary sources to provide important insights regarding the construction of artillery and the types that were produced by the royal government. See, for example, Michael Prestwich, "The Trebuchets of the Tower", in *The Medieval Way of War: Studies in Military History in Honor of Bernard S. Bachrach*, ed. Gregory Halfond (Farnham, 2015), 283–294. Some scholars remain doctrinaire in their rejection of the value of administrative documents for understanding the types of artillery produced in the high and late Middle Ages. See, for example, Peter Purton, *The Medieval Military Engineer: From the Roman Empire to the Sixteenth Century* (Woodbridge, 2018).

7 Some scholars have questioned the reliability of royal clerks who were assigned the duty of copying into the parchment records of the royal government those texts produced by the officers in charge of producing and keeping in repair the king's artillery. See, for example, Maurice Powicke, *The Loss of Normandy 1189–1204: Studies in the History of the Angevin Empire*, 2nd edn (Manchester, 1960, repr. 1999), 224–225. However, an exhaustive survey of all of the surviving administrative records dealing with arms production makes it clear that when an original document issued by an officer in charge of producing or repairing artillery survives and can be compared with a later redaction of this document by a royal clerk, the later redaction maintains both the content and the terminology employed by the original text. See the following and also David S. Bachrach, "Crossbows for the King: The Crossbow during the Reigns of John and Henry III of England", *Technology and Culture* 45 (2004), 102–119; and idem, "The Royal Crossbow Makers of England, 1204–1272", *Nottingham Medieval Studies* 47 (2003), 168–197, both in this volume.

8 For a full discussion of these sources, see the first essay in this volume.

9 See Rogers, *Siege Warfare*, 254–273; Paul E. Chevedden, "Artillery in Late Antiquity: Prelude to the Middle Ages", in *The Medieval City under Siege*, ed. Ivy A. Corfis and Michael Wolf (Woodbridge, 1995), 121–173, at 131–138.

horsehair and hempen rope, into kinetic energy that drove a wooden beam. The wooden beam, which could be equipped with a basket attached directly to the beam, or with a sling attached to its end, then transferred this kinetic energy to a projectile, usually a stone, located in the basket or sling.[10]

2. Tension engines used the same principle as handheld bows and crossbows, transferring the potential energy of the bow to the projectile, usually a long thin shaft equipped with an iron head, which looked like a large arrow or crossbow bolt.[11]

3. Engines employing the lever principle were essentially long beams fixed to a fulcrum. The front, shorter end of the beam, that is, the end closest to the target, was the target end, and the other, longer end was the projectile end, because the projectile was attached there. Energy was generated by the rapid descent of the target end and the concomitant rapid rise of the projectile end. There were two means of causing the rapid descent of the target end. The first of these was to have a large number of well-trained men pull down, in unison, on the ropes attached to the target end. Engines employing this method have been identified by scholars as a "traction type". The second method used to cause the rapid descent of the target end was to attach a very heavy weight to it. The projectile end, in this type of engine, although substantially longer, was much lighter than the target end. In order to use this engine, the artillerymen had to drag down the projectile end and secure it. After it was loaded, the projectile end was set free, and the much heavier weight on the target end fell rapidly and caused the projectile end to rise rapidly with the result that the projectile was sent on its way. Engines equipped with weights on their target ends have been designated by scholars as "counterweight lever engines".[12]

Spear-casting engines

The English royal government produced two types of engine during the thirteenth century that shot long sharps called *quarelli*.[13] The first of these engines, known as the *balista*, was essentially a large crossbow, and operated on the tension principle. In fact, royal clerks and other government officials used the term *balista* to refer to both handheld crossbows and light artillery that used the same means of

---

10 E. W. Marsden, *Greek and Roman Artillery: Historical Development* (Oxford, 1969), 16–33; and now the important study by Tracey Rihll, *Catapult: A History* (Yardley, PA, 2007).

11 Marsden, *Greek and Roman Artillery*, 5–12.

12 Rogers, *Siege Warfare*, 266–269, provides a valuable discussion of the types of lever engines in use up to 1200. Also see Chevedden *et al.*, "Traction Trebuchet", passim.

13 The term *quarellus* also was used by royal clerks and other royal officers to designate the ammunition for crossbows.

propulsion.[14] As a result, it is sometimes difficult to ascertain whether a *balista* being discussed in a government document is a handheld weapon or a piece of light artillery. In most cases, however, it is possible to make this determination from the context provided by the surviving documents. For example, when on 25 November 1287, the Exchequer received orders from the Chancery to pay Thomas de Veffinis, the sheriff of Canterbury, for the production of sixty-eight *balistae*, it is almost certainly the case that the text is describing crossbows rather than engines.[15] Here, the sheer number of weapons under consideration makes it very unlikely that these *balistae* were artillery pieces. In other documents, the government officials are ordered to produce or purchase particular types of *balistae* that only can have been crossbows. *Balistae ad unum pedem* and *balistae ad duos pedes*, for example, can only refer to crossbows and not to engines, because the foot in the 'one-foot' and 'two-foot' weapons refers to the metal stirrup attached to the back side of the bow of the hand-held weapons.[16]

In other cases, the context in which the *balista* is deployed makes it clear whether we are dealing with a piece of artillery or a crossbow. For example, a writ of *liberate* issued in 1298 notes that the sheriff of Northumberland had expended resources in building a parapet (*bretagium*) on the wall of Newcastle on Tyne on which to place an engine (*ingenium*) that could span *balistae*.[17] In this case, the building of a platform on the wall to hold a piece of equipment that could be used as part of a *balista* indicates that the latter was itself of substantial size and, therefore, not a handheld weapon. In still other documents, the use of the adjectives *magna* or *gros* can sometimes indicate that a particular *balista* is a piece of artillery rather than a handheld crossbow.

An account of the expenses undertaken by the sheriff and bailiff of Newcastle in 1304 for shipping military supplies to the siege of Stirling Castle includes the costs of transporting two *balistae magnae* and the winches (*ingenia*) used for spanning them.[18] The use of an entire wagon to transport two *balistae* suggests that they were pieces of artillery rather than small handheld weapons. Moreover, if these had been handheld weapons, we would expect to see the terms *turnus* or *vica*, invariably used by royal clerks to denote the winches used to span crossbows

---

14 The term *balista* originally had been used by Roman authors to refer to two-armed torsion, stone-throwing engines. By the fourth century, however, the term had come to be used for engines that had the shape and means of propulsion of very large crossbows. See Rogers, *Siege Warfare*, 264; Bradbury, *Medieval Siege*, 250; Ralph Payne-Gallwey, *The Crossbow* (New York, 1903, repr. 1958), 310–308; Kelly DeVries, *Military Technology*, 132; and Bachrach, "Crossbows for the King," (Part 1), 103.

15 National Archives C62/64 1 r.

16 On this point, see Bachrach, "Crossbows for the King", (Part 1), passim.

17 National Archives C62/74 5r.

18 National Archives C47/22/4 nr 38.

rather than the term *ingenium*, the word often used for the winches designed to span artillery.[19]

The use of the adjectives *magna* or *gros* in an administrative document, however, does not prove that a *balista* was an artillery piece. In 1297, for example, the ship's captain William Kingston issued a receipt for the arms delivered to his ship, *La Plente*, which included twenty-four crossbows of the 'one-foot' type, twelve crossbows of the 'two-foot' type, and finally twenty-four *arbalastes gros de tourn*, meaning twenty-four large crossbows equipped with winches. The identification of the last named *arbalastes* as crossbows rather than as artillery pieces is indicated first by their inclusion in a list of what are clearly crossbows, and secondly by the fact that a single ship could hardly transport twenty-four pieces of artillery while fully loaded with other arms, food supplies, and water.[20]

Finally, some documents list materials used in the construction of *balistae* that can refer only to the larger artillery pieces rather than to handheld weapons. The Pipe Roll account for 1214, for example, records that Richard de Marisco, the bishop of Durham, was credited for his expenditures on iron (*ferrum*) and cables (*cablae*) used in the production of *balistae*.[21] Handheld crossbows did not require either iron or cables in their construction, although crossbow quarrels did have iron heads.

The second type of dart-throwing artillery piece produced by the royal government was called a *springaldus*, or *espringald* in those records that were written in French.[22] The first reference to a *springaldus* that I have found in the surviving administrative sources appear in an inventory of arms issued on 13 February 1276 by Robert Warren, then serving as royal commander (*constabularius*) of Chepstow Castle (Striguil).[23] According to the constable, the castle at Chepstow

---

19 By 1261, the royal government had developed replaceable spanning devices which could be detached from one crossbow and attached to another. The terms used to describe these winches were *turnus* and *vica*, sometimes written as *viz* or *vicia*. See, for example, *Close Rolls of the Reign of Henry III* 14 vols (London, 1902–1938), here *CR (1259–1261)*, 449; National Archives E213/118 and E107/7/1 nr 7.

20 National Archives E101/6/20/14. These supplies included 300 quarters of unmilled wheat, twenty tuns of milled wheat, three *springalds* (engines to be discussed in this chapter), sixty-four cases of crossbow quarrels, as well as the crossbows noted earlier.

21 *The Great Roll of the Pipe for the Sixteenth Year of the Reign of King John Michaelmas 1214* (Pipe Roll 60), ed. Patricia M. Barnes (London, 1962), 106.

22 According to Prestwich, *Armies and Warfare*, 291, *springaldi* were huge crossbows mounted on wheeled frames. However, he revised his view in "The Trebuchets of the Tower", arguing instead that they were torsion-powered engines. Bradbury, *Medieval Siege*, 253, suggests that the *springaldus* may have been a type of *mangonellus* (see more later in the chapter) and therefore a torsion-powered rather than a tension-powered engine. Also see in this context, Jean Liebel, *Springalds and Great Crossbows* (Leeds, 1998), who saw the *springaldus* as a torsion-powered engine.

23 National Archives E101/14/27. I would like to thank Michael Prestwich for bringing to my attention that Striguil was Chepstow Castle rather than Stirling Castle as appears in the original version of this essay.

had in stock several artillery pieces including one *springaldus* with all of its equipment (*attilia*), and two *springaldi* that did not have ropes or the remainder of their equipment. This text makes clear that the *springaldus* was a spear-casting rather than a stone-throwing engine. Alongside the *springaldi*, Robert Warren reported that the depot at Chepstow contained 150 *quarelli pennati pro springaldis*, that is feathered quarrels for *springalds*.[24] A similar reference to the ammunition used by *springaldi* survives in a document issued on 4 February 1303 by John of Cambridge, the outgoing sheriff of Northumberland. According to John's memorandum, he handed over a *springaldus* with 400 *quarelli* to his successor when the latter took office in January 1303.[25]

This memorandum is of particular interest from an administrative perspective because its content is confirmed by two subsequent documents, each of which used the same terminology for the transferred equipment that is found in John of Cambridge's text. First, a clerk named Adam de Benton, who worked for the incoming sheriff of Northumberland, wrote out a memorandum stating that his lord had received the *springaldus* along with 400 *quarelli*.[26] Adam de Benton's text was then confirmed by the royal clerk John de Kingham, who worked for the royal Wardrobe, which served as a clerical clearing house for much of the military expenditure made by Edward I's government.[27] John de Kingham's text also states that the transfer of one *springaldus* and 400 *quarelli* took place. It should be noted that in each of the three documents under consideration here, each written by a separate clerk in a different office, the term *springaldus* continued to be used, strongly suggesting that it was understood by all three men as a *terminus technicus*.

It is not a simple matter to tease out a basic description of the *springaldus* from surviving administrative records. Two documents, however, shed light on this question. An inventory of the arms, issued to the royal officer John Kirkeby from the magazine at Newcastle on Tyne in 1300, lists three *cordae ad tenendum archum springaldi*.[28] This text indicates that a *springald* was equipped with a bow (*archus*), which was to spanned (*tendere*) when shot. The second document, an account issued in 1303 dealing with the military expenses of Sheriff John Cambridge of Northumberland, notes that he purchased bows (*arcus*) to be used in the construction (*operandum*) of several *springaldi*.[29] It therefore seems clear that, at least superficially, the *springaldi* resembled the large, tension-powered *balistae* that had been deployed by the English government since at least the late twelfth century. However, the *springald* utilized a fundamentally different

24   Ibid.
25   National Archives E101/579/16 1r.
26   Ibid., 3r.
27   Ibid., 1r.
28   National Archives E372/145 2v.
29   National Archives E101/579/6.

means of propulsion than the *balista*, in that it operated on the principle of torsion rather than tension, as demonstrated clearly by Thom Richardson and Michael Prestwich.[30]

Early stone-casting engines

In contrast to the general scholarly agreement that tension engines were in use throughout the Middle Ages, including in twelfth- and thirteenth-century England, considerable controversy still remains regarding the deployment of both torsion and lever artillery. Indeed, this uncertainty extends to the meaning of the terms employed by medieval authors of narrative sources to designate different types of artillery. In considering the administrative evidence for England, it is clear that by the reign of Richard I, royal scribes routinely discussed two types of stone-throwing artillery. These were *petrariae* and *mangonelli*, which scribes consistently contrasted with one another as different engines.[31]

Both *mangonelli* and *petrariae* were equipped with slings made of leather that were suitable for throwing stones rather than spears or large arrows. Numerous documents make reference to these slings. In 1194, for example, the constable of Windsor Castle was credited at the Exchequer for the funds he used to repair the hides (*coria*) used to make slings (*fundae*) for use on the *mangonelli* being stored in the magazine at Windsor.[32] The same account notes that the royal engineer Urric also was credited for payments he made to have hides repaired for use in the *petrariae* stored at Windsor. Similarly, the Norman Exchequer accounts for 1198 record the use of hides in the production of *petrariae*, specifically for making the slings used in these engines (*fondae*).[33] On 12 April 1221, during the reign of Henry III, the English Chancery issued a writ to the barons of the Exchequer

---

30 Thom Richardson, *the Tower Armoury in the Fourteenth Century* (Leeds, 2016); and Prestwich, "The Trebuchets of the Tower," passim.

31 It is clear that these terms were used to refer to two distinct types of artillery because a very large number of documents refer to the production of both of them side by side. The terms were not use as synonyms in any texts as understood by Amt, "Besieging Bedford", 109 who stresses that *petrariae* and *mangonelli* were different types of engine. For examples of orders issued by the royal government to produce both *mangonelli* and *petrariae*, see *The Great Roll of the Pipe for the Fifth Year of the Reign of King Richard the First Michaelmas 1193* (Pipe Roll 39), ed. Doris M. Stenton (London, 1927), 69, 74, 141; *The Great Roll of the Pipe for the Sixth Year of the Reign of King Richard the First Michaelmas 1194* (Pipe Roll 40), ed. Doris M. Stenton (London, 1928), 95, 251; *The Great Roll of the Pipe for the Tenth Year of the Reign of King Richard the First Michaelmas 1198* (Pipe Roll 44), ed. Doris M. Stenton (London, 1932), 76; *Rotuli literarum clausarum in turri Londonensi asservati 1204–1227*, 2 vols, ed. Thomas D. Hardy (London, 1833–1834), here *CR I*: 82, 87, 108, 123, 138, 191, 448, 449, 617; *CR II*: 98, 198; *Calendar of Liberate Rolls 1226–1272* (London, 1916–1964), hereafter *CLR 1226–1240*, 44; and National Archives E372/75 2v.

32 *Pipe Roll 6 Richard*, 176.

33 *Magni rotuli scaccarii normanniae sub regibus anglie*, vol. 2, ed. Thomas Stapleton (London, 1844), 464.

instructing them to credit the account of the royal officer Fawkes de Breauté for the expenses he had undertaken at the request of the crown. These included the purchase of two white hides, which were to be used to make slings (*fundae*) for the king's *petrariae* and *mangonelli*.[34]

The fact that these slings were used to throw stones is confirmed by the purchase of stone ammunition for use by *petrariae* and *mangonelli*. The Pipe Roll account for 1193 notes that the sheriff of Buckingham and Bedford was credited at the Exchequer for the money that he had paid to William de Semeilli for having transported stones to Winchester for use by the *petraria*, and other stone-throwing machines (*alia ingenia*) stored there.[35] Moreover, archaeological research at Bedford Castle, which was the site of a siege in 1224 in which both *petrariae* and *mangonelli* were employed, has brought to light a large number of stones that appear to have been cast by these engines.[36]

In light of the consistent distinction drawn by royal clerks between *petrariae* and *mangonelli*, there would need to be very good reason to doubt that they were not discussing different types of artillery. As observed previously, the royal clerks were quite precise in their use of terminology. This was the case because they, unlike the authors of narrative texts, were experts regarding these engines, or dealt with the reports of individuals who were experts regarding these engines and faithfully recorded their expense reports. Consequently, it must also be asked whether these same administrative documents shed light on the particularities of each type of machine, and particularly whether these documents shed light on the question of the use of torsion technology for stone-throwing engines.[37]

One very important piece of evidence, heretofore neglected by scholars, that illuminates the difference between the two types of artillery is contained in a writ issued on 14 October 1225 by the Chancery to the Exchequer. This Chancery writ ordered the barons of the Exchequer to credit the account of the sheriff of Bedford for his expenses during the siege of Bedford Castle. These expenses included fifty slings for *petrariae* and *mangonelli*. Much more significant in the present context, however, is the record of the sheriff's purchase of "two circles of iron used in making winches (*turnus*) for *mangonelli*".[38] The term *turnus*, as we have seen, had the specific meaning of a tool, almost certainly a winch, used to span crossbows. Obviously, the *mangonellus*, which was a stone-throwing engine equipped with a

---

34 *CR I*: 452, "*v s. et vi d. quos posuit in duobus coriis albis empties apud Northampton ad fundas petrariarum et mangonellorum nostrorum facias per preceptum nostrum*".

35 *Pipe Roll 5 Richard*, 141. The question of what these *alia ingenia* are is dealt with in this chapter.

36 On this point, see Amt, "Besieging Bedford", 111 n. 47.

37 Amt, "Besieging Bedford", 109 is of the view that most or all of the *mangonelli* and *petrariae* employed at the siege of Bedford were traction engines, meaning lever action artillery. The fact that both types were sling equipped stone throwers does not, however, shed light on this question because both torsion and lever-action engines could be equipped with slings.

38 *CR II*, 65, "*in duobus circulis ferri ad turnos mangonellos*". Amt does not mention this text in her article.

sling, could not be spanned in the same manner as a crossbow. Rather, the *turnus* used on a *mangonellus* had to be used to draw the rotating beam of the engine into the firing position.[39]

A *mangonellus* equipped with a *turnus,* therefore, could not be a traction lever engine of the type that existed in England in 1224, that is one that was powered by a trained team of pullers. The projectile end (the back end) was much longer and therefore much heavier than the target or front end. The natural resting position of the projectile end was down on the ground, and did not need to be levered into position. The role of the pullers was to bring down the target end and launch the projectile. Under no circumstances would it ever be necessary for a traction lever engine, utilizing pullers, to have a winch to bring down the projectile end. The winch also would be useless on the target end because this end of the rotating beam had to be brought down with great velocity, hence a team of pullers, rather than being winched down slowly with a *turnus.*

This leaves two possibilities for the identification of the construction of the *mangonellus.* It must either have been a counterweight lever engine or a torsion-powered engine. The first of these possibilities is very unlikely because of the absolute absence of any references to counterweights or the construction of counterweights in administrative documents from this period. By contrast, hides, wood, and iron fittings appear regularly in the contemporary administrative records.[40] In fact, as will be discussed later in the chapter, there are no references to counterweight engines of any type before the mid-1220s. The most reasonable conclusion to draw, therefore, is that *mangonelli* were not supplied with counterweights and that they were, in fact, torsion engines.[41] This means that the *mangonelli* worked on the "rubber-band" principle. The arm of the *mangonellus,* having been drawn back by a winch against twisted fibrous material, whether gut or horse hair, cast its load when the locking mechanism was released.

This leaves the identification of the *petrariae* deployed by Richard I and John. Given that the *petraria* was a stone thrower with a sling, the possibility that it was a tension engine can be excluded, because tension engines cast only long bolts. This still leaves the problem of whether the *petraria* was a torsion or lever engine. The first possibility is that the *petrariae* and *mangonelli* were both torsion engines different only in the means by which they were drawn into the firing position; the *mangonelli* through a winch and the *petrariae* by hand. This seems unlikely, however, for one main reason. As noted previously, royal clerks and royal officials charged with building these engines consistently treat them as entirely different types of artillery. The terms *mangonellus* and *petraria* are never used as synonyms. This is not what one would expect if these were fundamentally

---

39   See, for example, the image of a *mangonellus* equipped in this manner in Bradbury, *Medieval Siege,* 253.

40   The earliest reference to a counterweight that I have found is *CLR 1240–1245,* 245.

41   See Bradbury, *Medieval Siege,* 253.

the same type of engine differing only in the means by which they were brought into a firing position.

If we consider briefly the vocabulary used by royal clerks when dealing with crossbows, this point becomes very clear. Some crossbows were equipped with a mechanical spanning device called a *turnus*, and others, the 'one-foot' and 'two-foot' types mentioned already, were spanned by hand.[42] Royal clerks and officials nevertheless called all of these weapons *balistae*. In the view of the royal officials responsible for writing about the king's armaments, *balistae* equipped with different types of spanning technology were still the same kind of weapon. Given this administrative reality, it seems unlikely that a mere difference in the manner in which the *petrariae* and *mangonelli* were spanned, that is drawn into firing position, would have led royal officials to use two entirely different terms for these two types of artillery.

Consequently, the second possible identification for the construction of the *petrariae* as lever artillery would seem to be more likely. In this context, it must first be emphasized that *petrariae*, like *mangonelli*, were produced regularly in England during the reign of Richard I (1189–1199) more than two decades before the first reported introduction of a counterweight engine into England in 1216, during the invasion by Prince Louis of France, and more than three decades before the first reported construction of counterweight engines in England in 1225, that is the trebuchet.[43] Secondly, as is true of the *mangonellus,* the surviving administrative sources make frequent references to the materials used in the construction of *petrariae*, but make no mention of counterweights. This is a strong indication that *petrariae* were not equipped with counterweights. These factors combined make clear that is very unlikely the *petrariae* were counterweight lever engines. This only remaining plausible identification of the *petraria*, therefore, is as traction lever artillery, that is engines powered by teams of pullers on the target end. Happily, this conclusion fits well with the accounts of contemporary chroniclers who comment on the large number of men who were mobilized to operate the *petrariae* at the siege of Bedford Castle in 1224.[44]

The information from administrative documents indicates that the *mangonelli* and *petrariae* were, respectively, torsion and traction lever engines. In addition, these same sources make clear that not all of the engines within a particular type were built to the same specifications. By 1211, royal clerks began to make reference to "Turkish" *petrariae*.[45] In this year, for example, royal officers in charge

---

42 Bachrach, "Crossbows for the King", (Part 1), passim.
43 Prestwich, *Armies and Warfare*, 289; John France, *Western Warfare in the Age of the Crusades 1000–1300* (Ithaca, 1999), 122–123; and Sayers, "The Name of the Siege Engine Trebuchet", 189–196.
44 On this point, see *Annales Monastici*, ed. Henry Richard Luard (London, 1864–1869), bk 3, pp. 86–87, and the commentary on this text by Amt, "Besieging Bedford", 109–110.
45 Nicolle, *Arms and Armour*, 212 suggests that Turkish engines, and specifically Turkish *mangonelli* may be considered a simpler design in use by nomads.

of the vacant see of Durham were credited by the Exchequer for the expenses that they incurred in producing four *petrariae*. The first two weapons are characterized as large (*magnae*), and the latter two are characterized as "Turkish".[46] It would seem to be a reasonable interpretation that the "Turkish" *petrariae* were smaller weapons. The production by royal officers of two different types of *petrariae* characterized by their different sizes is confirmed in an order issued to the royal officer Peter de Maulay on 9 March 1214.[47] Peter was ordered to purchase ropes (*cordae*) suitable for both small (*parvae*) and large (*magnae*) *petrariae*.[48]

"Turkish" engines appear several times over the next two years in the surviving royal administrative records. On 2 August 1212, the Chancery issued a writ to Philip Mark, the sheriff of Nottingham, informing this officer that two master carpenters named Nicholas and Ralph, along with a team of assistants (*socii*) were being sent to him to build "*duas petrarias turkesias*".[49] Philip Mark received credit for the expenses he incurred in building these weapons, which were recorded in the Pipe Roll account for 1214.[50] Evidently, "Turkish" was used as an administrative *terminus technicus* by both Chancery and Exchequer clerks. On 2 May 1216, the Chancery issued a writ to Roel Bloet, the royal keeper of the forest at Knap (Sussex), informing him that Nicholas was being sent to produce as many *petrariae turkesiae* as possible. Once the *petrariae* were completed, Roel was ordered to send them along with their ropes (*funes*) and other equipment (*attilia*) to Dover.[51] In 1216, for the first time in the surviving administrative records, the adjective "Turkish" was applied to a *mangonellus* rather than to a *petraria*. The Pipe Roll for 1216 includes the administrative account submitted by Brian de L'Isle for his expenses as commander of the fortress of Knaresborough in Yorkshire.[52] These expenses included the pay of five master carpenters, who constructed two *petrariae* and "*tres mangunellos turkesios*".[53]

Thus far, the discussion of the torsion and lever engines produced under King Richard and John, and in the first decade of the reign of Henry III, has focused on *petrariae* and *mangonelli*. However, royal clerks in this period (1189–c. 1225) routinely employed a third term for stone-throwing artillery, namely *ingenium*. It would appear, however, that the term *ingenium* referred not to a third type of artillery, but rather was used as a synonym, at least down to 1225, for the

46 *The Great Roll of the Pipe for the Thirteenth Year of the Reign of King John Michaelmas 1211* (Pipe Roll 57), ed. Doris M. Stenton (London, 1953), 39.
47 *CR I*, 141.
48 Ibid., "*quod emere faciat cordas tam ad parvas petrarias quam ad magnas usque ad summam xx libr. Piccavie*".
49 *CR I*, 122.
50 *The Great Roll of the Pipe for the Sixteenth Year of the Reign of King John Michaelmas 1214* (Pipe Roll 60), ed. Patricia M. Barnes (London, 1962), 156.
51 *CR I, 267.*
52 *Pipe Roll 17 John*, ed. R. A. Brown (London, 1964), 13.
53 Ibid.

mangonellus. Throughout the records of both Richard and John, the royal clerks consistently contrast *petrariae* with *ingenia*, but never *mangonellus* with *ingenium*. As already noted, the Pipe Roll for 1193 deals with the purchase of stones to be used as ammunition for the king's *petrariae* and *alia ingenia regis*.[54] This same pattern of contrasting *petrariae* with *ingenia* appears in numerous other documents. For example, Ralph, the son of Stephen, is credited at the Exchequer in the Surrey Pipe Roll account of 1193 with providing hides and iron for constructing two *petrariae* and for transporting wood for the construction of *ingenia*.[55] In 1194, Reginald Basset was credited at the Exchequer for the expenses he incurred in transporting *petrariae* and *plurima ingenia* to the army at Nottingham.[56] In the same year, the royal engineer Urric was authorized to receive reimbursement for the money he spent on ropes for *ingenia* and *petraria* stored at Nottingham Castle.[57] In March 1221, the royal officer Alexander of Sawbridgeworth was credited at the Exchequer for the money he spent to have master engineer William build *ingenia* as well as for the money he spent on ropes for the king's *petrariae*.[58]

By contrast, the administrative documents from the reigns of kings Richard, John, and Henry III down to the year 1225 do not ever contrast the term *mangonellus* with the term *ingenium*. *Mangonelli* appear in the royal documents either alone or in conjunction with *petrariae*.[59] In light of the consistency in the terminology used by the clerks of the royal Chancery and Exchequer it seems reasonable to draw the conclusion that up to 1225, these officials used the terms *ingenium* and *mangonellus* as synonyms for torsion-powered, stone-throwing artillery as contrasted with the *petrariae*, which were traction lever engines that employed pullers.

The *mangonellus* appears to have remained in service throughout most of Henry III's reign. In August 1227, for example, master carpenters Thomas and Nicholas began production of three *mangonelli* at the forest of Trivel.[60] In March 1235, two *mangonelli* were shipped from storage in Winchester to Porcester for use in Gascony.[61] An inventory of Corfe Castle, conducted in 1252, found *mangonelli* stored there in good repair.[62] Elyias de Rayban, who carried out the

---

54 *Pipe Roll 5 Richard*, 141.
55 Ibid., 154.
56 *Pipe Roll 6 Richard*, 43.
57 Ibid., 176.
58 *CR I*, 453.
59 The single instance in the period 1189–1225 in which I have found the term *mangonellus* being used in conjunction with the term *ingenium* is from Chinon in Normandy. On 30 May 1200, the provost of Chinon was issued orders to obtain sufficient supplies of wood for the master carpenter Urric to build *petrariae, mangonelli* and *ingenia nostra*. See *Rotuli Normannie*, 24. The fact that this order was issued in Normandy rather than England may explain the difference in terminological usage.
60 *CR II*, 198.
61 *CR 1234–1237*, 65.
62 National Archives C47/2/1.

inventory, subsequently obtained supplies sufficient to construct two additional *mangonelli* at Corfe in the same year.[63] In his expense report for Rochester Castle in 1264, which was submitted to the Exchequer, Roger de Leyburn, the constable, recorded that he had purchased three ropes for the *mangonellus* stored there.[64]

After 1264, however, *mangonelli* no longer appear in English administrative records. The absolute silence of sources that previously included frequent references to the production, repair, storage, maintenance, and transport of *mangonelli* must be given serious consideration. If the *mangonelli* continued to be produced and used after 1264, why are they no longer mentioned under this name by the men who were responsible for building, storing, and most importantly, paying for them? There are two likely possibilities. The first is that the royal government introduced a new term to designate these torsion engines. But no new terms appear in the royal records in 1264, or at any other point after that year through the end of Edward I's reign in 1307 that conceivably could have been used to denote torsion engines. The other, more likely, possibility is that after 1264, the government ceased to purchase or produce new *mangonelli* and no longer repaired those that survived in royal arsenals and magazines.

As noted already, *petrariae* were produced in large numbers during the first decade of Henry III's reign, and they were deployed in sieges of Bytham (1220) and Bedford (1224). The royal government appears, however, to have ceased deploying *petrariae* in significant numbers by the mid-1220s, and completely phased them out of service by the mid-1230s. The final reference to a *petraria* that I have found in the royal administrative documents is a report in a Pipe Roll account for 1236 dealing with the lands of the Clare family which records that a royal carpenter Peter and his team of assistants (*socii*) had cut forty planks (*virgae*) for use in the repair of the king's *mangonelli* and *petrarii*.[65] As was the case with respect to *mangonelli*, it seems that the disappearance of the term *petraria* from royal records did not result from a decision to call these engines by another name. No other new terms for artillery appear in the royal records in 1236, or indeed, at any point up to the 1240s.[66] Rather, the disappearance of *petrariae* from the royal administrative records likely was caused by the decision of the government to phase out use of these traction lever engines in favor of the newer and better counterweight engine known to modern scholars as the trebuchet.

---

63 National Archives C47/2/1/4.
64 National Archives E101/3/3 2r.
65 National Archives E372/80 1r.
66 Beginning in c. 1241, the royal records begin to deal with an engine called a *blida*. This type of artillery will be discussed in detail later in this chapter.

Later stone-casting engines

The English term trebuchet frequently is used by scholars in a generic manner to refer to all large lever action engines whether of the traction or the counterweight type.[67] In this discussion, however, the English term trebuchet will be reserved for a specific type of counterweight lever engine introduced into England in 1225. The later term *trubechetum* was used by English royal clerks to denote a relatively small type of counterweight lever artillery. Larger counterweight lever engines, of a type of described by scholars as trebuchets, were denoted royal clerks and officers as *blidae*.[68] To complicate matters even further, in the decades after 1245 until the end of Edward I's reign in 1307, royal clerks generally used the generic term *ingenium* to denote both *trubecheta* and *blidae*, so that distinguishing between the two types depends on the context in which they are mentioned.

The first indication in the administrative records that the royal government had begun to deploy counterweight lever artillery in England is an order issued to the Exchequer to the Chancery on 19 April 1225 that authorized the master carpenter Jordan to receive 6 marks, in partial payment of his wages, for work on the king's *trubechetum* at Dover Castle.[69] Jordan appears numerous times in the royal records between 1225 and 1230 working on the king's trebuchets.[70] On 19 September 1225, for example, the Chancery issued orders to Adam de Bendenges, the royal forester at Odiham, to send two logs to Winchester.[71] The wood was to be delivered to Jordan so that he could make two beams for the king's *trubechetum* that he was building there.[72] By 8 June 1226, Jordan was building another *trubechetum*, this time at Windsor Castle, where he received 3 marks in partial payment of his wages.[73] Windsor subsequently became Jordan's center of operations as he appears serving there regularly until the end of 1229.[74]

In addition to being described by the royal clerks as the man who built the king's *trubecheta*, Jordan was also accorded the title of *trubechetarius*, that is the king's trebuchet builder.[75] Jordan is the only man to be called *trubechetarius* by royal clerks. Other specialists in the construction of counterweight lever artillery were called either engineer (*ingeniator*) or master carpenter (*magister carpentarius*). Not even Jordan's successors in the building of *trubecheta* were called *trubechetarius*. On 15 December 1233, for example, the royal officer Nicholas de Molis was issued orders by the Chancery to provide lumber from the Forest

---

67 See, for example, Rogers, *Siege Warfare*, 266–267; and France, *Western Warfare*, 119–124.
68 These *blidae* will be discussed in the next section.
69 *CR II*, 31.
70 Jordan last appears in the records on 28 February 1230. See *CLR 1226–1240*, 169.
71 *CR II*, 62.
72 Ibid.
73 *CR II*, 119.
74 *CLR 1226–1240*, 8, 26, 94, 128, 138.
75 See *CLR 1226–1240*, 110, 113, 121, 128, 129, 141, 147, 155, 169.

of Dean to Master Nicholas, *carpentarius regis*, and his team of assistants so that they could build the king's *trubechetum* there.[76]

The concomitant introduction of a new term for artillery (*trubechetum*) and the special appellation (*trubechetarius*) for the man who was in charge of building these engines, makes it very clear that the royal clerks were dealing with an entirely new type of artillery. But what type of artillery was this? As will be argued in this chapter, it seems certain that the *trubechetum*, as contrasted with the *petraria* which it replaced, was a counterweight lever engine rather than a traction lever engine.

The one uncertainty in this interpretation is the lack of evidence for counterweights in the surviving administrative sources for the 1220s and 1230s. The first specific reference to the purchase of materials, in this case large quantities of lead that were required for counterweights, comes in 1245, some two decades after Jordan began his work at Dover Castle. At first glance, this lacuna in the government documents poses a significant problem. However, a closer examination of the records for the production of *trubecheta* should serve to alleviate concerns about the silence of royal clerks about counterweights. As noted, the texts dealing with the actual production of both *petrariae* and *mangonelli* routinely referred to the types of materials purchased by royal officials in order to build them.[77] By contrast, the texts dealing with the production of *trubecheta* deal almost exclusively with the wages paid to the specialists building these engines, or with the transportation of the wood that was needed for their construction.[78] Therefore, while one would expect to find references to counterweights or materials for building them if they had been used on *petrariae* or *mangonelli*, one would not expect to find references to these materials with respect to the construction of *trubecheta*, at least up to 1245.[79]

This discussion of the sources regarding materials that were mentioned by royal clerks is essentially a negative argument with respect to the construction of *trubecheta*. What is required is positive evidence. The first point to emphasize, in this context, is that the traction lever engine, that is the *petraria*, had been in used by the royal government for many decades prior to 1225. Moreover, the *petraria* came in at least two sizes. It, therefore, seems very unlikely that the introduction of a new traction lever engine, even one that was substantially larger than those currently in use, would have caused the king's officials, who had already

---

76 *CR 1231–1234*, 352.

77 In addition to the examples provided here, also see *Pipe Roll 5 Richard*, 74, 141, 154, 158; *Rotuli Normannie*, 24; *The Great Roll of the Pipe for the Tenth Year of the Reign of King John Michaelmas 1208* (Pipe Roll 54), ed. Doris M. Stenton (London, 1947), 201–202; *CR I*, 108, 123, 191, 452, 454; *CR II*, 65; *CLR 1226–1240*, 47–48.

78 *CLR 1226–1240*, 8, 26. 71, 94–110, 113, 121, 128, 129, 138, 141, 147, 155, 169, 320; *CR II*, 44, 62, 119; *CR 1231–1234*, 352.

79 In 1245, and thereafter, royal clerks began to describe in greater detail the materials used in the construction of trebuchets. It is not clear why they began to do this.

demonstrated great conservatism in their use of terminology, to coin new terms for essentially the same technology. They would have been even less likely to coin a new term as a title for Jordan, who had been employed by the royal government to build these engines.[80]

Secondly, as discussed, it is important to keep in mind that royal clerks cease to mention *petraria* in the period after 1236. Given that for many decades the governments of Richard I, John, and Henry III considered it valuable to expend considerable resources to produce and maintain these engines, it seems reasonable to conclude that the *petrariae* only ceased to be used when they were replaced by something better. As noted, Jordan the *trebuchetarius* worked steadily for five years from 1225 to 1230, to fill the king's arsenal with the new *trubucheta* at Dover, Winchester, and finally at Windsor. He, in turn, was succeeded no later than 1233 by the master carpenter Nicholas, and then by the engineer Gerard, who appears for the first time in the royal administrative records in 1238.[81] The *petrariae* disappear from the royal records after 1236, following a decade of steady production of the *trubucheta*. The timing may simply be a coincidence, but it seems rather more likely that Jordan, and then Nicholas and Gerard, were overseeing the production of counterweight lever engines (*trubucheta*) as replacements for the king's traction lever *petrariae*.

The identification of the *trubucheta* as a relatively small counterweight lever engine as contrasted with the giant counterweight machines featured in manuscript illustrations rests on three main points. First, in order to replace the scores, if not hundreds of stone-throwing *petrariae*, which were used so effectively during Henry III's minority, the royal government required a tactically flexible and relatively inexpensive piece of easily constructed artillery. These factors point toward a smaller rather than an exceptionally large engine. Secondly, the documents dealing with the production of the *trubucheta* do not present the image of immense construction projects. Rather, they seem to indicate relatively small-scale operations. Typical in this regard is an order issued in September 1225 to Adam de Bendenges, mentioned already, to ship two beams (*virgae*) to Jordan at Winchester for his work on a *trubuchetum* there.[82] Thirdly, an inventory of arms stored at Beaumarais Castle, conducted in 1306, lists "*unum parvum ingenium stans super murum quod vocatur trubechetum*".[83] The identification in this document of the *trubuchetum* as a "small engine" that stands atop the wall of the castle certainly excludes the possibility that *trubucheta*, or at least this *trubuchetum*, is

---

80 The same reasoning applies to the introduction of the larger *mangonellus*. In this case, moreover, the use of the term *trubuchetum* to designate a torsion engine would contradict the settled scholarly consensus that a trebuchet was, by definition, a lever engine.

81 Concerning their service in the production of trebuchets, see *CR 1231–1234*, 352; and *CLR 1226–1240, 320*.

82 *CR II*, 62.

83 National Archives E101/486/20.

to be identified with the giant wall-breaking *ingenia* such as the famous *Warwolf*, which was employed by Edward I at the siege of Stirling Castle in 1304.[84]

It has been observed recently that thirteenth-century English narrative sources rarely used the term trebuchet.[85] This failure may be explained, in part, by the fact that the royal government used the term *trubechetum* very rarely after 1245.[86] Unlike the situation with both the *petraria* and the *mangonellus*, however, the disappearance of the term *trubechetum* from royal administrative records was accompanied by the introduction of a new term to take its place. This was *ingenium*, which no longer was used for *mangonelli* after this point. In 1244, for example, Bertram de Criol was issued orders by the Chancery to take possession of two *ingenia* that were being sent to him, to find appropriate storage for them, and to have them repaired.[87] These engines were identified by the royal clerk as "*videlicet unum ingenium quod vocatur blideh et unum trubechetum*".[88] The Pipe Roll account for Kent for this year, which was written out by clerks of the Exchequer rather than the clerks of the Chancery, noted that Bertram had received these *ingenia*.[89] Moreover, the Exchequer clerks also identified these *ingenia* as a *trubechetum* and a *blida*.[90] These two examples make clear that by 1244, at the latest, *ingenium* was considered a suitable synonym for the terms *trubechetum* and *blida* at both the Exchequer and at the Chancery.

From an administrative perspective, the use of the apparently generic term "engine" to designate a specific type of artillery was not unprecedented in royal administrative practice.[91] As discussed, it appears that from at least 1193 up to 1225, royal clerks had used *ingenium* as a synonym for *mangonellus*. Between 1225 and 1241, however, royal clerks ceased to use *ingenium* to discuss any type

---

84 Michael Prestwich, *War, Politics, and Finance under Edward I* (Totowa, NJ, 1972), 53.

85 France, *Western Warfare*, 123. France notes the fact that Jordan built trebuchets at Dover and Windsor but has the incorrect dates, and does not mention that Jordan also constructed a trebuchet at Winchester. More importantly, however, France does not seem to appreciate the fact that Jordan worked continuously for almost five years on the construction of trebuchets, indicating an exceptional commitment by the royal government to produce large numbers of these engines in a short period.

86 The final reference to a *trubechetum* from the reign of Henry III appears in a text issued on 13 September 1244. See *Calendar of Liberate Rolls 1240–1245* (London, 1930), 265. As discussed, the term *trubechetum* does appear at least once in the reign of Edward I in the inventory of arms at Beaumarais Castle from 1306. See National Archives E101/486/20.

87 *CR 1242–1247*, 219.

88 Ibid.

89 National Archives E372/89 5r.

90 Ibid.

91 Royal clerks sometimes used the term *ingenium* to refer to devices that were parts of artillery rather than artillery itself. For example, the term was used to designate a winch used to draw *balistae* into firing position in National Archives E101/14/27.

of artillery. As a result, the term was now free for use as a new attribution for the *trubechetum* as well as the *blida*.[92]

It has been argued here that the term *trubechetum* was used by royal clerks to designate a counterweight lever engine. The new engine would appear to have replaced the *petraria*, but not the *mangonellus*, in rapid order because the *petraria* disappears from royal government records after 1236. The phasing out of use by the royal government of its traction lever engines but not of its torsion engines suggest that we are *not* seeing the wholesale replacement of older equipment but rather a selective replacement that worked out over a period of time consistent with royal resources, needs, and the availability of specialist personnel to construct new engines. This finding, in turn, indicates that the *trubechetum* was seen by contemporaries as superior to the *petraria*. One likely explanation for this superiority is the replacement of large teams of pullers with a single counterweight. The former had to be trained and paid by the government on an ongoing basis, while a counterweight, once constructed, was available thereafter at no further cost, other than transportation. One final point to be made in this discussion is that the *parvum ingenium*, identified as a *trubechetum* at Beaumarais in 1306, cannot have been traction lever action engine. There would have been no room for a team of pullers to operate on the narrow parapet of this fortification.

After 1244, when government records begin to record in detail the materials that were required for the construction of the *ingenia*, it is clear that these supplies included lead, whose only use for artillery was in the making of counterweights. For example, on 27 June 1244, the Chancery issued orders to the sheriff of London to purchase twenty cart loads of lead at the Boston fair and to transport this very heavy cargo to Newcastle on Tyne for delivery to the engineer (*ingeniator*) Gerard so that he could build the king's engines there. This passage demonstrates conclusively that the term *ingenium* was being used to denote a counterweight engine.[93] A similar shipment of lead for use in the king's *ingenia*, on this occasion in Gascony, is recorded in the Patent Roll for 1254. On 20 October of this year, a merchant named William de Forges was authorized to receive payment for the lead he delivered to the king's engineer Gerard, for use on the king's *ingenia*.[94]

As we have already seen, in addition to the *trubechetum*, Henry III's government began to produce a second type counterweight lever engine, that is the *blida*, no later than the early 1240s. The term *blida* appears for the first time in the royal record on 8 August 1241, when a Chancery writ issued to the sheriff of Hereford ordered him to construct a *blida* under the direction of Master Gerard, who was

---

92   I have found no examples of the term *ingenium* in any royal administrative documents between 6 June 1225 and 4 June 1241. The term reappears in the royal record on 4 June. See *CLR 1240– 1245*, 67.

93   *CLR 1240–1245*, 245.

94   *CPR 1247–1258*, 348.

being sent to Wales to oversee the project.[95] The expression used by the clerk in this writ, namely "which is called a blida", suggests that we are dealing with an early instance of the term *blida* being employed by the Chancery. Even four years later, in August 1244, a Chancery writ to the constable of Dover Castle used the expression "*quod vocatur blida*" to describe one of the two *ingenia* being shipped to his castle.[96] By contrast, the clerk apparently did not feel any need to qualify the term *trubechetum* with the phrase "*quod vocatur*", which makes sense because by then the term *trubechetum* had been part of the administrative vocabulary for almost twenty years.[97] In a similar vein, after its initial years of deployment, royal clerks no longer used the expression *ut vocatur* when discussing the *blida*. Indeed, by late 1244, Chancery clerks already were using the term *blida* without any qualification.[98]

The *blida*, like the *trubechetum*, clearly was a stone-throwing engine. On 20 September 1245, the Chancery issued orders to John Lestrange, the justiciar of Chester, directing him to cooperate with the royal engineer Gerard in selecting supplies for the construction of a *blida* and several *mangonelli* at Gannoc Castle.[99] These supplies included tanned hides (*coria tannata*) to be used to make slings for both types of weapons, which are called here *machinae*.

It is of significant interest that the royal clerks used the generic term *machinae* rather than *ingenia* as a collective noun for the *blida* and *mangonelli*. The plural *machinae* was used by royal officials as a generic term for all kinds of large military equipment, including towers.[100] The use of *machinae* here, therefore, is a clear indication that the royal clerks recognized that the *mangonelli* were not *ingenia*. The obvious conclusion to be drawn here is that although both *mangonelli* and the *blida* were stone throwers, the *blida* was a counterweight lever engine, like the *trubechetum*, while the *mangonelli*, as discussed previously, were

---

95 National Archives E372/85 1r, "*Precipimus tibi quod ingenium nostrum quod vocatur blithe per consilium magistri Gerardi facias*".

96 *CR 1242–1247*, 219.

97 Ibid.

98 National Archive E372/88 5r.

99 National Archives C62/25 3r. The production of slings for *blidae* is also noted in *Calendar of Liberate Rolls 1251–1260* (London, 1259), 267.

100 It does not appear that the royal clerks serving during the reigns of either Richard or John ever used a generic term for large, stone-throwing weapons. It is not until the reign of Henry III that the royal clerks introduced the practice of using a collective term to designate the king's siege weapons. On 19 August 1224, the Chancery issued a writ to the sheriff of Bedford commanding him to have *petrariae*, *mangonelli*, and a siege tower (*belefridum*), which had been used during the siege of Bedford Castle, dismantled and shipped to Northampton to be delivered to the sheriff of Northampton. See *CR I*, 617. The writ went on to add that a similar writ had been sent to the sheriff of Northampton ordering him to receive *praedictas machinas*. The term *machinae* as a generic description of the king's siege engines appears periodically in the surviving royal administrative documents through the remainder of Henry III's reign, but would seem to have dropped out of use before the accession of Edward I in 1272. For the use of the term *machinae* by Henry III's clerks, see *CLR 1240–1245*, 135, 323; and *CR 1259–1261*, 258.

torsion engines. This identification of the *blida* as a counterweight lever engine is confirmed by the fact that among the supplies shipped to the engineer Gerard at Gannoc Castle were six cart loads of lead, as discussed. The only purpose that this lead could have served was to make a counterweight.[101]

From the time the *blida* was introduced as a new type of counterweight lever artillery, it is clear that the royal clerks used the terms *ingenium* and *blida* as synonyms. The first surviving reference to a *blida* from 1241 notes that Master Gerard, who had worked previously on the king's *trubecheta*, was now in charge of building an *ingenium*, which is called a *blida*.[102] In some cases, the clerks used both terms together. A Pipe Roll account for 1244, discussed previously, mentions the shipment of the king's *ingenia* from Sandwich to Dover, and records that these engines comprised one *blida* and one *trebuchetum*.[103] It was far more usual, however, to find that the records simply refer to *ingenia*, without specifying whether these were *trubecheta* or *blidae*. It is, therefore, difficult to determine whether a particular *ingenium* is one or the other type of counterweight artillery. However, because the *trubecheta* were smaller, they likely were more numerous.

Finally, as was true regarding both the *petrariae* and the *mangonelli*, it would appear that there were at least two different sizes of *blida*. On 20 January 1256, the Chancery issued orders to the sheriff of Cumberland to complete two large (*magnae*) *blidae* that were under construction at Carlisle under the direction of the royal engineer Gerard.[104] How smaller *blidae* compared in size with *trubecheta* cannot be determined from the surviving administrative documents. However, the shipment, noted earlier, of six cart loads of lead to Gannoc Castle in 1245 for use in the counterweight of a single *blida* certainly suggests that this was a large piece of artillery.

In considering the evidence developed thus far, it would appear that by the time Edward I ascended the throne in 1272, the royal government had discontinued the use of both the torsion-powered *mangonellus*, and the traction lever engine (*petraria*). The counterweight engines known originally as *trubucheta* and the *blida*, both of which were introduced during Henry III's reign, would appear to have been the basic stone-throwing artillery used during the final three decades of the thirteenth century and the first decade of the fourteenth century. As had been true throughout the final twenty-five years of Henry III's reign, both types of artillery continued to be identified by royal clerks as *ingenia*.

A Pipe Roll account for 1287, for example, records that during the Welsh revolt of that year, royal officials hired master mason (*cementarius*) Adam and his team of assistants to quarry and prepare stone ammunition (*lapides*) for use by the

---

101 National Archives C62/25 3r.
102 National Archives E372/85 1r.
103 National Archives E372/88 5r.
104 National Archives C62/32 15r.

king's *ingenia*.[105] The account of Robert Tibetot for his expenses in commanding Newcastle Emlyn in 1288 records that he spent money to have 480 stones produced for use as ammunition by his *ingenia*.[106] Robert also purchased ropes and cords for use on the *ingenia*, hides for making slings (*funda*), and boards for making a basket (*cista*), likely to hold the ammunition, to attach to one of the *ingenia* stored at his castle.[107] Robert's greatest expense, however, was paying the smiths to produce iron fittings (*ferramenta*) that were constructed for the *ingenia*.[108] Similarly, in 1299 Walter de Langton, the bishop of Coventry and Lichfield, was credited at the Exchequer for the expenses that he incurred in 1296–1297 in the production of four *ingenia*. These expenses included purchases of iron, bronze, and hemp; the purchase and transport of timber; and the wages paid to rope makers.[109]

Because the royal clerks serving Edward I maintained the policy which had become tradition, of denoting both *trubecheta* and *blidae* as *ingenia*, it is not possible, except in rare circumstances, to identify a specific piece of stone-throwing artillery as one or the other. One important exception, discussed here, was the trebuchet stationed at Beaumaris Castle in 1306. Nevertheless, the numerous financial accounts submitted by royal officials permit the observation that the royal government built not only small artillery pieces for use in the defense of fortifications, but also a significant number of very large stone-throwing engines that had the destruction of fortifications as their main task. One famous engine, the *Warwolf*, was mentioned previously in this chapter. But most of these very large counterweight lever engines did not receive names, or at least official or semi-official names that were recorded in administrative documents.

A Pipe Roll account for 1279, for example, records that Egidius de Adenarde, the constable of the Tower of London, paid out in excess of £870 to build three *ingenia* at the Tower under the direction of Master Bertram the engineer.[110] These costs included fifteen ship loads (*batella*) of timber, over sixty-one cart loads of lead purchased for counterweights (*contraponda*), and 4,000 pounds of copper (*cuprum*) to provide shielding (*scuta*) for two of the engines.[111] Clearly, we are dealing here with large pieces of artillery.

We can see similar evidence for the building of large pieces of artillery during Edward I's siege of Stirling Castle. Three Exchequer documents from 1304 record that the royal government required a number of ecclesiastical institutions in Scotland to support the king's campaign through the sale of the lead contained

---

105 National Archives E372/132 1r.
106 National Archives E101/4/21.
107 Ibid.
108 Ibid.
109 National Archives C62/75 8r.
110 National Archives E372/123 21r. Concerning Bertram's career, see A. J. Taylor, "Master Bertram, Ingeniator Regis", in *Studies in Medieval History Presented to R. Allen Brown* (Woodbridge, 1989), 289–315.
111 National Archives E372/123 21r.

in the roofs of their churches. Bishop John of Brechin was paid in excess of £17 for five cart loads of lead taken *"pro pondere ingeniarum regis"*.[112] The prior and convent of St. Andrew's received £78 for twenty-two cart loads of lead, and the abbot and brothers of the monastery of Dunferm received over £41 for twelve cart loads of lead.[113]

Once these large *ingenia* were constructed, it required a great deal of effort to move them, including the assembling of ships, wagons, horses, sailors, and drivers, and providing pay and food for all of the men involved in the operation. In 1288, for example, royal officials recruited twenty-four men, forty oxen, and four wagons to transport a single *ingenium* to Carmarthen Castle.[114] The same text records that a ship transported over three tons of lead to the new castle of Emlyn, already mentioned, for use as engine counterweights.[115] In 1300, the royal government employed twenty-one ox carts to transfer a single *magnum ingenium*, the equipment of some carpenters, lead, and stones from Linlithgow to Stirling, a journey that took four days and cost a total of £6.[116]

Conclusion

A comprehensive examination of all of the surviving administrative documents from the reigns of Richard, John, Henry III, and Edward I makes it clear, by contrast with numerous narrative sources, that the royal officials in charge of building the king's artillery and the royal clerks responsible for recording information about its construction, movement, and storage provide an exceptionally important corpus of information about what types of artillery were constructed and deployed by the royal government from the late twelfth through the early fourteenth century. During the reigns of Richard and John, royal engineers built three different types of engine, the tension-powered *balista*, the torsion-powered *mangonellus*, and the traction lever *petraria*. Perhaps inspired by the new counterweight lever engine deployed by Prince Louis during his invasion of England in 1216, the royal government under Henry III began to construct these engines as well. The *trube-chetum*, as it was denoted by royal clerks, was not a large wall-breaking engine of the type featured in many manuscript illustrations of a later date and used by

---

112 National Archives E101/12/28. In this case, the possibility cannot be excluded the lead was taken to produce counterweights for numerous smaller engines rather than few larger counterweights for giant stone-throwing machines.

113 Ibid. There is some evidence to suggest that the royal government used other materials in addition to lead to construct counterweights. The liberate roll for 1299, for example, records that Walter Langton, Bishop of Coventry and Lichfield and royal treasurer, spent in excess of £40 purchasing cart loads of stone (*petra*) and clay (*argillum*) *"ad pondus"* of four *ingenia* being built at Carlisle. See National Archives C62/75 8r.

114 National Archives E101/14/21.

115 Ibid.

116 National Archives E101/12/9.

scholars to represent earlier technology, but rather a smaller type of artillery intended to replace the relatively awkward traction lever *petraria*. By 1236, at the latest, the royal government no longer deployed the *petraria* and had replaced it with two distinct types of counterweight engines, namely the *trubechetum* and the *blida*. By the last decade of Henry III's reign, the torsion-powered *mangonellus*, a mainstay of the royal artillery since at least the reign of King Richard, had also been phased out of use. King Edward's government continued to deploy both the *trubechetum* and the *blida* as stone-throwing artillery into the early fourteenth century. The *trubechetum* likely served the role of the smaller, anti-personnel weapon, which could also be deployed as defensive artillery on fortress and city walls. The *blida* likely was the larger wall-smashing artillery of the type identified with the well-known *Warwolf*. Edward's government also introduced a new type of torsion-powered engine called a *springaldus*, which cast long arrow or bolt-shaped ammunition and was deployed alongside the seemingly ageless *balista*.

When considered from an administrative perspective, it is clear that the English government possessed a highly professional and well-organized bureaucracy to oversee military affairs for well over a century. Royal officers and clerks maintained careful records regarding all aspects of the production, maintenance, storage, and deployment of a wide range of types of artillery. Even more importantly, royal officials demonstrated an appreciation for the development and use of a highly specialized technical vocabulary to describe these engines. Indeed, it is their regular and systematic use of this vocabulary that makes it possible to identify the rather dramatic efforts by the royal government to deploy newer and better types of artillery over the course of the long thirteenth century.

Part 2

MILITARY LOGISTICS

6

THE MILITARY ADMINISTRATION OF ENGLAND

The royal artillery (1216 –1272)[1]

It is commonly believed that King Edward I of England (1272–1307) revolutionized the military organization of England. A typical example of this view is Michael Powicke's argument that "Edward I effected what amounted to a revolution in the English army and laid the foundation for Creçy and Poitiers".[2] Despite this general consensus, however, it is the burden of this paper to suggest that Edward's reputation as a "revolutionary" is a considerable exaggeration. It will be shown here that in regard to military administration, Edward's government had available the expertise of at least two generations of a previously well-developed military bureaucracy. Because the overall military administration was so large, detailed, and all-encompassing, this study examines only a small part to make the point that in this area Edward did not carry out a revolution.

1 This article was first presented as a paper at the second annual conference of the German His-torical Institute which was held in Berlin on 25–28 October 2002. I would like to thank the participants at the conference, particularly Professors Patrick Geary, Caroline Bynum, Michael Borgolte, Johannes Fried, and Dr. Benjamin Scheller, for their helpful comments and suggestions. Additional research for this article was made possible by the generous support of the Center for the Humanities and the Office of the Dean at the University of New Hampshire, USA. The dates in this paper refer to the reign of Henry III, King Edward I's father and predecessor.
2 Michael Powicke, *Military Obligation in Medieval England: A Study in Liberty and Duty* (Oxford, 1962, repr. 1996), 96. The military organization utilized by the royal government under Edward is regularly treated by specialists as the beginning of a new era in military affairs rather than as a continuation of the system that had been in place for many decades. Typical in this regard are Michael Prestwich, *The Three Edwards: War and State in England 1272 –1377* (London, 1980, repr. 1996); and Andrew Ayton, "Sir Thomas Ughtred and the Edwardian Military Revolution", in *The Age of Edward III*, ed. J. S. Bothwell (Woodbridge, 2001), 107–132. The focus on the military innovations and achievements of Edward I as compared with his father Henry III is also evident in the wide spectrum of scholarly attention that the former has received. See, for example, John Edward Morris, *The Welsh Wars of Edward I: A Contribution to Medieval History Based on Original Documents* (1901, repr. New York, 1969); Michael Prestwich, *War, Politics and Finance under Edward I* (Totowa, NJ, 1972); A. Z. Freeman, "Wall-Breakers and River-Bridgers: Military Engineers in the Scottish Wars of Edward I", *Journal of British Studies* 10 (1971); and Thomas Avril, "Interconnections between the Lands of Edward I: A Welsh-English Mercenary Force in Ireland 1285–1304", *Bulletin of the Board of Celtic Studies* 40 (1993), 135–147.

The particular focus of this study is on the military administration that made possible the production, storage, and transportation of the royal artillery during the half-century before Edward's accession.[3]

The overwhelming majority of the evidence for the royal military administration of the thirteenth century is to be found in surviving government records produced by two of the offices of the central or royal government, the Chancery and the Exchequer, whose major duties included, respectively, serving as a royal writing office and as a center for the collection of taxes and disbursement of cash.[4] Numerous chronicles survive from the thirteenth century, and many of these provide valuable information concerning a variety of military topics.[5] However, aside from the many difficulties inherent in narrative sources, including the *parti pris* and level of expertise of the author, these chronicles do not provide the type of information required for a study of military administration. In particular, chronicle writers do not discuss the detailed procedures utilized by royal servants to transfer information by parchment concerning the actions of other agents of the royal government, who were engaged in activities such as cutting down timber, moving timber, purchasing lead, building storage sheds, and paying the wages of carpenters engaged in the construction of siege artillery.[6]

3   The royal artillery provides a valuable point of focus for this study because of its role in the conduct of sieges which dominated medieval warfare not only during the thirteenth century but also the whole of the Middle Ages. See, in this regard, Michael Prestwich, *Armies and Warfare in the Middle Ages: The English Experience* (New Haven, CT, 1996), 281, "sieges dominated medieval warfare in a way that battles never did". The basic works on medieval siege warfare are Jim Bradbury, *The Medieval Siege* (Woodbridge, 1992); R. Rogers, *Latin Siege Warfare in the Twelfth Century* (Oxford, 1992); Bernard. S. Bachrach, "Medieval Siege Warfare: A Reconnaissance", *Journal of Military History* 58 (1994), 119–133, repr. with the same pagination in Bernard. S. Bachrach, *Warfare and Military Organization in Pre-Crusade Europe* (Bury St Edmunds, 2002); Peter Purton, *A History of the Early Medieval Siege: c. 450–1220* (Woodbridge, 2009); and idem, *A History of the Late Medieval Siege, 1200–1500* (Woodbridge, 2010).

4   The collections of documents used in this article are listed here: *Rotuli Litterarum Clausarum in Turri Londonensi Asservati 1204–1227*, ed. Thomas D. Hardy, 2 vols (1833–1834), hereafter *CR I* and *CR II*; *The Close Rolls 1227–1272* (London, 1892–1938), hereafter *CR* with specific dates; *The Calendar of Liberate Rolls 1226–1272* (London, 1916–1964), hereafter, *CLR*; and *The Calendar of Patent Rolls 1216–1272* (London, 1891–1913), hereafter *CPR*. The Pipe Rolls for the reigns of Henry II, Richard I, and John have all been edited by the Pipe Roll Society individually. Each roll will be cited individually in this chapter.

5   Antonia Gransden, *Historical Writing in England c. 550–c. 1307* (Ithaca, NY, 1974), provides an easily accessible discussion of all of the surviving narrative sources from this period.

6   In the context of using narrative sources for writing military administrative history, see Emilie Amt, "Besieging Bedford: Military Logistics in 1224", *Journal of Medieval Military History* 1 (2002), 101–124, who makes clear (102–107) that narrative and epistolary sources are invaluable for establishing both the political context of the siege of Bedford and the general course of the military action. However, in order to recreate the logistics of the campaign, Amt was forced to rely entirely on administrative records (108–116), principally documents from the close rolls and Pipe Rolls.

Administrative procedures for the construction of siege engines

Once it was decided by the king and his advisors that artillery was needed in a particular place at a particular time to sustain England's military needs, orders were issued to a master carpenter or carpenters (*magister carpentarius*) who specialized in the construction of artillery. These men, who were specialists in the construction of siege engines, were in charge of building artillery.[7] In the period before 1240, these master carpenters generally worked with teams of assistants (*socii*) to aid them in their efforts.[8] Frequently, these master carpenters were resident within the royal household, and it is not clear whether they always received written orders detailing the task at hand to which they had been assigned. As we shall see in this chapter, when master carpenters were not resident in the king's household, it was necessary to issue written orders to them making clear what kinds of artillery they were to build and in what quantity, and where the work was to be done.

In order to transport the carpenters, their assistants, and especially their tools to a chosen work site, it was necessary to have transportation assets made available, usually a wagon or wagons as well as horses and drivers, although sometimes riverine assets were assigned as well. These transportation resources were not provided directly by the royal household. Rather, the responsible officials of the central government required local royal officers, e.g., sheriffs, constables,

---

7 Specialists in medieval military history use the term artillery to describe a wide range of mechanical devices that were used to hurl stones, missiles such as spears, and lead balls. These engines were constructed from a variety of materials including wood, hide, rope, and iron fittings, and used either torsion or counterweight action for their power. The projectiles thrown by these engines were generally larger than those shot by handheld missile weapons such as self-bows and crossbows. Artillery was used both in an anti-personnel function and to destroy hard-point fortifications such as city and castle walls. For a useful introduction to artillery, see Kelly DeVries, *Medieval Military Technology* (Peterborough, 1992, now available in a second edition, Toronto, 2012), 127–142. For the artillery used in medieval England during the thirteenth century, now also see David S. Bachrach, "English Artillery 1189–1307: The Implications of Terminology", *The English Historical Review* 121.494 (2006), 1408–1430, and in this volume.

8 The practice of sending master carpenters to build siege engines accompanied by a team of *socii* went back at least to John's reign. In a letter to the royal military officer Philip Mark, issued on 24 August 1212, King John stated, "we are sending the master carpenters Ralph and Nicholas to build two Turkish *petraria* without delay. We order that you provide them and their assistants what they need" ("*mittimus ad vos magistrum Radulfum et magistrum Nicholas carpentarios et vobis mandamus quod ab eis fieri faciatis duas petrarias turkesias sine dilacione et eis et sociis suis necessaria inveniatis*"), *CR I*, 122. Similar orders stress the presence of these *socii* operating with master carpenters during Henry III's reign. See *CLR 1226–1240*, 47–48; and *CR II*, 198. At some point around 1240, however, Henry III's administration altered this policy of sending master craftsmen to worksites accompanied by teams of assistants. Instead, a single master carpenter was given oversight responsibilities for all building operations and local royal officials were given the task of finding suitable carpenters to build the king's engines. See, for example, *CLR 1240–1245*, 67.

and bailiffs, to provide the necessary vehicles and drivers.[9] It was generally the case that these transportation resources were drawn from the locality in which the master carpenters and their assistants were resident. Thus, for example, when they were at London, it was usually the constable of the Tower of London or the sheriffs of the city who were issued written orders by the officers of the central government to provide transportation.

These local officials either had to provide wagons and drivers from their own resources such as a team normally assigned to the Tower of London, or the responsible official had to obtain these assets from other local sources in a timely manner. The most common recipient of such requests for transportation from sheriffs and constables, as well as the royal bailiffs of towns to supply this equipment were ecclesiastical officials such as abbots, priors, and cathedral deans.[10] Indeed, church officials would appear to have been the largest non-governmental source for providing the equipment for the transportation of military personnel and supplies in both peace and wartime.[11]

The costs involved in providing the vehicles and personnel for transporting the royal carpenters and their tools, including paying the wages of the drivers, feeding the horses, or paying the fees charged by church officials, were not part of the normal financial obligations of the sheriffs, castle constables, or bailiffs. Thus, the Chancery can be seen to have issued writs of *computabitur* (literally, it will be accounted) which stated that the local official was permitted to obtain credit at the Exchequer during his twice-yearly audit there for the expenses he had incurred in regard to the cost of providing transportation for artillery construction crews and their tools. These local officers, including sheriffs and constables, therefore kept a detailed account of all of the costs involved in such operations.[12] In order to obtain this credit, the constable, sheriff, or bailiff was required to submit his

---

9 This system was very common, with the result that local officials regularly received orders requiring them to provide transportation for the king's servants. See, for example, *CR I*, 198; *CR 1251–1253*, 431; *CLR 1240–1245*, 258. Local officials had also been required to provide transportation to the king's servants during John's reign. See *CR I*, 4, 102, 205, 450. It is important to distinguish between officials of the central government, who worked in the presence of the king, or of his designated representative, at the royal court, and local royal officials who worked far from the presence of the king. Local officials such as sheriffs, constables, and bailiffs, either were appointed by the king or the king's designated representative, but had a great deal of autonomy in carrying out certain of their duties, including the collection of taxes and rents as well as the administration of justice. It should be emphasized, however, that they did not have autonomy in carrying out orders pertaining to the royal military administration, as we shall see in this chapter.

10 In a typical order issued on 20 July 1244, the sheriff of Westminster was commanded to secure transportation resources from the abbots and priors of his county. See *CR 1242–1247*, 257–258.

11 This topic is addressed in more detail in David S. Bachrach, "Military Logistics during the Reign of Edward I of England, 1272–1307", *War in History* 13 (2006), 423–440, and in this volume.

12 See, for example, *CR I*, 551, where the sheriffs of London are promised that "the costs that you incur, which have been vetted by the testimony of honest men, will be credited to your account at the exchequer" ("*custum quod ad hoc posueris per visum et testimonium legalium hominum comutabitur vobis ad scaccarum*"). This document is a standard writ of *computabitur*.

writ of *computabitur* to the clerks of the Exchequer along with a detailed written list of his expenses, including the number of vehicles and drivers employed, and how much each individual item had cost.[13] In order to avoid fraud, the central government required that this account had to be confirmed as accurate by a group of local men.[14] The standard phrase used in government documents to describe this vetting process is *"per testimonium legalium hominum"*.[15]

However, if a local official did not receive a writ of *computabitur* from the Chancery, but rather was sent a direct royal order to carry out a particular task (frequently called a *brevis* in the administrative documents), he could petition the central government for repayment or credit. In this case too, the local official was required to keep a detailed record of his expenses that was to be validated by the oaths of local witnesses, who were then listed by name in the document. This account was then submitted to the Chancery. Once this written account had been received and accepted as valid by the king's officials, a written order was then issued by the Chancery to the barons of the Exchequer informing them of the expenses incurred by the local officer and requiring them to credit his account for this amount.[16]

Before the master carpenters and their assistants set out for the building site, they frequently were given a sum of money at royal command to pay their personal expenses, usually food and lodging, for the duration of their journey. Here too, written orders were required. The normal disbursing agent in this situation was the Exchequer. However, before the officials of the Exchequer could release any cash, they required an order of "liberate" from the Chancery. Thus, before the carpenters set out to build siege engines, a Chancery official had to issue a document, validated by the Chancery seal, authorizing the Exchequer to disburse a money payment to the master carpenter. For example, the master carpenter Jordan, a specialist in the construction of counterweight artillery called trebuchets, was supposed to receive 5 marks for his expenses while at the royal fortress of Dover.[17] It is likely that this document originally was given directly to the mas-

---

13 The royal office of the Exchequer had a number of tasks during most of the thirteenth century, including collecting and counting taxes that had been gathered by the sheriffs from their shires, keeping records of monies collected and owed, and paying out sums to individuals who had a proper writ sealed by the Chancery. The titular heads of the Exchequer were the so-called barons, although most of the work was done by lower-ranking clerks (*clerici*).

14 *CR I*, 100, where the barons of the Exchequer received the order, "credit the costs incurred by the keepers of the bishopric of Lincoln that have been vetted by the testimony of honest men" (*"computate custodibus episcopatus Lincolnensis custum quod possunt per visum et testimonium legalium hominum"*).

15 See the previous two notes.

16 These orders of "liberate" are ubiquitous in the surviving Chancery rolls. See, for example, *CR I*, 641; *CLR 1240–1245*, 259; *CLR 1267–1272*, 40.

17 See, for example, *CR II*, 44, where an order was issued to the barons of the Exchequer *"liberate de thesauro nostro Jordano carpentario facienti trubechetum nostrum apud Dover v. m. ad expensas suas"*.

ter carpenter, who was in charge of the construction crew, so that he could then take it to the Exchequer.

In summary, the process of moving the required personnel to the appropriate site in order to build the king's artillery relied on the production of a matrix of documents and a complex bureaucratic organization. A written order was required to obtain transportation assets from local royal officials such as the king's constable at the Tower of London, or the sheriffs of a particular shire. This local official was required to keep a detailed account of his expenditures, to have this account verified by local witnesses, and then to submit it in writing to the king's Chancery officials. These officers had in turn to accept the claim from the local official and issue their own written order to the barons of the Exchequer to credit the local official's account. In addition, a further written document was required so that the master carpenter and his team could obtain cash to purchase food and lodging during their journey.

The entire process, however, was somewhat more complicated when the carpenters resided away from the royal household. In these instances, it was necessary to send a written order to the local official with jurisdiction in the area where the craftsmen were then resident, e.g. castle constables, sheriffs, and town bailiffs. This written order stated where the carpenters were to go and what types of engines they were to build once they arrived there.[18] The process for securing transportation for the carpenters and their tools was the same as that noted previously. So too was the process employed by the local official to obtain credit for the costs he had incurred in providing this transportation. However, providing a cash advance to the carpenters for the expenses of their journey required a different procedure, because it was not expected that these craftsmen would or could go to the officers of the Exchequer. Rather, the central government issued orders to the local royal official in charge, whether sheriff, constable, or bailiff, requiring him to provide the carpenters with money and/or supplies for their journey.[19] Once again, in order to obtain credit at the Exchequer, the local official was required to submit a written account that detailed his expenses and which was vetted by local witnesses. Once this request for payment with its supporting documents was received by the central government, written orders were then issued by the Chancery to the barons of the Exchequer that informed them of the local official's expenses and required them to credit his account.[20]

As these preparations were underway to send the artillery construction crew to the building site with transportation and satisfactory supplies, a second administrative process was in train to ensure that the craftsmen would be received in the

---

18 On 18 July 1231, for example, orders were issued to the constable of Windsor Castle to send all of the royal carpenters resident there, with the exception of Nicholas, to County Salop. Nicholas was to remain and continue to oversee the royal operations at Windsor. See *CR 1227–1231*, 531.

19 See *CR I*, 450.

20 Ibid.

proper manner at their destination and that the required building materials would be provided to them once they had arrived. The first step here was the issue of an order to the local officer in charge of the building site, which was usually one of the royal castles or royal forests. The officers in question were constables, sheriffs, or the keepers of the royal forest lands. This order informed the relevant local official that one or two named master carpenters along with a specified number of assistants would soon be arriving to build a particular number of siege engines of a particular type or types, e.g. *trubecheta, mangonelli, balistae,* or *petrariae.* A representative example of this type of order was issued by the Chancery on 18 August 1227 to Hugh de Kilpec, overseer of the royal forest at Trivel. He was informed that two master carpenters named Thomas and Nicholas as well as four assistants were be sent to Trivel to build five pieces of siege artillery there called *petraria* (2) and *mangonelli* (3).[21] The local official was required to find lodgings for these men and to pay them as well. Consequently, his orders also included information regarding the regular daily wages of the carpenters and their assistants.[22] The local official in charge of the building site was permitted to obtain credit for all the expenses incurred in housing and paying the carpenters. In order to do so, he submitted a detailed written account to the central government that had been approved by local witnesses.[23] The process for obtaining credit at the Exchequer was the same as that already explained with regard to obtaining payment for providing transportation resources to move royal artillery construction crews as well as their tools to their building sites.

In addition to assuring that the carpenters were housed and paid, the order to the relevant local official from the central government also required him to provide the supplies necessary for the artillery construction crew to carry out the task of building siege engines. The most common supplies noted in various of these royal orders included timber, ropes, cables, iron fittings, lead for counterweights, ox hides for slings, and nails. It was frequently the case that artillery construction

---

21   A representative example is the order issued on 18 August 1227 to Hugh de Kilpec, the overseer of the royal forest at Trivel announcing, "*mittimus carpentarios nostros magistros Thomas et Nicholas et quatuor eorum socios ad forestam nostram de Trivel ad duas petrarias et tres mangonellos in ea faciendo*". See *CR II,* 198. There is, at present, no agreement among specialists about the meaning of the terms trebuchet, mangonel, and petrary. Furthermore, there is not yet a systematic study of the terms used by royal clerks to discuss artillery produced in England during the thirteenth century. I hope to write such a study in the near future. For an introduction to the state of the question on the terms used for artillery, see Rogers, *Latin Siege Warfare,* 254–273, and Prestwich, *Armies and Warfare,* 287–292. However, now see, Bachrach, "English Artillery 1189–1307: The Implications of Terminology", passim, where the meaning of these terms are treated in detail.

22   On 19 February 1221, for example, the sheriff of Nottingham was ordered to pay master carpenters Thomas, Burnellus, and Robert, "the same wages that they were accustomed to receive during the reign of our father King John" ("*liberationes suas sicut eas habere consueverunt in tempore domini J. rex patris nostri*"). See *CR I,* 449.

23   Ibid., the sheriff was promised that these expenses "would be credited to him at the exchequer". ("*computabitur tibi ad scaccarum*").

crews were sent to build engines at a particular royal fortress or royal forest, such as Windsor or the Forest of Dean, because these sites served as depots for the storage of military supplies, particularly the types of supplies required for the construction of artillery. The local sheriff, constable, or forest keeper, therefore, had the responsibility to acquire and store all or most of the materials required by the builders to carry out their assigned duties.[24]

The actual provision of the necessary supplies to the carpenters was simply a matter of moving the required timber, iron fitting, ropes, and other materials from their storage areas to the building site. This movement of supplies, however, also required a substantial commitment of information to parchment. Each magazine commander was required to keep track through a detailed written procedure of exactly how much materiél, of what types, and in what condition, was maintained in his storage areas.[25] When these supplies were used in the construction of siege engines, the local officer was required to emend his accounts by subtracting the appropriate number of logs and other raw materials from the inventory list. Once the building project had been completed, the officer was further required to submit a new written inventory of the supplies kept in the depot in which he detailed exactly what had been used by the carpenters. This written account had to be verified by the carpenters themselves before it was submitted to the central government.[26] Obviously, in order to keep track of his own supplies, the local

---

24 Detailed orders of this type were issued to the sheriff of Northampton informing him that Master Robert de Hotot was arriving to build engines at Brikestock, which was under the sheriff's jurisdiction. The sheriff was required to pay Robert's wages and it was further required that "you transport to an appropriate place the wood that has been cut in those regions for the purpose of building mangonels, just as Master Robert will tell you. The costs that you entail, which are [confirmed by the testimony of honest men] will be credited to you at the exchequer" ("*maeremium quod perstaverit in partibus illis ad ipsos petrarias et mangonellos faciendos cariari facias ad locum competentem sicut idem magister Robertus tibi dicet et custum quod ad hoc posueris per visum etc. computabitur tibi ad scaccarum*"). See *CR I*, 621.

25 For examples of inventory lists, see *CR 1231–1234*, 181, 212, 268, *CR 1234–1237*, 282; *CR 1237–1242*, 82–83, 183–84; *CR 1242–1247*, 440; *CR 1254–1256*, 112; and *CLR 1226–1240*, 219, and 205. There are also numerous examples of unpublished inventory accounts for castles surviving in Chancery and Exchequer accounts. See, for example, National Archives C47/10/13/2, which describes the supplies at Dublin Castle in 1224, including *duo mangonelli*, C47/2/1/3 which notes the purchase of six bases (*fundae*) for mangonels at Corfe Castle by its constable Elyas de Rabban in 1252, and E101/3/3 in which the constable Roger de Leyburn notes the purchase of three *cordas ad mangonellum* at Rochester Castle in 1264.

26 There was a clear expectation among officers of the central government not only that local depot commanders would have detailed records of what supplies were on hand, but also from where these supplies had come. See, for example, *CR I*, 123, "We order that all of the ropes used for petraries and mangonels, which were transported from Bristol and are now in Winchester, be carried back to Bristol. Keep all of the ropes used for ships" ("*Rex Stephano de Turneha*' [Turnham] etc. *Mandamus vobis quod omnes cordas ad petrarias et mongonellas quod sunt apud Wint' quod venerunt a Bristol faciatis presencium latori deferendum usque Bristol, et cablas ad mare penes vos retineatis*").

commander kept a copy of the inventory list for himself, but it is not clear from the surviving records whether this document was in the form of a chirograph.[27]

Matters became more complicated when the depot at the building site had an insufficient quantity of one or another type of raw material needed to build the siege engines required by the government. In these cases, it became necessary to bring the required supplies from elsewhere. There were two basic methods for obtaining additional materials: either through purchasing them on the private market, or having them transported from another royal supply depot. When purchasing materials for use in the construction of siege engines from private sources, local officials were required in the initial phase of the process to use money drawn from their own revenues.[28] These costs included obtaining vehicles for transportation and paying drivers and guards, as well as the actual purchase price of the goods. As was true of all other aspects of the building process, these costs were to be redeemed by the local official at the Exchequer, provided he submitted a written account to the Chancery detailing his expenses and had this account vetted by local witnesses. If the claim for expenses was accepted by the central government, an order was issued by the Chancery to the barons of the Exchequer ordering them to credit the account of the local official.[29]

The shipping of materials from one royal depot to another imposed yet another level of complexity on the administrative system which, in turn, required the production of a further matrix of written documents. The decision to move supplies was made either in response to a request from the local official where the engines were being built, or because officers from the central government knew from their own records that an insufficient supply of materials was available at a site to complete the job.[30] In the first case, the local officer sent a letter to the central government asking for materials, either because he could not obtain them locally, or did not wish to expend his own resources in purchasing them. It should be emphasized here, that without a prior writ of *computabitur* from the central government to purchase supplies with a concomitant assurance that the costs would be credited to his account at the Exchequer, a local constable or sheriff had no guarantee that he would be reimbursed.

27 When English clerks used the term chirograph to describe a document, they meant that a report was written in duplicate or triplicate on a single piece of parchment. This parchment was then divided into two or three parts each of which contained a copy of the written report. The distinctive edge dividing the two or three pieces of the parchment could be matched against one another to confirm at a later date that these were the original copies of the written report.

28 See, for example, *CR I*, 641; and *CLR 1240–1245*, 245. In the latter case, the sheriff of Lincoln was ordered to purchase twenty wagon loads of lead for use in the construction of siege engines at Newcastle on Tyne.

29 These expenses of the local officials can be traced through orders of "liberate" issued by the Chancery to the Exchequer.

30 As we shall see in this chapter, the officers of the central government were regularly informed about the state of supplies at royal depots throughout England.

To ensure that the proper supplies were available, the central government normally either issued a writ of *computabitur* to the sheriff, constable, or other local official to purchase the supplies locally, thereby providing him with a guarantee that he would be credited for the cost at the Exchequer, or put in motion the procedures to have the materials delivered from another royal supply depot. In the latter case, the central government set in train two complementary bureaucratic procedures. For the sake of clarity, we will call the local official in charge of site where the engines were being built constable A and the official in command of the site from which additional supplies were being transported constable B. In the first step of the process, the central government sent a written order to constable B requiring him to transport a specified quantity of supplies to the site where the siege engines were being built, the site which was under the command of constable A.[31] At the same time, a second written order was issued to constable A. This second order listed the materials that were being shipped to him. It also required constable A to inventory the materials once they had arrived, and then to prepare a chirograph in which he recorded the findings of this inventory.[32] He was to keep one portion of this chirograph for his own records and to send a second portion on to the central government. A third copy might also be produced and provided to constable B who had shipped the supplies.

Once constable B had shipped the required supplies to the building site, he was permitted to claim a credit at the Exchequer for the expenses he had undertaken in their transportation. As we have seen, in order to obtain this credit, it was necessary for constable B to submit a written account in which he listed his expenses.[33] This account had then to be vetted "*per testimonium legalium hominum*". After this account was accepted as valid by the officers of the central government, an order was issued by the Chancery to the Exchequer ordering the barons to credit the local officer's account.

As is clear from this description, the royal government imposed bureaucratic redundancy at both the local and central level whenever supplies were shipped from one depot to another. At the local level, constable B's account of the quantity of materiél transported and the costs involved in its transportation were audited by

---

31 See *CR I*, 62, for the orders issued to Adam de Bendenges to ship logs from the forest of Odiham, where he served as royal keeper, to Windsor Castle for the use of Jordan who was building a trebuchet there.

32 See *CLR 1240–1245*, 265.

33 See, for example, National Archives C47/10/13/2, C47/2/1/3, and E101/3/3. It is also possible to detect much of their original content in the orders of "liberate" issued to the Exchequer by the Chancery. These instructions to credit the accounts of royal officials frequently included detailed accounts of the supplies that they had shipped and the costs involved in their transportation. In order for the Chancery to provide this information to the Exchequer, the information first had to have been provided to the Chancery officers. The latter, of course, were not in the field with local royal officials and relied on written reports to obtain their information. For a representative example of an order of "liberate" in which Chancery officers had included detailed information regarding the transportation of military supplies, see *CLR 1245–1251*, 245–246.

local witnesses. This process was duplicated, on the receiving end when constable A inventoried the materials that were shipped to him and also issued a written report in the form of a chirograph in which he noted his findings. Constable A was able to check these findings against the orders sent to him by the central government in which the constable was informed about the types and quantities of supplies he was to expect.

The officers at the central level similarly had access to redundant accounts that detailed the types and quantities of supplies that had been shipped from one depot to another. In the first case, the officers of the central government received a detailed written report from constable B in which he listed what materials had been transported and how much this had cost. This report had, of course, been vetted by local witnesses. Constable B's account could then be matched against the copy of the chirograph sent to the central government by constable A. As a consequence, the officers of the central government were in a position not only to know whether fraud had been committed, but also to keep very close track of where and in what quantities supplies were located in the various royal depots at any particular time. Because these redundant systems were employed whenever any military supplies were shipped between any of the royal depots in England, the officers of the central government had available to them in the aggregate a precise account of the total quantity of materials under direct royal control that were available in the kingdom at any time. This information was, of course, crucial to those responsible for making decisions about how to allocate royal resources for military purposes.

The organization of artillery production dealt with thus far was the norm under peacetime conditions within England. This system was altered, however, in order to accommodate the special conditions imposed by military campaigns when artillery was built *in situ* at sieges. In these circumstances, massive quantities of matériel, including huge stores of ropes, timber, iron fittings, and lead were transported from all over England to a single location. As a consequence, the normal bureaucratic redundancies that had been instituted to avoid fraud and establish precise accounts of where and in what quantities royal military supplies were located were not operative. In place of a single local official awaiting shipment of a specified load of matériel, timber and other supplies were being transported into a very large but temporary army camp that had been established on the site of the siege. In order to keep control over the logistical situation, the central government maintained the normal system to the extent that this was possible. Thus, writs of *computabitur* were issued by the central government to local officers all over England, which specified the precise quantities of matériel that were required from them.[34] In order to obtain credit for the costs involved in transporting these

---

34 On 2 February 1221, for example, Sheriff Philip Mark of Nottingham was ordered to join the royal siege at Bytham in Lincolnshire with a large quantity of supplies, including ropes and slings for use in siege engines. See *CR I*, 448.

supplies, local officials were still required to submit vetted accounts of their expenditures to the royal government.[35]

A major development in administrative practice took place on the receiving end at the royal army camp. In order to alleviate the immense record-keeping burden placed on royal clerks accompanying the army, each local official charged with transporting supplies to a siege encampment also was required to send along a clerk to help in the process of maintaining a precise written account of the supplies that had been shipped and received.[36] Once a convoy arrived in camp and had been met by one of the king's supply officers, the clerk of the local official and the royal supply officer were required to inventory the materials that had been shipped. After this inventory was written up and witnessed by the royal supply officer, this document served both as a confirmation that the local officer, e.g. the sheriff, constable, or bailiff, had shipped the required ox hides, ropes, and other materials, and as a basis for ascertaining the overall quantities of supplies that were in camp. This document also provided the local official with a written receipt that proved he had fulfilled his orders.[37]

Like the beginning of a military campaign, the end of a siege brought with it enormous logistical challenges. It was then necessary to ascertain what materials had not been expended and thus were still available for use. These supplies then had to be transported to appropriate storage areas. The first step in this process was to conduct an exhaustive inventory of what supplies were left and then to compare this result with the stack of written documents produced when supplies had been brought into camp. It is possible that the various reports detailing the delivery of supplies into camp were rationalized into one document.[38] At this point, if there appeared to be significant discrepancies between the quantity of supplies that had been used in the construction of siege artillery, and the remaining stocks, it was possible to conduct an investigation into the possibility of theft.[39] Following the

35 See ibid., where the barons of the Exchequer were ordered to credit the account of Philip Mark for "the costs that he entailed, which were validated by the testimony of honest men" (*"custum quod posuit per visum et testimonium legalium hominum"*).

36 Thus, for example, the sheriffs of London were required to send, "one of your clerks" (*"unum de clericis vestris"*) to the siege of Bedford in the summer of 1224. See *CR I,* 605.

37 *CR I,* 605, the king's order notes specifically that the clerk from London was present so that "we will be able to send our orders to you about the allocation of the costs entailed in this effort" (*"vobis mittere possimus litteras nostras de allocatione custi ad hoc opponiti"*).

38 We can see this process of rationalization at work in other military contexts. For example, at the conclusion of the barons war in 1265, the clerks of the Exchequer created a summary document listing dozens of expense reports submitted by Roger de Leyburn, then serving as constable of Rochester Castle and as one of King Henry's chief military officers in the field. See National Archives E101/3/6.

39 Concerning the provision of guards for the materiél stored in camp, see *CR I,* 452, 605, and 641; and *Rolls of Divers Accounts for the Early Years of the Reign of Henry III: Accounts of the Escheats for the Sixteenth, Seventeenth, and Eighteenth Years of the Reign of Henry III, Wardrobe Receipt Rolls, and Fragments of the Household Roll 10 Henry III,* ed. Frederick A. Cazel (London, 1982), 52.

completion of this initial audit, decisions had to be made about where the remaining stocks of material were to be sent. It would appear to have been the normal practice to send supplies back to their place of origin in so far as this was possible. Once again, the costs involved in transporting supplies from the siege site back to storage depots fell on the local official who had brought them in the first place. This was also the case regarding the costs for paying the carters, drivers, and guards who had transported and guarded these supplies on the road and in the siege camp.[40] These costs could be redeemed in the form of credit at the Exchequer provided that the local officials submitted a written account of their expenses with the appropriately vetted supporting documentation.

As we have seen, the building of siege engines in England required close cooperation between the central government and local officials which was sustained by a very complex bureaucratic organization and which, in turn, generated an extensive parchment trail. Although the bureaucratic procedures differed to a certain extent in peacetime and in war, sheriffs, constables, bailiffs, and the keepers of the royal forest played a crucial role in assuring that the artillery construction crews were provided with all of the materials they needed to carry out their duties. In Gascony during the mid-thirteenth century, however, the English government instituted a fundamentally different administrative regime. In the absence of local royal officials, such as sheriffs and constables, the central government chose not to rely on Gascon officers or to work through his seneschal in Bordeaux to obtain building materials for royal carpenters engaged in the construction of artillery. Instead, the king or his designated agent was accompanied by a cadre of clerks who were responsible for purchasing supplies of iron, lead, steel, timber, and other goods directly from Gascon and Iberian merchants.[41] Obviously, these men had to be familiar with the specialized requirements of the royal artillery construction crew in order to purchase the correct types of ropes, iron fittings, and other supplies necessary for the construction of siege engines. It is not surprising, therefore, that the same clerks appear regularly in the surviving royal documents as the agents responsible for the purchase of these military supplies.[42]

Rather than providing these clerks with chests of money for their purchasing expeditions, the royal agents instead were authorized to issue letters patent to local merchants that could later be redeemed for cash.[43] When he issued a letter patent to a local merchant, the king's clerk recorded the types and quantities of supplies purchased, and the price that had been agreed on between him and the merchant. The clerk also kept a separate written account in which he recorded this information. This record of purchases, which initially may have been kept

40 See *The Great Roll of the Pipe for the Fourth Year of the Reign of Henry III, Michaelmas 1220* (London, 1987), 74 and 99–100.
41 *CPR 1247–1258*, 358; and *CLR 1251–1260*, 217.
42 See, for example, *CLR 1251–1260*, 217, 225, 288, and 398.
43 Letters patent were unsealed letters issued by the Chancery or Chancery officials traveling with the king. They were all sealed with the Chancery seal.

on a wax tablet rather than on parchment, ultimately included all of the purchase agreements that the clerk made with local merchants. It is not clear from the surviving records whether the king's clerk or the merchant was responsible for actually transporting the supplies to the building site. However, we do know that in order to be paid, the local merchants had to travel to Bordeaux and there present their letters patent to the Gascon financial officers.[44]

After the king's clerk returned from his purchasing expedition, he was required to make a full written report detailing the types, quantities, and costs of the supplies that he had acquired. This information was then recorded in the king's Wardrobe account.[45] The Wardrobe frequently was the royal office responsible for authorizing the expenditure of cash while the king was traveling outside of England. Once the Wardrobe officials had recorded all of the information provided to them by the clerk who had purchased the supplies, they in turn issued written orders to the Gascon financial bureau at Bordeaux called the office of the receiver. These orders authorized the Gascon financial officers to disburse cash to the merchants with whom the king's clerk had done business. Thus, when the local merchant appeared at Bordeaux with his letter patent, the information contained there could be checked by the local fiscal office against the orders issued to him by the king's Wardrobe officials.[46] In Gascony, therefore, as in England, the royal government insisted on bureaucratic redundancy in all matters relating to the purchase and shipment of military supplies. Two documents were required for the foreign merchants to be paid at Bordeaux. Furthermore, a record of the quantity and cost of supplies that had been purchased was kept in two places, namely in the royal Wardrobe and by the receivers at Bordeaux. Because the building of siege engines in Gascony was essentially an *ad hoc* endeavor, however, it seems that supplies were not stockpiled over the long term there and it was, therefore, not necessary to keep detailed records of where supplies were located.

Administrative procedures for the storage and transportation of artillery

Once siege engines had been built, it was necessary not only to provide secure locations for keeping the artillery until it was needed, but the central government also had to be provided with a detailed record of how many pieces of artillery, of what type, and in what condition were in the government's possession. It was also

---

44 An example of this practice is dealt with in *CLR 1251–1260*, 225.
45 *CLR 1251–1260*, 398. The Wardrobe account originally was intended to record the expenses of the king's personal household. Over time, however, this account developed into an all-purpose record for the king while he traveled. However, despite the argument by Prestwich, *War, Politics and Finance*, 120, that the Wardrobe took on a markedly new function during the reign of Edward I, it is clear that the Wardrobe accounts were being used to record military expenses many decades before.
46 *CLR 1251–1260*, 225.

necessary to know their location. As might be expected, siege engines were normally stored at royal castles. Major depots were located at Dover, Windsor, Corfe, and the Tower of London. At these locations, access to the artillery was limited to those individuals whose duties justified their being granted a royal license (*licencia regis*).[47]

Thus, for example, when a specialist was sent to repair siege artillery at a depot such as Corfe, he was given a written document in which he was identified as the king's agent. The written document noted the engines that the specialist was ordered to repair, and also included a list of the supplies that would be required for him to carry out his duties.[48] A second written order was sent directly to the local official in charge of the depot informing him of the artillery engineer's arrival.[49] This order noted what particular engines were to be examined and repaired—information that was obtained from the lists maintained by the central government which detailed not only the number and types of siege engines situated in royal depots, but their condition as well.[50] The documents issued to the local depot commanders also required them to provide the visiting specialists with accommodations and supplies, and occasionally to pay his wages as well.[51] In order to obtain credit for these expenses at the Exchequer, local officials were required to submit detailed written reports to the central government in which they noted the costs

---

47 An order issued to the constable of St Briavels Castle and to the keepers of the Forest of Dean insisted that they "guard the engines and wood in the same place that they are now located and not permit them to be moved by anybody or be taken anywhere without a special license from the king" ("*machinas et maeremium ... custodiri faciant in eodem loco in quo nunc sunt, non permittentes ea per quoscumque alicubi amoveri seu aliquid inde distrahi sine licencia regis speciali*"). See *CR 1259–1261*, 258.

48 See, for example *CR 1251–1253*, 431.

49 One of the royal carpenters most frequently entrusted with this task during the 1240s and 1250s was a master carpenter named Gerard. See, for example, *CR 1247–1251*, 324, "the king is sending his engineer Master Gerard to Alan la Zusch, the justiciar of Chester, to inspect and to set in order the king's works at the royal castles of Gannoc and Dissard just as Gerard had discussed with the king. We order that he be admitted and that he and his requirements be attended to diligently" ("*Rex mittit magistrum Gerardum ingeniatorum suum ad Alanum la Zusch, justiciarum Cestrie, ad ordinandum et videndum opera regis in castris regis de Gannoc et Dissard secundum quod inter regem et ipsum prelocutum fuit. Mandans quod ipsum admittat, et ad negocia illa expendienda una cum ipso diligenter intendat*"). In the previous year, a large quantity of supplies had been shipped to both Dissard and Gannoc to build siege engines there. See *CLR 1245–1251*, 245-6.

50 As we shall see, each commander of a royal storage depot was required to submit a written report detailing the number, type, and condition of engines that were transported to him from other depots.

51 Again regarding Gerard at Gannoc and Dissard, the order issued to Alan la Zusch noted, "and because he is not able to delay there or return to the king without incurring costs, the justiciar is ordered to provide Master Gerard with two marks that the king allocated for his use" ("*et quia ibidem morari et inde ad regem sine sumptibus reverti non poterit, mandatum est eidem justiciario eidem magistro G. duas marcas habere faciat, quas rex ei faciat allocari*"). See *CR 1247–1251*, 324.

that they had incurred. As was true of virtually all such accounting documents, these expenses had to be vetted by proverbial *probes homines legales*. Once an account had been received and accepted by the central government, an order was issued by the Chancery to the Exchequer requiring the barons to credit the local official's account there.

In addition to requiring that even royal officials obtain written authorization to gain access to siege engines, the king's artillery was further protected through the construction of warehouses that were specially designed to hold these weapons. Orders for the construction of these warehouses came from the central government, but the immediate costs were assumed initially by the relevant local officials, e.g. the constables, sheriffs, bailiffs, and forest keepers where the engines were being stored.[52] These officers were required to obtain the necessary supplies and builders to construct these storage facilities. Once again, the costs for these building efforts could be redeemed in the form of credit at the Exchequer once the local officials had gone through the standard accounting process.[53] The central government kept copies of both the original orders requiring the construction of these warehouses, and the subsequent financial accounts issued by the local officials. As a result, it was possible for the king's officers of the central government to maintain a close account of which royal castles and other sites administered by royal officers were equipped with these buildings, and not only how many siege engines each structure could accommodate, but also how many actually were stored at each facility.

As was true with regard to the transportation of supplies used in the construction of artillery, noted earlier, moving siege engines required close cooperation between officers of the central government and local officials which resulted in the production of a wide range of documents. In the simplest case, the process was begun when the central government issued an order to the commander of a royal depot, such as the constable of Dover Castle, requiring him to transport artillery to another facility. This order listed which engines were to be moved; how they were to be moved, e.g. by land transport or by water; and by which date they were to arrive at their destination.[54] When the entire transportation effort was conducted by only a single local official and his staff, the costs that he incurred were redeemable at the Exchequer provided he followed standard auditing procedure. As we have seen, he was obliged to submit a written account detailing his expenses that had been vetted by local witnesses.[55]

---

52 See *CLR 1240–1245*, 258; and *CLR 1260–1267*, 175.

53 Ibid.

54 In one case, the sheriff of Kent was ordered to have the royal engines located in the castle at Rochester carried by water, probably along the Medway River, to Sandwich. From there, the engines were to be taken by ship to Portsmouth where they were to be kept pending the king's crossing of the channel. See *CLR 1226–1240*, 41.

55 See, for example, *Great Roll of the Pipe for the Fourth Year of the Reign of King Henry III*, 14.

When two or more officials at separate localities, e.g. the sheriff of Northampton and the sheriff of Bedford, were involved in the transportation of one or more engines, each of these men received a set of written orders from the central government. These documents recorded the transportation duties that were incumbent on each of these local officers.[56] Each official thereby was informed when he could expect the engines to be delivered to him and to whom they were to be delivered on the next stage of their journey. All of these orders were accompanied by a timetable. At the same time that the officials on the delivery end were receiving their orders, the ultimate recipient of the siege engines also received a document from the central government. These documents listed the particulars of the shipment he would be receiving and an order to inventory the weapons when they arrived. The responsible official then was required to produce a chirograph that detailed his findings.[57] This officer was to keep one copy of the chirograph for his own records and to send a second copy on to the central government. This document not only indicated how many engines had been transported and of what type they were, but also described their condition upon arrival.

This system of redundant documents assured the central government of an accurate account of how many engines, of what type, and in what condition had been moved from place to place. The account submitted by the sending officer or officers could be checked against the chirograph issued by the receiving officer. As noted already with regard to supplies, because these documents were issued every time an engine was moved from one site to another, the central government was able to keep track of the total number of artillery pieces in England, where they were located, and their state of readiness.[58] When this information was added to the data concerning the building of new engines, discussed earlier, officials of the central government had a very clear picture of the artillery available for military campaign, information that was crucial to any military planning efforts. Although far fewer records survive which detail the transportation of siege engines within Gascony, it would appear that the same system applied there as did in England.[59]

The redundant bureaucratic procedures put into place to assure a careful count of the siege engines available for use in military campaigns were crucial to combating fraud, mismanagement, and loss once the artillery was safely stored in warehouses. However, in order to protect the artillery in transit, the royal government routinely required local officials to provide armed guards to accompany the engines. Like all other expenses incurred in the course of transporting the engines,

---

56 See, for example, *CR I*, 617, where the order to the sheriff of Northampton to transport engines from Bedford to his county survives as a *fragmentum* in an order to the sheriff of Bedford to transport these same *mangonelli*.

57 For a representative example of this type of order, see *CLR 1240–1245*, 265.

58 This attention to the movement of engines extended even to the transportation of privately owned artillery. See, for example, *CR I*, 545.

59 See *CR 1242–1247*, 69.

the wages for these armed guards could be claimed by local officials when they submitted their accounts to the central government.[60]

Of no little importance in our evaluation of this system is the fact that all of these local officials operated on very tight schedules. These officers were given specific dates by which artillery had to be moved from point A to point B so that the engines could be deployed in the king's military operations. The seriousness with which military planners of the central government regarded these transportation schedules is indicated by a letter issued to the sheriff of Westminster in 1244.[61] The sheriff was ordered to ask the local abbots and priors to provide wagons and carts for the transportation of the king's engines to Newcastle on Tyne. If they were unwilling to do so, the sheriff was to show them the king's letter and ask again. If, however, the local church officials were still unwilling to provide transportation resources, the sheriff was ordered to find the necessary vehicles anywhere he could in his county and send them to Newcastle no later than the feast of St. Peter in Chains so that the king's plans would not be disturbed "*pro defectu sui*".[62] To demonstrate the serious consequences that the sheriff faced should he fail in his task, the king's order emphasized that these vehicles were to be sent "in so far as the sheriff loved his own body" ("*idem vicecomes sicut corpus suum diligit*").[63]

Conclusion

However innovative and revolutionary Edward I was in many aspects of military affairs, it is clear that his government had at least two generations of sophisticated military administration upon which to draw when going about the business of producing, storing, and transporting the artillery that was so important for the conduct of siege operations. During the long half-century preceding Edward's reign, royal officers routinely produced, transferred, and stored the huge quantities of documents necessary to ensure the continued allocation of men, money, and resources that made it possible to purchase nails, iron fittings, lead, and hides; to cut down and finish trees; to transport tools and workers; to pay carpenters, bargemen, carters, waggoneers, sailors, and guards; and to build storage sheds. In short, for more than five decades before Edward became king, the English government had in place the administrative resources that made the deployment of the royal artillery possible.

60 References to the payment of these guards can be seen, for example, in *CR I*, 450, 605, 641.
61 *CR 1242–1247*, 257–258.
62 Ibid.
63 Ibid.

7

MILITARY PLANNING IN THIRTEENTH-CENTURY ENGLAND

The important questions that medieval military planners had to consider when preparing for an offensive campaign or the defense of fortifications and territory included how many weapons are available for use, what types of weapons are available, where are these weapons stored, and in what condition are they to be found? Without answers to these questions, officials could not make plans about how many troops effectively could be mobilized, where transportation resources for the shipment of arms should be assembled, which fortifications or regions required additional arms, and how many additional arms, including ammunition, had to be produced or purchased. In sum, without accurate and current information about the weapons and ammunition available for use by the government's fighting men, medieval officials could not make military plans. Unfortunately, there is a dearth of studies concerning the development of accurate, timely, and regularly updated information concerning the arms and ammunition available for use by medieval armies.[1]

The burden of the following study is to identify the efforts of the English royal government during the thirteenth century to obtain, collate, update, and use information concerning the location, number, type, and condition of the arms and ammunition at its disposal. The sources used in this study consist largely of the administrative documents produced by the royal government's bureaux of the

---

1 Despite some very good work on military administration, this area of military history generally has not benefited from significant scholarly attention. Indeed, in some quarters there appears to be an actual bias against administrative studies as un-military. For example, Matthew Bennett, "The Development of Battle Tactics in the Hundred Years War", in *Arms, Armies and Fortifications in the Hundred Years War*, ed. Anne Curry and Michael Hughes (Woodbridge, 1994), 1–20, here 1, argues, "It is a common aphorism that the history of war is too important to be left to military historians. They tend to be obsessed with battle with no further interest or wider understanding of the warring societies. Hence the growth of the 'War and Society' school of history, in which the study of warfare is 'legitimized' by reference to its social context. Unfortunately, and all too frequently, war often drops out of what become simply administrative studies". This notice of Bennett's comment is not to be understood as a critique of his study on tactics. Nevertheless, Bennett's remarks in this context are indicative of a school of thought that sees military history in an either/or paradigm, with administration falling outside the scope of "real" military history.

Chancery and Exchequer, responsible for the government's correspondence, tax collection, audits, and expenditures, and by individual royal officers in command of fortresses, magazines, arms factories, and other production sites. Many of the surviving documents for the reigns of John (1199–1216) and Henry III (1216–1272) have been published in full text or as calendars.[2] Most of the documents from the reign of Edward I (1272–1307) have not been published.[3] By contrast with the administrative records produced by the royal government, the very rich corpus of narrative sources surviving from thirteenth-century England, most of which were written by clerics, shed a great deal of light on politics and some aspects of warfare, but have very little information about administration, particularly military administration.

---

2   The Chancery was the royal writing office, and the Exchequer was the office in charge of auditing the accounts of royal officials and receiving royal income, including taxes and fines, collected by royal officials working at the local level. The Exchequer also served as center for the disbursement of funds to royal officials. Over the course of the later thirteenth century, this last function of the Exchequer gradually was taken over by the officials of the royal Wardrobe. The basic collections of published Chancery documents from the reigns of John and Henry III are *Rotuli Litterarum Patentium in Turri Londinensi Asservati*, ed. Thomas D. Hardy (London, 1835), hereafter *RLP*; and *Rotuli Litterarum Clausarum in Turri Londonensi Asservati 1204–1227*, Thomas D. Hardy, 2 vols (London, 1833–1834), hereafter *CR I* and *CR II*. These are supplemented by the Pipe Rolls which were assembled by the Exchequer on the basis of semi-annual audits of royal officials working in the counties. The Pipe Rolls for the reign of John have all been edited separately by the Pipe Rolls Society. Several of the Pipe Rolls from Henry III's reign have been edited by the Pipe Roll Society and will be cited individually. The majority of the Pipe Rolls for the reign of Henry III have not been edited. These will be cited by their catalogue numbers in the National Archives at Kew (formerly the Public Record Office). The major series of administrative documents from the Chancery and Exchequer are supplemented during John's reign by the *misae* accounts and *praestita* rolls which are recorded in *Rotuli de Liberate ac de Misis et Praestitis regnante Johanne*, ed. Thomas D. Hardy (London, 1844), hereafter *Rotuli*. For the Norman rolls, see *Rotuli Normannie in Turri asservati Johanne et Henrico Quinto Anglie Regibus*, ed. Thomas D. Hardy (London, 1835), hereafter *Rot. Norm.* Editions of the *Close Roll* texts for the reign of Henry III appear in *Close Rolls 1227–1272* (London, 1902–1938), hereafter *CR* with the appriopriate year ranges. Calendars of the Patent Rolls for the reign of Henry appear in *Calendar of Patent Rolls 1216–1272* (London, 1901–1903), hereafter *CPR* with the appropriate year ranges.

3   The Pipe Rolls for the reign Edward I have not been edited. These will be cited by their catalogue numbers in the National Archives. Calendars of the Close Rolls for the reign of Edward I appear in *Calendar of Close Rolls 1272–1307* (London, 1900–1908), hereafter *CCR* with appropriate year ranges. Calendars of the Patent Rolls for the Edward I appear in *Calendar of Patent Rolls 1272–1307* (London, 1893–1901), hereafter *CPR* with appropriate year ranges. The liberate rolls for the reign of Edward I have not been published and are cited in this chapter according to their catalogue numbers at the National Archives. In addition to these large enrolled collections, there are thousands of surviving letters, writs, memoranda, receipts, and other documents relating to the military administration of Edward I's reign. The overwhelming majority of these texts are unedited and unpublished. They are cited in this chapter according to their catalogue numbers at the National Archives.

Part 1: The entry of arms into royal possession

The English royal government employed a wide variety of administrative processes over the course of the thirteenth century to keep track of its stocks of arms
and ammunition. This section considers the bureaucratic procedures put in place
by the royal government to ensure that newly acquired arms were inventoried
properly by royal officers at the local level and that this information was transmitted to the central government for the purpose of collation and assessment. The
royal government acquired new stocks of arms and ammunition through production in the king's own workshops and through purchase on the private market.
Although there are many similarities in the administrative procedures used by
royal clerks and officers to keep track of these two types of acquisitions, there are
also important differences so that it is necessary to consider each set of procedures
separately.

Royal arms production

Throughout the thirteenth century, the royal government produced enormous
quantities of crossbow quarrels, numbering in the millions; tens of thousands of
crossbows; and many hundreds of artillery pieces of a wide variety of types.[4]
The royal government concentrated production of crossbows and quarrels in fortresses, including the Tower of London, Windsor Castle, Corfe Castle, and at St.
Briavels Castle located in the Forest of Dean.[5] The royal officials (*constabularii*)
in command of these fortresses were responsible for keeping detailed records
about every stage of the production process, from the purchasing of supplies to
the storage of arms in their magazines in specially prepared containers. The quarrel production facility located near St. Briavels Castle in the Forest of Dean offers
a particularly good example of how royal officials implemented these administrative procedures.

---

4   Concerning royal efforts to produce these weapons, see David S. Bachrach, "The Royal Cross-
     bow Makers of England, 1204–1272", *Nottingham Medieval Studies* 47 (2003), 168–197); idem,
     "Origins of the Crossbow Industry in England", *Journal of Medieval Military History* 2 (2004),
     73–88; idem, "Crossbows for the King: The Crossbow during the Reigns of John and Henry III of
     England", *Technology and Culture* 45 (2004), 102–119; and idem, "The Military Administration
     of England: The Royal Artillery (1216–1272)", *Journal of Military History* (2004), 1083–1104,
     all of which are also in this volume. The surviving administrative sources indicate that the royal
     government did not produce other types of arms and ammunition in its own workshops but rather
     purchased them on the private market. Following the conquest of Wales in 1282, King Edward I's
     government transferred much of its crossbow production to Welsh castles, particularly Caer-
     narvon. Several of these production facilities will be discussed here.
5   During John's reign, crossbows were produced in five centers, including Nottingham, Salisbury,
     Northampton, Marlborough, and Gloucester. By 1222, however, production had been concen-
     trated at the Tower of London and Corfe Castle. See "Royal Crossbow Makers", 175–181.

From 1230 to 1278, a smith named John Malemort oversaw the largest work-shop producing quarrels for the king in the Forest of Dean.[6] John was, himself, under the command of the series of men who served as constable of St. Briavels Castle. In some cases, the constable of St. Briavels Castle also held the office of sheriff of Gloucestershire. Each of these constables, as part of the duties of his office, was required to submit detailed written reports (*compoti*) to the office of the Exchequer, noting the income he had collected for the central government and his expenses on behalf of the king. In the second portion of these reports, the con-stables listed the supplies they had provided to John Malemort, how much these supplies had cost, and how many quarrels John had produced. These reports were then collated with similar written reports submitted by other royal officials work-ing at the county level and issued in the Exchequer's annual Pipe Roll. The 1265 Pipe Roll account for Gloucestershire, for example, records that John Malemort received a salary of 30 marks for producing 30,000 quarrels.[7]

The clerks at the Exchequer noted in the Pipe Roll that this figure of 30,000 quarrels matched what John Malemort had produced in 1261, and far exceeded the 23,000 quarrels put out by John's workshop in 1262.[8] The clerks included these figures for 1261 and 1262 in the Pipe Roll for 1265 in order to put the last named year into historical context. Up to this time John Malemort had produced at most 30,000 quarrels in the course of a single year using his normal staff. The fewest numbers of quarrels produced by John Malemort's workshop was 23,000.[9] From an administrative standpoint, this document is exceptionally important because it makes clear not only that the Exchequer collected information about the number of quarrels produced by John Malemort's workshop on a yearly basis, but that this information was available for use and that the information was consulted by the clerks at the Exchequer.

The officers in charge of production facilities for crossbows followed similar administrative procedures to ensure that the central government was aware of how many weapons they had constructed. On 1 June 1290, for example, the Chancery issued an order to the Exchequer to credit the account of Robert Delura, the royal

---

6   For a brief but useful introduction to the Forest of Dean as a royal arsenal and the work done by John Malemort, see Alf Webb, "John Malemort—King's Quarreler: The King's Great Arsenal, St. Briavels and the Royal Forest of Dean", *Society of Archer Antiquaries* 31 (1988), 40–46. The sec-ond major royal production center for quarrels was the Tower of London. At least eleven men can be identified working as smiths and fletchers producing quarrels there in the period 1220–1274.

7   National Archives E372/109 10r.

8   Ibid.

9   The normal production quota for John Malemort's workshop was 25,000 quarrels. On 15 June 1255, the Chancery issued an order to James Fresel, the constable of St. Briavels Castle, requiring that he provide sufficient supplies to John Malemort to produce 25,000 quarrels. *CR 1254–1256*, 96–97. The Chancery order emphasizes that the constable is to pay John Malemort 25 marks a year, every year, so long as the latter continues to produce 25,000 quarrels. Ibid., "*singulis annis sequentibus faciat habere eidem Johanni xxv. marcas, quamdiu idem Jacobus fuerit constabu-larius regis loci predicti*".

controller at Caernarvon Castle in Wales, for the money he had spent to provide the supplies necessary for William the crossbow maker (*atilliator*) to build 300 crossbows in the workshop located in this castle.[10] This text, which survives in the 1290 liberate roll produced by the Chancery, is itself the penultimate step in a chain of documents that extends back to February 1287. The writ of liberate, noted here, contains two pieces of information that make it possible to establish the "parchment trail" that led to William's production of 300 crossbows at Caernarvon. First, the writ requires that the Exchequer credit Robert Delura for the money listed *in compoto suo*, that is in his record of accounts submitted to the Chancery. Second, the writ notes that Robert spent in excess of £17 on 300 crossbow bowstaves (*baculi pro balistis*) at the order of John de Bonvillars, the lieutenant of Otto de Grandson, the justiciar of North Wales.[11]

Based on the information contained in the writ of liberate, which is itself a summary of the original document sent to the Exchequer, it is clear that the first document, leading to the production of 300 crossbows by William, was an order issued by John de Bonvillars to Robert Delura requiring the latter to purchase 300 bowstaves for crossbows. The second document was Robert Delura's account book (*compotus*) in which he listed all of the expenses he incurred as the controller of Caernarvon Castle, including the costs for the 300 bowstaves. Given standard administrative practice, it is likely that the *compotus* entry for the bowstaves included a copy of the order by John de Bonvillars.[12] Robert then submitted his *compotus* to the Chancery where it was examined and accepted as a valid account of his expenses.[13] The next step was for the clerks at the Chancery to write a writ of liberate ordering the clerks at the Exchequer to credit Robert's account for the money he had spent purchasing the 300 bowstaves and paying the wages of William the *atilliator* who had turned these bowstaves into crossbows. Finally, the clerks at the Exchequer had to record the information included in this writ in their own records. It is a copy of this writ that is included in the liberate roll

---

10   National Archives C62/66 4r.

11   Concerning the administrative system established by King Edward in Wales after the conquest and particularly after the revolt of 1287, see Michael Prestwich, *Edward I*, 2nd edn (New Haven, CT, 1997), 206–207. This order clearly was issued before John de Bonvillars was killed at Dryslwyn Castle later that year.

12   It was standard practice for officials to record a copy of the order requiring them to make purchases on behalf of the king in their own account books so that they would have proof at a later date that they had authorization to undertake these expenses and should, therefore, be credited for them. In 1304, for example, King Edward I issued orders to the sheriffs of London instructing them to purchase all of the crossbows, bows, arrows, and quarrels that were available in the city and send them to the royal army encamped at Stirling. The sheriffs included a copy of this royal order in their report (*compotus*) in which they listed the arms that they had purchased and how much these arms had cost. See National Archives E101/12/5.

13   As will be seen, officials at the Chancery on occasion asked the officials at the Exchequer to conduct an audit of the account books (*compoti*) submitted by royal officials.

for 1290 and survives today. At this point the Exchequer clerks had a permanent record that Caernarvon Castle now housed an additional 300 crossbows.

In contrast to both quarrels and crossbows, the royal government built artillery, including both anti-personnel weapons and large wall-breaking engines, in a large number of royal castles and royal forests rather than in specialized workshops.[14] In addition, rather than being informed about how many engines had been built in a given year, as was the case with respect to crossbow and quarrel production, the central government, through the bureau of the Chancery, required castle constables, the keepers of royal forest lands, sheriffs, and other royal officials at the local level to construct a specified number of engines under the direction of royal engineers. For example, on 20 January 1256, the Chancery issued orders to the sheriff of Cumberland to have two large engines called *blidae* built at Carlisle under the supervision of the royal engineer named Gerard.[15] The Chancery also issued orders to other royal officers at the local level to provide supplies for the construction of specified numbers of engines. In 1299, for example, the Chancery issued a writ of liberate to the Exchequer requiring that the clerks there credit the account of Walter Langton, who held the three offices of royal treasurer, keeper of the royal wardrobe, and bishop of Coventry and Lichfield, for the money he spent at the king's command (*per preceptum nostrum*) on supplies for building four engines (*ingenia*) at Carlisle.[16]

Of course, that an engine was intended to be built did not mean that it was built. The king's administrative officials were well aware that the acquisition of large quantities of supplies by royal officers, including engineers, carpenters, and smiths, as well as castle constables, keepers of royal forests, and sheriffs, could lead to fraud, graft, and other financial malfeasance. Consequently, they put into place rigorous auditing processes to ensure that money authorized to be spent on engines was spent on engines. In November 1255, for example, the Chancery issued orders to the sheriff of Northumberland to provide the royal engineer Gerard with the supplies he needed to complete several *blidae* being constructed at Carlisle.[17] The Chancery sent a second order to the mayor and bailiffs of Carlisle to chose three or four *probos et legales homines*, that is honest men in good legal standing, to witness (*videre*) and swear (*testificare*) that the engines actually were being built.[18] Finally, the Chancery issued a third order, this one to Gerard, requiring that he finish the construction of the engines under the supervision (*per visum*) of these men.[19]

---

14 On this point, see Bachrach, "Military Administration of England", passim.
15 National Archives C62/32 15r.
16 National Archives C62/75 8r.
17 *CR 1254–1256*, 235. *Blidae* are large counterweight stone-throwing engines. See the discussion by David S. Bachrach, "English Artillery 1189–1307: The Implications of Terminology", *The English Historical Review* 121.494 (2006), 1408–1430 and in this volume.
18 *CR 1254–1256*, 235.
19 Ibid.

Once the artillery pieces were finished, the royal officers who had spent money on supplies and the wages of engineers, smiths, and carpenters submitted their vetted accounts (*compoti*). In some instances, as was the case with the expenses incurred by Bishop Walter Langton, noted earlier, the *compotus* was submitted to the Chancery. The Chancery officials then reviewed the account, and, if they found it acceptable, they issued a writ of liberate to the Exchequer instructing that the officials there disburse funds to repay expenses undertaken at the order of the king. This writ of liberate listed the amount of money that had been spent, the types of supplies that had been purchased, the number and type of engines that had been constructed, and the place where they had been built.[20] As a consequence, the Exchequer officially was informed about the type and number of the artillery pieces that had been added to the royal inventory. The second way in which the Exchequer officially was informed about the types and number of engines built by royal officials was during the semi-annual audits of the accounts of these officials at the Exchequer. The Pipe Roll for 1276–1277, for example, records that Giles Auden, the constable of the Tower of London, claimed the costs he incurred for purchasing four oak beams, cables, ropes, and iron fittings necessary to build a new engine (*ingenium novum*) at the Tower.[21] Two years later, the Pipe Roll for 1278–1279 recorded that Giles' *compotus* listed the expenses that the constable incurred in shipping ten oaks from the royal forest at Odiham to build three *ingenia* at the Tower.[22] When officials submitted their *compoti* directly to the Exchequer, all of the information concerning the number and types of artillery built naturally was available to the Exchequer officials.

The royal government produced crossbows, quarrels, and a variety of types of artillery in a large number of workshops in England, Wales, and Scotland. Royal officials at both the local level and in the central government bureaux of the Chancery and Exchequer ensured that detailed information about these arms were collected, collated, and prepared for use by the king's officers who were responsible for planning military operations. Indeed, as we saw already, clerks at the Exchequer, which was the ultimate repository for this information about royal arms production, were able to work back through their records to identify past production levels for the king's workshops.

Royal arms purchases

Virtually all purchases of arms by royal officers were initiated by letters sent to them by Chancery officials requiring the expenditure of funds.[23] In May 1267, for example, at the tail end of the Montfortian rebellion (1264–1267), the Chancery

---

20 In the case of Walter Langton, what we are seeing is the sending of money from one royal bureau, the Exchequer, to another royal bureau, that is the Wardrobe.

21 National Archives E372/121 22v.

22 National Archives E372/123 21r.

23 Many hundreds of these letters survive from the reigns of Henry III and Edward I, usually as *fragmenta*, that is copies of the original documents imbedded within other texts.

issued orders to the sheriff of Hampshire to purchase ten new crossbows and 2,000 quarrels to be used specifically for the defense of Winchester Castle.[24] Similarly, in May 1304, Exchequer officials sent orders to the sheriffs of London requiring that they purchase all of the crossbows, quarrels, and arrows available in their bailiwick and send them to Stirling Castle where King Edward was engaged in a siege.[25]

As noted earlier, however, anyone with experience dealing with bureaucracy and bureaucrats knows that the simple sending of an order to have something done, in this case purchasing arms, does not mean that it will be done. This is particularly true when there is scope for corruption and graft. The men who designed the royal military administrative system were fully aware that even the dedicated royal officers commanding the king's fortresses and overseeing the localities on behalf of the central government might fail to carry out their duties because of simple negligence or for more mercenary reasons. As a result, rather than relying on the proper behavior of the royal officers, who were commissioned to purchase arms on behalf of the government, the king's administrators required that constables, sheriffs, and other officials submit written expense reports either to the Chancery or to the Exchequer noting the type, quantity, and condition of the arms that they purchased. Moreover, these accounts had to be vetted by honest local men in good legal standing (*probi homines legales*).[26] In August 1224, for example, the Chancery issued orders to the bailiffs of Northampton to have the smiths in their town work day and night (*tam de die quam de nocte*) to produce 4,000 quarrels and to have them sent with all possible speed to the royal army then besieging Bedford Castle.[27] The Chancery order concludes with the formula "*et custum quod ad hoc posueritis per visum et computabitur etc*".[28] This means, the money that you spend on this, which has been vetted (*per visum*), will be credited (*computabitur*) [to your account at the Exchequer (*scaccarum*)].

Once the local officials spent the money to purchase arms, and then had their accounts of these expenses vetted by the *probi homines legales*, the constables, sheriffs, bailiffs, and other local officers submitted these accounts to the authorities working in the bureaux of the central government. In many cases, these vetted accounts (*compoti*) were submitted by sheriffs, bailiffs, and constables, directly to the Exchequer. The Pipe Roll for 1282, for example, records that the *compotus* of Peter de la Mare, the constable of Bristol Castle, included claims for the expenses he had incurred purchasing 50,000 quarrels, ninety-two crossbows,

24 *CLR 1260–1267*, 273.
25 National Archives E101/12/5 part 1. This order to the sheriffs of London survives as a *fragmentum* in their *compotus*, which was submitted to the Exchequer.
26 For a detailed discussion of this vetting process, see Bachrach, "Military Administration of England", *passim*.
27 *CR I*, 613.
28 Ibid.

and forty baldrics.[29] Walter Cambio, the sheriff of Northumberland, similarly was credited for the twelve crossbows he purchased for Bamburgh Castle in 1283.[30] The same system was in place six decades earlier, from the very beginning of Henry III's reign. The Pipe Roll for 1221, for example, records that Adam, the sheriff of Lancashire, was credited for the 10,000 quarrels he had purchased at the order of King John, Henry III's father, for the defense of the royal castles in both Lancashire and West Derbyshire.[31] Much as was the case in the production of arms by royal officials, when *compoti* were submitted directly to the Exchequer, the officials in this bureau were made aware of both the types and quantities of arms purchased by the king's officers.

Frequently, however, the accounts (*compoti*) of royal officers were submitted first to the Chancery, since it was almost always a Chancery letter that initiated the purchase of the arms. The Chancery officials then took one of two steps. The most common procedure was to issue a writ of liberate to the Exchequer authorizing the reimbursement or crediting of the royal officer who had purchased the arms. In January 1223, for example, the Chancery issued a writ of liberate to the Exchequer requiring that John de Ferentin, the constable of Bristol Castle, be credited for the 100 s. he spent on forty wooden crossbows at the order of the king (*per preceptum nostrum*).[32] The bureaucratic language was much the same fifty years later when the Chancery issued a writ of liberate in June 1274 to the Exchequer requiring that John de Havering be credited for the 70 s. he spent on twelve crossbows, twelve baldrics, and 1,000 quarrels purchased for the defense of Dover Castle.[33] Less frequently, the Chancery issued orders to the Exchequer to conduct an audit of an account submitted by a royal official. An audit of this type was ordered in May 1276 for the account of Robert de Neville who recently had stepped down as constable of York Castle.[34] According to the Chancery letter, this audit was to focus on all of the expenses Robert claimed in providing food, arms, and other supplies necessary for the defense of the castle.

As is clear from the previous discussion, in the relatively few instances when the Exchequer was called upon to audit the vetted expense reports (*compoti*) submitted by royal officials to the Chancery, the information in these *compoti* concerning the types and quantities of arms that had been purchased were made available to the Exchequer officials. Similarly, when the Chancery issued writs of liberate to the Exchequer on behalf of royal officials who had purchased arms at the king's orders, these writs also provided detailed information about the types and quantities of arms that were purchased. Indeed, in this context, it is worth

---

29 National Archives E372/126 6r.
30 National Archives E372/128 5v.
31 *The Great Roll of the Pipe for the Fifth Year of the Reign of King Henry III Michaelmas 1221* (London, 1990), 63.
32 *CR I*, 530.
33 National Archives C62/50 5r. John de Havering was the constable of Dover Castle at this time.
34 National Archives C54/93 12r., *De compoto Roberti de Neville audiendo*.

emphasizing that inclusion in writs of liberate of detailed information about the types, quantity, and condition of arms purchased by royal officers on behalf of the government illustrates the concern of the king's administrators that the officials at the Exchequer have all of the pertinent information regarding the numbers and types of weapons and ammunition in the king's possession. Indeed, if it were not deemed important for officials at the Exchequer to have this information, there certainly was no need to take up valuable parchment space sending out detailed writs of liberate when a single line of text would have been sufficient to obtain reimbursement or credit for the constables, sheriffs, and other officers who had purchased arms for the government.

Part 2: Arms in transit

The purchase and production by the royal government over the course of the thirteenth century of very large quantities of military supplies was necessary to provide arms and ammunition to soldiers serving in the field and in garrisons. As a result, royal officials at the local level, especially those employed at major magazines and depots such as the Tower of London, St. Briavels Castle, Caernarvon Castle, Newcastle on Tyne, and Berwick on Tweed, frequently were engaged in the transport of crossbows, bows, lances, shields, helmets, armor, arrows, crossbow bolts, and artillery throughout England, Wales, and Scotland, and overseas to Gascony and Flanders. As was true of the acquisition of arms, each step in the process of moving weapons and ammunition in the English administrative system necessitated the production of a wide spectrum of documents at both the local level and by the central bureaux of the Chancery and Exchequer. The ultimate purpose of all of these administrative documents was to ensure that the royal officials in charge of developing the king's military plans had accurate and up-to-date information about the types, quantity, and condition of the arms and ammunition available to the royal government in the British Isles and royal possessions on the continent.

The simplest and most straightforward transfer of arms was the movement of weapons and ammunition from storage in one magazine or depot to another. These transfers of arms were initiated by a letter from the Chancery to the constable in command of a royal castle, or other magazine, requiring him to send a specific number of a specific type or types of weapons and ammunition to a specified destination. In April 1216, for example, the Chancery issued orders to Philip Mark, the sheriff of Nottingham, requiring him to send six composite crossbows and two wooden crossbows equipped with winches (*ad turnum*) to Nicholas de Haya, constable of Lincoln, for the defense of the castle there.[35] The Chancery then issued a second letter to the intended recipient of the arms informing him what types of weapons and ammunition he should expect to receive. Thus, in September 1244,

---

35   *CR I*, 196.

the Chancery issued a letter to the sheriff of Kent ordering him to expect delivery of three pieces of siege equipment, namely a large stone-throwing engine called a *blida*, a smaller stone-throwing engine called a *trubechetum*, and a ram (*multo*).[36]

This first set of orders, to the constable responsible for sending the arms and to the officer responsible for receiving them, set the weapons and ammunition in motion. At this juncture it is worth emphasizing that the transfer of arms from place to place cost money, with expenses for the wages of carters, wagonneers, bargemen, and even sailors; the hire of carts, wagons, barges, and ships; and the feeding of horses and oxen. In order to recoup these expenses, the official who withdrew arms from the magazine or depot under his command and transported them to another storage facility was required to submit an itemized expense report (*compotus*), usually to the Chancery. These *compoti* recorded not only the costs involved in matters such as purchasing barrels and horse feed, but also the type and number of arms that were shipped. In 1277, for example, Giles de Adenarde, the constable of the Tower of London, submitted a report to the Chancery in which he recorded the money he spent to ship 10,000 quarrels, forty crossbows, and forty baldrics from the Tower to Bristol, a round trip of ten days.[37] These expenses included obtaining a four-horse cart along with four horses, producing and repairing buckets for storing quarrels, and paying a mounted guard to accompany the shipment of arms to Bristol and to return with the wagon and driver after the arms had been delivered.[38] Once this *compotus*, properly vetted by the proverbial honest men of legal standing, was submitted and accepted at the Chancery, clerks from this bureau issued orders to the Exchequer requiring that the royal officer, who had arranged and paid for the transportation of arms, receive compensation, usually by having his account credited at the Exchequer. Thus, the Pipe Roll issued by the Exchequer covering the period 1278–1279 includes the *compotus* of Giles de Adenarde, which lists his expenses on arms and ammunition.[39]

However, an additional document was required before the Chancery issued a writ of liberate to the Exchequer. In this document, the Chancery clerks listed the arms that had been transported, the place to which they had been transported, and the amount of money that was to be credited to the account of the officer who had overseen their transportation. The royal officer who received the arms was required to submit to the Chancery a detailed report of the type, quantity, and condition of the weapons and ammunition that were delivered to him. On 24 May 1304, for example, Walter Bedewind, a royal clerk working at Stirling Castle, affixed his seal to a memorandum which stated that he had received from Richard de Bremesgrave, the chief logistics officer at Berwick on Tweed, a shipment of

---

36 *CLR 1240–1245*, 265.
37 National Archives C47/2/2 #12. The official in charge of shipping the arms was Robert of Sandwich.
38 National Archives C47/2/2 #12.
39 National Archives E372/123 21r.

lead used for counterweights (*pondera*) on artillery (*ingenia*), twenty crossbows (*balistae*) of the "one-foot" type, four crossbows of the "two-foot" type, twenty-four baldrics, 6,000 quarrels designed for crossbows of the "two-foot" type, and 17,000 quarrels designed for crossbows of the "one-foot" type. The quarrels were packed in nine chests (*coffrae*).[40] The transportation of these crossbows and quarrels from Berwick to Stirling was overseen by Richard de Bremesgrave's subordinate (*garcio*) named Roger de Lande. Walter de Bedewind kept one copy of this memorandum for himself and gave a second copy to Roger de Lande. This second copy then made its way to Richard de Bremesgrave and ultimately was submitted by him to the Chancery. It was only when the memorandum, with Walter Bedewind's seal affixed to it, was submitted to the Chancery that Richard de Bremesgrave's *compotus*, in which the latter listed all of his expenses, including those incurred transporting arms to Stirling, could be accepted and a writ of liberate drafted to be sent to the Exchequer to credit Richard de Bremesgrave's account in that bureau.

In the final analysis, the straightforward transportation of arms from storage in one magazine or depot to another required the production of not fewer than five discrete documents, a least one of which had to be written in duplicate. First, the Chancery issued letters to the two constables involved in the transaction, requiring the first to transport the arms, and the second to receive the arms. In the second stage, the constable who had transported the arms submitted to the Chancery a list of his expenses, which usually was vetted by local witnesses. The constable who had received the arms drew up in duplicate a detailed list of the weapons and ammunition that had been delivered. He kept one copy for himself. The second copy either was submitted directly to the Chancery or, as was the case with Walter de Bedewind, noted previously, the copy was returned to the constable who had sent the arms, to be submitted by him to the Chancery. The final document was a writ of liberate issued by the Chancery to the clerks at the Exchequer to credit the account of the constable who had paid for the arms to be sent. At the end of the process, the full and up-to-date details of the type, quantity, and condition of the weapons, ammunition, and other supplies that had been removed from one magazine and transported to another were on record both at the Chancery and at the Exchequer, and were available for use by the king's military planners.

Frequently, the transfer of arms was more complicated than the straightforward shipment of weapons and ammunition from one magazine to another. It was often necessary for royal officers to take temporary possession of a shipment of arms and subsequently to send them on to other royal officials. As the number of royal officers and the number of transfer points increased, so too did the quantity of documents that were necessary to provide the king's military planners with up-to-date and accurate information. During Edward I's reign, one of the

---

40 National Archives C47/22/9 #70. Concerning the types of crossbows under discussion here, see David S. Bachrach, "Crossbows for the King", (Part 1), passim.

most frequently used routes for the transfer of arms began at St. Briavels castle located in the Forest of Dean in the southern march lands between England and Wales. Crossbow quarrels, as well as other arms produced here, were shipped to Bristol Castle, which lay south across the Severn River. From here, weapons and ammunition were taken by sea to Caernarvon Castle on the west coast of Wales. A large quantity of arms were stored at Caernarvon Castle to serve as a strategic reserve for all of the royal forces in Wales. However, significant quantities of arms also were transferred from Caernarvon to other royal fortresses, including Harlech, Conway, Criccieth, and Beaumaris. At every step of the process, from the initial decision to move arms from St. Briavels Castle to the final storage of these arms at Harlech and other strongholds in Wales, royal officials in the central bureaux of the Chancery and Exchequer as well as royal officers commanding the king's magazines were required to produce a wide spectrum of documents whose purpose was first to ensure that the arms were delivered where they were needed and second to ensure that information about the location, quantity, types, and condition of the arms were available to the king's military planners. The following description of one set of arms transfers serves to make clear what this administrative process entailed.

The Pipe Roll account for 1295–1296 records that John Boteturte, the constable of St. Briavels Castle, spent in excess of £120 to purchase 50,000 quarrels designed for crossbows of the "two-foot" type and 100,000 quarrels for crossbows of the "one-foot" type. The constable spent an additional £5 to construct 300 chests (*coffrae*), in which to store the quarrels, and then to ship the 150,000 quarrels south across the Severn to be delivered to Nicholas Fermbaud, the constable of Bristol Castle and the commander of the port located there.[41] This report included in the Pipe Roll for 1295–1296 was the final link in a chain of documents that began with an order issued by the Chancery to John Boteturte to purchase 150,000 quarrels and to transport them safely to Bristol. John Boteturte subsequently submitted to the Chancery an account (*compotus*) of his expenses. The Chancery then compared this *compotus* with a memorandum, affixed with the seal of Nicholas Fermbaud, confirming the delivery of the quarrels to Bristol, and issued a writ of liberate to the Exchequer to credit John Boteturte for his expenses in purchasing and delivering the quarrels.

Ordinarily, given the relatively fragmentary state—as contrasted with modern archives—of the surviving corpus of royal documents from thirteenth-century England, the bureaucratic texts just listed would have to be inferred from normal administrative practice. In this case, however, modern scholars are fortunate to have available a writ of liberate, enrolled in the liberate roll for 1296–1297, but to be dated to the previous year, issued by the Chancery to the Exchequer on behalf of John Boteturte.[42] The enrolled writ requires that the officials at the Exchequer

---

41   National Archives E372/141 12v.
42   National Archives C62/73 5r.

allocate (*allocare*) to John Boteturte money for the expenses he had incurred over the previous three years in fulfilling the government's need for arms. These included purchasing and transporting 140,000 quarrels to Nicholas Fermbaud at Bristol in 1293, purchasing 6,000 quarrels and transporting them to Richard de Bosco, the constable of Corfe Castle in 1294, and purchasing and transporting 150,000 quarrels to Nicholas Fermbaud in 1295.[43] The clerks at the Chancery emphasize in the writ of liberate that the decision to confirm John Boteturte's expenses and to authorize the Exchequer to reimburse him was based on letters patent (*litterae patentes*) issued by Richard de Bosco and Nicholas Fermbaud confirming their receipt of the quarrels in 1293, 1294, and 1295.[44]

The two surviving administrative documents noted here, the text in the Pipe Roll and the enrolled writ of liberate, between them provide concrete evidence for the entire chain of texts, postulated in the previous passage, regarding the transfer of arms from one magazine to another. However, the quarrels shipped from St. Briavels Castle to Bristol did not remain in Bristol, but rather were transshipped from there to Wales, which required the production of a further matrix of documents. A writ of liberate enrolled in the liberate roll for 1296–1297, discussed earlier, authorized the Exchequer to credit the account of Nicholas Fermbaud for the roughly £7 he spent to transfer 50,000 quarrels, received from the constable of St. Briavels Castle, to Hugh de Leominster, the chamberlain at Caernarvon Castle in 1296.[45] These expenses included the costs of shipping (*fretum*) the arms and wages paid to the master of the ship, as well as wages paid to a valet (*valetus*) who served as a guard on this ship for sixty-six days.[46]

This writ of liberate issued by the Chancery to the Exchequer on behalf of Nicholas Fermbaud, as noted, marks the penultimate step in the chain of documents required to provide accurate and up-to-date information to the king's planners about the location, condition, type, and quantity of arms available for use by royal military forces. First, the Chancery sent an order to Nicholas requiring him to transport the quarrels, delivered to him by John Boteturte, to Hugh de Leominster at Caernarvon Castle. This order from the Chancery does not survive. However, an exactly analogous order issued by the Chancery to Nicholas Fermbaud in 1298 does survive as a *fragmentum*, that is as a copy of a text imbedded within another document. This latter document is in the *compotus* submitted by Nicholas Fermbaud regarding his expenses which is entitled "the *compotus* of Nicholas Fermbaud constable of Bristol regarding his expenses and the actions he undertook at the order of the king from the feast of St. Michael in the 25th year of the reign of King Edward to the feast of St. Michael in the 26th year of the reign of

---

43 Ibid.
44 Ibid.
45 National Archives C62/73 4r.
46 Ibid.

King Edward".[47] In this *compotus*, Nicholas had his clerk transcribe the Chancery order to him requiring that he, as the constable of Bristol, transport 100,000 quarrels and nineteen barrels of honey to the royal castle of Caernarvon and have these supplies delivered to Hugh de Leominster, the royal chamberlain there. The Chancery letter requires that the delivery of these supplies be confirmed by a document, called an indenture (*indentura*), drawn up between the man Nicholas chose to deliver the supplies and Hugh de Leominster.[48] Although the surviving *fragmentum* does not mention this, it is almost certainly the case that two copies of this *indentura* were to be drawn up, one for Hugh de Leominster and one for Nicholas Fermbaud. Finally, the Chancery letter assures Nicholas Fermbaud that his expenses will be credited to him in his account at the Exchequer. The Latin text, which deserves to be quoted in full, is as follows: "*Et custum quod ad hoc posuistis cum illud solvimus vobis in compoto vestro ad scaccarum nostrum allocari faciemus*".[49]

As this discussion of the second stage of the transportation of arms, which originated at St. Briavels Castle and then were shipped from Bristol to Wales, makes clear, each additional step required the production of additional administrative documents. Indeed, the ultimate arrival of the quarrels in Wales is confirmed by yet another administrative document. The Pipe Roll for 1300–1301 records that in 1296, the twenty-fourth year of King Edward's reign, Hugh de Leominster submitted his *compotus* to the Exchequer in which he included the expenses he had incurred in transporting 40,000 quarrels that he had received from Bristol to the royal castles of Criccieth, Harlech, Conway, and Beaumarais.[50] As noted, the inclusion of Hugh Leominster's *compotus* in the Pipe Roll is the last step in an entire series of administrative acts, each marked by the production of a discrete document. The Pipe Roll account is significant not only because it makes clear that a full range of documents was produced at the third and final stage of shipment of arms from St. Briavels Castle to the king's garrisons in Wales, but also because it demonstrates, again, that documents, archived at the Exchequer, dealing with the location, types, quantities, and condition of arms not only were available for use, but that they were used by the king's officials years after they first were composed.

47 National Archives E101/6/4.

48 Ibid.

49 Ibid. The Pipe Rolls do not record that Nicholas Fermbaud was credited for the expenses he incurred for transporting these 100,000 quarrels to Caernarvon Castle. It is possible that this information was left out of the Pipe Rolls, either accidentally or intentionally, by the clerks at the Exchequer. It is also possible that Nicholas Fermbaud was compensated in some other manner, perhaps through the bureau of the royal Wardrobe, which took over many of the tasks of the Exchequer, especially in military matters.

50 National Archives E372/146 24v–25r.

Part 3: Inventories and audits

The regular updating of records, kept at the Exchequer, about the types, quantity, condition, and location of arms available for use by the king's soldiers required, as noted earlier, obtaining information about new arms being added to royal magazines and the transfer of these arms among the king's fortresses, magazines, and depots. In order to maintain a truly accurate picture of what arms were available, however, the king's military planners also had to be concerned with the negative side of the balance sheet. Naturally, in wartime, stockpiles of ammunition were drawn down at a rapid rate, and weapons were damaged, destroyed, and even captured. Even in peacetime, normal wear and tear took their toll on both arms and armor. Moreover, supplies of ammunition were diminished through use in training exercises. The king's administrators therefore found it necessary to conduct regular investigations of royal magazines and arms depots to determine both the quantity and condition of the arms in storage. The officers in charge of these investigations then drew up detailed inventory lists that were submitted, ultimately, to the Exchequer where they were stored for use by the king's military planners.[51] Hundreds of these inventories survive for thirteenth- and early fourteenth-century England, either as independent texts or as *fragmenta* or *perdita*. The last-named are references imbedded within surviving texts to no longer surviving documents. The following section discusses several of these inventories from the reigns of John, Henry III, and Edward I in an effort to demonstrate the continuity over time of the royal government's efforts to gather and collate information for use by the king's military planners.

On 3 January 1214, while preparing for King John's planned military expedition to the west of France, the Chancery issued orders to Hugh Neville, the constable of Marlborough Castle, requiring him to send to Portsmouth all of the iron horse armor (*coopertae ferreae*) and linen horse coverings, and all of the other arms (*omnes aliae armaturae*) that Walter of St. Owen had left in Hugh Neville's care.[52] This text is not, itself, an inventory of the arms at Marlborough Castle. The Chancery letter does demonstrate, however, that the officials working in the central bureaux of the royal government had available detailed information about the types of arms being stored at Marlborough Castle. Moreover, the officers at the Chancery were able to distinguish between those arms stored at Marlborough that had been deposited there by Walter of St. Owen, and other arms that were being stored there in early 1214.

The first surviving example of an actual inventory is a fragmentary report written in 1224 regarding the arms stored at the royal fortresses of Athlone, Limerick,

---

51 There is reason to believe that during John's reign, and early in the reign of Henry III, the written reports regarding the arms stored at the king's castles were kept at the Chancery rather than at the Exchequer.

52 *CR I*, 140.

and Dublin in Ireland.[53] According to the text, Roger, the constable at Athlone, had in his stores a wide range of armor and arms, including six coats of mail (*loricae*), four of which were equipped with crests (*corphae*) and two which did not have them; nine iron caps (*capelli ferri*); a helmet (*galea*); one crossbow (*balista*) equipped with a mechanical winch (*ad troil*); 2,000 quarrels; and two pieces of stone-throwing artillery called *mangonelli*. The inventory also listed 101 ropes (*cordae*), and cured hides used in slings (*fundae*).[54]

An inventory of the royal castle of Corfe, conducted in 1252 by four investigators designated as *nobiles*, noted thirty iron caps (*capelli ferri*), twenty old helmets (*gallenae veteres*), and two coats of mail (*loricae*).[55] An inventory of Shireburn Castle, conducted by the same four investigators in the same year, found nine coats of mail, four hauberks (*haubriones*), four helmets, eight iron caps, and fourteen old and broken-down crossbows (*balistae veteres debiles*), five of which were built of composite materials (*de cornu*) and nine of which were constructed of wood (*ligneae*). The inventory further specified that three of the composite crossbows were of the "one-foot" type and two were of the "two-foot" type, and that seven of the wooden crossbows were of the "two-foot" type.[56]

As is clear from the inventories from Henry III's reign discussed here, the investigators recorded not only the type and quantity of the arms stored in the royal castles, but their condition as well. The same concerns marked the inventory reports from the reign of Edward I. A representative example is an inventory conducted at Beaumarais Castle in 1306. According to the surviving report, which is divided into eleven sections dealing with arms, the garrison had available[57]

Arms (*armatura*)

    6 damaged helmets of little value

    4 battle axes

    4 damaged hauberks of little value

    2 iron coats of mail

    30 old, damaged, and unrepared shields

Crossbows (*balistae*)

    1 composite crossbow equipped with a winch

    1 composite crossbow of the "two-foot" type

    1 composite crossbow of the "one-foot" type

    2 crossbows constructed of yew wood (*de iffo*) of the "two-foot" type that recently had been repaired

    2 crossbows constructed of elm that also recently had been repaired by the constable

53   National Archives C47/10/3 #2.

54   Ibid.

55   National Archives C47/2/1.

56   Ibid.

57   National Archives E101/486/20.

Crossbows (*balistae*)

28 crossbows constructed of yew wood of which 14 have been repaired and 14 have not been repaired because they cannot be spanned

20 crossbows constructed from elm of the "one-foot" type which also are damaged in that they cannot be spanned

Baldrics (*baldrici*)

4 damaged baldrics of limited value designed to span crossbows of the "one-foot" type

Quarrels (*quarelli*)

312 chests of quarrels (approximately 150,000 individual quarrels)

Bows (*arcae*)

29 self bows constructed of elm

Engines (*ingenia*)

One small engine, which is called a trebuchet, which is standing atop the wall

Nuts (*nuces*)

7 brass nuts used for springalds[58]

Springalds (*springaldi*)

4 old springalds lying about in an unrepaired state along with their damaged iron parts

Supplies (*necessaria*)

108 pounds of woven horse hair

88 pounds of woven cannabis for the aforementioned springalds

Large Quarrels (*quarelli magni*)

700 large quarrels fletched with wax that are intended for the aforementioned springalds

Inventories, of the type just discussed, of royal magazines, depots, and other facilities used to store the king's arms, were conducted on a regular basis throughout England and Ireland, and during Edward I's reign, in Wales and Scotland as well. The inventories served to update the records stored in the central bureaux of the Chancery and especially the Exchequer regarding the type, quantity, and condition of the arms available for both offensive and defensive military operations. Special action was taken, however, to expedite this process of updating the royal records stored by the central government when command of a castle, magazine, or depot changed hands. In these circumstances, the central government invariably required that a detailed audit be conducted that identified what arms were stored in the facility and what, if any, losses in equipment the outgoing commander had to make good. On 3 March 1273, for example, William of Brebelshute handed

---

58 A *springald* is a torsion-powered, double-armed spear caster. See the discussion by Michael Prestwich, "The Trebuchets of the Tower", in *The Medieval Way of War: Studies in Military History in Honor of Bernard S. Bachrach*, ed. Gregory Halfond (Farnham, 2015), 283–294.

over command of the castle of Dryslwyn in Wales to Thomas de Roshale.[59] The transfer of command was marked administratively by a memorandum, vetted by Roger Mortimer, who held the office of royal justiciar in Wales, that included a detailed inventory of the arms stored at Dryslwyn Castle. These included fifteen battle axes (*haketones*); one gambeson; ten helmets (*galenae*), of which four were old and six were in good condition one iron coif; nine hauberks; six iron coats of mail (*corsetti*); one iron gorget; nine sets of iron plate armor (*platea*), of which three were new and six had iron gorges; twelve small and large shields (*targiae et scuta*); twelve lances; twenty-four spears (*tela*); two *springalds* with their equipment (*utilia*); 108 quarrels and quarrel heads for the *springalds*; thirty-six crossbows of various types; fifteen baldrics; eighteen self-bows; 4,000 quarrels; and 300 arrows.[60] As is clear from this list, the audit of the *armatura* of Dryslwyn Castle was quite thorough.

Such close auditing of the royal arms stored in the king's castles and other depots and magazines when there was a transfer of command was necessary not only to maintain up-to-date information for the king's planners but also to ensure that no confusion arose over the ownership of the weapons and ammunition stored in a particular facility. The concern among royal administrators over the question of proper title to arms is made clear in a Chancery letter issued to Adam de Chetewind, a royal clerk, in October 1276.[61] Adam had overseen the audit of Chartley Castle when Roger Lestrange was relieved of his post as commander there. The Chancery order required Adam to deliver to Roger all of the military equipment, including iron fittings (*ferramenta*) used in engines (*ingenia*), crossbows, quarrels, and armor, and all of the rest of the property that Roger had left in the castle when he handed it over to Adam de Chetewind.[62]

As is evident from the Chancery letter, Roger Lestrange was not permitted to take anything from the castle in the immediate aftermath of giving up command. Instead, before he was allowed to take the arms, armor, engine parts, and other supplies that were his personal property, an audit had to be conducted of the entire inventory of the castle. This audit included both the king's property, that is the normal complement of arms, armor, and other supplies stored there, and Roger's property that came and went with him and was used in the defense of the castle only so long as Roger was there. Clearly, the ability to differentiate between the king's military property and Roger's military property at the end of Roger's tenure entailed a systematic keeping of records regarding both sets of property from the beginning of Roger's tenure as commander of the castle. This means that there must have been an audit of the arms, armor, and other supplies of the fortress before Roger took command. Furthermore, as noted, any additional

---

59 National Archives E213/118.
60 Ibid.
61 *CCR 1272–1279*, 316.
62 Ibid.

arms and armor purchased by Roger on behalf of the king, or additional arms and armor shipped to the castle by the royal government had to be recorded. From the point of view of the royal government, it was not necessary for Roger to have kept detailed records of his own property, because the king's officials really only were interested in making sure that the king's property stayed in the castle. From Roger's point of view, however, it may well have been important to keep detailed records of his arms, armor, and other supplies to keep the royal government or any other party from trying to take it away from him.[63]

In Roger's case, the audit of his command made clear that he had not made off with royal property. This was not true, however, of every royal official given command over a castle, magazine, or depot. The Pipe Roll for 1299–1300 records the Robert Balliol, the outgoing sheriff of Northumberland, had not yet given sufficient information about a wide range of weapons, ammunition, and armor that had been delivered to him during the time he held office.[64] The Pipe Roll accounts for 1300–1301, and 1301–1302, also record that Robert Balliol had not yet made a sufficient response to the Exchequer to explain the missing arms and armor.[65] It was not until the Pipe Roll of 1302–1303 that the clerks at the Exchequer recorded that Robert had paid £22 in order to make good the missing arms and armor.[66] Clearly, in this case at least, the clerks at the Exchequer not only kept detailed records about the type, quantity, and condition of the arms that were supposed to be stored in the king's magazines, depots, and castles, but also pursued discrepancies in these records until the royal officer in charge paid the necessary fines.

Conclusion

English government officials maintained a highly structured administrative system that effectively provided military planners with well-organized and coherent information about the types, quantities, and condition of the arms available for use by the king's troops. This study has focused on only one aspect of English military administration, and much work remains to be done to understand the full panoply of administrative systems that made possible the conduct of war by the kings of England. It is time that medieval military historians, and especially those working on medieval England, follow the lead set by their fellow historians in areas such as the English economy, where the thorough study of the vast body of surviving royal administrative documents has led to significant advances in our understanding of that world.

---

63 This document also indicates that magnates such as Roger did keep personal arsenals that included arms, armor, crossbows, quarrels, and even engines, or at least the iron fittings that could be used to put together engines. This is significant when trying to piece together the military resources available to the royal government.

64 National Archives E372/145 2v.

65 National Archives E372/146 20r and E372/147 14r.

66 National Archives E372/148 5r–5v.

8

MILITARY LOGISTICS DURING THE REIGN OF EDWARD I OF ENGLAND, 1272–1307

Vegetius, the great authority on military matters throughout the Middle Ages, wrote in his exceptionally widely known handbook *Epitoma rei militaris* that "armies are more often destroyed by starvation than by battle, and hunger is more savage than the sword".[1] Vegetius added, "other misfortunes can in time be alleviated: fodder and grain supply have no remedy in a crisis except storage in advance".[2] Successful military commanders throughout the Middle Ages took these *dicta* very seriously, doing everything in their power to ensure that sufficient quantities of grain, meat, wine, and other supplies were available for their troops on campaign and in garrison.[3] King Edward I of England (1272–1307), whose military administration is the focus of this study, is widely recognized by scholars to have been an effective military leader and, indeed, conqueror, whose campaigns met with frequent success in Wales, Scotland, and Gascony, if not in Flanders.[4]

The logistical systems that made possible Edward's military campaigns over a period of more than three decades are exceptionally complex and have, as yet, received only cursory attention from scholars.[5] Before a general study of these

---

1   Vegetius, *Epitoma rei militaris*, ed. Alf Önnerfors (Stuttgart, 1995), 3.3. I am quoting the translation of this passage by N. P. Milner, *Vegetius: Epitome of Military Science* 2nd revised edn (Liverpool, 1996), 67.
2   Ibid. Concerning the wide diffusion of Vegetius manuscripts during the Middle Ages, see Charles R. Schrader, "A Handlist of Extant Manuscripts Containing the *De re militari* of Flavius Vegetius Renatus", *Scriptorium* 33 (1979), 280–305. Now also see the important study Christopher Allmand, *The "De Re Militari" of Vegetius: The Reception, Transmission and Legacy of a Roman Text in the Middle Ages* (Cambridge, 2011).
3   For a valuable introduction to the general problem of logistics in the Middle Ages, see Bernard S. Bachrach, "Logistics in Pre-Crusade Europe", in *Feeding Mars: Logistics in Western Warfare from the Middle Ages to the Present*, ed. John A Lynn (Boulder, CO, 1993), 57–78.
4   The most thorough monographic work dealing with Edward's military organization is Michael Prestwich, *War, Politics and Finance under Edward I* (Totowa, NJ, 1972).
5   For the current state of the question regarding logistics during the reign of Edward I, see Prestwich, *War, Politics and Finance*, 114–136; and (idem), *Edward I*, 2nd edn (Yale, 1997), where he reiterates several elements of his earlier work, drawing particular attention to some of the royal administrators who helped to direct Edward's logistical operations, particularly in Scotland (480–483, 486–487, 513, and 527).

logistical systems can be undertaken, each of the numerous facets of administration that made possible the supply of Edward's armies must be examined in detail. Among the many problems that require elucidation are royal efforts to acquire food supplies and wine from territories in England, Ireland, and Gascony, including the development of a corps of royal clerks skilled in the many tasks necessary for the selection and purchase of these supplies. Just as important as the identification of the bureaucratic procedures and administration undergirding the acquisition of food and wine is the investigation of the means by which these supplies, once acquired, actually arrived in the hands of the soldiers who needed them. Crucial in this regard is an investigation of the system of warehouses and other storage facilities that were utilized by royal officials from the time grain, animals, and wine were purchased until the time the supplies were delivered to the troops. Of particular importance are the massive magazines such as those established at Newcastle and Berwick for Edward's Scottish wars from the late 1290s through 1307. Finally, it is necessary to consider the means by which supplies were moved from their point of origin to soldiers serving in the field and in garrisons. Transportation took place by ship, by barge, and by land. It is the administrative system that made possible this last mode of transportation that is the focus of the following study.[6]

In the pre-modern period, land transportation always was substantially more expensive than transportation over the same distance by water. The cost of transporting goods by cart or wagon over land in thirteenth- and fourteenth-century England has been calculated to be roughly twice the cost of river transport and eight times the cost of transport by sea.[7] When possible, therefore, water transportation of supplies was preferred by the royal government. Nevertheless, certain stages of the transportation system required land conveyance. The initial acquisition of grain from the countryside and its transportation to regional collection points on rivers or on the sea was done over land.[8] Similarly, the transportation of supplies from major supply centers in the campaigning zones, to be discussed

---

6   Although the narrative sources for thirteenth- and early fourteenth-century England are exceptionally rich, the authors of these texts had very little to say about matters of military administration, particularly such mundane questions as the mobilization of land transportation. Fortunately, scholars working in this period have available an enormous corpus of administrative documents produced by all levels of the royal government concerning virtually every aspect of military administration. Several of the major sets of documents have been published in calendared form: *Calendar of Patent Rolls Edward I 1272–1307* (London, 1893–1901, repr. 1971), hereafter *CPR* with date range; and *Calendar of Close Rolls 1272–1307* (London, 1900–1908, repr. 1970), hereafter *CCR* with date range. Most of the surviving documents, however, from Edward I's reign have not been published. These include the liberate rolls and pipe rolls, and many tens of thousands of indentures, writs, letters, Wardrobe accounts, tax rolls, and property lists. These texts are cited individually according to their catalogue numbers in the National Archives.

7   James Masschaele, "Transport Costs in Medieval England", *The Economic History Review* ns 46 (1993), 266–279, here 273.

8   On this point, see the valuable observations by Masschaele, "Transport Costs", 266–268.

in this chapter, frequently had a land component. In Wales, supplies deployed to English fortresses along the coast had to be moved inland to support royal armies marching toward the interior. In Scotland, supplies were moved west by barge and ship along the Tweed, Forth, and Tay rivers.[9] However, the transportation of supplies north or south of these river systems required land vehicles and draught animals. As a consequence, the provision of carts, wagons, horses, and oxen for transportation duties was crucially important to the success of the entire military logistical system.

Background

When Edward I came to power in 1272, he inherited from his father Henry III (1216–1272) an efficiently functioning system of transportation resources designed to supply the royal household everywhere in England. The central government possessed under its direct control a substantial stock of carts, wagons, and horses.[10] As a rule, these transportation resources were distributed throughout the kingdom in order to facilitate the supply of the royal household wherever it might be. In August 1229, for example, a letter from the Chancery to the sheriff of Southampton makes clear that several long carts (*longi carrecti*) were stationed at Winchester Castle.[11] The purpose of this particular Chancery letter was to inform the sheriff of Southampton that the royal clerk William Hardel was coming to Winchester to inspect the state of the carts being stored there. If William decided that it was necessary, the sheriff was to employ several smiths and carpenters to carry out any repairs needed to the carts. The sheriff also was to arrange for the work to be inspected by several legally competent men (*homines legales*) from the area and pay the smiths and carpenters for their labor.[12] From an administrative perspective, this Chancery document makes

---

9   There are numerous shipping accounts for the transportation of supplies by royal officials along the Tweed, Forth, and Tay. See in this regard, for example, the Wardrobe account for 1301–1302 in British Library ADD 17360, 21r–25r.

10 The use by Henry III's government of royal officials at the local level to mobilize transportation resources was by no means a new practice. King John (1199–1216) regularly required his sheriffs to find the necessary carts, wagons, and draught animals to move supplies. On 4 August 1204, for example, King John ordered the sheriff of Kent to provide transportation (*carragium*) to the crossbow maker Roger so that he could move his tools (*utensilia sua*) to Nottingham. See *Rotuli Litterarum Clausarum in Turri Londonensi Asservati 1204–1227*, ed. Thomas D. Hardy, 2 vols (1833–1834) I: 4.

11 *Close Rolls of the Reign of Henry III 1216–1272* (London, 1902–1938), here *CR 1227–1231*, 200.

12 Ibid. With respect to the oversight process insisted upon by the royal government when authorizing payments made by local officials, see David S. Bachrach, "The Military Administration of England: The Royal Artillery (1216–1272)", *Journal of Military History* 68 (2004), 1083–1104, passim, and in this volume.

clear that the central government kept detailed records regarding its vehicles and draught animals.[13]

When the transportation resources held directly by the crown proved insufficient to supply the royal court, local officials, particularly town bailiffs and county sheriffs, were ordered to requisition vehicles and animals from the areas under their jurisdiction. In November 1232, for example, the Chancery issued orders to the bailiffs of Coventry, Banbury, Bristol, Stratford, Brackley, Oxford, Hereford, and Gloucester requiring them to receive royal officers (*servientes*) who were being sent to them to purchase fish and other supplies for the use of the king through the royal right of purveyance. Once the *servientes* had made their purchases, the bailiffs were to secure transport (*carragium*) for these supplies all the way to Worcester.[14] The vehicles requisitioned by the bailiffs of these towns had then to make substantial round-trip journeys ranging from 75 to 265 kilometers, requiring between three and eleven days on the road.[15] Although not specified in the Chancery document, it seems likely that the *carragium* was to be provided by the merchants from whom the *servientes* had made their purchases. In general, however, it appears the sheriffs were responsible for supplying from the resources of their offices the vehicles and animals necessary for transporting both food supplies and matériel to the royal court and to royal installations around the kingdom.[16]

13 It appears from the surviving administrative documents that the responsibility for building new carts and wagons was assigned by the royal government to the sheriffs. On 26 October 1251, for example, the Chancery issued an order to the sheriff of Yorkshire requiring him to have built immediately two long wagons with all of their equipment (*attilium et harnesium*) to be completed by the time the king arrived at the city. See *CR 1247–1251*, 520. An exceptionally detailed list of costs for the production of long carts was recorded on a writ of liberate issued by the Chancery to the Exchequer on 20 April 1242. According to the text of the writ, a wheelwright named Richard was owed in excess of £21 for the construction of twelve long wagons (*cartae longae*), and a saddle maker named Simon de Barking was owed just over £37 for twenty-four saddles, two dozen pairs of curry combs (*strigilia*), two dozen leather girths, four dozen shafts fitted with both large and small buckles, twelve poles, two dozen pairs of leather traces (*tractuus*), two dozen sets of ropes for the wagons and horses, five dozen horse collars, and twelve large tarpaulins for the wagons. See *Calendar of Liberate Rolls 1226–1272* (London, 1916–1964), here *CLR 1240–1245*, 118.

14 *CR 1231–1234*, 171.

15 It is of parenthetical interest that the clerk, who drew up the requisition order, wrote down the first five towns from which supplies were to be requisitioned in order of their distance from Worcester: Coventry 73 kilometers, Banbury 96 kilometers, Bristol 100 kilometers, Brackley 105 kilometers, and Oxford 265 kilometers. It seems unlikely that the clerk's action was accidental, which suggests that the officials at the royal court had a very good understanding of the practical geography of England, including the relative distances of the towns from which supplies were provided to the royal court.

16 In this regard, see, for example, *CR 1251–1253*, 73, 125, 388, 430, 466; *CR 1253–1254*, 63, 194, 205, 208, 258, 297; *CR 1254–1256*, 127; *CR 1256–1259*, 69, 77, 220–221, 238, 247, 271, 337; *CR 1268–1272*, 54, 446–447, 459–460,

For the most part, ecclesiastical institutions during Henry III's reign were exempt from having their vehicles and animals requisitioned for use by the government. There were exemptions, however. On 10 August 1245, for example, the Chancery issued an order to the prior of Dunstable to supply two good carts (*bonae carettae*) to transport the king's supplies that were located at Dunstable to Chester, 260 kilometers away.[17] Similarly, in May 1263, Henry's government sought a cart horse (*summarius*), and a cart driver (*carettarius*) from the abbot of Wautham.[18] In this case, the letter from the Chancery makes clear that it was the dearth of transportation and all other supplies for the king's campaign in Wales that forced him to make this request of the abbot "under the debt of affection in which you hold us".[19]

The tenor of this latter request for material support, couched in the terms of affection rather than command, indicates the reluctance of the royal government to pressure the church into contributing its transportation resources.[20] The only major exception to this practice would appear to be those occasions on which ecclesiastical institutions came into the hands of the crown. Thus, for example, in 1228, the Chancery issued orders to Stephen Lacy, the royal administrator of the bishopric of Durham, to provide well-made carts (*bonae carectae*) to ship crossbow bolts (*quarellae*) from Durham to Winchester.[21] Similarly, in 1261, Walter de Burges, the royal custodian of the bishopric of Winchester, received an order from the Chancery requiring him to find the resources to transport supplies to the castle of Farnham.[22]

---

17   *CR 1242–1247*, 335.
18   *CR 1261–1264*, 306.
19   Ibid., "*indigemus tam pro cariagiis quam negotiis aliis factum expeditionis nostre contingentibus, vobis rogamus ut sub debito dilectionis qua nobis tenemini*".
20   The reluctance of the royal government to requisition vehicles and animals from ecclesiastical institutions may, perhaps, be explained in part by a Chancery writ issued in July 1244 to the sheriff of Westminster. See *CR 1242–1247*, 257–258. The sheriff was ordered to request (*perquire*) that the abbots and priors in his jurisdiction provide wagons (*carrae*) to help transport the king's engines (*ingenia*) to Newcastle on Tyne. The text of the writ, however, makes clear that the sheriff very well could experience difficulties in obtaining these wagons. He is instructed to show the royal writ to the various abbots and priors in order to help convince them to help, implying that the sheriff's word alone would not be sufficient. The writ then goes on to require that if the abbots and priors refused to hand over the wagons (*si ea regi dare aut commodare noluerint*), then the sheriff is to seize (*capere*) the wagons both from the ecclesiastical officials and from others in the county, "as he loves his body". The difficulties envisioned by the author of this writ in gaining the voluntary support of ecclesiastical institutions may well, in the long run, have convinced Henry III's officials that requisitioning transportation resources from the church was not worth the effort.
21   *CR 1227–1231*, 81.
22   *CR 1261–1264*, 1.

Edward I's early career

The first major test of the royal logistical system during Edward I's reign came during the Welsh war of 1277. In the course of this very brief campaign, Edward's government put into motion two separate systems to obtain supplies for the army that was preparing to march into Wales. The first element of the royal plan was, essentially, an expansion of the purveyance system by which the royal court obtained its supplies. Clerks and other officers were dispatched from the court to the counties to purchase supplies and arrange for them to be shipped to the king and the army.[23] A letter patent issued by the Chancery on 17 July 1277 to the sheriff of Nottingham and Derby provides an overview of how this system was supposed to work.[24] The sheriff was informed that Hugh de Kendal, a royal clerk, and Ralph Maloure, a royal sergeant, were being sent to his counties to purchase grain for the royal army. The sheriff was ordered to aid these two officials in every way that he could, and ensure that the grain that Hugh and Ralph purchased was sent to Chester, for transshipment to the English troops operating in Wales.[25] Similar orders were issued to the sheriffs of Leicestershire and Warwickshire, Lancashire, Shropshire and Staffordshire, and Gloucestershire.[26]

In order to facilitate the transfer of the food supplies from these counties, the Chancery ordered in a second letter patent issued on 17 July, that the sheriffs in question *request* carts and wagons (*carectae, carrae*) from the bishops, abbots, priors, and other church officials located in their jurisdictions.[27] There is no mention in the letter patent that the sheriffs were to coerce the churchmen to permit the requisition of these vehicles. Indeed, the royal government seems to have gone out of its way to avoid any appearance of demanding that the church provide transportation resources for the war. On 3 August 1277, for example, letters of protection were issued to the abbot and convent of Bildewas and to the abbot and convent of Pippewell, stating that the two houses were not required to provide *carragium* despite the great need of the army for supplies.[28] In the event that they were unable to gain the consent of the religious authorities to use their vehicles and animals, the sheriffs were bound to find other sources of transportation. In 1277, given the relatively small size and short duration of the campaign, this probably meant that the sheriffs deployed the carts, wagons, horses, and oxen available

---

23 For an overview of this system with respect the provisioning of royal forces in Edward I's Welsh wars, see Prestwich, *War, Politics and Finance*, 118–120.
24 *CPR 1272–1281*, 219.
25 Ibid.
26 Ibid.
27 *CPR 1272–1281*, 219.
28 *CPR*, 224. For similar grants of exemption from having their transportation resources seized by the royal government, see ibid, 226, and 232.

to them as part of the *impedimenta* of their offices, although the surviving administrative documents are not explicit on this point.[29]

In order to supplement the direct purchase of supplies by royal officials, the second element of the crown's logistical plan was to encourage private merchants to bring food supplies directly to the army.[30] On 7 July 1277, the Chancery issued orders to the sheriffs of Lancashire, Worcestershire, Shropshire and Staffordshire, Derbyshire, Gloucestershire, and Herefordshire, as well as to the bailiffs of Kermerdin and Cardigan in Wales, requiring that all local markets be banned and that all merchants be sent with their goods to the royal army.[31] The Chancery subsequently issued letters of protection to dozens of merchants, protecting their vehicles, animals, and goods from seizure by any officials. On 12 August 1277, for example, the merchant Sybil de la Pere of Bruges was issued a letter of protection for a cart load of grain and other food supplies being carried to Chester for sale to the royal forces there.[32] Similar letters of protection were issued on 25 August to John le Spencer and Ernold de Depe, both of whom were leading wagon trains loaded with provisions to Wales.[33]

The limited extent of the 1277 campaign, the relatively small numbers of English troops involved, and the fact that the royal army was able to use the Welsh harvests in Anglesey in August and September of 1277, all helped to disguise the fundamental problems created by having two entirely separate logistical systems in operation at the same time.[34] In 1277, at least, the sheriffs were able to acquire and transport supplies without interfering with the operations of the merchants. The Second Welsh War (1282–1284), however, was much longer and involved far more troops than the operations of 1277. The resulting demands on the logistical system exposed considerable problems, particularly in the ability of royal officials to find sufficient transportation resources to move supplies to the army.

---

29 The campaign began in July 1277 and concluded in September of that year. On this point, see Prestwich, *War, Politics and Finance*, 28. Prestwich, (ibid.), 92, suggests that there may have been as many as 15,000 men in royal pay during the summer of 1277, but that the vast majority of them were Welsh. The surviving administrative documents do not make clear whether English resources were employed to feed Welsh troops operating in Wales.

30 Some magnates also provided supplies for their own troops. See, in this regard, *Welsh Rolls in The Calendar of Various Chancery Rolls AD 1277–1326* (London, 1912), 246, where the men of Earl John Warren of Surrey and Sussex are granted letters of protection on 7 November 1282 to obtain and bring food for the earl's troops serving in Wales. However, this element of the logistical system was relatively minor in comparison to the royal government's efforts to provide for the many thousands of men serving in the shire levies. See in this regard Prestwich, *War, Politics and Finance*, 117–118. Indeed, given that the magnates were granted letters of protection for their men, and for merchants, to bring supplies to them, the logistical efforts of the magnates may well be understood to fall within the rubric of the market element of the overall royal logistical system.

31 *CCR 1272–1279*, 426. On this point, see Prestwich, *War, Politics and Finance*, 119.

32 *CPR 1272–1281*, 226.

33 *CPR 1272–1281*, 227. For similar letters of protection, see ibid., 228–229.

34 Concerning the harvesting of grain in Wales by Edward's army, see Prestwich, *War, Politics and Finance*, 28.

The Second Welsh War (1282–1284)

The apparent success of the logistical operations in 1277 led royal planners again to use two independent systems to obtain supplies for the royal army. As had been done five years earlier, the royal government sent clerks and other officials from the court to oversee the purchase of supplies directly from producers at the county level using the royal right of purveyance. On 14 April 1282, for example, the Chancery sent a letter to the sheriff of Essex noting that John Maidstone was being sent to his county to acquire 1,500 quarters of wheat and 2,000 quarters of oats, peas, cheese, and other food supplies to be taken to the port of Winchelsea for transport to the royal army.[35] At approximately 500 modern pounds to the quarter, the rate fixed by the royal government in 1296, this amounted to 1,750,000 pounds or 875 tons of supplies.[36] The Chancery order required the sheriff to second one of his own men to the service of John Maidstone to help him in his work, and to use the king's revenues within the county to pay for the food supplies. In the present context, it is important to note that the sheriff and his man also were to find the transport necessary to get the supplies to Winchelsea.[37] Similar orders were sent to the sheriffs of Surrey, Sussex, Kent, and Southampton.[38] Some of the costs for the purchase and transport of these supplies can be traced through the pipe rolls for the war years. Sheriff Roger Springhouse of Shropshire, for example, was credited at the Exchequer for £17 he spent on the purchase and transport of grain (*frumentum*) from Shropshire to the royal army at Aberconway in Wales, a distance of 140 kilometers from the county seat at Shrewsbury.[39]

In addition to mobilizing the efforts of his sheriffs, the king's men also continued to exploit royal control over those church lands that the government held in the absence of duly elected abbots and bishops. On 10 April 1282, therefore, the Chancery ordered the royal administrators at Winchester to procure 1000 quarters of wheat, 600 quarters of oats, and 200 quarters of barley. Again, the locally based officials were responsible for transporting all of this grain to Chester for shipment to the royal army.[40]

However, in addition to requiring royal officials at the local level to purchase and ship supplies to troops in Wales and those preparing to depart, Edward's government again relied to a considerable degree on merchants during the Second

---

35   *Welsh Rolls*, 217.
36   Concerning the weight of the quarter, see Ronald Edward Zupko, *British Weights and Measures: A History from Antiquity to the Seventeenth Century* (Madison, WI, 1977), 22. Michael Prestwich, "Victualling estimates for English Garrisons in Scotland during the early Fourteenth Century", *The English Historical Review* 82 (1967), 536–543, here 537, suggests a quarter weight of 380 pounds of 16 ounces each.
37   *Welsh Rolls*, 117. For a brief overview of the logistical operations for the Second Welsh War of 1282–1284, see Prestwich, *War, Politics and Finance*, 119–120.
38   *Welsh Rolls*, 217.
39   National Archives E372/28 6r.
40   *CCR 1279–1288*, 150.

Welsh War to bring supplies directly to the army. The government encouraged this, on the one hand, by granting hundreds of writs of safe conduct and letters of protection to merchants bringing grain, meat, wine, and other supplies to the mustering areas for the army, particularly at Chester.[41] In case this proved insufficient, however, the government also required that merchants within several counties only sell their goods to the army, that is they were prohibited from bringing their goods to local markets. Thus, for example, on 24 May 1282, the Chancery issued orders to the mayor and sheriffs of London requiring them to issue a proclamation throughout the city that any merchants with goods for sale had to bring them to the royal army at Chester. Similar orders were issued to the sheriffs of Warwickshire and Leicestershire, Nottinghamshire and Derbyshire, Lincolnshire, Yorkshire, and Northampton.[42]

The government again ordered the establishment of army markets in the spring of 1283. On 21 March 1283, for example, the Chancery sent writs to the sheriff of Shropshire and Staffordshire requiring that royal proclamations be read in all of the boroughs and market towns in these two counties summoning merchants there to bring their food supplies to Montgomery for sale to the royal army and the king.[43] Similar orders were issued to the sheriffs of Gloucestershire, Herefordshire, Nottinghamshire and Derbyshire, Warwickshire and Leicestershire, and Worcestershire.[44]

In practice, therefore, the central government established two rival systems of supply that competed with each other both for food stuffs and, even more crucially, for the means to move these goods to the army.[45] The sheriffs, their officers, and the royal officials sent by the king to the counties to purchase grain, all had a strong interest in ensuring that they fulfilled the specific tasks allotted to them. John Maidstone and the sheriff of Essex, for example, were responsible for finding, purchasing, and transporting 3,500 quarters of supplies, amounting, as noted, to some 875 tons. This meant that the two men, and their staffs, were responsible for the transportation necessary to move approximately 875 wagon loads or twice as many cart loads of grain, peas, and beans.[46] The merchants, for their part, had

---

41 *Welsh Rolls* for 1282, 221–230, 232–238, 241, 243–246, 259, 260. *Welsh Rolls* for 1283, 262, 265–275; and *CPR 1281–1292*, 25, 59, 67.
42 *Welsh Rolls*, 250.
43 *Welsh Rolls*, 279.
44 Ibid.
45 As noted, some magnates also provided supplies to their military households independently of the overall royal logistical effort. In so far as the efforts of these magnates can be considered to have played a role in the depriving the sheriffs of land transportation resources, they had an impact similar to that of merchants who also had the benefit of letters of protection from the crown.
46 The carrying capacity of medieval wagons generally, and those of late thirteenth and early fourteenth century, in particular, has not yet been settled. There is general scholarly agreement that four-wheeled wagons and two-wheeled ox-drawn carts had approximately twice the carrying capacity of two-wheeled horse-drawn carts. See, in this regard, James Field Willard, "Inland Transportation in England during the Fourteenth Century", *Speculum* 1 (1926), 361–374, here

a strong interest in bringing their supplies directly to the army in the hope of getting high prices for their goods. It is for this reason that so many hundreds of merchants sought letters of protection to go to Chester, and even to Wales, rather than simply selling their goods to the sheriffs of their counties who might have imposed fixed prices through the royal right of purveyance. Of course, this also meant that the merchants used their vehicles and animals to transport their own goods, thereby depriving the sheriffs and other royal officials of a large portion of the transportation resources that might otherwise be available in their counties.

The dearth of vehicles and animals available to the sheriffs was exacerbated by the fact that Edward's government maintained its policy of not requiring religious institutions to provide transportation resources for military campaigns during the Second Welsh War of 1282–1284. A letter patent issued by the Chancery in June 1282 to the abbot of St. Wereburg in Chester, for example, promises that the latter's *voluntary* contribution of horses and carts for the king's expedition into Wales will not be treated as a precedent by the royal government to the detriment of the monastery.[47] But this voluntary grant of vehicles and horses was rare. Much more common was the exemption of ecclesiastical institutions from having their vehicles and horses requisitioned. Many scores of letters of protection were issued to monasteries, priories, convents, parishes, and bishoprics throughout 1282 and 1283 that protected their property from any requisitions at all.[48] As a result of royal policy toward ecclesiastical institutions, the number of vehicles and animals

---

366–367; Marjorie Nice Boyer, "Medieval Pivoted Axles", *Technology and Culture* 1 (1960), 128–138, here 133; and John Langdon, *Horses, Oxen and Technological Innovation: The Use of Draught Animals in English Farming from 1066 to 1500* (Cambridge, 1986), 151. The carrying capacity of a cart remains a difficult question. Albert C. Leighton, *Transport and Communication in Early Medieval Europe AD 500–1100* (New York, 1972), 72, gives the figure of 1,000 pounds for the carrying capacity of a two-wheeled Roman vehicle. Marcel Girault, *Attelages et Charrois au Mayen-Age* (Paris, 1992), 138, sees pulling capacity of medieval carts limited to 500 kilograms, or 1,100 pounds. If Girault is correct, then the carts in use by the English government during Edward's reign could carry approximately half a ton, and the wagons as well as ox-drawn carts (*palustra*) could carry about a ton. Masschaele, "Transport Costs", 268–269, identifies several texts from the fourteenth century in which vehicles drawn by four horses are reported to have transported 4 quarters, or 2,000 pounds, of supplies. It is not clear from Masschaele's description of the texts he cites whether these vehicles are two-wheeled *carettae* or four-wheeled *cartae*.

47 *CPR 1281–1292*, 29.
48 See in this regard, *CPR 1281–1292*, 17, and 19; and *Welsh Rolls*, 221, 223, 224–225, 228, 232, 234, 235, 236, 239, 241, 242, 243, 244, 245, 246, 259, 260, 261, 262, (1283), 262, 263, 264, 265, 266, 267, 268, 270, 271, 272, 273. Nevertheless, as had been true during Henry III's reign, the church was not entirely exempt from royal exactions. On 16 December 1282, for example, the Chancery issued orders to the abbot of Chester informing him of the desperate need of the king for transport and draught horses. See *Welsh Rolls*, 277. The abbot was therefore required to send all of his wagons (*carrae*) and carts (*carettae*) with drivers to Chester. In order to oversee the mobilization of these resources, the king sent the royal clerk William de Perton. Similar writs were issued to the abbots of Vale Royal, Grace Dieu in Cumberland, Stanlowe, the priors of Norton and Birkenhead, and the justice of Chester.

available for transporting supplies to the royal army was, from the beginning of the Second Welsh War, artificially reduced to a significant degree.

Given this set of circumstances, it is hardly surprising that difficulties arose in the logistical plans made by the government. The sheriffs could not obtain vehicles from most ecclesiastical institutions. The sheriffs and royal officials also were prohibited from requisitioning supplies and transport from the hundreds of merchants who had goods to sell and vehicles to transport them. On an *ad hoc* basis, the sheriffs could use their own limited resources and requisition additional vehicles and animals from individual landowners in their counties. But this latter solution imposed its own burdens, most importantly identifying who had these transportation resources and who could afford to be without them. The sheriff of Essex, who had to find transportation for 875 tons of supplies quickly, hardly had the time to go searching through every farm and village to find well-built carts and wagons as well as healthy animals. In the final result, many royal officials operating at the local level, including some sheriffs and clerks dispatched to the counties by the king, considered it better to risk the royal wrath by violating letters of protection than by failing to fulfill the tasks assigned to them. Staying clear of the ecclesiastical institutions, which might have considerable political influence, these royal officials seized the supplies and, more importantly, the vehicles and animals, of merchants who were bringing their goods to the royal army. In effect, one element of the logistical system cannibalized the other.

In recognition of this problem, the Chancery issued orders on 8 November 1282 to the sheriffs through southern and central England, requiring them to crack down on the abuses being carried out in their jurisdictions.[49] The royal order specifically names members of the royal household, other royal *ministerii*, and bailiffs, as being responsible for hindering the passage of food and other supplies through the counties to the army.[50] The sheriffs were to enforce all letters of protection granted to merchants, and were to jail any official who violated them.[51]

Land transportation in a new logistical system

The brief revolt in Wales in 1287 by Rhys ap Maredudd did not cause the royal government to alter its logistical system to a significant degree, probably for two reasons. First, the English campaign commanded by the regent, Edmund of Cornwall, was very brief, much like the war of 1277. Secondly, and perhaps more importantly, Edward I was in Gascony during the revolt by Rhys, and it was not possible to innovate on a major scale in his absence. It should be noted that the unexpected nature of the revolt by Rhys, long an English ally in Wales, also militated against the organization of purchasing commissions at the county level so

---

49 *Welsh Rolls*, 257–258.
50 Ibid.
51 Ibid.

that the sheriffs were largely excluded from the logistical preparations in 1287. Instead, the royal government appears initially to have relied almost entirely on merchants to bring food to the army. On 23 June 1287, the Chancery issued orders to the sheriffs of Shropshire, Worcestershire, Gloucestershire, and Herefordshire, to have the merchants of their counties carry supplies for sale to Ludlow, located in Shropshire on the Welsh frontier.[52] One month later, on 17 July 1287, the Chancery issued orders to the sheriffs of Shropshire, Gloucestershire, Worcestershire, and Warwickshire to have them direct the merchants of their counties to the town of Hereford to sell supplies to the army of Edmund of Cornwall. The sheriff of Somerset was to have the merchants of his county bring their supplies either to Bristol or to Bridgewater.[53]

Growing frustrated with the lack of merchant response, however, the Chancery finally issued orders on 5 August to the sheriffs of Shropshire, Worcestershire, and Herefordshire commanding them to take over the collection of supplies and to provide transport (*carragium*), leaving aside all of their other duties until this task was completed.[54] In order to help ensure that the sheriffs did what they were ordered, royal clerks were sent to help oversee the logistical operations.[55] The surviving administrative records do not note whether the sheriffs and other royal officials committed the same kinds of abuses that plagued the government's logistical operations during the Second Welsh War.

Relative peace in Britain in the period 1287–1294 and the lack of major military operations on the island obviated the need for a major logistical effort for a period of seven years. As a consequence, it is not until the mid-1290s that it is possible to discern the ways in which the royal government applied the lessons of the logistical problems of the Welsh campaigns of 1282–1284 and 1287. In assessing the decisions made by Edward's officials regarding logistical preparations in the 1290s, it appears that having observed the difficulties of employing two competing supply systems, one based on obtaining supplies through the royal right of purveyance and other through the market, and the potential unreliability of merchants to provide adequate provisions in a timely manner, the royal government shifted the major responsibility for acquiring and transporting supplies from the merchants to the sheriffs, with the latter being overseen by officials sent from the court. One additional factor that should be considered in this context is that the transition to a system of supply acquisition based almost entirely on the royal right of purveyance may have been intended to save money for the government by imposing a fixed price on food supplies in a period when grain prices, in particular, were rising rapidly.[56]

---

52 *Welsh Rolls*, 314.
53 *Welsh Rolls*, 312.
54 *Welsh Rolls*, 314–315.
55 Ibid.
56 Grain prices may have reached a high point in 1295 and thereafter remained high for the remainder of the decade in England. On this point, see D. L. Farmer, "Some Grain Price Movements in

The initial transition from a logistical system depending heavily on merchants to one depending almost entirely on the royal right of purveyance and administered directly by royal officials can be discerned in the Welsh revolt of 1294–1295.[57] In the initial stages of this campaign, the royal government had the advantage of already having in place major military forces and substantial supplies destined for service in Gascony.[58] These troops and supplies immediately were redirected toward Wales.[59] Additional supplies were shipped to Wales by sea from Ireland.[60] It appears that the resupply of the royal forces in Wales was overseen by administrative officers sent by the court to coordinate activities in the counties with the sheriffs and other local officials. The most senior of the royal officials charged with acquiring and transporting supplies to the king's troops in Wales was John Maidstone, who had held similar responsibilities during the Welsh campaigns of 1282–1284.[61] Late in the second year of the Welsh revolt, on 3 October 1295, writs of aid were issued by the Chancery to the sheriffs of Kent and Sussex requiring them to work with John de Burne and John Maidstone to acquire grain and other food supplies and to transport these to Winchelsea for transshipment to the royal forces in Wales.[62] Conspicuously missing from the surviving Chancery documents concerning the 1294–1295 campaign are letters of protection issued to merchants and requirements for sheriffs to hold army markets.

A major consequence of the government's decision to transform its logistical operations and expand the use of the royal right of purveyance to obtain supplies for the army was an increase in the responsibilities of the sheriffs. In conjunction with royal officials sent from the court, they not only were required to obtain supplies but also had the task of transporting them over land either to ports for transshipment, or directly to royal magazines. This reformed logistical system, and its land transportation component, was tested and refined through eleven years of war in Scotland during the last third of Edward's reign (1296–1207).

Thirteenth-Century England", *Economic History Review* 2nd series 10 (1957), 207–220, here 212; and Prestwich, *War, Politics and Finance*, 128. Now, however, see the study by David S. Bachrach, "Prices, Price Controls, and Market Forces in England under Edward I c. 1294–1307", *Haskins Society Journal* 20 (2009), 204–220 and in this volume, with the finding that royal officials tended to pay the going market rate in individual regions rather than imposing a fixed price set by the government.

57 Commenting on other aspects of royal military organization in this war, Prestwich, *Edward I*, 224 argues, "A study of the campaign of 1294–5 shows a well-oiled war machine in operation".

58 See the important discussion by Mark Kennedy Vaughn, "'Mount the War-Horses, Take your Lance in your Grip ...': Logistics Preparations for the Gascon Campaign of 1294", in *Thirteenth Century England VIII: Proceedings of the Durham Conference 1999*, ed. Michael Prestwich, Richard Britnell, and Robin Frame (Woodbridge, 2001), 97–111.

59 On this point, see Prestwich, *War, Politics and Finance*, 120.

60 *Calendar of Close Rolls 1288–1296*, 374.

61 With respect to John Maidstone's work in the Second Welsh War, see Prestwich, *War, Politics and Finance*, 119–120.

62 *CPR 1292–1301*, 151.

Land transportation during the Scottish Wars, 1296–1307

The intervention by the English government in Scottish affairs and particularly the decision by Edward to seize the Scottish crown resulted in an ongoing series of military campaigns over a period of eleven years to break local resistance and implant English rule. The military resources devoted to Edward I's Scottish wars were substantially larger than the commitments in manpower, supplies, and materiél that had been deployed to Wales.[63] As a consequence, the logistical system required to keep the many tens of thousands of royal troops supplied for years at a time grew correspondingly large and complex.

The quantities of supplies acquired and transported by sheriffs and royal clerks during the late 1290s and first years of the fourteenth century were exceptionally large.[64] In November 1297, royal clerks were appointed to work with the sheriffs of Lincolnshire, Yorkshire, Cambridgeshire and Huntingdonshire, and Nottinghamshire, to collect 18,050 quarters of wheat and oats for transport to blue-water and riverine ports from which the grain could be transshipped to the royal magazine and warehouses at Newcastle.[65] The sheriffs had to find vehicles and animals, therefore, to transport over 4,500 tons of supplies, entailing 4,500 wagon loads or 9,000 cart loads or most likely some combination of the two. In August 1301, Sheriff Hugh de Bushey of Lincolnshire, alone, received orders to transport 2,000 quarters, of wheat, oats, and beans to the royal magazine at Berwick.[66] In November 1301, additional Chancery writs were issued to the sheriffs of Surrey and Sussex, Worcestershire, and Gloucestershire, as well as Somerset and Dorset, requiring the acquisition and transport of 4,500 quarters of wheat and oats.[67] In May 1302, writs were issued to the sheriffs of Yorkshire, Lincolnshire, Norfolk and Suffolk, Cambridgeshire and Huntingdonshire, Nottinghamshire and Derbyshire, Essex, Sussex, Berkshire, and Middlesex requiring 15,000 quarters of oats, malt, and wheat to be transported overland to Berwick on Tweed, which had become the central magazine for operations in Scotland.[68] In December of that year, orders were issued by the Chancery to the sheriffs of nine counties requiring the delivery to Berwick of 19,300 quarters of grain, salt, beans, and peas, a total of almost 4,900 tons.[69]

---

63 For an overview of the manpower resources devoted to Edward's Scottish campaigns, see Prestwich, *War, Politics and Finance*, 94–99.
64 The efforts of magnates to secure supplies for their households outside of this system were rare and exceptionally minor in comparison to the tasks undertaken by the royal government through the sheriffs. On this point, see Prestwich, *War, Politics, and Finance*, 117–118.
65 *CPR 1292–1301*, 314.
66 *CPR 1296–1302*, 498.
67 *CPR 130–1307*, 3.
68 Ibid., 35
69 Ibid., 98–99. For similar orders throughout the period 1301–1307, see ibid., 109, 126, 129, 207, 208, 218, 417, 419, 423, 471, and 509.

The confirmation that these massive quantities of supplies were actually delivered by the sheriffs can be found in the accounts of the clerks and royal logistics officers stationed at the major royal magazines on the Scottish frontier and in Scotland. Thus, for example, Richard de Bremesgrave, the chief of the royal logistics office at Berwick, recorded that during the month of July 1299 Sheriff Richard Draycote of Lincolnshire sent 603 quarters of malt, beans, peas, and oats to Berwick. In August, the total was 1,291 quarters.[70] Richard Draycote sent an additional 707 quarters of malt and oats in July of that year that were recorded in the accounts of Robert Heron and John de Weston, two of Richard de Bremesgrave's senior aides.[71]

The royal government took three steps to help the sheriffs and the royal clerks sent to oversee their work obtain sufficient vehicles and animals to carry supplies to ports for transshipment to the royal magazines, to carry supplies directly over land to these magazines, and to provide vehicles and animals for use by the king's logistics officers operating in Scotland, itself. First, sheriffs were required to increase the number of vehicles and animals in their direct possession, or, more precisely, in the direct possession of their offices. The Pipe Roll for 1298–1299 shows, for example, that the sheriff of Yorkshire purchased nine carts (*carettae*) and twenty-seven cart horses.[72] These efforts, although they may have helped to fulfill some of the required carrying capacity, nevertheless were far from sufficient for the sheriffs' needs. In May 1302, alone, the sheriff of Yorkshire was required to purchase and transport 3,500 quarters of wheat, oats, and malt to Berwick.[73] This quantity of supplies amounted to 875 wagon loads or twice as many cartloads far outstripping the resources directly under the sheriff's control. Large numbers of additional vehicles and animals had to be found by the sheriffs to carry out their duties.

The second step taken by the royal government to ensure that the sheriffs had available sufficient transportation resources to carry out their duties was to have local authorities draw up detailed lists of the vehicles and animals in their jurisdictions suitable for use carrying the government's supplies. These lists were, in effect, highly specialized forms of the subsidy rolls drawn up by royal officials throughout Edward's reign to help facilitate the collection of taxes in money authorized by various parliaments to pay for the king's wars.[74] The original subsidy rolls detailed all of the property of the potential taxpayers. The transportation lists recorded only the types of vehicles and draught animals that individuals within local jurisdictions possessed.[75]

---

70 British Library ADD 37654 1v.
71 Ibid., 2v.
72 National Archives E 372/144 13v.
73 *CPR 1301–1307*, 35.
74 Concerning the organization of the subsidy rolls and royal taxation, see Prestwich, *War, Politics and Finance*, 177–185; and Langdon, *Horses, Oxen*, 184.
75 Ibid.

A document drawn up at the Exchequer from information gathered at Carlisle, for example, shows the efforts made by sheriffs and other royal officials to fulfill the insatiable need of the king's armies for transport during the Scottish wars.[76] The title of the Exchequer document makes clear that the information contained within was witnessed and sworn by twelve witnesses. The text is then divided into three portions. The first section, titled *De libertate episcopi* of Carlisle, gives the names of twenty-six men, each of whom has a number either of carts (*carettae*) or horses (*equi*) listed after his name. The aggregate total is thirteen carts and thirty-four horses. The second section titled *De libertate prioris* of Carlisle lists ten men having a total of nine carts and sixteen horses. The third section titled *De villata* of Carlisle lists sixty-five men having a total of thirty-four carts and 102 horses.[77] In sum, the royal government through its local officials, in this case the constable of Carlisle Castle, had a list of men in the town of Carlisle and in the immunities of priory and bishopric who could be called on to provide fifty-six carts and 154 horses for use by the army. A similar list produced early in the reign of Edward II, in 1309, by the sheriff of Sussex for the region of Chichester shows the continuation of royal policy regarding the identification of transportation resources.[78] This particular list included fifty-one men owning a total of fourteen carts, forty-seven horses, seven wagons, and seventy oxen.[79] It seems reasonable to conclude, based on the thoroughness of this particular document, that royal officials expected that it might be necessary to coerce individuals, through the right of purveyance, to provide transportation resources to the crown, and intended lists, such as the one compiled at Carlisle, to serve as the basis for this mobilization.

The effectiveness of these lists of vehicles and animals in facilitating the mobilization of transportation resources by the sheriffs and other officials is made clear in the records of the Wardrobe, which served as a major administrative office under Edward I for military affairs. The Wardrobe account for 1301, for example, notes explicitly that the thirty carts and 121 cart horses delivered to Berwick by Sheriff Richard Draycote of Lincolnshire in July of that year were obtained "*de diversibus hominibus ballive sue ... de Lincoln*".[80] The same Wardrobe account credits Ralph, the sheriff of Nottinghamshire and Derbyshire, for the money he spent to pay for the services of carts and horses from his county for transport duty to and from Newcastle. This included just over 20 s. that he had to pay to refurbish the carts that he had requisitioned from the people living in his county.[81] The same Wardrobe account records the rates paid by the government for animals and vehicles sent from the counties of Nottinghamshire and Derbyshire. Two-horse carts were paid at a rate of 14 d. per day on the outward trip and 9 d. per day on

76 National Archives E101/371/6.
77 Ibid.
78 E163/3/7.
79 Ibid.
80 British Library ADD 7966A 57v.
81 Ibid., 55r.

the return, when they were empty. Three horse carts were paid at the higher rate of 18 d. per day on the outward trip, but again only 9 d. per day on the return journey when the vehicles were empty.[82]

As the Exchequer document dealing with the mobilization of vehicles and animals at Carlisle, noted previously, suggests, the third step taken by the royal government to facilitate the efforts by sheriffs to transport supplies to the army was to eliminate the exemption from requisitions long enjoyed by ecclesiastical institutions. A circular letter issued by the Exchequer in 1306 provides detailed instructions to the sheriffs of thirteen counties, emphasizing both the types of equipment sought by the royal government and the types of animals that were required from the ecclesiastical institutions located in their jurisdictions.[83] Each cart (*charette*) was to be drawn by three horses. Each of the horses was to have a value of not less than 30 s. each but preferably of 40 s. Each wagon (*charr*) was to be drawn by six oxen. The sheriffs were to obtain these vehicles and animals from the abbots and priors in their jurisdictions, and were to provide these officials in turn with a duplicate copy of a *bone endenture*. These "good indentures" were to list the price of the carts and horses, or wagons and oxen, including all of the equipment (*tut latir*). The abbots and priors were to provide two men to drive each of the carts or wagons that were requisitioned from them. Both the sheriffs and the ecclesiastical officials were to keep a copy of the indenture affixed with the seals of both men. The ecclesiastical officials could then submit their copies of the indentures to the Wardrobe for payment. In the absence of significant damage to their vehicles or the loss of their animals, the abbots and priors were to received 12 d. (1 s.) a day for each day that their wagons and carts were in use by the king.[84] According to the final report issued by the Exchequer, the sheriffs in question mobilized eighty-four carts and thirty wagons, with 252 horses and 180 oxen.[85]

These church officials were paid a substantially lower daily rate for their vehicles, animals, and drivers than individuals whose two-horse carts were mobilized six years earlier by the sheriff of Nottinghamshire and Derbyshire, noted already. The difference in the rates granted to the ecclesiastical officials is even more striking when it is taken into account that the churchmen were required to send either three-horse carts, or the even larger wagons pulled by six oxen. Given the very large number of churchmen whose transportation resources were mobilized and the large number of counties involved, this can hardly be seen as an isolated incident, and may well represent the policy of the royal government of mobilizing the resources of the church to the benefit of the crown at a higher rate than that demanded of individual laymen.

---

82 Ibid., 55r.
83 E101/5/24.
84 Ibid.
85 Ibid.

Conclusion

The English government faced an increasingly difficult set of logistical challenges over the course of Edward I's reign as the size and duration of the royal military campaigns increased. During Edward's first Welsh campaign in 1277, the system of logistics inherited from Henry III proved sufficient for the limited aims of the royal government. The longer and substantially larger military undertaking of the Second Welsh War, which culminated in the conquest of this land, brought into clear focus the insufficiencies, particularly in the area of transport, of the English logistical systems. In particular, the use of two separate and competing supply networks caused delays and disruptions in the transportation of food and other goods to the royal armies operating in Wales in 1282–1283, and the Welsh campaign of 1287 made clear that merchants could not be relied upon to provide sufficient supplies in the absence of governmental mobilization of resources through its right of purveyance. The logistical system visible during the Welsh revolt of 1294–1295 and particularly during the Scottish campaigns of 1296–1307 show that the government had learned from the problems of the previous decade and had taken direct control over the provision of supplies to soldiers in the field and in garrisons. In order to facilitate the efforts of the sheriffs to carry out their now enormous responsibility for acquiring and transporting supplies, Edward's government vastly increased both the numbers of vehicles and draught animals subject to requisition. The church was now required to play its part materially in the king's wars, and perhaps even to help subsidize royal military efforts by accepting lower rates of reimbursement for transportation resources. In addition, the highly developed system of taxation with its extensive rolls of taxpayers' property was turned toward the identification of additional transportation resources subject to requisition by the sheriffs. In sum, the developments in the administrative systems undergirding the organization of land transport mirror the major developments of the English logistical system as a whole over the course of Edward I's reign. With respect to the broader question of the capabilities and responsibilities of government in thirteenth- and early fourteenth-century England, the changes in the land transportation system demonstrate the ability of Edward's officials to adjust to the evolving realities of warfare in a dynamic manner, solving problems not faced by their predecessors in the previous reign.

9

PRICES, PRICE CONTROLS, AND MARKET FORCES IN ENGLAND UNDER EDWARD I, C. 1294–1307[1]

Historians long have debated whether participation by the "state" in economic affairs in the West should be characterized, at the extremes, by a so-called command economy or rather by the free functioning of market forces. Because of a dearth of data that can be analyzed in a statistically significant manner, debates regarding economic affairs in the Classical Greek world, Rome, Late Antiquity, the Carolingian Empire, and its successor states up to Anglo-Norman England often have drawn on scattered pieces of pseudo-statistical information located largely in narrative sources. This rather thin corpus of information has provided considerable scope for the imposition by scholars of models that sustain their preconceived views regarding the organization of economic affairs.[2]

By contrast, the explosion of surviving administrative records in England from the reign of Henry II (1154–1189) onwards permits a far different approach to economic history. Rather than relying primarily on the information provided by laconic narrative sources, Domesday book and the Pipe Roll of 1130 are the major exception in the earlier period, scholars have available hundreds of thousands of documents that record the actual participation by the royal government in a very wide range of economic affairs. Documents stored at the National Archives and British Library, including those found in the liberate rolls, pipe rolls, patent rolls, close rolls, and Wardrobe Books, as well as writs, memoranda, letters,

---

1   I would like to thank my brother Professor Daniel Bachrach for his help with the statistics developed in this paper.

2   For an exceptionally valuable survey of economic historical theory of the ancient and late antique periods as it has developed over the past seventy years, see Ian Morris, "Foreword", to the M. I. Finley, *The Ancient Economy*, revised edn (Berkeley, CA, 1999), ix–xxxvi. Morris criticizes, in particular (xxvi–xxvii), empiricist critiques of Finley's economic model of the ancient and economy as being "undertheorized", arguing that "Their [empiricist] models are likely to be more realistic, in the sense that they account for more data and are contradicted by fewer facts, but they are also less likely to interest the large communities of social scientists and comparativists that Finley, Polanyi, and Weber reached". Now also see Michael Leese, "Kapêloi and Economic Rationality in Fourth-Century B.C.E. Athens", *Illinois Classical Studies* 42.1 (2017), 41–59, and the literature cited there, who makes clear that empiricist models are essential to understand real economic behavior.

inventories, and *compoti* produced by royal officials provide detailed and specific information about the prices paid by the kings of England for many scores of different types of items.

Despite the vast store of economic data available from this treasure trove of royal documents, however, it remains an open question whether the English kings permitted the free functioning of markets in England or imposed price controls on goods purchased by government officials. Some scholars, relying primarily on narrative sources, read as plain text, have argued that the English government imposed uniform rates of compensation on suppliers at lower than current market prices throughout the kingdom on a consistent basis.[3] Other scholars, most notably Michael Prestwich, have been less convinced regarding the widespread imposition of price controls.[4]

The enormous volume of data available for England makes it is necessary to limit this investigation into government policy toward price controls to a relatively brief period. In choosing a temporal focus, I have been influenced by the observations of numerous scholars who have identified societal stress, and particularly times of war, as significant stimuli toward governmental efforts to limit the functioning of markets through the imposition of various types of price controls.[5] A second important

---

3   J. L. Bolton, *The Medieval English Economy 1150–1500* (Totowa NY, 1980), for example, concludes (181) regarding the peasantry that "[T]hey were also liable to have crops and animals seized to provision the armies as the Crown exercised its right of purveyance—of taking supplies which might later be paid for, often at ridiculously low prices". Although Bolton provides no documentary evidence to support this conclusion, he does cite an unnamed "fourteenth-century rhymer" (185) to the effect that peasants were being crushed by the demands of the government for their cows and even their clothing. This "rhymer" may be the author of "song against the king's taxes", printed in *The Political Songs of England from the Reign of King John to that of Edward II*, ed. Thomas Wright (London, 1839, and repr. 1968), 182–187. J. R. Maddicott, *The English Peasantry and the Demands of the Crown, 1204–1341* (Oxford, 1975), 26–27, argues that the crown did occasionally offer less than market rates, or, at least, that royal officials did so. It is not clear from Maddicott's discussion whether he sees this as an abuse by royal officials at the local level, or whether this was royal policy. W. M. Ormrod, "The Crown and the English Economy, 1290–1348", in *Before the Black Death: Studies in the "Crisis" of the Early Fourteenth Century*, ed. Bruce M. S. Campbell (Manchester, 1991), 149–183, here, 175 emphasizes the purveyance of wool, which has less direct importance for military matters. Also see Ilana Krug, "Wartime Corruption and Complaints of the English Peasantry", in *Noble Ideals and Bloody Realities. Warfare in the Middle Ages*, ed. Niall Christie and Maya Yagizi (Leiden, 2006), 177–196, who argues for extensive abuse of purveyance during the reign of Edward I and his successors.

4   Michael Prestwich, *War, Politics and Finance under Edward I* (Totowa, NJ, 1972), 135.

5   On this point, see Richard Bonney, "France, 1494–1815," in *The Rise of the Fiscal State in Europe, c. 1200–1815*, ed. idem (Oxford, 1999), 123–176, here 161, who emphasizes that "The motor of fiscal change in France, as for all the major European monarchies was expenditure on war"; Gwynne Lewis, "'Fiscal States': Taxes, War, Privilege and the Emergence of the European 'Nation State', c. 1200–1800", *French History* 15 (2001), 51–63, where she reviews the state of the field and argues (54) for a consensus that the costs of waging war played a central role in the creation of the centralized taxation structures, and a thorough exploitation of the economy to fund governmental policies. This consensus reiterates the position taken by Charles Tilly, in his

factor in my selection of a period for a focused investigation is the fact that Edward I's government (1272–1307) was reported by many contemporaries to have undertaken very substantial measures to intervene in the market economy.

Among the many charges leveled against Edward I was the complaint that royal officials imposed draconian burdens on the population to pay for the king's wars and to obtain supplies for the king's armies.[6] Walter of Guisborough, for example, writing shortly after the events in question, described the king as excusing himself in the aftermath of the crisis of 1297 "for the exactions and prises which he had taken from the people".[7] Making the case for popular opposition to Edward's exactions, Walter presents the supporters of Humphrey de Bohun, earl of Hereford and marshal, as saying that "they and the whole community of the land were burdened more than they could bear by the unjust exactions, tallages, and prises".[8]

Perhaps the single most widely criticized tool employed by royal officials was the *prise*, mentioned by Walter, often referred to as purveyance.[9] The kings of England long had possessed the right to compel the sale of supplies to the crown with payment to be made at later date. During the reigns of Henry II and his successors, this tool generally had been limited to use in supplying the court, although there were some exceptions. Henry II, for example, used the royal right of *prise* to collect more than 2,000 tons of wheat, oats, and beans, as well as thousands of pigs to provide supplies to army invading Ireland in 1171.[10]

---

influential study, *Coercion, Capital and European States, AD 990-1992*, 2nd edn (Cambridge, 1992). With respect to the Angevin context, see the recent study by Nick Barratt, "Finance on a Shoestring: The Exchequer in the Thirteenth Century", in *English Government in the Thirteenth Century*, ed. Adrian Jobson (Woodbridge, 2004), 71–86, here, 80.

6 For a detailed discussion of the complaints raised against the use of purveyance by Edward's officials, see Prestwich, *War, Politics and Finance*, 129–136; idem *Documents Illustrating the Crisis of 1297–1298 in England* (London, 1980), 12–13; and Maddicott, *The English Peasantry*, 15–34. More recently with specific attention to the purveyance of transportation resources, see David S. Bachrach, "Military Logistics in the Reign of Edward I of England, 1272–1307", *War in History* 13.4 (2006), 421–438, and also in this volume.

7 *The Chronicle of Walter of Guisborough*, ed. H. Rothwell (London, 1957), 291, "*Excusavit etiam se rex de exaccionibus et prisis quas a populo susceperat*". This passage is discussed in some detail by J. R. Maddicott, "'1258' and '1297': Some Comparisons and Contrasts", in *Thirteenth-Century England IX: Proceedings of the Durham Conference 2001*, ed. Michael Prestwich, Richard Britnell, and Robin Frame (Woodbridge, 2003), 1–14, here 4.

8 *Walter of Guisborough*, 291, "*non solum ipsi sed tota communitas terre gravata erat et utlra modum de iniustis vexationibus tallagiis et prisis*".

9 The most thorough treatment of purveyance is now Krug, "Wartime Corruption", 177–196 . Also see Bachrach, "Military Logistics", 421–438.

10 The payments for these supplies by sheriffs are recorded in *The Great Roll of the Pipe for the Seventeenth Year of the Reign of King Henry the Second, AD 1170–1171* (London, 1893); and *The Great Roll of the Pipe for the Eighteenth Year of the Reign of King Henry the Second, AD 1171–1172* (London, 1894). For a discussion of the supplying of this expedition, see Prestwich, *War, Politics and Finance*, 118; and David L. Farmer, "Some Price Fluctuations in Angevin England", *The Economic History Review* new series 9 (1956), 34–43, who provides details regarding

However, the massively increased level of military activity under Edward I, who launched wars of conquest in Wales and Scotland, and fought defensive wars against the French in both Flanders and Gascony, required an enormous expansion of the use of the prise/purveyance to assure the regular supply of provisions to royal armies in the field and to garrisons stationed in royal fortifications.[11] The increased scope and size of the royal requisitioning of supplies brought with it an increased number of instances of corruption, graft, violence, theft, and other malfeasance by royal officials against a larger number of subjects. This group of affected agricultural producers included a substantial number of influential churchmen and gentry, as can be seen not only in complaints by the authors of narrative sources, but also in the proliferation of suits brought in royal courts against royal officials.[12]

The tempo of military campaigning and, therefore, of the need for enormous quantities of supplies increased markedly during the mid-1290s, and continued throughout the remainder of Edward's reign. The final third of Edward's reign, therefore, which included the Welsh war of 1294–1295, the Flanders campaign of 1297, the wars against the French in Gascony 1294–1298, and the Scottish wars of 1296–1307, is particularly important for assessing whether royal participation in the grain and livestock markets of England, e.g. two of the most important aspects of the English economy, was based on a policy of using royal edicts to impose price controls.[13]

Quantitative studies

Any assessment of royal participation in agricultural markets in England broadly must begin with a discussion of David Farmer's studies on grain and livestock prices for the thirteenth and early fourteenth centuries, first published in 1957 and 1969, and then recapitulated in 1988.[14] Farmer identified a "national price" level

---

the actual prices paid by Henry II's officials. For a discussion of the campaign, now see John D. Hosler, *Henry II: A Medieval Soldier at War, 1147–1189* (Leiden, 2007), 70–76.

11 For an overview of Edward's campaigns during the final third of his reign, see Prestwich, *War, Politics and Finance*, passim; idem, *Edward I*, 2nd edn (New Haven, CT, 1997), 376–555; and Bachrach, "Military Logistics", 421–438.

12 Regarding legal complaints made against royal officials with citations to the documents, see Prestwich, *War, Politics and Finance*, 132; and Krug, "Wartime Corruption", 177–196 and the literature cited there.

13 Prestwich, *War, Politics and Finance*, 134–135, indicates that there were no complaints that Edward I's officials imposed abnormally low prices on sellers, although there were numerous complaints regarding the failure to pay for supplies that were taken. When considering this question, however, Prestwich focuses his attention on the plea rolls rather than on the actual prices paid by royal officials for grain over the course of Edward's reign and across various regions.

14 D. L. Farmer, "Some Grain Price Movements in Thirteenth-Century England", *Economic History Review* new series 2 (1957), 207–220; idem, "Some Livestock Price Movements in Thirteenth Century England", *Economic History Review* second series 22 (1969), 1–16; and idem, "Prices

for four types of grain: wheat, rye, barley, and oats; as well as six types of animals used for labor and food: oxen, plough horses, cart horses, pigs, cows, and sheep. Farmer derived this "national price" level from the average price obtained for these agricultural commodities within fifteen regional districts, located in central, eastern, and southern England. Most of the price data was taken from the extensive series of pipe rolls produced from the records of the estates of the bishops of Winchester covering the long century from 1205–1325, with substantial additional information provided for the early thirteenth century from published pipe rolls from the reign of King John.[15] For the period c. 1240 onwards, Farmer supplemented the Winchester material, with price data obtained from the accounts of the stewards of sixty-six manors held by earls of Norfolk, Merton College Oxford, Westminster Abbey, Crowland Abbey, and several smaller estates.[16]

Farmer used the data from the Winchester pipe rolls and supporting materials to draw several conclusions about the general price structure of grain and livestock prices over the course of the thirteenth century and about the effects of various stimuli on those prices. He concluded that long-term price structure, at least as defined by the prices obtained by the manor stewards surveyed, was inflationary with respect to the cost of grain and livestock in silver, as represented by the minted silver coins of the Angevin and Plantagenet kings. The rise in value of grain and livestock relative to silver was particularly pronounced in the period after c. 1265. Within this overall inflationary trend, four major currency reforms under John, Henry III, and Edward I had the effect, in Farmer's view, of lowering of the cost of grain and livestock, as measured in silver, at least over the short term.[17]

From a methodological perspective, it must be noted that in presenting a "national price" that was, itself, an average of the average prices of the fifteen regions, Farmer's data is problematic. First, it is to be noted that Farmer's sources provide virtually no price data from the southwest or from the north, including the exceptional important region of Yorkshire, in the period that included Edward

---

and Wages", in *The Agrarian History of England and Wales: II 1042–1350*, ed. Joan Thirsk (Cambridge, 1988), 715–817. Regarding local markets, with a specific focus on London and its hinterland, see Bruce M. S. Campbell, James A. Galloway, Derek Keene, and Margaret Murphy, *A Medieval Capital and its Grain Supply: Agrarian Production and Distribution in the London Region c. 1300* (London, 1993).

15 See Farmer, "Grain", 210–211, and idem, "Livestock", 1.

16 Farmer, "Grain", 210.

17 Farmer, "Livestock", 12–13. Farmer's general conclusions regarding the role of the supply of silver coins on the nominal price of agricultural products were supported by P. D. A. Harvey, "The English Inflation of 1180–1220", *Past and Present* 61 (1973), 3–30. More recently, however, Farmer's conclusions have been called into question, at least for the first half of the thirteenth century, by J. L. Bolton, "Inflation, Economics and Politics in Thirteenth-Century England", in *Thirteenth Century England IV: Proceedings of the Newcastle upon Tyne Conference 1991*, ed. P. R. Coss and S. D. Lloyd (Woodbridge, 1992), 1–14.

I's reign.[18] In addition, Farmer does not provide the range of prices obtained by estate stewards within each district, the modal prices in each district, or the weighted average prices for commodities within these districts. The absence of this information makes it impossible to determine whether there was a standard price in the districts, and whether there were significant price variations within and between districts over time. As a result, it is not possible to ascertain whether the data obtained from the stewards of the bishops of Winchester are indicative of the prices obtained by other agricultural producers in these same localities and regions. In effect, Farmer does not solve the problem of whether the bishops of Winchester enjoyed "market power", that is the ability of a major seller to alter current market conditions in its own interest.[19] In addition, without information about the price variations within regions, it is not possible to determine whether there were regional or, instead, local markets and prices.

In discussing livestock prices, Farmer addresses these issues at a macro level when he compares average prices for all livestock within five of the regions to his 'national price'. (Such a comparison assumes, of course, that the markets were regional rather than local). Farmer concludes, for example, that in the south Hampshire region the average prices for the six types of livestock noted earlier were approximately 10 percent below the 'national price level' in the decade from 1295–1305.[20] While such a comparison suggests differential prices between large regions, it does not shed light on the question of price variability within regions, e.g. whether there were local as well as regional markets prices for pigs. A further problem is that Farmer does not provide detailed price information for individual types of livestock within regions. Therefore, it is not clear whether the prices for the six types of livestock move uniformly in the same direction.

It is important to note the limitations on the information presented by Farmer because scholars have tended to use the "national price" rates for various grains and livestock to provide a context for a discussion of royal purchases of these same commodities.[21] However, royal officials did not purchase goods on a national

---

18 Farmer, "Grain", 210.
19 With regard to the danger that the "context" of a particular sale might skew the price of an item, see Latimer, "Early Thirteenth-Century Prices", 43.
20 Farmer, "Livestock", 11.
21 Prestwich, *War, Politics and Finance*, 135, uses Farmer's grain price data to conclude that royal officials obtained better prices for their own produce from the purveyors than were paid to other men. N. J. Mayhew, "Money and Prices in England from Henry II to Edward III", *Agricultural History Review* 35 (1987), 121–132, here 23, identifies Farmer's grain price data as the preferred index to use for calculating inflation in grain markets. W. M. Ormrod, "Royal Finance in Thirteenth-Century England", in *Thirteenth Century England V: Proceedings of the Newcastle upon Tyne Conference 1993*, ed. P. R. Coss and S. D. Lloyd (Woodbridge, 1995), 141–164, here 142 and 163–164, uses Farmer's 'national price' to calculate the quantity of wheat and the number of oxen that the money of account held by the crown would purchase over four extended periods. Paul Latimer, "Early Thirteenth-Century Prices", in *King John: New Interpretations*, ed. S. D. Church (Woodbridge, 1999), 41–73, here 41–46, provides a detailed overview of some

level, but rather on a local level, so that such comparisons are, at best, problematic. Moreover, when discussing the massive quantities of supplies obtained by royal officials in the north, particularly from Yorkshire, and also the significant purchases made by royal officials in the far west, in Devon and Cornwall, Farmer's 'national price' provides no guidance at all because he provides no data from these regions.

In light, therefore, of the importance of Farmer's studies in shaping discussions regarding the economic history of Angevin and Plantagenet England, this paper has two goals. First, it seeks to ascertain whether the government's use of purveyance to obtain supplies for the army was coupled with an effort to control prices. As such, what is at issue is whether the price levels for grain and livestock appear to have been fixed by government agents either within regions or across regions. Secondly, by offering an analysis of the prices paid by royal officials for grain and livestock, this study will clarify the value of Farmer's 'national price' for contextualizing the purchase of grain and livestock by the king's officials

The price data used in this study is derived from a random sample of the information provided by account books of royal clerks engaged in the purchase of grain and livestock, Wardrobe accounts for the payments of debts incurred by

---

of the methodological pitfalls that can be anticipated in Farmer's development of data, most of which, in Latimer's view, Farmer successfully avoids. These difficulties include the possibility that any particular price might be atypical, that the samples of prices might be biased toward particular localities, and that prices might be distorted by the particular contexts in which goods are sold. However, Latimer does suggest (43–44) that Farmer's data does not avoid the problem that when, "the geographical or the contextual bias in the sample of prices undergoes a definite and sustained change, there is the risk that the price series before this change cannot be treated as at all comparable to the price series after this change". Latimer identifies this source problem chiefly in the Exchequer Pipe Roll records used by Farmer for the early part of his price ranges rather than in the Winchester Pipe Roll data from which he extracted most of his data regarding prices in the second half of the thirteenth century and the early fourteenth century. Most recently, Maryanne Kowaleski, "A Consumer Economy", in *A Social History of England, 1200–1500*, ed. Rosemary Horrox and W. Mark Ormrod (Cambridge, 2006), 238–259, here 241, uses Farmer's data in "Prices and Wages", in *The Agrarian History of England and Wales, II* (Cambridge, 1988), 715–817, as the basis for calculating the amount of labor that was necessary to purchase a fixed "market-basket" of consumables over time.

Some skepticism regarding the value of some of Farmer's findings has been raised. Bolton, "Inflation", 5, notes that Farmer may have been more aware of the limitations on the value of his data than have been scholars who have used his studies. In this regard, Bolton points specifically to A. R. Bridbury, "Thirteenth-Century Prices and the Money Supply", *Agricultural History Review* 33 (1985), 1–21. In particular, Bridbury (2) states, "As a result of Dr. Farmer's exhaustive labours in the archives, we can be reasonably confident of knowing as much as we are ever likely to know about the trends of grain prices in the thirteenth century".

An important exception to the reliance on Farmer's data is Campbell *et al.*, *A Medieval Capital*, in which the authors make use of London city records, chronicle sources, royal judicial records, and royal administrative records, including some purveyance documents, inquisitions *post mortem*, as well as the types of manorial records utilized by Farmer. See the discussion of the sources in *A Medieval Capital*, 13–23.

royal officials, writs of *liberate* to royal officials who had paid for supplies out of local revenues, and receipt records of royal officials at major supply bases, such as Berwick, Carlisle, and Perth during the period 1294–1307. The broader corpus of texts dealing with prices paid by royal officials, from which this sample is drawn, is provided as Appendix 1. The value of a random sample is that it provides a statistically valid representation of the total corpus of data. In statistical terms, because we simply cannot "know" the full extent of the data set, much of which is now lost, the random sample is the only way we can really have any confidence that the data upon which we are basing our conclusions is in any way representative of the population from which it is drawn, or more accurately, that the sample does not in any *systematic way*, bias the conclusions we can draw about the population from which the sample is drawn. Because the price data here has been derived from a random sample, the patterns of prices paid by royal officials that are attested in the set of documents used in this study can be understood to reflect the general practices of the royal government officials with respect to their participation in the grain and livestock markets over the last third of Edward I's reign. In addition, the actual prices paid by royal officials in a given region and year can be understood to reflect the prices paid for the broader set of purchases made by royal officials in those regions during those years.

Purchases of grain and livestock by royal officials

In early 1294, negotiations between French and English representatives regarding the settlement of damages done to French merchants in the Channel by English "pirates" broke down. In anticipation of punitive action by King Philip IV (1285–1314) against Gascony, Edward I ordered the mobilization of an English force. These troops were to be sent to the continent to undertake a campaign of disruption against French-held cities and other fortifications along the Gascon frontiers.[22] The authority for obtaining and transporting supplies for this campaign was placed in the hands of John Maidstone, who had held a similar office during the Second Welsh War of 1282–1284.[23] The *compotus* that John submitted for audit at the Exchequer after the campaign of 1294–1295 included a detailed list of the quantities of grain obtained from Sussex, Surrey, Somerset, and Dorset. This document indicates by name and location the individuals from whom the grain

---

22 For an account of the 1294 expedition, see Prestwich, *Edward I*, 376–382; and Mark Kennedy Vaughn, "'Mount the War-Horses, Take your Lance in your Grip ...': Logistics Preparations for the Gascon Campaign of 1294", in *Thirteenth Century England VIII: Proceedings of the Durham Conference 1999*, ed. Michael Prestwich, Richard Britnell, and Robin Frame (Woodbridge, 2001), 97–111.

23 Prestwich, *War, Politics and Finance*, 120, for John Maidstone's service in the Welsh war. See National Archives E101/4/30 for the *compotus* of John for the planned 1294 campaign in Gascony. Maidstone's accounts for the 1294 Gascon campaign, receive particular attention from Vaughn, "Logistics", 97–111.

was purchased, the prices that each individual was paid per quarter of grain, and the transportation costs for this grain from the counties to Portsmouth.[24]

In reviewing John's accounts, it immediately becomes clear that royal officials operating in these four counties purchased oats at a wide variety of prices. The modal price paid by royal officials in Surrey and Sussex per quarter of oats was 3 s.[25] Dozens of landowners in these two counties, however, received substantially higher prices for their oats. The knight Henry of Guildford, for example, was paid 3 s. 4 d. per quarter for his twenty quarters.[26] The abbot of Beaulieu, located in Hampshire, similarly received 3 s. 4 d. for oats from the monastery's Surrey properties, as did the rectors of the churches of Clearfield and Droxford.[27] The same and even higher prices were paid to a dozen other property holders in Surrey, including John de Warenne, earl of Surrey (1240–1304), who was paid 3 s. 6 d. for nine quarters of oats from his estates.[28]

High social status was not, however, a guarantee of receiving a particularly high price for one's oats. The knight Roger de Insula, for example, received only 3 s. per quarter for his oats.[29] At the other end of the social spectrum, many scores of farmers were paid substantially lower prices for their oats by royal officials. By contrast with higher prices paid in Surrey and Sussex, the modal price per quarter oats remitted by royal officials in Somerset and Dorset was 2 s. 4 d. Moreover, in these western counties, royal clerks paid as little as 1 s. 1 d. to several dozen sellers for a total of 185 quarters of oats.[30]

In considering this random sample of data from Surrey, Sussex, Dorset, and Somerset, in the summer of 1294, the wide range of prices paid by royal officials for oats makes clear that Edward's government did not impose a fixed price per quarter of oats on farmers in these counties. In general, higher ranking individuals, both ecclesiastical and lay, appear to have received a higher price for their oats than did other farmers. This premium may indicate a desire by royal officials to avoid conflicts with important individuals, or even to win their support for royal policies. However, the premium over the modal price certainly was not limited to

---

24 A quarter, which consisted of 8 bushels, was fixed by the royal government at 504 pounds in 1296. Concerning the weight of the quarter, see Ronald Edward Zupko, *British Weights and Measures: A History from Antiquity to the Seventeenth Century* (Madison, WI, 1977), 22. Michael Prestwich, "Victualling Estimates for English Garrisons in Scotland during the Early Fourteenth Century", *The English Historical Review* 82 (1967), 536–543, here 537, suggests a quarter weight of 380 pounds of 16 ounces each.

25 National Archives E101/4/30 3v. Vaughn, "Logistics", 106, is concerned only with the oats purchased in Surrey and Sussex, not in Somerset and Dorset, and is not concerned with the differing prices paid by royal officials, or local officials acting on behalf of John Maidstone. Vaughn places the total quantity of oats purchased in Surrey and Sussex at 2,686.75 quarters.

26 National Archives E101/4/30 3v.

27 Ibid., 4r.

28 Ibid., 4r.

29 Ibid.

30 Ibid., 8v–9r.

high-ranking individuals. Among the highest prices obtained from royal officials in all four counties was 3 s. 8 d. per quarter paid to an untitled man named Galfrid Damel in Surrey.[31] Several other fortunate but untitled farmers received as much as 4 s. 3 d. for their total of forty-seven quarters of oats in Surrey.[32] Factors other than the social status of the seller may have played a role in the price paid by royal officials for oats. These include the quality of the grain, and the negotiating skills of the farmer.

John Maidstone's account records the payments made for more than 400 wagons that transported the grain that had been purchased to Portsmouth.[33] The expedition to Gascony departed in October 1294, which provides a *terminus ante quem* for the arrival of the grain at Portsmouth, allowing time for the recording and loading of the cargoes of oats and other supplies. As a result, price differences that were caused by the changes in supply and demand over the course of the year can be excluded as having had a bearing on the costs incurred on behalf of the royal government by John Maidstone and his staff in 1294.

A similar pattern of price diversity can be seen in a Wardrobe account for the regnal year running from November 1300 to November 1301, which recorded, among many other matters, the receipt of supplies at Berwick by Richard de Bremesgrave, the chief logistics officer at this supply base.[34] Four Gascon merchants, who arrived at Berwick in the late summer of 1301, received two separate prices for their wine. William Bidal, Bernardus de Scander, both from the town of Montsak, as well as Durandus de Compessours and John de Viners were paid 53 s. 4 d. each for 29 tuns (*dolia*) and 50 s. each for 20 tuns.[35] As was true regarding oats and other grains, discussed earlier, the quality of the product may well have been a factor in determining the price paid by Richard de Bremesgrave for these tuns, although his account does not shed additional light on this matter.[36] More important, perhaps, when considering the question of governmental price controls, is the decision made by these four Gascon merchants to sail from southwestern France some 850 nautical miles all the way up the eastern coast of England to sell their wares. It seems unlikely that they undertook this arduous and potentially dangerous journey in the expectation of receiving a low fixed price for their wine.

A Wardrobe account for the next year (Nov. 1301– Nov. 1302), provides exceptionally detailed records regarding the prices paid by royal officials for both

---

31 Ibid., 4v.

32 Ibid., 3r.

33 Ibid., 2r. Concerning the importance of the time of year in effecting the price of grain, see Farmer, "Grain", 215.

34 British Library MS ADD 37654.

35 Ibid., 11v.

36 Richard de Bremesgrave's accounts tend to emphasize when goods were of poor quality, but not when they were of good quality. See in this context National Archives E101/12/32 nr 2 where Richard reports that the grain that he received from the Isle of Wight was "fere putrefacti".

grain supplies and livestock that subsequently were transported to Berwick.[37] Again, it is clear that price diversity is the rule. The sheriff of Norfolk and Suffolk, for example, dispatched 500 quarters of wheat to the supply base on the Scottish frontier. Roughly half of the wheat, 260 quarters or about 65 tons, had been purchased for a price of 4 s. 6 d. per quarter. The remaining 240 quarters had been purchased for 4 s. 2 d., for a difference of almost 8 percent.[38]

This important price variation was not limited to wheat. The sheriff of Southampton, for example, purchased 300 pigs for six separate prices from 3 s. 6 d. to 4 s. 6 d., a range of almost 20 percent.[39] The sheriff of Lincolnshire, for his part, shipped to Berwick 886 quarters of oats, for which he paid two separate prices, and 1,072 quarters of malted barley, for which he paid five separate prices ranging from 3 s. to 4 s. 2 d. per quarter.[40] The range in the prices paid by the sheriff of Lincolnshire for this barley was more than 35 percent.

In 1304, the royal clerk Ralph Dalton, who was responsible for overseeing purveyance for Edward's army in the north, undertook a major purchasing operation in Yorkshire. There, he and his subordinates, working with the sheriff's clerks, collected 2,598 quarters of wheat, barley, beans, and oats, which were then transported by ship to forces operating in Scotland.[41] Of the 800 quarters of wheat purchased by Ralph in the city of York and its environs, 280 cost 5 s. per quarter, 320 cost 4 s. 6 d., and 250 cost 4 s. This works out to a range of 20 percent from lowest to highest price.

Wardrobe accounts for the Scottish war in 1306 present a very similar pattern of price diversity.[42] John Dean, the sheriff of Shropshire and Staffordshire, paid two separate prices for 1,180 quarters of wheat, at 5 s. and 4 s. 6 d. per quarter, as well as two separate prices for 1,187 quarters of oats, at 3 s. and 2 s. 6 d. per quarter.[43] Information in this particular Wardrobe account is corroborated by a memorandum issued earlier in the year by the Exchequer noting these same purchases by the sheriff.[44] John Dean's colleagues in Norfolk and Suffolk, Cornwall, Yorkshire, the Holderness region of Yorkshire, as well as the royal official Walter de Huntercombe at Edinburgh similarly participated in the various local grain markets rather than imposing fixed rates of compensation, paying several different prices for each type of commodity.[45] The sheriff of Yorkshire, for example, purchased 1,091 quarters of wheat, paying two prices for this commodity, 5 s. and

---

37 British Library MS ADD 7699A.
38 Ibid., 51v.
39 Ibid., 52r.
40 Ibid., 52r.
41 National Archives E101/12/8 1r, 4r, 5r.
42 National Archives E101/369/11.
43 Ibid., 71v.
44 National Archives E101/13/11.
45 National Archives E101/369/11 71r–75r, and 90r.

4 s. 6 d. Similarly, he paid two different prices, 2 s. 8 d. and 2 s. 6 d., for 1,720 quarters of oats.[46]

The evidence of variable prices makes clear that King Edward's government permitted the free functioning of markets within and between counties and did not attempt to impose price controls through the *prise* or right of purveyance. The time of the year in which purchases were made certainly affected the costs of agricultural commodities. However, even when it is clear, as is the case with the data from 1294, discussed earlier, that all of the purchases of a particular commodity were made in the same season, the same pattern of price diversity holds. This conclusion regarding the functioning of regional and even local markets is supported not only by the variability in the prices paid by royal officials, but also by the fact that there exists only a single order that requires the imposition of a fixed price.[47] This point requires emphasis. Arguments *ex silentio* for the imposition of price controls would require that *all* but one such order for a dozen campaigns have disappeared while an enormous quantity of other data survived.

This is not to say that royal involvement in the market was free of coercion and fraud. The volume of complaints lodged against royal officials for malfeasance during this period certainly permits the conclusion that some individual sellers, having been compelled to part with their grain and livestock, were then cheated. In addition, it seems clear that despite royal commands to the contrary, some farmers with small holdings were forced to sell grain and livestock they required to sustain their own households.[48] However, in the aggregate, payment by royal officials of several, and in some cases, many prices for the same commodity in the same region in the same year and in the same season make clear that numerous factors other than royally sanctioned price-fixing were at work. On the question of price controls, Edward's government appears to have eschewed an extreme version of the so-called command economy, preferring to permit local markets to function.

The "national price" in perspective

Despite Farmer's observation that "the term 'national price level' is perhaps a little misleading", many scholars have used his longitudinal price studies to provide a context for discussions of the economic behavior of the royal government, without the serious qualifications needed to make clear the statistical problems inherent in Farmer's data.[49] Aside from the methodological difficulties regarding Farmer's selective presentation of his data, discussed already, scholars hoping to

---

46   Ibid., 73v.
47   This set of fixed prices was set out in 1296 and can be found in National Archives E159/70 mm 119–120. On this point, see Prestwich, *War, Politics and Finance*, 128.
48   Prestwich, *War, Politics and Finance*, 136.
49   For Farmer's comment, see "Grain Price Movements", 210. With regard to the use of Farmer's data, see n. 20.

use his year to year price calculations and the "national price" face an even more important question. Is it legitimate to consider the prices obtained by the bishops of Winchester for their agricultural commodities as representative of the prices obtained by other agricultural producers?

Although Farmer does not provide data regarding the aggregate quantities of grain and numbers sold by Winchester's stewards, it is undeniable that these were dwarfed by the sales of hundreds of thousands of tons of grain, and tens of thousands of pigs, cows, sheep, and oxen to the royal government during the period 1294–1307 by myriad agricultural producers throughout England.[50] Farmer's calculation of a "national price" simply does not take into account the prices paid by the royal government to a vast number of sellers for enormous quantities of agricultural commodities in this period. It is clear, therefore, that the price data generated by a very small number of estates in a limited region of England cannot represent a "national price". It is also clear that scholars cannot use this limited amount of data to draw general conclusions, at least in this period, about royal policies, inflation, or other economic matters.

The following two examples, which could be multiplied many times, demonstrate that Farmer's data from Winchester's estates is insufficiently robust either to draw conclusions about royal participation in agricultural markets in those regions of England where Winchester held estates or to develop a super-regional price for central, eastern, and southern England. They further show the dangers that can arise when trying to generalize from Farmer's data.

According to Farmer's calculations for pigs, the "national price" in 1301 was 2 s. 9.75 d. per pig.[51] In the south Hampshire region, however, Farmer calculated that the bishops of Winchester received, on average, only 90 percent of the "national price" in the decade ending in 1305. Farmer did not have sufficient data points from the Winchester material to provide averages over the shorter term. As a result, it is not possible to determine, on the basis of his reported findings, whether there were statistically significant fluctuations in any given year from the lower "regional price" in the south Hampshire region. Nevertheless, if one takes the 90 percent rate for the decade ending in 1305 as being valid for 1301, then the south Hampshire "regional price" should be just a fraction over 2 s. 6.5 d. Table 9.1 lists the prices paid by royal officials in Southampton, located in the south Hampshire region, for pigs in 1301, and compares this price in percentage terms with both the "national price" for 1301 and the south Hampshire "regional price/adjusted national price" calculated on the basis of the 90 percent rate provided by Farmer for the decade ending in 1305.[52]

---

50 Regarding the extraordinarily large quantities of food stuffs purchased by the royal government during this period, see Prestwich, *War, Politics and Finance*, 114–136; and more recently Bachrach, "Military Logistics in the Reign of Edward I of England", passim.

51 Farmer, "Livestock Price Movements", 5.

52 This data is taken from British Library ADD 7699A 52r.

Table 9.1   Pig prices in Southampton in 1301

Number of pigs	Price per pig	Percentage difference from national price	Percentage difference from adjusted national price
15	3 s. 6 d.	+24%	+36%
30	3 s. 10 d.	+36%	+50%
55	4 s.	+42%	+56%
95	4 s. 2 d.	+48%	+63%
45	4 s. 4 d.	+54%	+69%
60	4 s. 6 d.	+60%	+76%

As this table makes clear, the lowest price paid by royal officials for pigs in 1301 in the south Hampshire region was 24 percent higher than Farmer's figure for the "national price" that year. Moreover, and even more strikingly, the lowest price paid for pigs in Southampton in 1301 was 36 percent higher than one would expect following Farmer's guide to the adjusted "national price" or "regional price" for livestock. The differences are even more compelling when considering the modal price of 4 s. 2 d. paid to the royal government to numerous sellers, which gives a 48 percent higher unit cost than the "national price" and a 63 percent higher unit cost for the "regional price". Clearly, scholars who attempt to use Farmer's data to calculate the purchasing power of the royal shilling in 1301 would be seriously misled with regard to the costs of pigs, at least in the south Hampshire region.

From a statistical perspective regarding the broader corpus of data from which this commodity sample was drawn, that is pigs, it should be noted that these animals serve as an operational proxy as a mechanism to test the utility of a sample in order to draw conclusions about the characteristics of the population from which it is drawn. Given the enormous divergence from what would be expected given Farmer's figures for regional livestock prices in South Hampshire, the pig data seriously diminishes the trust that scholars can have in the descriptive value of Farmer's data set as a whole.

The second set of data to be considered here concerns the prices paid by the royal government per quarter of oats in 1306. As noted earlier, Farmer does not provide information regarding the underlying "regional prices" that made up the national price for oats. As a result, it is not possible to provide the more detailed comparison found in the last column of the first table. Table 9.2, therefore, compares the price paid by royal officials for oats in percentage terms with Farmer's "national price". The "national price" calculated by Farmer for a quarter of oats in 1306 was 2 s. 6 d.

In considering the information in Table 9.2, it is clear that the prices paid for these oats varied considerably between counties, and also within some counties. In addition, it can be seen that the royal government paid a full third more for oats in Essex and Hereford than one might expect based on Farmer's "national price". Royal officials paid 20 percent less than Farmer's "national price" in Norfolk and Suffolk.

172

Table 9.2   Price per quarter of oats in central, eastern, and southern England in 1306[a]

County	Number of quarters	Price per quarter	Difference from "national price"
Norfolk and Suffolk	950	2 s.	−20%
Salop and Stafford	180	3 s.	+20%
Salop and Stafford	1,006	2 s. 6 d.	no difference
Essex and Hereford	500	3 s. 4 d.	+33%
Canterbury and Huntingdon	485	2 s. 8 d.	+7%

[a] This data is taken from National Archives E101/13/4 71r–75r.

This enormous range in prices paid by royal officials helps to illustrate the additional considerable problems involved in using Farmer's data to draw conclusions about economic matters, generally, and about royal economic policies, in particular. An unwary scholar attempting to use Farmer's "national price" to discuss, for example, the price paid to an abbot in Essex for his oats might well come away with the impression that this ecclesiastical official was receiving extraordinarily good treatment at the hands of royal officials. Conversely, a scholar might conclude on the basis of the price paid to a peasant in Lancashire for his oats that this peasant was receiving far less than the "national price" and, therefore, was being cheated by royal officials. Neither of these conclusions, however, would be warranted.

There are two related problems here. First, as suggested by the data regarding pigs, discussed earlier, it is not at all clear that the Winchester data compiled by Farmer actually is representative of contemporary prices for agricultural commodities. It is not, therefore, justifiable to use Farmer's price data as the baseline against which other price data must be compared. Secondly, even if we were to grant Farmer's data the benefit of the doubt with regard to its status as representative of contemporary prices, it is inappropriate to compare prices paid in Essex or Suffolk against a "national price" when attempting to understand the activities of royal officials who are purchasing agricultural commodities at the local level. Farmer, himself, as noted, describes his "national price" as the average of fifteen regional prices. However, Farmer does not provide any information about these regional prices for grain or, for that matter, for individual types of livestock. As a consequence, on the basis of the information provided by Farmer, it is not possible to know whether, for example, 2 s. for a quarter of oats in Suffolk represents a good or a bad price for a peasant selling his grain to the sheriff.[53]

---

53   The possible misinterpretation of Farmer's data in this manner is not an idle concern. In discussing the corruption involved in Edward I's purveyance system, Prestwich, *War, Politics and Finance*, 135, argues that "a comparison of the prices offered by purveyors with the national averages that have been calculated by Farmer reveals that the former were consistently lower". As suggested by the data discussed here, such a comparison is not valid unless it can be ascertained what range of prices was being paid for particular commodities in a particular region.

The information presented here regarding royal purchases of pigs and oats represents only a small fraction of the data that is available regarding royal participation in agricultural markets in the period 1294–1307. However, even the two data sets charted above make clear the considerable problems and dangers inherent in generalizing from Farmer's data regarding prices in England, or in using his data to draw conclusions about specific examples of economic behavior by royal officials. During the final third of King Edward I's reign, the royal government purchased enormous quantities of agricultural commodities. These purchases must be included in any calculation of regional or national prices for grain or livestock that purports to provide an accurate presentation of contemporary commodity costs.[54] What is required at this point, therefore, is a detailed study of royal commodity purchases that takes advantage of the vast corpus of documents in the National Archives and the British Library. Only then will scholars begin to have a realistic picture of commodity prices in England in a given year, and of changes in these prices over time.

Appendix 1

The following list is the database from which I have drawn the random sample of documents discussed in the text. This list includes all of those unenrolled documents that I have identified, in the digital catalogue of the National Archive, as containing information regarding the purchases of agricultural commodities by the royal government during the reign of Edward I. This list does not include the documents that appear as *fragmenta* in the Pipe Rolls, liberate rolls, close rolls, or patent rolls.[55] Many of these *fragmenta* duplicate the information found in the documents below. The texts here are listed in numerical order as identified in the archive catalogue rather than by the dates on which they were issued. I hope that this form of presentation will facilitate the use of the list by scholars who are working on economic questions.

E39/3/55
E101/3/16, 20, 25, 28, 29, 31
E101/4/1, 3, 6, 15, 17, 18, 22, 29, 30
E101/5/3 4–6, 13, 14, 17, 22
E101/6/2, 9, 11–18, 20, 23–26, 32, 33, 35, 38
E101/7/1–3, 9, 11, 13–19, 23, 28, 29
E101/8/1–4, 6, 8–15, 18, 19, 24, 27–30

---

54 This use of data from royal administrative records is what differentiates a study such as Campbell *et al.*, *A Medieval Capital*, from Farmer's studies that relied almost entirely on a limited range of manorial accounts for the period under discussion here.

55 *Fragmenta* are partial transcriptions of texts that are imbedded in other texts. In the case of the Pipe Rolls, it was frequently the case that the royal clerks who drew them up included pieces of other documents in recording the accounts of the sheriffs at the Exchequer.

E101/10/4, 7, 9, 16–19, 22, 25, 28
E101/11/6, 8, 9, 12–15, 17–19, 23, 26, 27, 29, 30
E101/12/1, 2, 4, 7, 8, 14, 19, 21, 22, 26, 27, 32, 34–37, 40
E101/13/1-3, 10, 11, 14, 16–20, 25, 27, 29
E101/98/5, 7, 12, 14, 16, 25, 29, 31-33, 36–38
E101/99/3
E101/351/6
E101/352/28, 29
E101/353/20
E101/354/31
E101/357/9
E101/358/3, 6, 9, 10–12, 24, 25, 30
E101/360/3, 4, 6, 19
E101/361/1, 29, 30
E101/3624–7, 9, 10–12, 16, 19, 21, 23, 26
E101/364/6–8, 10
E101/366/11, 18, 19, 21–23
E101/367/9, 30
E101/368/19, 20
E101/369/8, 9, 13, 18
E101/531/7–10
E101/540/23
E101/550/1, 3–8, 10
E101/552/4–7
E101/556/1–5
E101/559/1–4
E101/561/1
E101/566/3–7
E101/568/1–3, 5–13, 15, 17–19, 21–26
E101/571/2
E101/574/4–15, 18
E101/579/1, 3–5, 7, 8
E101/580/2, 3, 5, 7
E101/82/2, 3, 5, 7
E101/585/1, 2, 5–8
E101/588/1–6
E101/590/1–3
E101/592/1
E101/593/1–3
E101/597/1–8, 10–13
E101/612/5
E101/612/23
E101/684/12, 19, 21–45
E101/699/28

E213/16, 193, 195-197, 199, 290, 291, 297
C47/2/16–19, 23
C47/3/17, 20, 21, 332, 52
C47/22/1–13
C47/35/8
C148, 118, 121, 122, 124, 126

10

MILITARY INDUSTRIAL PRODUCTION IN THIRTEENTH-CENTURY ENGLAND

The case of the crossbow bolt

Introduction

When I first began studying the administrative history of England, Professor Lyon's works provided the crucial grounding in the sources that helped me to navigate the tremendous volume and variety of texts collected at the National Archives in London that make this field so rewarding. But I owe an even deeper debt of gratitude to Professor Lyon for stimulating my very interest in this fascinating field. One of the very first works of medieval history that I read, encouraged by one of Lyon' former students, was *From Fief to Indenture*. I am, therefore, doubly grateful for the opportunity to participate in this memorial volume honoring Bryce Lyon.

The focus of the present study is on the production and acquisition by the English government of ammunition for the many thousands of crossbows used by royal troops from the reign of Richard I (1189–1199) to the reign of Edward I (1272–1307).[1] Over this long century, the English government devoted a considerable quantity of resources to produce and purchase millions of crossbow quarrels, of a variety of types. The regular employment of crossbowmen in the royal armed forces meant that the government had to have available a steady stream of ammunition supplies. This led kings from Richard to Edward I to maintain ammunition production facilities on a regular footing in peacetime as well as during periods of overt military operations. However, in periods of intense military

---

1   Regarding the important role of crossbows in English warfare from the late twelfth through the early fourteenth century, see David S. Bachrach, "The Origins of the English Crossbow Industry", *Journal of Medieval Military History* 2 (2003), 73–87; idem, "The Crossbow Makers of England, 1204–1272", *Nottingham Medieval Studies* 47 (2003), 168–197; idem, "The Royal Arms Makers of England 1199–1216: A Prosopographical Survey", *Medieval Prosopography* 25 (2004, appearing 2008), 49–75; idem, "Crossbows for the King: Some Observations on the Development of the Crossbow during the Reigns of King John and Henry III of England, 1204–1272", *Technology and Culture* 45 (2004), 102–119; idem, "Crossbows for the King (Part Two): The Crossbow during the Reign of Edward I of England (1272–1307)", *Technology and Culture* 47 (2006), 81–90; and idem, "The Crossbow in English Warfare from King John to Edward I, An Administrative Perspective", *Cithara* 52 (2012), 3–21. All of these studies are also published in this volume.

activity, the royal government found it necessary to supplement production from its own facilities with purchases on the private market.[2]

The reigns of Richard and John, 1189–1216

It was not until the reign of King John that we have evidence for the royal government's involvement in crossbow production in England.[3] By contrast, the production of ammunition for crossbows significantly antedates John's successful effort to transplant a crossbow industry across the channel in 1203–1204. By Richard I's reign, at the latest, the royal government already had spent considerable sums purchasing, producing, and stockpiling crossbow quarrels for use in the king's military campaigns on land and on the sea. In 1192, for example, the

---

2   Due, in no small part, to Professor Lyon's extensive work and publications, the legal and administrative sources for thirteenth- and early fourteenth-century England are accessible to scholars. Bryce D. Lyon, *A Constitutional and Legal History of Medieval England* 2nd edn (New York, 1980), provides an essential introduction to the numerous corpora of administrative documents that shed light on the actions of the royal government from King John onward. Similarly, Professor Lyon's publication with Mary Lyon of *The Wardrobe Book of William de Norwell: 12 July 1338 to 27 May 1340* (Brussels, 1983) and *The Wardrobe Book of 1296–1297: A Financial and Logistical Record of Edward I's 1297 Autumn Campaign in Flanders Against Philip IV of France* (Brussels, 2004), have helped illuminate the value of the voluminous Wardrobe accounts for numerous aspects of administrative history, including military affairs.

The pipe rolls for the reigns of Henry II, Richard I, and John have all been edited separately by the Pipe Roll Society. Each roll will be cited individually in this chapter. Several of the pipe rolls from Henry III's reign have been edited by the Pipe Roll Society and will be cited individually. The majority of the pipe rolls for the reigns of Henry III and Edward I, however, have not been edited. These will be cited by their catalogue numbers in the National Archives at Kew Gardens (formerly the Public Record Office). For a valuable introduction to the pipe rolls, see Lyon, *A Constitutional History of Medieval England*, 257–265. The basic published collections of documents that provide information for this study are *Rotuli Litterarum Patentium in Turri Londinensi Asservati*, ed. Thomas D. Hardy (London, 1835), hereafter *RLP*; and *Rotuli Litterarum Clausarum in Turri Londonensi Asservati 1204–1227*, Thomas D. Hardy, 2 vols (London, 1833–1844), hereafter *CR I* and *CR II*; The *misae* accounts and *praestita* rolls are recorded in *Rotuli de Liberate ac de Misis et Praestitis regnante Johanne*, ed. Thomas D. Hardy (London, 1844), hereafter *Rotuli*. For the Norman rolls, see *Rotuli Normannie in Turri asservati Johanne et Henrico Quinto Anglie Regibus*, ed. Thomas D. Hardy (London, 1835), hereafter *Rot. Norm*. Editions of the close roll texts for the reign of Henry III appear in *Close Rolls 1227–1272* (London, 1902–1938) hereafter *CR*. Calendars of the close rolls for the reign of Edward I appear in *Calendar of Close Rolls 1272–1307* (London, 1900–1908), hereafter *CCR*. Calendars of the patent rolls for the reigns of Henry III and Edward I appear in *Calendar of Patent Rolls 1216–1272* (London, 1901–1903), and *Calendar of Patent Rolls 1272–1307* (London, 1893–1901) hereafter *CPR*. The liberate rolls for Henry III's reign are in *Calendar of Liberate Rolls 1226–1272* (London, 1916–1964), hereafter *CLR* with year ranges. The liberate rolls for the reign of Edward I have not been published and are cited here according to their call numbers at the National Archives. Many thousands of other documents have not been published and also are published according to their record numbers in the National Archives.

3   Bachrach, "The Origins of the English Crossbow Industry", 73–87.

pipe roll entry for London and Middlesex records that the sheriffs of London were stockpiling *quarellae*, along with other war materiél, including stone-throwing engines (*petrariae*), stones, and shields at the Tower of London, which was one of England's main magazines.[4] Two years later, in 1194, the pipe roll account for Hampshire and Winchester notes the expenditure of funds by the sheriff on iron to be used for the production of quarrel heads.[5] In 1196, William the son of Alan, the sheriff of Shropshire, was credited 4 s. in the pipe roll for his purchase of *quarellae*.[6]

During King John's reign, the pipe rolls record a significant increase both in the sums spent by the government to produce quarrels in royal workshops and on the purchase of this ammunition from private sources. The pipe roll account in 1200, for example, records that Reginald Cornhill, the sheriff of Kent, spent 50 s. for 5,000 quarrels.[7] After the opening of the earliest royal crossbow workshops, first in Nottingham and then in five other centers during the summer of 1204, the pipe rolls show an even more dramatic rise in the quantity of quarrels obtained by the government.[8] In 1207, the royal officials administering the bishopric of Lincoln for King John are credited in the pipe roll for spending in excess of £70 to purchase 92,000 crossbow bolts as well as chests and barrels in which to store them.[9] That same year, the sheriff of Nottingham spent an additional £5 on about 7,000 quarrels.[10] The pipe rolls record a second major series of expenditures on crossbow bolts in 1211. The royal keepers of the bishopric of Durham purchased just under 86,000 quarrels that year.[11] The sheriff of Yorkshire purchased 40,000 quarrels.[12] The royal officer Brian de L'Isle spent in excess of £21 on 32,000

---

4 *The Great Roll of the Pipe for the Third and Fourth Years of the Reign of King Richard the First Michaelmas 1191 and Michaelmas 1192* (Pipe Rolls 37 and 38), ed. Doris M. Stenton (London, 1926), 158.

5 *The Great Roll of the Pipe for the Sixth Year of the Reign of King Richard the First Michaelmas 1194* (Pipe Roll 40), ed. Doris M. Stenton (London, 1928), 212, "*et pro ferro ad fabricandas quarellas ad opus R*".

6 *The Chancellory Roll for the Eighth Year of the Reign of King Richard the First Michaelmas 1196* (Pipe Roll 42), ed. Doris M. Stenton (London, 1930), 42.

7 *The Great Roll of the Pipe for the Second Year of the Reign of King John Michaelmas 1200* (Pipe Roll 46), ed. Doris M. Stenton (London, 1934), 209.

8 Regarding the establishment of these production facilities in England, see Bachrach, "The Origins of the English Crossbow Industry", 73–87.

9 *The Great Roll of the Pipe for the Ninth Year of the Reign of King John Michaelmas 1207* (Pipe Roll 53), ed. A. Mary Kirkus (London, 1946), 14. The see of Lincoln was vacant in 1207 following the death of Bishop Walter of Coutance.

10 Ibid., 114. The next year, the royal officials overseeing the vacant see of Lincoln purchased an additional 42,000 quarrels for use in the garrisons in the Poitou, and at Winchester Castle. See *CR I*, 100.

11 *The Great Roll of the Pipe for the Thirteenth Year of the Reign of King John Michaelmas 1211* (Pipe Roll 57), ed. Doris M. Stenton (London, 1953), 39.

12 Ibid., 43.

crossbow bolts.[13] Finally, a royal officer named John Fitzhugh purchased 34,500 quarrels, for a grand total of just under 200,000 bolts.[14]

Purchases of this order of magnitude continue to characterize royal arms acquisitions up through King John's failed French expedition of 1214. The pipe roll for 1212 records purchases of 140,000 quarrels by the royal officials overseeing the vacant see of Durham, as well as by Bishop Mauger of Worcester, and by the sheriff of Derby.[15] In addition to these large purchases of ready-to-use quarrels, John Fitzhugh, noted in the preceding paragraph, was credited for the expenses he incurred to have 28,000 bolt heads fitted with shafts and feathers.[16] The pipe roll for 1213 is lost, but the evidence from 1214 indicates that the large-scale purchases of quarrels continued up to the eve of King John's final continental campaign. The sheriff of Gloucester, for example, purchased 45,000 quarrels in 1214.[17] Brian de L'Lisle, now serving as the constable of Knaresborough Castle in Yorkshire's West Riding, purchased an additional 15,000 crossbow bolts. Moreover, he sent a shipment of 30,000 bolts to Portsmouth to be transported to the English fleet gathering there for the invasion of France.[18] Finally, William Saint John, the sheriff of Southampton, added a further 10,000 quarrels to the royal stockpiles.[19]

Even without the undoubtedly large number of quarrels purchased in 1213, the four years before King John's final continental campaign saw the acquisition of least half a million quarrels on the private market.[20] Of course, this number must be seen as a minimum figure. Not only are all of the records for 1213 lost, but a great majority of the pertinent documents produced by the royal Chancery and Exchequer also have not survived. As we shall see in this chapter, the surviving

---

13 Ibid., 88.

14 Ibid., 108 and 111.

15 *The Great Roll of the Pipe for the Fourteenth Year of the Reign of King John Michaelmas 1212* (Pipe Roll 58), ed. Patricia M. Barnes (London, 1955), 47, 61, and 169. The bishopric of Durham was without a prelate following the death of Philip of Poitou in 1208, who was not replaced until 1217 by Richard Marsh.

16 Ibid., 44.

17 *The Great Roll of the Pipe for the Sixteenth Year of the Reign of King John Michaelmas 1214* (Pipe Roll 60), ed. Patricia M. Barnes (London, 1962), 55.

18 Ibid., 67. Alan was originally ordered to produce as many quarrels as possible in a writ issued by the Chancery on 23 May 1214. See *CR I*, 206, "*Dei gratia etc. dilecto sibi Alano de S. Georgio* [sic] *constabulario de Gnaresburgh salutem. Mandamus vobis quod fieri faciatis omnes quarellos quos poteritis et eos mitti usque Portsmouth, retentis ad garnesturam castri de Gnaresburgh uno millario is opus fuerit. Et custum quod in opere et in cariagum posueritis vobis faciemus computari*". A similar order was sent the same day to Reginald Cornhill, one of King John's chief procurement officers. See *CR I*, 206.

19 PR 14 John, 126.

20 Some indication of royal expenditures on crossbow bolts in 1213 can be gleaned from a letter issued by the Chancery to the Exchequer authorizing the barons to credit Brian de L'Isle the expenses he incurred for purchasing 10,000 quarrels and transporting them from Knaresborough Castle, where he served as constable, to Portsmouth. See *CR I*, 148.

administrative records of this type from the reigns of Henry III and Edward I also refer to the purchases of very substantial numbers of quarrels by the crown.

The purchase by royal officials of large numbers of quarrels from private producers was complemented in John's reign by the regular output of crossbow bolts from royal workshops. The latter can be understood as operating in conjunction with the crossbow workshops established by John in the period 1203–1212.[21] At least three fletchers, Denis, Philip, and Thomas, who specialized in the fabrication of crossbow quarrels, as contrasted with fletchers making arrows, can be identified in King John's service.[22] In addition to these three men, the pipe roll from 1214 records the service of smiths who produced iron heads for crossbow bolts for the royal government during John's reign. These records do not provide the names of the smiths.[23]

The evidence from the pipe rolls makes clear that John's government maintained workshops for the production of crossbow quarrels, with a major center at the Tower of London. In addition, the royal government supplemented the supplies of quarrels available from its own workshops with the purchase of this ammunition on the private market. Indeed, as noted, many of these purchases were very large, that is in excess of 10,000 units, and it is clear that government obtained many hundreds of thousands of quarrels from private producers.

The reign of King Henry, 1216–1272

Henry III's government continued the policies of King John regarding both the production and purchase of quarrels. The much larger corpus of surviving administrative documents in the period after 1216, however, permits a far more detailed understanding of royal efforts both to purchase crossbow bolts on the private market as well as to maintain, and even expand, royal workshops that specialized in the production of ammunition. Before the spring of 1221, as noted earlier, the royal government already had in place a major production facility for crossbow bolts at the Tower of London. A letter from the Chancery on 25 May 1221 instructed the officers of the Exchequer to disburse £10 to a royal officer named Alex of Dorset to pay the wages of the smiths and crossbow makers producing *quarelli* and *balistae* at the Tower.[24] A second royal production facility was

---

21 Bachrach, "The Origins of the English Crossbow Industry", 73–87.
22 See *The Great Roll of the Pipe for the First Year of the Reign of King John Michaelmas 1199*, ed. Doris M. Stenton (London, 1933), 132; PR 13 John, 171; *CR I*, 2, respectively.
23 *Pipe Roll 16 John*, 136. In this case, William Saint John, the sheriff of Southampton, noted already, was credited with the expenses he incurred for transporting the smiths from Winchester to Portsmouth. The original order to dispatch the smiths was issued on 23 May 1214 by Bishop Peter de Roches of Winchester. He wrote to the sheriff of Southampton to instruct him to find transportation for the smiths serving there along with their wives, children, and tools, as well as the quarrels they had produced, and to send them to Portsmouth. See *CR I*, 205.
24 *CR I*, 460.

in full operation no later than 1222. The pipe roll for this year records that the sheriff of Gloucester and the constable of St. Briavels Castle paid the wages of William Malemort, a smith, his two assistants (*garciones*), and a fletcher named William, who were all engaged in producing crossbow bolts for the crown in a workshop located in the Forest of Dean.[25] In addition to paying the wages of the two Williams and their assistants, the sheriff and constable also purchased iron, coal, a forge, bellows, and hammers, for use in the workshop.[26]

The surviving administrative records suggest that the two workshops at the Tower of London and the Forest of Dean produced a sufficient quantity of crossbow bolts for peacetime needs. In periods of intense conflict, however, the royal government sought additional quarrels from private makers. The royal response to the siege of Bedford Castle in 1224 exemplifies this pattern.[27] On 20 June 1224, the Chancery issued an order to the sheriff of London requiring that he send a large quantity of military supplies to the royal forces encamped outside Bedford Castle. Of particular importance in this context, the sheriff was ordered to send as many quarrels as he could.[28] The text emphasizes that the sheriff was to send these supplies *sub omni festinacione*, indicating that the war matériel was to be taken out of current stocks stored in the magazines.

That same day, however, the Chancery sent a second order to the sheriff of London ordering him to find five or six smiths (*fabri*) to work non-stop, literally day and night (*de die et nocte*), to produce as many quarrels as possible for use at the siege of Bedford Castle.[29] Within eight days, that is by 28 June 1224, the sheriff of London was able to acquire an additional 3,000 quarrels which he then sent to Bedford.[30] However, even the additional supplies of crossbow bolts sent from London proved to be insufficient, and the government sought further shipments of ammunition. On 23 July 1224, the Chancery issued orders to the bailiffs of Northampton to mobilize all of the smiths in town who knew how to make quarrels to produce 4,000 of them as quickly as possible.[31] On 24 July, the next day,

---

25 *The Great Roll of the Pipe for the Sixth Year of the Reign of King Henry III Michaelmas 1222* (London, 1999), 39.

26 *Pipe Roll 6 Henry III*, 39. Concerning the role of St Briavels Castle and the Forest of Dean as an important arsenal during the reign of Edward I, see Cyril E. Hart, *Royal Forest: A History of Dean's Woods as Producers of Timber* (Oxford, 1966).

27 For a detailed discussion of the logistical efforts undertaken by the royal government during the siege, see Emilie Amt, "Besieging Bedford: Military Logistics in 1224", *The Journal of Medieval Military History* 1 (2002), 101–124.

28 *CR I*, 605, "*Mandamus vobis sicut nos diligitis sub omni festinacione qua poteritis ad nos mittatis usque Bedeford duas carectatas vel tres de cordis et xx funas ad mangonellos et petrarias et targias et quarellos quotquot poteritis*".

29 *CR I*, 605.

30 Ibid., 608.

31 *CR I*, 613, "*mandamus vobis quod ... visis litteris tam die quam de nocte fieri faciatis per omnes fabros ville Northampton qui in arte fabricanti quarellos sunt instructi, quatuor milia quarellorum*". A letter issued by the Chancery on 19 August 1224 to the constable of the castle at

further orders were issued to the royal bailiffs of Oxford, as well as to the sheriffs of London, requiring that they have the local smiths produce 6,000 and 10,000 quarrels, respectively.[32] It should be noted that this was the second lot of crossbow bolts required from the sheriffs of London in the space of a month.

The pattern of quarrel production and purchases established by the royal government during the early 1220s remained the norm throughout the remainder of Henry III's reign. Henry's government employed no fewer than thirteen master smiths and fletchers in royal workshops between 1225 and 1272, and several of these men, including William Malemort noted above, employed teams of assistants.[33] Perhaps the best known of these men was William Malemort's brother John, who began working with William in 1225, and subsequently supervised his own workshop at the Forest of Dean from 1230 until at least 1278, during the reign of Edward I.[34] The Tower of London also continued to house a major production facility through the end of Henry's reign, although the smiths and fletchers there served for much shorter terms of service than John Malemort.[35] In addition to these major facilities, Henry III's government established at least one subsidiary production center for crossbow quarrels in 1261 at Dover Castle under the direction of a smith named Adam.[36]

The annual output of the two major production centers at the Forest of Dean and the Tower of London reached 50,000 quarrels by 1229. On 18 November of that year, the Chancery issued orders to the bailiff of St. Briavels Castle, located in the Forest of Dean, to increase the pay of William Malemort, his brother John, and William the Fletcher on the condition that they raise their daily level of production to 200 from 100 quarrels.[37] Other surviving letters in the liberate rolls make clear that the Malemort brothers, William the Fletcher, and their assistants were expected to work on average five days a week, that is 250 days, to produce a

---

Northampton required him to store at his castle 900 of the 4,000 quarrels, which were produced by the smiths of the city. See *CR I*, 617.

32 *CR I*, 638.

33 I intend to write a prosopographical study of all of the arms makers who served during the reign of Henry III, including the smiths, fletchers, crossbow makers, and artillery builders. Concerning the arms makers employed by the royal government during the reign of King John, see Bachrach, "Arms Makers", 49–75.

34 *CR II*, 54; *CR 1272–1279*, 438. John Malemort's career has been studied by Alf Webb, "John Malemort—King's Quarreler: The King's Great Arsenal, St. Briavels and the Royal Forest of Dean", *Society of Archer Antiquaries* 31 (1988), 40–46; and part 2, in ibid., 32 (1989), 52–58.

35 At least six master smiths can be identified serving as quarrel makers at the Tower of London between 1225 and 1273. They are Thomas, Roger, Ogerus, Henry, Alan, and Richard. For Thomas see *CR II*, 45, 55, 58, 68, 84, 115, 140, 143, and *CLR 1226–1240*, 5, 15, 24, 32, 39, 43–44; for Roger see E372/76 8v and *CLR 1251–1260*, 376, 401; for Ogerus see National Archives E372/77 12r and *CLR 1226–1240*, 203; for Henry see *CR 1261–1264*, 205–206 and *CLR 1260–1267*, 3, 7, 70–71, 112; for Alan see *CR 1261–1264*, 205–206 and *CLR 1260–1267*, 119, 144, 220, 221, 224, 253, 282; and for Richard see *CLR 1267–1272*, 24, 32.

36 *CLR 1260–1267*, 53.

37 *CLR 1226–1240*, 157–158.

total of 50,000 quarrels per year.[38] In 1230, however, William Malemort left royal service, and John Malemort's daily production quota was reduced to 100 quarrels a day, where it remained until the end of Henry III's reign.[39] This level of output likely was matched by the royal production facility at the Tower of London, although the surviving records do not record how many quarrels the master smiths and fletchers working there were supposed to produce on a daily basis.

This substantial output of crossbow bolts from the production facilities at the Tower of London and the Forest of Dean were deemed by the royal government to be sufficient for peacetime conditions. During Henry III's many military actions on the continent, in Wales, and in civil wars in England, however, the government found it prudent to continue to supplement its normal supplies of quarrels with purchases from private manufacturers. For example, before undertaking the Welsh campaign of 1228, the royal government first ordered substantial additional stocks of quarrels. On 15 July 1227, the Chancery issued orders to the sheriff of Cumberland to have the smiths in his shire produce 100,000 quarrels at the cost of the royal government.[40] In February of the same year, Stephen de Lucy, the royal official administering the vacant see of Durham, was ordered to have suitable smiths in the bishopric produce as many quarrels as possible at royal cost.[41] In the end, this royal officer succeeded in acquiring no fewer than 25,000 bolts for the central government.[42] The Welsh campaign of 1242 saw similar preparations. The constable of Windsor Castle purchased 50,000 iron heads for crossbow bolts from local smiths, and on 27 August 1242 the Chancery issued an order to the royal bailiffs of Windsor to provide shafts and feathers for them.[43]

In one final example, following the defeat of the baronial forces at Evesham (4 August 1265), Henry III and his son Edward spent much of the next two years hunting down and defeating isolated pockets of rebel resistance. The most important of these centers was the castle of Kenilworth, which fell in December 1266, although scattered resistance continued into 1267.[44] In order to conduct these military operations, the royal government first sought to increase production at its own facilities. In July 1266, John Malemort was asked to produce an additional 6,000 quarrels above his normal quota.[45] But this proved insufficient. The royal government therefore ordered the sheriffs of the city of London to have the local

---

38 See *CR 1254–1256*, 96–97; *CLR 1251–1260*, 373.
39 See *CLR 1226–1240*, 181–182, 103–104, 228, 240, 263, 320, 381–382, 468; *CLR 1240–1245*, 77–78, 175; *CLR 1245–1251*, 41, 119, 204, 229, 357; *CLR 1251–1260*, 45, 151, 226, 373; *CLR 1260–1267*, 192. The one exception to this pattern was in December 1257 when the royal government asked John Malemort to double his production from 25,000 to 50,000 quarrels for use in the king's Welsh campaign. See *CLR 1245–1251*, 415.
40 *CLR 1226–1240*, 44.
41 *CLR 1226–1240*, 19. This order was repeated on 21 September 1228. See *CR 1227–1231*, 81.
42 *CLR 1226–1240*, 164.
43 *CLR 1240–1245*, 146.
44 Michael Prestwich, *Edward I*, 2nd edn (Yale, 1997), 51–59.
45 *CLR 1260–1267*, 221–2.

smiths produce 20,000 quarrels, of which 13,200 were produced and shipped to the king's forces.[46] The next year, in March 1267, the government sought an additional 50,000 quarrels from the sheriffs of London and 30,000 from the bailiffs of Colchester, which were supposed to be produced by local smiths.[47]

During Henry III's reign, the government established its main production centers for quarrels at the Forest of Dean and the Tower of London. The annual output of these two facilities was 25,000 quarrels each, although in times of crisis, output at these centers was doubled. This regular production was supplemented during periods of war by very large purchases of quarrels on the private market. Given the consistently large production of quarrels by royal workshops over half a century, and the continuing effort by the government to purchase quarrels on the private market, it seems clear that the numbers of quarrels obtained by Henry III's logistics officers numbered in the millions.

The reign of Edward I, 1272–1307

The early years of King Edward's reign saw the continued production of quarrels at the traditional workshops located in the Tower of London and the Forest of Dean. John Malemort, noted earlier, produced quarrels for the government at S. Briavels Castle, located in the Forest of Dean, until at least 1278.[48] The production staff at the Tower of London in 1273 and 1274 included a smith named Henry and two fletchers named Hugh and Peter.[49]

Nevertheless, the surviving evidence indicates that Edward's government made a decision at some point in the 1270s both to decentralize its production facilities and perhaps to rely more heavily on private producers to supply quarrels. John Malemort, the chief of the production facility at St. Briavels Castle, does not appear in the surviving royal records after 1278, and he does not appear to have been replaced. It is likely that he died at this time, having been in royal service for the better part of four decades. As will be clear in this chapter, however, the constables of St. Briavels Castle continued to have responsibility for the large-scale production of crossbow bolts, at least sporadically, throughout Edward I's reign. Evidence for the production of quarrels at the Tower of London becomes scarce in the surviving administrative documents after 1274, although some master smiths and fletchers can still be identified working there. Thus, for example, in 1294, the smith John of Northampton and the carpenter Robert de Colbroke are authorized in a writ of liberate to receive their daily wages of 9 d. and 4 d., respectively, for producing quarrels at the Tower.[50]

---

46 *CLR 1260–1267*, 230 and 263.
47 Ibid., 264 and 276.
48 *CR 1272–1279*, 438.
49 National Archives C 62/49 5r; C62/50 2r, 6r, and 15r.
50 National Archives C62/71 2r.

In place of this centralization of quarrel production in two government work-shops, which was the norm throughout most of Henry III's reign, Edward's gov-ernment would appear to have hired smiths and carpenters to produce crossbow bolts in the same places that crossbows were now being made, namely in the royal castles of Wales, Scotland, and the marches.[51] This decentralization had the benefit of lowering transportation costs for the finished products. In 1294, for example, Reginald de Grey, the commander of the royal army in Wales, employed a smith at Chester Castle to make quarrels for his troops as they prepared to deal with Welsh rebels. The smith was accompanied in his work by an *atilliator* who was repairing the crossbows of Reginald de Grey's troops.[52]

King Edward's wars in Scotland and the consolidation of his conquests saw the establishment of several centers for the production of quarrels there. The liberate roll for 1298 records, for example, that John Kirkeby, the sheriff of Northumberland, paid the wages of fletchers who completed 2415 quarrels at Newcastle.[53] The sheriff also paid the wages of two smiths who repaired 10,000 old bolt heads so that they could be reused.[54] The English garrison town of Berwick also served as a major center for the production of quarrels for use by royal gar-risons in Scotland. A garrison roster for Berwick Castle, issued in 1300, indicates that the specialists on staff there included a crossbow maker, and two smiths.[55]

The significant level of quarrel production achieved at Berwick is indicated by several surviving administrative documents. In 1298, for example, the account of John Burdon, the constable of Berwick Castle, includes expenses for the pro-duction of 4,300 quarrels designed for "two-foot" crossbows.[56] A memorandum issued in September 1302 records that Richard de Bremesgrave, the chief logistics officer at Berwick, transported large quantities of food as well as crossbows and 5,000 quarrels from his magazine to the garrison at Selkirk Castle.[57] A memoran-dum issued two years later in May 1304 by a royal officer named Walter Bedewind, recorded that he had received 23,000 quarrels from Richard de Bremesgrave for the garrison at Stirling Castle. Another memorandum, issued in August of 1304, recorded that the ship captain Robert, the son of Walter, carried a further load of "*quarellos pro balistis preparatos apud dictum Berwick*" to Stirling Castle.[58] Other surviving documents from the English officers in Scotland indicate that the

---

51   Regarding production of crossbows in fortresses in Scotland and Wales, see Bachrach, "The Crossbow in English Warfare", passim.
52   National Archives C62/75 6r. The payment to Reginald de Grey for his expenses were recorded in the liberate roll for 1298.
53   National Archives C62/74 5r.
54   Ibid.
55   National Archives E101/8/24.
56   National Archives E101/7/6. Regarding the types of crossbows deployed by the royal government during Edward I's reign, see Bachrach, "Crossbows for the King (Part Two)", 81–90.
57   National Archives E101/9/30 #14.
58   National Archives C47/22/9 #70 and #71.

garrisons at Roxburgh and Dumfries Castles also had smiths and fletchers on staff to produce quarrels in each of these fortresses in 1303.[59]

As had been true during Henry III's reign, however, Edward I's government also found it necessary to supplement the regular supply of quarrels from its own workshops with purchases from private producers. The bulk of these purchases by the crown came in the context of royal military campaigns. The Welsh campaigns of 1277, 1282–1284, 1287, and 1294–1295 all saw exceptionally large purchases of crossbow bolts. A writ to the Exchequer issued on 23 June 1277, for example, ordered the clerks there to credit the account of Robert, a royal treasury official, for almost £70 he had spent on the production of 100,000 quarrels, and a further £7 for the costs in involved in transporting 77,000 of these quarrels to the fortresses of Chester and Montgomery.[60] Earlier that year, on 12 March, the king issued orders to the royal steward, Ralph of Sandwich, to have 200,000 quarrels produced at St. Briavels Castle, the site of the major workshop earlier overseen by John Malemort.[61]

The Welsh campaigns of 1282–1284 saw even larger purchases of quarrels by the royal government. The chief logistics officer for the royal army in Wales, a clerk named Ralph, recorded in his *compotus*, that in 1283 he had received and subsequently distributed to garrisons and troops in Wales 164,000 completed quarrels and an additional 18,750 iron heads. This included in excess of 80,000 quarrels and heads shipped into England from Gascony.[62] In January and May 1283, additional purchases of crossbow bolts numbering 90,000 and 30,000, respectively, were shipped by Peter de la Mare, constable of Bristol Castle, and Grimbald Pauncefoot, constable of St. Briavels, to the royal garrisons at Chester, Carmarthen, and Rothelan.[63] In December 1284, King Edward ordered Peter de la Mare to purchase a further 200,000 quarrels for use by the royal garrisons in Wales.[64]

Purchases of quarrels on a similar scale marked the Welsh campaigns of 1287 and 1294–1295. On 25 November 1287, for example, a writ of liberate was issued to the Exchequer authorizing the payment of £120 to Thomas, the sheriff of Canterbury, for the purchase and shipment of just under 150,000 quarrels to

---

59 National Archives E101/9/30 #25 and E101/14/1. The second of these documents, which is not dated, notes that James Dalilegh, one of the chief royal logistics officers for the Scottish war, sent glue *pro quarellis* to the castle at Bonfres. James was appointed receiver at Stirling in 1300. Concerning James Dalilegh's career in Scotland, see Michael Prestwich, *War, Politics and Finance under Edward I* (Totowa, NJ, 1972), 122, 136, 165.

60 National Archives C62/54 2r.

61 *CR 1272–1279*, 373.

62 National Archives E101/4/6/1. On 14 April 1282, Edward I ordered a royal official in London named Gregory Rokesleye to purchase 4,000 quarrels for use on the king's ships preparing to set sail for Wales. See *CR 1279–1288*, 153.

63 National Archives C62/59 8r and 6r.

64 *CR 1279–1288*, 308.

the royal garrison at Carmarthen.[65] Similarly, in 1296, John Botetourt, the constable of St. Briavels, was authorized to receive almost £130 for the purchase and production of 146,000 quarrels to be stored at the magazine at Corfe Castle and for the royal garrisons in Wales. This sum also included the costs for producing 312 chests that were used to carry these quarrels and an additional 150,000 bolts that were transported to the royal arms depot at Bristol Castle, i.e. roughly 1,000 crossbow bolts were carried in each chest.[66]

Edward's Gascon campaigns also saw large-scale purchases of crossbow bolts. In a turnabout from the state of affairs in 1283, the royal government now shipped quarrels produced in England to the continent. A *rotulus* drawn up in 1298 recorded the purchase of quarrels from five separate private workshops in England in July and August of that year. The document records the purchase of 88,200 quarrel heads at a cost of just under £50.[67]

If we turn our attention to Edward I's Scottish campaigns (1296–1307), the surviving administrative records suggest that the government relied more heavily on its own workshops rather than on the purchase of quarrels from private makers. The only year in which we see the acquisition of very large numbers of quarrels on the private market is 1298. In this year, Thomas of Suffolk and Adam Fulham, the sheriffs of London, purchased 104,000 crossbow bolts for use in Scotland, including 72,000 for "one-foot" weapons, 24,000 for "two-foot" weapons, and 8,000 for crossbows equipped with a winch (*turnus*).[68] The royal government made an additional purchase of 100,000 bolts in 1298, but for use in Wales. Nicholas Fermbaud, the constable of Bristol Castle, was issued orders on 18 December of that year, to send 100,000 quarrels to the royal fortress at Caernarvon, from where they would be sent to the castles at Conway, Beaumarais, Harlech, and Criccieth under the direction of John de Havering, the justiciar of North Wales.[69]

The surviving administrative documents make clear that the royal government purchased well in excess of one million crossbow bolts for use in Edward I's Welsh and Scottish wars. However, even this noteworthy number must be understood as representing only a fraction, and perhaps even a small fraction, of the total number of quarrels produced for the royal government in the thirty-five years between 1272 and 1307. The surviving administrative records, although numerous, are only a small percentage of the original volume of documents that dealt with military logistics. As a result, it is almost certain that a very large number of records dealing with the purchase of quarrels have been lost. In addition, the

---

65 National Archives C62/64 1r. In 1290, Peter de la Mare sent an additional 19,000 quarrels and forty crossbows to the garrison in Carmarthen. See C62/66 5r.
66 National Archives C62/73 5r.
67 National Archives E101/5/15.
68 National Archives C62/74 6r. Regarding the types of crossbows used in the armies of Edward I, see Bachrach, "Crossbows for the King (Part Two)", 81–90.
69 National Archives E101/6/4.

numbers of crossbow bolts discussed here does not include the normal production from the royal facilities in workshops at Chester, Berwick, Roxburgh, Dumfries, and perhaps other centers as well. As we saw already, the facility at Berwick alone was capable of producing many thousands of quarrels in a short period of time. Indeed, it would appear that the royal government relied largely on its own workshops in Scotland to produce quarrels for the forces stationed there. As a consequence, it seems likely that the total number of crossbow bolts acquired by the royal government during King Edward's reign should be numbered in the many millions.

Conclusion

Despite the fact that the surviving administrative documents from the reigns of John, Henry III, and Edward I are only a fraction of the original output produced by the royal government, they nevertheless illustrate the clear and continuing commitment of the crown to produce and acquire staggering quantities of quarrels from the late twelfth through the early fourteenth century. The royal government churned out tens of thousands of quarrels every year in its own workshops. In periods of war, the government purchased many hundreds of thousands more to supplement existing stockpiles. If one can measure the importance attached by government officials to particular policies by the resources they devote to them, then we can be reasonably sure that for well over a century, the royal government of England attached considerable importance to securing large supplies of crossbow quarrels for its troops.

11

THE CROSSBOW IN ENGLISH WARFARE FROM KING JOHN TO EDWARD I

An administrative perspective

Readers of *Cithara* will be familiar with the Hollywood cliché in medieval films that the heroes are armed with bows, while the villains are armed with crossbows. The recent *Lord of the Rings* trilogy, in which the elf Legolas was armed with a longbow, while the evil orcs were equipped with crossbows, offers a useful example of this dichotomy.[1] In reality, however, crossbows were widely used across the medieval world, so that the "good guys" in any particular conflict, and from any particular perspective, likely included men equipped with these weapons.

The reason for the broad diffusion of the crossbow was that these weapons could be used in ways that self-bows, that is bows drawn and held steady by the archer, could not. The most important advantage of the crossbow was that it could be held "cocked" without any effort on the part of the crossbowman. This meant that the crossbowman could wait until he had a target, and then release the firing mechanism. A second, concomitant advantage was that a crossbowman could take cover while waiting for a target. This was something that an archer operating a self-bow could not do. As a consequence of these two advantages, crossbowmen were particularly valuable in the defense of fortifications. Here, the slow rate of fire of the crossbow as compared with a self-bow was compensated for by the ability of the crossbowman to pick out his targets patiently, while at the same time taking advantage of the protection offered by the safety of the fortress.

In this context, specialists in continental military history have identified the crossbow as the most important handheld missile weapon in the armies of the West during the second half of the twelfth and throughout the thirteenth century.[2] Studies of medieval English military history similarly note the exceptionally

---

1   I would like to thank Professor Peter Burkholder of Fairleigh Dickinson University, NJ, USA, for bringing to my attention this Hollywood cliché.

2   Hans Delbrück, *History of the Art of War within the Framework of Political History III: The Middle Ages*, trans. Walter J. Renfroe Jr. (London, 1982), 395; Maurice Powicke, *The Loss of Normandy 1189–1204: Studies in the History of the Angevin Empire*, 2nd edn (Manchester, 1960, repr. 1999), 225; Ferdinand Lot, *L'Art militaire et les armées au moyen âge en Europe et dans le Proche Orient*, 2 vols (Paris, 1946), I: 313; Eric Christiansen, *The Northern Crusades: The Baltic*

important role of the crossbow for the twelfth and early thirteenth century, up through the end of the reign of King John (1199–1216).[3] However, some scholars argue that the role of the crossbow was eclipsed after this point by the self-bow, and was used in only small numbers during the reigns of Henry III and particularly Edward I.[4] This study, based on a thorough investigation of the pertinent surviving administrative documents from the period 1199–1307, shows instead that royal government during the reigns of Henry III (1216–1272) and Edward I (1272–1307), expended even greater resources on the production and acquisition of crossbows than was the case before 1216.[5]

---

and Catholic Frontier, 1100–1525 (Minneapolis, MN, 1980), 88; Philippe Contamine, War in the Middle Ages, trans. Michael Jones (Oxford, 1993), 71–72, first published as La guerre au moyen âge (Paris, 1980); Jim Bradbury, The Medieval Archer (New York, 1985), 76; N. J. G. Pounds, The Medieval Castle in Europe and Wales: A Social and Political History (Cambridge, 1990, repr. 1994), 108; Kelly DeVries, Medieval Military Technology (Peterborough, 1992, now available in 2nd edn Toronto, 2012), 41; David Nicolle, Medieval Warfare Source Book Volume I: Warfare in Western Christendom (London, 1995), 130; and Michael Prestwich, Armies and Warfare in the Middle Ages: The English Experience (New Haven, CT, 1996), 129.

3 Michael Powicke, Military Obligation in Medieval England: A Study in Liberty and Duty (Oxford, 1962, repr. 1975), 58–60; Matthew Strickland, War and Chivalry: The Conduct and Perception of War in England and Normandy, 1066–1217 (Cambridge, 1996), 175 and 180; and S. D. Church, The Household Knights of King John (Cambridge, 1999), 41–49.

4 See, for example, John E. Morris, The Welsh Wars of Edward I: A Contribution to Medieval Military History, Based on Original Documents (Oxford, 1901, repr. 1969), 27–28; Powicke, Military Obligation, 88–91; Philip Morgan, War and Society in Medieval Cheshire (Manchester, 1987), 40; Christopher Allmand, The Hundred Years War: England and France at War c. 1300–c. 1450 (Cambridge, 1988), 61–62; and Prestwich, Armies and Warfare, 131.

5 The sources available for the discussion of the production of crossbows are detailed in the first essay in this volume. The full references to the collections of documents cited in this volume are included in this note. The pipe rolls for the reigns of Henry II, Richard I, and John have all been edited separately by the Pipe Rolls Society, and will be cited individually in this chapter. Several of the pipe rolls from Henry III's reign have been edited by the Pipe Roll Society and also will be cited individually. The majority of the pipe rolls for the reigns of Henry III and Edward I, however, have not been edited. These will be cited by their catalogue numbers in the National Archives at Kew (formerly the Public Record Office). In addition, see Rotuli Litterarum Patentium in Turri Londinensi Asservati, ed. Thomas D. Hardy (London, 1835), hereafter Rotuli; and Rotuli Litterarum Clausarum in Turri Londonensi Asservati 1204–1227, ed. Thomas D. Hardy, 2 vols (London, 1833–1834), hereafter CR I and CR II; Rotuli de Liberate ac de Misis et Praestitis regnante Johanne, ed. Thomas D. Hardy (London, 1844), hereafter Rot. de Lib. For the Norman rolls, see Rotuli Normannie in Turri asservati Johanne et Henrico Quinto Anglie Regibus, ed. Thomas D. Hardy (London, 1835), hereafter Rot. Norm. Editions of the close roll texts for the reign of Henry III appear in Close Rolls 1227–1272 (London, 1902–1938), hereafter CR with specific dates. Calendars of the close rolls for the reign of Edward I appear in Calendar of Close Rolls 1272–1307 (London, 1900–1908), hereafter CCR. Calendars of the patent rolls for the reigns of Henry III and Edward I appear in Calendar of Patent Rolls 1216–1272 (London, 1901–1903) and Calendar of Patent Rolls 1272–1307 (London, 1893–1901), hereafter CPR. For Henry III's reign, see Calendar of Liberate Rolls 1226–1272 (London, 1916), hereafter CLR. The liberate rolls for the reign of Edward I have not been published and are cited according to their call numbers at the National Archives.

Crossbow production in England, 1202–1272

Although it is clear that many English soldiers of the later twelfth century were armed with crossbows, there is no evidence in the surviving royal administrative records to suggest that these crossbows were produced in England.[6] Rather, it is clear that the royal government imported noteworthy numbers of these weapons from abroad, largely from Italy, particularly Genoa.[7] The final surviving record of the purchase of crossbows from Italy by John's government is in 1207 from a Genoese merchant named Benedict, who sold the king just over £100 worth of crossbows.[8] Depending on the type of weapons purchased by the crown, Benedict may have delivered as many as 1,000 crossbows.[9] This importation of crossbows should not be confused with King John's employment of mercenaries armed with crossbows, a practice which would prove so contentious later in his reign, as evidenced by clause 51 of the Magna Carta (1215) that required foreign crossbowmen along with all other foreign mercenaries to be ousted from England.[10]

It was not until 1202 that King John began a sustained effort to develop a crossbow industry in England, which culminated in 1204 with the beginning of large-scale crossbow production at a variety of sites, including Nottingham, Gloucester, Northampton, Marlborough, and Salisbury.[11] Over the course of his reign, John employed at least ten specialists to serve as master crossbow makers in royal workshops, several of whom commanded teams of assistants.[12] It should be emphasized in this context that there is no evidence in the surviving administrative sources for the existence of private, that is non-governmental, workshops for the production of crossbows in England at any point in John's reign. More specifically, in contrast to the reigns of both Henry III and Edward I, there is

---

6 See David S. Bachrach, "Origins of the Crossbow Industry in England", *Journal of Medieval Military History* (2004), 73–88, here 81–83.

7 See Bachrach, "Origins", 81–83; (idem), "Royal Crossbow Makers of England, 1204–1272", *Nottingham Medieval Studies* 47 (2003), 168–197, here 170–71; and idem, "Royal Arms Makers of England 1199–1216: A Prosopographical Survey", *Journal of Medieval Prosopography* 25 (2004, appearing 2008), 49–75, here 62–70. All of these essays also appear in this volume.

8 *CR 1*, 76.

9 The least expensive crossbows, wooden weapons of the "one-foot" type, cost as little as 1 s. 6 d. each. Prices are discussed in more detail later in this chapter. For a full discussion of the types of crossbows that were constructed by the royal government over the course of the thirteenth century, see David S. Bachrach, "Crossbows for the King: A Note on the Technology of the Crossbow during the Reigns of John and Henry III of England", *Technology and Culture* 45 (2004), 102–119; and idem, "Crossbows for the King Part Two: The Crossbow during the Reign of Edward I of England (1272–1307)", in *Technology and Culture* 47 (2006), 81–90, and in this volume.

10 On this point, see Morris, *The Welsh Wars*, 28 and 89. For the text of the Magna Carta, see *Sources of English Constitutional History*, ed. and trans. Carl Stephenson and Frederick George Marcham (New York, 1937), 123.

11 Bachrach, "Crossbow Makers", 175–176.

12 Bachrach, "Royal Arms Makers of England 1199–1216", 62–70.

no evidence that John's government purchased crossbows from private sources within England.[13]

During Henry III's reign, the royal government continued to produce large numbers of crossbows in royal workshops. At least seventeen crossbow makers were employed by the royal government in the period 1216–1272, several of whom also had teams of assistants working for them.[14] However, whereas crossbow production during John's reign had been organized at a variety of regional centers, the first decade of Henry III's reign saw the concentration of manufacture at two facilities, located respectively at the Tower of London and Corfe Castle in Dorset.[15] During the late 1250s, an additional center for crossbow production was established at Windsor Castle.[16]

Despite the extensive production of crossbows in royal workshops, however, the king's crossbow makers did not keep up with the demands of the government for these weapons. Beginning no later than 1223, and probably even earlier, the central government supplemented the supplies of crossbows available from its own workshops with purchases from private manufacturers.[17] However, in contrast to the pattern of purchases from Italian (Genoese) merchants during King John's reign, noted earlier, the overwhelming majority of the crossbows obtained by Henry's government came from private makers located in England itself. In January 1223, for example, orders were issued to the Exchequer to credit the account of John Ferentin, then serving as the constable of Bristol, for the 100 s. that he had spent to purchase forty wooden crossbows for use in the castle there.[18] Later that same year, the Chancery issued orders to the Exchequer instructing the clerks there to issue £10 to a royal officer named Achard de Marsit to reimburse him for the purchase of five composite crossbows (bows which were produced using layers of bone, wood, and glue). This purchase included four units of the most advanced type of crossbow, which was equipped with a mechanical spanning device called a *turnus*.[19] This latter purchase would appear to have been relatively small by government standards. We see far more references to ten or more crossbows as is the case in 1241 with separate purchases of ten wooden and ten composite crossbows for 20 s. and £21, respectively, or twenty wooden

---

13 The purchase of crossbows from private English makers by the royal government in the period after 1216 will be discussed in detail in this chapter.
14 Bachrach, "Crossbow Makers", passim.
15 There is no evidence of production at Corfe after 1230. See Bachrach, "Crossbow Makers", 177.
16 Ibid, 175–181.
17 *CR I*, 530.
18 Ibid.
19 Concerning this purchase, see *CR I*, 558. With respect to the number and types of crossbows used by the royal government during the reign of Henry III, see Bachrach, "Crossbows for the King", (Part 1), 102–119.

crossbows in 1253 for 50 s.[20] Government purchases of crossbows from private sources continued throughout Henry III's reign.[21]

In contrast to the period before 1216, and specifically before 1207, none of the documents that record the purchase of crossbows by the royal government, except for one, mentions Genoese or Italian participants in the transaction.[22] The surviving evidence from royal administrative documents indicates that in the wake of King John's efforts to develop crossbow production in England, the technical expertise for building these weapons spread beyond the royal workshops into the private sphere. It would appear, in fact, that at least in some cases there was overlap in the craftsmen who worked in private and governmental workshops.

The clearest example of this pattern of mobility among the specialists in crossbow construction between private and royal manufacturing centers concerns a crossbow maker named Peter who made crossbows for Henry's government at Corfe Castle from 1225 to 1230.[23] Before his five-year term of employment for the king, however, Peter seems to have operated his own workshop, which sold some of its weapons to the crown. Indeed, Peter first appears in the surviving royal records on 20 August 1225, when the Chancery issued orders to the Exchequer to pay him 60 s. for six composite bows that he had sold to the king's officers responsible for acquiring weapons for the English garrisons serving in Gascony.[24]

The uneven nature of the surviving royal records during the early 1230s does not permit any firm conclusions about whether Peter returned to a private workshop after 1230 or simply retired or died. Peter's case does, however, offer a potential solution to the question of why the surviving royal records make no reference to the retirement or death of the majority of the crossbow makers who worked for the government.[25] If these craftsmen simply moved out of royal service into private workshops, which also produced weapons for the royal government,

---

20 *CLR 1240–1245*, 79 and 84. The final purchase noted here appears in a much later collection of government documents. See *CLR 1267–1272*, 261.

21 See, for example, *CLR 1260–1267*, 235 and 273.

22 The one exception is the purchase of £200 worth of crossbows from a Genoese merchant named Anselm in February 1228. *CLR 1226–1240*, 71. It is worth noting that £200 worth of crossbows did constitute a large purchase of these weapons. As we saw already, wooden crossbows, likely of the "one-foot" type, cost as little as 1 s. 6 d. If the entire shipment of crossbows from Genoa consisted of these weapons, and wooden crossbows of the one-foot type were the most common weapons used in England, we are looking at an order of almost 2,700 crossbows. Even if all of the crossbows were of the most expensive type, namely composite bows equipped with a *turnus*, this would still entail a shipment of 400 weapons each costing 10 s.

23 Concerning Peter's career, see Bachrach, "Crossbow Makers", 177.

24 See *CR II*, 58.

25 Concerning this problem, see Bachrach, "Royal Crossbow Makers", 193–196.

there would have been no need for royal clerks to make any further reference to these men, unless they sold arms to the government.[26]

In addition to direct purchases by King Henry III's government of crossbows from private sources, we also catch a glimpse of non-governmental production in the personal arsenals maintained by magnates. For example, following the death in 1246 of Earl William Marshal, the son of the famed marshal who served as regent for Henry III in 1216, the royal government exercised its right of first purchase of private arsenals, and the record of that sale was recorded by government clerks.[27] On 29 July 1246, orders were issued by the Chancery to the constable of the Tower of London instructing him to take possession of a large collection of weapons, including fifty-two wooden and composite crossbows of various types, which had been purchased from executors of the earl's will.[28] Given William Marshal's possession of these weapons, which clearly belonged to him (there would otherwise be no need to purchase them from his executors), the obvious question is where did he get them? King Henry's government maintained extensive records dealing with all aspects of its crossbow program, including the production, transportation, storage, and, as noted, purchase of these weapons.[29] There are no references, however, to the sale of these weapons by the government to any individuals or institutions. It therefore seems likely that magnates such as William Marshal purchased crossbows on the private market and, perhaps, also employed their own crossbow makers.[30]

There is evidence to suggest that at least some magnates did employ their own crossbow makers early in Henry III's reign. On 18 October 1224, Henry III's regency council issued an order to Archbishop Walter de Gray of York insisting that a crossbow maker employed at Knaresborough Castle, named Roger, along with his tools, be sent to serve at the newly established royal workshop at the Tower of London.[31] A second order making the same demand was issued on

---

26 The only case in which the royal clerks refer to the death of a crossbow maker in royal service was in respect to a man named James of Toulouse who was replaced at the Tower of London by Thomas de Sancto Sepulchro in the spring of 1252. See *CLR 1251–1260*, 48.

27 It seems likely that William Marshal inherited at least some of these weapons from his elder brother Richard who employed crossbowmen in numerous battles, including the siege of Monmouth in 1233. See *Matthaei Parisiensis, monachi sancti Albani, Chronica majora*, ed. H. R. Luard, 7 vols (London, 1872–1883), III: 256. Concerning this text, see Matthew Strickland, *War and Chivalry: The Conduct and Perception of War in England and Normandy, 1066–1217* (Cambridge, 1996), 175.

28 *CR 1242–1247*, 446.

29 Concerning the very large number of documents dealing with all aspects of crossbow production, storage, shipping, and repair, see Bachrach, "Royal Crossbow Makers", 168–197.

30 Similar royal efforts to acquire the arsenals of magnates, which included crossbows, can be seen earlier in Henry's reign, in 1233. The arsenals accumulated by Ranulph, earl of Chester and Lincoln, and by William Briwere, were both acquired by the royal government and sent to royal castles for storage. See *CR 1231–1234*, 181 and 256.

31 *CR I*, 620.

20 October 1224.[32] It would appear, however, that the archbishop was somewhat slow in carrying out the council's wishes, because on 9 January 1225 a third letter was issued ordering the prelate to send along all of Roger's remaining tools and materials that remained at Knaresborough Castle and to have them transported to the Tower of London where Roger now worked.[33]

If we consider the seven decades from 1202 to 1272 from an economic perspective with respect to the production of crossbows in England, it would appear that an initial royal monopoly during John's reign gave way to a mixed production scheme under Henry III, with both governmental and private sources. The production of crossbows by workers employed by magnates might be considered a mixed category of private and public. Nevertheless, the apparent spread of technical expertise regarding the production of crossbows into the private market does not seem to have undermined the leading role of government workshops in providing crossbows for royal use. The surviving evidence from Henry's fifty-six-year reign indicates that royal production at the Tower of London and Corfe Castle, and later at Windsor accounted for the majority of the crossbows deployed by the English government in garrisons and depots throughout the period 1216–1272. The dozen or so references to the purchase of crossbows from private sources are dwarfed in the administrative records by hundreds of documents concerning all aspects of crossbow production, including the purchase of prodigious quantities of materials and the pay and support of almost a full score of crossbow makers, some with teams of assistants, who were employed by Henry's government.[34]

Alongside this significant production of crossbows by and for the royal government, there would also appear to have been significant private production for private or semi-private purposes. As noted, magnates, such as William Marshal and perhaps Archbishop Walter de Gray of York, created their own arsenals, either to fulfill their military obligations to the crown or to pursue private local interests by violent means. It is likely that many of these weapons came from private producers.[35] In addition, some militia forces were also equipped with crossbows. During King John's reign, the royal government mobilized crossbowmen from the shire levies, as was the case, for example, prior to the invasion of France in 1213. According to Matthew Paris, the levies assembled at Dover,

---

32 Ibid.

33 *CR II*, 13.

34 All aspects of these crossbow makers' work, including the purchase of supplies, are dealt with in detail in Bachrach, "Crossbow Makers", passim.

35 While there are scores of references in the surviving government documents to the transfer of crossbows to royal fortresses, barely a handful attest to the delivery of weapons to individual magnates who were not serving as the constables of royal fortresses. According to the documents, even Prince Edward, the king's eldest son and heir, usually received crossbows in the context of providing weapons for a royal garrison. Thus, for example, on 21 November 1265, the Chancery sent orders to the constable of the Tower of London to issue five composite crossbows along with three buckets of crossbow bolts to Edward for garrison at Odiham Castle. See *CR 1264–1268*, 149.

Feversham, and Ipswich included not only archers (*sagitarii*) but crossbowmen (*balistarii*) as well.[36] This pattern of deploying crossbow-armed militiamen continued into Henry III's reign. The siege of the castle of Bedford in 1224, for example, included a noteworthy body of crossbowmen at least some of whom, it would appear, were drawn from the king's levies rather than from the ranks of Henry III's professional troops.[37]

Private producers of crossbows would also appear to have supplemented their income from the military market with crossbow production for hunting. Thus, for example, the forest ordinance issued by the royal government in 1243 makes specific reference to the possession of crossbows by men in the rural population of England.[38] In particular, selected knights in each county were to undertake an inquest in order to ascertain who had bows and arrows, and crossbows (*balistae*), as well as hunting dogs, or any other tool, which could be used to cause mischief in the king's forests.[39]

Crossbow production 1272–1307

During the first years of his reign up to 1275, Edward I's government would seem to have maintained the traditional policy with respect to the acquisition of crossbows for use by English troops. These weapons continued to be produced by royal

---

36 Matthew Paris, *Chronica majora*, II: 539. On this point, see Powicke, *Military Obligation*, 60.

37 Matthew Paris, *Chronica majora*, III: 85. For a useful introduction to the siege and the royal logistical efforts required to sustain it, see Emilie Amt, "Besieging Bedford: Military Logistics in 1224", *The Journal of Medieval Military History* 1 (2002), 101–124.
In 1221, the royal government similarly mobilized crossbowmen from the levies to serve at the siege of Bytham Castle in Lincoln. On 2 February 1221, the Chancery issued an order to Philip Mark, sheriff of Nottingham, to mobilize the local levies, including the *balistarii*, to participate in the siege. In this context it is significant that Philip Mark was instructed to leave the garrison of Nottingham, that is his professional soldiers, at home. See *CR I*, 448, "*mandamus vobis firmiter quod statim visis litteris istis sub quanta poteritis festinacione in propria persona vestra iter arripiatis veniendi in occursum nostrum usque Biha' (Bytham) cum tota gente armata qua vobiscum adducere poteritis baillia et familia vestra salva garnisione castri nostri Nottingham*" ("We firmly command that having seen this letter, you hurry as quickly as possible in person to meet us at Bytham with all of the armed men, whom you are able to mobilize from your bailiwick and your military household, leaving in place, however, the members of our garrison at Nottingham"). We also see the mobilization of levies armed with crossbows in the reigns of Edward I and Edward II. See the discussion by David S. Bachrach, "Urban Military Force of England and Germany c. 1240–c. 1315, A Comparison", in *Mercenaries and Paid Men: The Mercenary Identity in the Middle Ages*, ed. John France (Leiden, 2008), 231–242, here 236, and in this volume; and National Archives E372/132 1v and 22r; E372/133 18r and 29r; C62/63 4r; E101/5/19; E101/14/33.

38 *CR 1242–1247*, 126.

39 Ibid., "*Item milites debent attente inquirere in itinere suo, quis habuerit arcus et sagittas vel balistas ..., vel aliquod aliud ingenium ad malefaciendum domino regi de forestis suis*" ("The knights are to inquire diligently along their itinerary who possesses bows and arrows, and who possesses crossbows, and has undertaken anything to the detriment of the Lord King in his forests"). The same ordinance was reissued in 1251. See *CR 1251–1253*, 47.

officers in the long-established workshops at the Tower of London and Windsor Castle.[40] Furthermore, at least three members of Henry III's staff of crossbow makers, including Thomas de Sancto Sepulchro, Henry, and Conrad, noted as a specialist in the construction of composite crossbows, appear numerous times in the surviving administrative documents during the initial stages of Edward's reign, which include both his time on crusade and his first year back in England.[41]

Indeed, the commitment of the new government to the continued production of crossbows during the early years of Edward's reign is made clear by the expansion of the number of royal workshops in operation. Even before Edward returned to England for his coronation, a third royal workshop was established at Cambridge in February 1274, which complemented the efforts of the production centers at the Tower of London and Windsor Castle.[42] A fourth production center was established at Dover Castle in January 1275, about four months after Edward was crowned king on 19 August 1274.[43]

Within a decade, Edward's government again expanded the number of workshops that produced crossbows for government use. The impetus for this substantial increase in royal crossbow production was the Second Welsh War (1282–1284), which saw the establishment of English hegemony over Wales.[44] In order to maintain the hard-won English gains, Edward's government instituted a policy of building a system of massive fortifications along the Welsh coast that could be used as centers of regional control and as bases for further military action in case of Welsh revolts, such as those that occurred in 1287 and 1294–1295. In October 1284, following the temporary end of active fighting in Wales, the royal government issued orders for the establishment of professional garrisons in the

---

40 It should be noted that Edward did not return from crusade until 2 August 1274 and that the government administration up to this point was largely in the hands of his father's men. Nevertheless, Edward did continue to employ at least two of his father's leading crossbow makers until at least 1277, more than a year after his return to England. See the next note.

41 For the details of the service of these crossbow makers during Henry III's reign, see Bachrach "Crossbow Makers", 173–197. Thomas, Conrad, and Henry appear numerous times in the surviving records. See National Archives C62/49, C62/50, C62/51, *CR 1272–1279*, 6 and 26. Both Henry and Conrad remained in royal service until at least March and December 1275, respectively. See C62/51 10r and C62/52 10r. The references to Conrad during the final year of his service to the king show that he had been moved from Windsor to the Tower of London. This same Conrad accompanied royal troops on campaign in Wales in 1277, and is described as coming "from London". See E101/3/11 1r.

42 National Archives C62/50 7r.

43 National Archives C62/51 11r. The crossbow makers at Cambridge and Dover are not mentioned by name in the Chancery documents but are referred to as *atilliator*, the traditional term for crossbow makers in royal administrative documents since the mid-1240s. On this point, see Bachrach, "Crossbow Makers", 172.

44 The basic work on Edward's conquest of Wales remains Morris, *The Welsh Wars of Edward*. Also see Ifor Rowlands, "The Edwardian Conquest and its Military Consolidation", in *Edward I and Wales*, ed. Trevor Herbert and Gareth Elwyn Jones (Cardiff, 1988), 41–72.

Welsh fortresses of Criccieth, Conway, Bere, Harlech, and Caernarvon.[45] Each of the newly appointed castle constables was required to recruit ten to fifteen professional crossbowmen, and twenty to thirty foot sergeants, as well as a staff of specialists including a chaplain, a mason, and a carpenter.[46] Most significantly in the present context, each of the garrison commanders also was required to recruit a crossbow maker (*atilliator*) to serve in the castle.[47]

It would seem clear that it was not necessary to employ a full-time crossbow maker to supply the needs of the relatively small number of professional crossbowmen in each of these royal garrisons. Even in the aftermath of the Second Welsh War of 1282–1284, the number of crossbowmen assigned to these garrisons, including the English headquarters at Caernarvon, did not exceed fifteen men per garrison.[48] Rather, the five newly appointed crossbow makers almost certainly were intended to provide weapons to the loyal Welsh population of the region and to the English settlers who represented the bulk of the manpower for the defense of Caernarvon, Criccieth, and the other English-held fortifications.[49] Indeed, it seems likely that the Welsh castles were intended to serve as magazines or arms depots for these levies.

The importance of local forces, particularly local men armed with crossbows, for the defense of the Edwardian fortresses is made clear by the large numbers of crossbows and immense quantities of ammunition that were stored in these centers throughout the 1280s and 1290s up to King Edward's death in 1307. Criccieth Castle continued to boast a crossbow maker long after the 1282–1284 Welsh war convinced the royal government of the need to pursue an expanded policy of crossbow production. In 1295, for example, Richard Havering, the constable of Criccieth, recorded the wages of Robert the crossbow maker (*atilliator*) in the garrison account book.[50] Similarly, the surviving garrison and supply records for Caernarvon show continued large-scale production of crossbows there over a long period. On 1 June 1290, for example, the Chancery issued orders to the Exchequer to credit the account of Robert de Delura, the royal chancellor at Caernarvon, for in excess of £17 that he spent on materials for the construction at this fortress of 300 of these weapons under the direction of the *atilliator* William.[51] The latter, who was a highly paid professional earning 8 d. per day, continued to serve at Caernarvon until at least 1300.[52]

45 National Archives C77/5.
46 Ibid.
47 Ibid.
48 Ibid.
49 Concerning the use of the population around the fortresses as militia forces, see Rowlands, "The Edwardian Conquest", 52–53; and Frederick C. Suppe, *Military Institutions on the Welsh Marches: Shropshire AD 1066–1300* (Woodbridge, 1994), 17.
50 See National Archives E101/5/17.
51 National Archives C62/66 4r.
52 National Archives C62/67 2r; C62/69 1r; C62/76 7r.

Thus, even after the last major uprising in Wales ended in 1295, Edward's government continued to expend considerable resources there to produce crossbows. There was even an expansion of production in Wales in the early fourteenth century, with additional workshops established at Carmarthen and Dryslwyn Castles no later than 1301.[53] In addition to the Welsh production facilities, Edward's government also established a workshop for crossbow production on the Welsh frontier at Chester by 1297.[54] Before this point, Chester had served as a staging point and depot for the shipment of both crossbows and quarrels to Wales during periods of intense fighting.[55]

As was true in Wales, the English campaigns in Scotland during Edward I's reign (1296–1307) depended heavily on the control of fortified towns and castles, many of which were located on the coast. Here too, the royal government established new centers for the production of crossbows to support the king's forces in Scotland. The garrison records for Berwick, for example, include the wages of a crossbow maker stationed there in 1299.[56] The production facility at Berwick was still in operation five years later when a memorandum detailing the delivery of supplies from Berwick to Stirling Castle indicates that the royal officer in charge of logistics at Berwick had overseen the continuing production of crossbows there in 1304.[57] According to the text of the document, Robert, a ship captain from Alemouth, had carried a load of lead, iron, and crossbows (*balistae*), as well as quarrels for the *balistae* that had been produced (*preparatae*) at Berwick at the orders of Richard de Bremesgrave, the royal receiver there.[58] All told, pay records at Berwick show the continuous employment of *atilliatores* there from at least 1299–1307.

Elsewhere in Scotland, the garrison rolls for Roxburgh Castle record the continuous presence of an *atilliator* there for at least five years, 1300–1304.[59] Four other fortified centers, Jedburgh, Lochmaben, Dumfries, and Edinburgh, also had *atilliatores* on staff in the garrison throughout the period 1300–1304.[60] Two further production facilities, at Linlithgow and Kirkintilloch, were established no

---

53 National Archives E372/146 33v.
54 National Archives E372/143 33v; and C62/75 6v–7r.
55 On 12 January 1283, for example, the Chancery issued orders to the Exchequer to provide in excess of £86 to the royal officer Peter de la Mare for the twelve crossbows and 80,000 quarrels which he purchased and shipped to the fortress at Carmarthen. See National Archives C62/59 8r. In November 1287, the Chancery sent orders to the Exchequer to issue in excess of £88 to Thomas de Veffinis, the sheriff of Canterbury, for the purchase and dispatch of 120 bows for crossbows to Carmarthen, and for the purchase, production, and dispatch of 120,000 quarrels to the same castle. See C62/64 1r.
56 National Archives E101/7/10.
57 National Archives C47/22/9 #71.
58 Ibid.
59 National Archives E39/93/18; E101/9/9; E101/10/6 1v; E101/11/1 2r; E101/12/10.
60 National Archives E101/68/1 5r–12r; E39/93/18; E101/9/9; E101/8/27; E101/10/6; E101/12/10; E101/11/1 2r–2v; E101/12/18 2r–5r.

later than 1302, and similarly were in operation continuously up to at least 1304.[61] In sum, at least eight production facilities were opened in Scotland in the period 1299–1302.

As is clear from the previous discussion, Edward's government maintained the traditional policy of producing a substantial number of the crossbows required by its military forces in royal workshops staffed by royal officials. Nevertheless, the well-established centers at the Tower of London and Windsor Castle, which played a dominant role in this production during Henry III's reign, would seem to have given way to workshops located in areas of current or potential conflict in Wales and Scotland.[62] This pattern of change within an overall paradigm of continuity also characterized the efforts of King Edward's government to supplement the supplies of crossbows available from royal workshops with the purchase of these weapons from private manufacturers. As will be seen below, in addition to obtaining large numbers of crossbows from the local, English market, the royal government also began to participate again in the international arms trade.

As discussed, Henry III's government made regular purchases of crossbows from domestic manufacturers. The surviving records from this period, however, do not provide detailed information about who these manufacturers were or where they were based. For example, the Chancery order from 1223 that required the Exchequer to credit the account of the constable of Bristol castle for the forty wooden crossbows he had purchased does not mention from whom he bought these weapons.[63] The laconic nature of these texts from Henry's reign is explained by the fact that only the enrolled, that is the redacted version, of a far more extensive parchment trail has survived. By contrast, many thousands of original royal documents, many of which contain numerous circumstantial details, have survived from Edward's reign. As a consequence, it frequently is possible to ascertain the names of the craftsman who produced the crossbows and sometimes the location of their workshops as well.

For example, a memorandum issued in September 1302 pursuant to the king's demands for supplies, records that the mayor and burgesses of Newcastle delivered eighty-seven crossbows and other arms to William de Werk, the royal officer

---

61 National Archives E101/10/6 6r–6v; E101/11/1 3v and 10v; and E101/12/18 4r–5r.

62 The evidence from the surviving government documents indicates that Windsor continued to house a crossbow production facility up to 1278. See National Archives E372/122 1v. The facility at the Tower of London continued to produce crossbows until at least 1277. See E101/3/11. Production of crossbows at the Tower of London was renewed, apparently on an intensive scale, in 1294, perhaps in response to the need for more crossbows for the king's Welsh and Gascon campaigns during these years. The liberate roll accounts for 1293–1294 and 1294–1295 record that a crossbow maker named William Conrad oversaw a massive effort to produce a variety of missile weapons, including crossbows, self-bows, and *springalds* at the Tower of London with a total cost of over £566. See C62/70 2r; and C62/71 2r. This high level of production continued at the Tower until at least 1299. See E372/144 19v.

63 *CR I*, 533.

in charge of logistics for the king's Scottish castles.[64] In the context of setting out the sacrifices made by the good townspeople of Newcastle to the royal war effort, the memorandum notes that forty-five of the crossbows had been purchased from three separate men named John Wallas, Roger Archer, and Robert de Talten. The remainder of the crossbows appears to have come from the stores kept by the town of Newcastle, because the memorandum simply records that these weapons were delivered by the mayor and burgesses without any reference to how they were acquired. A similar memorandum, this one issued in 1304, records the purchase by the royal government of a wide variety of arms, including twenty-nine cross-bows.[65] The document records the names of a total of thirteen men engaged in the production of arms, including four crossbow makers: John of Wales, Robert de Talkari, Roger Doulker, and Hugh Doulker, who likely was related to Roger.[66] As was true of the memorandum concerning the delivery of arms by the officials of Newcastle, this document does not specify where the arms were produced. Nevertheless, it provides an additional indication that the private production of crossbows was not limited to a few individuals during the early fourteenth century.

In addition to providing the names of individual crossbow makers who sold their wares to the crown, some surviving government documents also shed light on where these weapons were produced. On 20 May 1304, for example, Edward issued an order to the sheriffs of London instructing them to send crossbows, self-bows, and bolts to the army at Stirling Castle.[67] The king specifically insisted that the sheriffs find all of the crossbows and bolts that were available for sale within their bailiwick and that they purchase them without delay.[68] After receiving this order, the two sheriffs of London, named William and John de Omeford, used the same parchment, on which the king had sent his directive to record their expenses in carrying out Edward's commands. According to their notes, the sheriffs pur-chased eighty-five crossbows in June of 1304 for just over £9, which provides a

---

64   *Calendar of Documents Relating to Scotland 1272–1307*, ed. Joseph Bain (Edinburgh, 1884), 339.

65   National Archives E101/12/12.

66   It is of interest in the present context that each of the crossbow makers listed in this memorandum would also appear to have been a bowyer as well. In addition to being paid for *balistae*, they are also paid for *arcubi*, which usually means a bow stave.

67   National Archives E101/12/5. A similar order survives from much earlier in Edward's reign. On 8 April 1288, for example, the Chancery issued orders to the sheriff of London to purchase forty-four crossbows, including forty of the "one-foot" type and four of the "two-foot" type, along with baldrics, for use by the king. See *CR 1279–1288*, 502.

68   National Archives E101/12/5, "*Vobis precipimus quod omnes balistas, quarellos, et sagittas quas infra balliam vestram venditoras expositas aliqualiter contigerit inveneretis sine dilatione aliqua dicto exitibus ballia vestro ad opus nostrum emi facitis*" ("We command you that you are to find, without any delay, all of the crossbows, bolts, and arrows, which are available for sale in your bailiwick, and you are to purchase them for our use with the revenues from your bailiwick").

glimpse at the number of crossbows that were in stock in the workshops of private manufacturers at a particular moment in the city of London.[69]

Several other texts provide additional hints that the crossbow makers of London were seen by the royal government as a valuable source for these weapons. Standard administrative procedure during Edward's reign required that castle constables, as well as other royal officers who commanded arsenals and arms depots, keep detailed accounts so that the central government would have as complete as possible a record of how many weapons of each type in the royal arsenal were available in working order at any particular moment.[70] In order to meet these requirements, the clerks of these constables and royal officers kept running accounts of all the weapons that were received or dispatched by their commanders, and noted their condition. In addition, these same clerks kept written accounts of all of the constable's expenses in repairing, storing, and transporting weapons. Finally, these clerks kept detailed records of how much money the constables had spent to acquire or build new weapons.

In the present context, an example of a running account of this type from the Tower of London, written in 1294, gives an indication that the constable there purchased significant numbers of crossbows from the local market. In particular, the clerk recorded that the constable Ralph of Sandwich sent forty crossbows to the royal forces operating in Wales, of which thirty-six were purchased by the constable and four were withdrawn from the Tower's arsenal.[71] Three points seem rather clear from the clerk's account. First, Ralph of Sandwich had received orders to send forty crossbows to Wales. Second, these orders authorized him, in a manner similar to the orders issued to the sheriffs of London in 1304, noted earlier, to purchase as many weapons as possible. Third, Ralph was only able to purchase thirty-six crossbows and therefore had to make up the difference from the stocks maintained at the Tower of London.[72]

---

69   By way of context, it should be noted that the sheriffs were able to purchase 120 self-bows at the same time for a total price of just over 82 s. See ibid.

70   Regarding the enormous "paper trail" that was required for this kind of administrative oversight, see David S. Bachrach, "Military Planning in Thirteenth-Century England", *Nottingham Medieval Studies* 49 (2005), 43–63, and in this volume.

71   National Archives C47/2/2 #12. The text adds that Ralph also dispatched forty-five baldrics, which had also been purchased, and 10,000 quarrels that had been withdrawn from the stocks stored at the Tower of London.

72   The practice by the royal government of purchasing crossbows from private makers in London is also suggested by a receipt issued in 1303, by John Droxford, who served as the receiver or logistics officer of the king's Wardrobe, to James of Malines, for the purchase of forty crossbows, extra cords, and 3,000 quarrels. According to the text of the receipt, James shipped these weapons in two wagons from London to the Scottish fortress of Linlithgow. See National Archives C47/22/2. Evidence from an even larger purchase of eighty-four crossbows, including "one-foot", "two-foot", and *turnus*-equipped varieties, from London makers can be seen in the liberate rolls for 1298–1299. In this case, funds were issued to Thomas of Suffolk and Adam of Fuleham, until recently the sheriffs of London, for the money they spent purchasing four dozen crossbows *de uno pede*, two dozen crossbows *ad duos pedes*, and one dozen crossbows *de turno*, as well as 104,000 quarrels for these weapons. See C62/75 4r.

The increased number and variety of documents surviving from the reign of Edward I permit a clearer picture than is possible for the period before 1272 of royal efforts to supplement its own production of crossbows with purchases from private makers. This far more nuanced picture concerning the names and even the locations of these private arms makers confirms that Edward's government maintained considerable continuity with the practices of royal officers serving Henry III. It is important to emphasize, however, that just as the production of crossbows by the royal government during Edward's reign was characterized by change within an overall pattern of continuity in royal practice, so too the purchase of weapons from private suppliers demonstrates the desire of the king's officials to expand their efforts to obtain crossbows for the king's troops. In particular, Edward I's officials began to import significant numbers of crossbows from abroad, particularly from Gascony.

A memorandum issued 21 November 1297 by Earl Henry de Lacy of Lincoln, then serving as the royal governor in Gascony, makes clear how this trade in crossbows was conducted.[73] The memorandum states that Henry de Lacy had disbursed in excess of £20 to a professional crossbowman named Richard, identified as an Englishman in the text, for the purchase of crossbows. These crossbows were then handed over to a royal clerk named John de Sandale for transport back to England.[74] To put this purchase in context, the prices for crossbows in the 1290s ranged from 1 s. 6 d. for the most common and simple wooden crossbows equipped with a stirrup of the "one-foot" type, to 4s. for crossbows equipped with a "two-foot" stirrup, to 10 s. for the most expensive composite bows equipped with a mechanical spanning device known as a *turnus*.[75] Richard therefore purchased

---

73 National Archives E210/6478.

74 Ibid. We can see a similar shipment of crossbows from Gascony in a document detailing the cargo of a ship sailing from Bordeaux to London in March 1285, including twenty crossbows among other munitions. The ship sank on route, and royal officials made a record of material that had been lost in the accident. See National Archives C47/2/16 #24.

75 These prices come from a memorandum issued by John Droxford, logistics officer for the royal Wardrobe, on behalf of James de Maline, noted previously, who had purchased and transported "one-foot", "two-foot", and *turnus*-equipped crossbows from London to the royal forces stationed at the Scottish castle of Linlithgow. See National Archives C47/22/2. These prices are similar to those paid by royal officers in others situations. In 1280, for example, the royal officer Peter de la Mare paid 26 s. for twelve crossbows, or 2 s. 2 d. each. These weapons likely were of the "one-foot" variety. See C62/59 8r. In 1298, Walter Beauchamp, the constable of Gloucester Castle, paid 5 s. apiece for "two-foot" crossbows, which he had purchased for the garrison under his command. See C62/74 5r. In 1301, Bishop John of Carlisle spent 26 s. on eight "one-foot" crossbows and two crossbows *ad turnum* for use at Lochmaben Castle. See C62/77 4r. Although the text from the liberate roll does not specify how much the bishop spent for each type of weapon, it seems clear that they were rather less expensive than those discussed. In September 1302, the mayor and burgesses of Newcastle delivered a significant quantity of crossbows to the royal army in Scotland, including twelve priced at 2 s. 2 d., twenty-one for 2 s., and a further twelve for 2 s. each. See *Calendar of Documents Relating to Scotland 1272–1307*, 339. It is almost certainly the case that these were crossbows of the "one-foot" type. Finally, a memorandum concerning the purchase of

a minimum of forty weapons, if all of them were of the most expensive type, or perhaps as many 266 basic wooden crossbows.

Conclusion

The crossbow was an important, perhaps the most important, handheld missile weapon in use by English forces during the late twelfth century, that is before the beginning of noteworthy production of them in England during the reign of King John. The surviving administrative records from the thirteenth and early fourteenth century demonstrate that royal government continued to expend considerable resources on both the production and acquisition of crossbows throughout the reigns of Henry III and Edward I. Indeed, it would appear that the crown expended greater resources to equip its troops with crossbows than had been the case during the early thirteenth century. This is evident both in the greater number of royal production facilities in operation during the reign of Edward I, and in the greater numbers of crossbows procured by the government on the private market during his reign.

In the two decades between 1282–1302, the royal government opened at least sixteen new production facilities in Wales, in Scotland, and in Chester Castle, and re-opened on a massive scale production at the Tower of London. Moreover, even this extraordinary level of government production was insufficient to meet royal logistical demands. Purchases of crossbows from private sources in England continued unabated throughout Edward's reign. Even this combination of government and private production was insufficient, however, to supply all of the crossbowmen in Edward I's armies. As a result, Edward's government renewed the policies of John's reign by beginning large-scale importation of crossbows from the continent.

Much of this increase, particularly after 1272, may be explained by the significantly greater scale of the military operations conducted by Edward I as contrasted with either his father or his grandfather. Edward, although ruling for thirty-five years as compared with the fifty-six years of his father, conducted significantly more large military campaigns. What is incontestable is that the crossbow was an exceptionally important missile weapon on an enormous scale throughout the thirteenth century, and particularly during Edward I's reign.

---

a variety of weapons by the royal government, issued in 1304, records that John of Wales was paid 24 s. for ten crossbows, Robert Talkari was paid 12 s. 6 d. for six crossbows, Roger Doulker was paid 20 s. for ten crossbows, and Hugh Doulker was paid 6 s. for three crossbows. On average the price for these crossbows was just over 2 s. each. See E/101/12/12. The brief discussion of prices for crossbows in Morris, *Welsh Wars*, 91–92, does not take into account the majority of the documents cited here.

12

KING EDWARD I'S MILITARY BUREAUCRACY

The case of Peter of Dunwich

It is common in collections of this type to recall how the honoree helped in shaping one's career or intellectual development, and generally provided some *beneficium* (one of the honoree's favorite words) in the course of academic interchange. But in my case, the situation is rather different and quite rare. My earliest memories of our honoree go back more than forty-five years to when he held my hand in the station in Angoulême as my family waited for the train to go back to Poitiers. Over the intervening years, the honoree taught me how to skip so that I could pass kindergarten, took me and my younger brother on nature walks, coached my soccer team, drove me to swim meets, and helped me with my Latin homework. Long before I knew anything about Bernie the scholar, I just knew him as my dad. My intellectual debts to him are incalculable, but far more important has been the almost fifty years of a father's love. So this one is for you, Dad.

Introduction

Over the course of his thirty-five-year reign, Edward I of England (1272–1307) enjoyed enormous military success, particularly in Wales and Scotland, and held his own on the continent against King Philip IV of France (1285–1314).[1] However, Edward's military achievements owed relatively little to his personal command of armies in the field. Indeed, his successes in this area were limited to just three encounters. Early in his career, at the battle of Lewes (1264), Edward's contingent defeated the city militia of London under Simon de Montfort's command in an otherwise losing effort for the royal army. At Evesham (1265), Prince Edward led the royalist army to a crushing victory over Simon de Montfort's baronial forces. Later in his career, Edward commanded

---

1 For a survey of Edward I's reign, which offers considerable attention to military affairs, see Michael Prestwich, *Edward I*, 2nd edn (New Haven, CT, and London, 1997); and also idem, *War, Politics and Finance under Edward I* (Totowa, NJ, 1972).

the English forces at the battle of Falkirk (1298), where he defeated the Scots under the command of William Wallace.[2]

Rather than in battlefield command, Edward's genius lay in the mobilization of vast material, financial, and human resources with which English armies ground down and eventually overwhelmed their opponents.[3] Over the course of the 1280s, 1290s, and early fourteenth century, the English royal government raised and supplied armies numbering in the tens of thousands of men for sustained military operations lasting many months.[4] The English royal government would not mobilize armies of comparable size again until the early modern era. What makes Edward I's achievement even more remarkable is the very small scale of the military administration that he inherited from his father Henry III (1216–1272).[5]

As the great mass of surviving documents from the late thirteenth and early fourteenth century make clear, the vast increase in the size of the royal armies, and the concomitant vast increase in the capacity of the institutions that supported them, was the result of Edward I's own policy decisions.[6] However, the implementation of these policies was the work of many dedicated professionals, who remained in the royal service for many years, and even decades. Several of King Edward's chief advisors and ministers have received some attention from scholars. These include Walter Langton, who served as royal treasurer and held office as bishop of Lichfield; John Droxford, who served as keeper of the Wardrobe; and John Sandale, who held a variety of high level offices, including chamberlain of Scotland.[7] For the most part, however, the mid-level administrators, that is the men who traveled throughout England, Wales, and Scotland, and overseas to implement royal policy, have not benefited from a thorough scholarly investigation of their entire careers. The following study, therefore, is intended to highlight the career of one man, Peter of Dunwich, whose service helps to illuminate the range of administrative duties of a large cadre of royal bureaucrats who labored

---

2   Among the first scholars to take serious note of Edward I's success in mobilizing military resources on a grand scale was A. Z. Freeman, "The King's Penny: The Headquarters Paymasters under Edward I, 1295–1307", *Journal of British Studies* 6 (1966), 1–22.

3   See, for example, Prestwich, *War, Politics*, 114–136.

4   Ibid., 92–113.

5   Regarding the relatively small inheritance that Edward I received in terms of military administration from his father Henry III, see David S. Bachrach, "Military Logistics in the Reign of Edward I of England, 1272–1307", *War in History* 13.4 (2006), 421–438, particularly 421–424.

6   Edward I's role as a decisive decision maker comes through clearly in the biography by Prestwich, *Edward I*. See, for example, ibid., 62, 76, 272, and 350–351. Also see the important study by Caroline Burt, *Edward I and the Governance of England, 1272–1307* (Cambridge, 2012), who emphasizes Edward's personal leadership in the legal reforms instituted during his reign.

7   See, for example, Freeman, "King's Penny", 1–22; and Prestwich, *Edward I*, 138, 142, 154, 169, 399, 429, 445, 504, 510, 512, 534, 541, 563.

on behalf of the English government and facilitated the military successes of Edward I's reign.[8]

Peter of Dunwich in royal service

Peter, apparently, came into the royal service during the summer of 1295. There is no surviving reference to his having undertaken any tasks directly on behalf of the king before this date. Rather, two letters sent by Peter in the spring of 1295, both to Hugh de Cressingham, then a leading clerk in the royal financial administration, indicate that Peter was, at this time, in the service of the knight Nicholas de Stuteville, and through him in the entourage of Roger Bigod, the earl of Norfolk (1270–1306).[9] The first of these letters provided a report on Peter's interaction with a man named Michael Pichard regarding the collection of customs duties at Lincoln.[10] In the second letter, Peter passed on the wishes of Nicholas de Stuteville that Hugh de Cressingham have a speedy recovery from his current illness.[11] In light of this correspondence, it would appear that some arrangement was made between Hugh de Cressingham and Nicholas de Stuteville, or perhaps Roger Bigod, himself, to have Peter enter royal service.

Just a few months later, in August 1295, Peter of Dunwich was appointed by Edward I to oversee the implementation of a coastal defensive system that was intended to protect eastern England from invasion by the French.[12] Among his important duties, Peter was responsible for meeting in person with every major secular and ecclesiastical magnate in coastal counties of Essex, Norfolk, and Suffolk and providing them with detailed instructions for the mobilization of their military households and tenants to provide garrisons at key points along the entire coast. These magnates included the abbots and priors of half a dozen major

---

8 Peter has received some limited attention from scholars, principally for his role in the coastal defensive program organized in 1295 (more on this later), and for his service as the royal receiver at Berwick in 1297. See A. Z. Freeman, "A Moat Defensive: The Coast Defense Scheme of 1295", *Speculum* 42 (1967), 442–462; Prestwich, *War, Politics*, 122, 139, 146, and 148. Peter also was noted by John Edward Morris, *The Welsh Wars of Edward I: A Contribution to Mediaeval Military History* (Oxford, 1901), 287, to have mobilized levies of foot soldiers in Lancaster and Chester for the Falkirk campaign.

9 Hugh de Cressingham, who was killed at the battle of Stirling Bridge in 1297, is another mid-level administrator whose career would repay detailed investigation. For a brief survey of his career, see Freeman, "The King's Penny", particularly 7–10.

10 National Archives SC1/48/2.

11 National Archives SC1/28/1.

12 The details of Peter's duties in organizing the coastal defenses in this period are preserved in *Parliamentary Writs and Writs of Military Summons*, 2 vols in 4, ed. F. Palgrave (London, 1827–1834), here I: 269/10–11; *Manuscripts of the Corporations of Southampton and King's Lynn* (King's Lynn, 1887), 189; and *Calendar of Close Rolls 1288–1296* (London, 1904), 544–5.

monasteries, Roger Bigod, noted in the previous paragraph, and Humphrey de Bohun, earl of Hereford and Essex.[13]

In addition, Peter was given responsibility for coordinating the implementation of the coastal defense plans, devised by the royal court, with all of the royal officials who had responsibilities for local defense in these three counties. These men included the sheriffs of Essex, Suffolk, and Norfolk; the royal constables of all of the towns and castles in these three counties; and the specially appointed "guardians of the sea" (*custodes maris*), who were tasked by the king with organizing the defenses in specially designated defensive regions along the coast. Finally, Peter was responsible for coordinating the defensive preparations made by the civic authorities in all of coastal towns in both Norfolk and Suffolk.[14] The successful implementation of this defensive system was seen the very next year, in 1296, when many hundreds of men organized through Peter's efforts were mobilized to defend the coast again against potential French attack.[15]

In the meantime, however, Peter had formally joined the royal household, and was acting as one of the king's paymasters for the army operating in Wales during the autumn and winter of 1295.[16] The next spring, in March 1296, Peter received a letter of protection, which freed him from being harassed by any lawsuits or other legal matters while in the king's service.[17] Later that same year, Peter followed his new patron in the royal household, Hugh de Cressingham, to Scotland. The latter was established as the royal treasurer in Scotland in September 1296. That same month, Peter received a new letter of protection to last for one year as a consequence of his work in Scotland in the king's service.[18] Peter's main duties from the autumn of 1296 through the summer of 1297 consisted of organizing and administering the royal magazine at Berwick on Tweed, which was the main center of supply for all English military operations in Scotland.[19]

The English defeat at the battle of Stirling Bridge at the hands of William Wallace and Andrew Murray on 11 September 1297 led to a substantial reorganization of Edward I's military administration in Scotland. Hugh de Cressingham was killed in the battle, and one of the ramifications of his death was the departure of Peter of Dunwich from his role as receiver at Berwick, to be replaced by Richard de Bremesgrave.[20] But although he no longer served in the English royal

---

13 The coastal defense system as a whole is discussed in considerable detail by Freeman, "A Moat Defensive", 442–462, and for Peter's role, 447 and 450.

14 Ibid.

15 National Archives E101/5/29.

16 *Book of Prests of the King's Wardrobe for 1294–1295: Presented to John Goronwy Edwards*, ed. E. B. Fryde (Oxford, 1962), 153.

17 National Archives C67/11 m 5.

18 *Calendar of the Patent Rolls AD 1292–1301* (London, 1895), 197.

19 For Peter's service during this period, see *Calendar of Close Rolls 1296–1302* (London, 1908), 17; and National Archives E101/6/9, which is Peter's account (*compotus*) of his expenses while serving as the receiver at Berwick.

20 Richard de Bremesgrave's career is another that would repay detailed investigation.

administration in Scotland, Peter remained in Edward I's service. A letter patent issued on 23 October 1297, just six weeks after the defeat at Stirling Bridge, shows that Peter, along with another royal clerk named John de Hodelston, was being dispatched to mobilize a force of 11,000 foot soldiers in the counties of Lancashire, Cumberland, and Westmoreland.[21] This mobilization effort, which was intended to raise an army to avenge the loss at Stirling, took some time, and Peter was still in Lancashire in late December 1297.[22]

Peter, along with his staff and armed retainers, subsequently accompanied the royal army north to Scotland, and saw his work contribute to Edward I's victory at Falkirk on 22 July 1298.[23] While in Scotland, Peter was again given the task of organizing supplies for the royal army at Berwick. While there, Peter and his fellow royal clerk Robert Heron undertook the purchase of food and other supplies from English merchants who had traveled north in the hope of making a profit.[24] There was, however, some disagreement about how much money was paid out, and how much was still owed to the merchants, who brought suit against the two royal clerks. The issue dragged on for several years with the result that Peter and Robert wrote a letter to the king in November 1303, asking him to command the royal chamberlain to examine their records from the 1298 campaign, and pay the merchants so that the lawsuits could be brought to an end.[25]

Political difficulties in England and ongoing negotiations with the French meant that no major military campaign was undertaken in Scotland during the spring and summer campaigning season of 1299.[26] Peter of Dunwich was among the royal officials who were detailed to undertake other, non-military tasks, and he is visible in the surviving records acting as an itinerant royal justice in Suffolk in September 1299.[27] However, King Edward did lead an army into Galloway in the summer of 1300, and Peter of Dunwich was again in the company of his royal master, receiving considerable quantities of wine (three barrels) and half a metric ton of grain for himself, and his staff.[28]

From 1300 onward, the English undertook almost continuous military operations in Scotland, and Peter of Dunwich was to play an important role both in mobilizing supplies, and in naval operations for the next six years. In March of 1301, Peter was busy obtaining almost 1,000 metric tons of grain supplies in the counties of Norfolk and Suffolk for shipment to Edward's forces in Scotland.[29] Peter undertook this same task in Essex the following month, where he procured

---

21   See *Calendar of Patent Rolls 1292–1301*, 313.
22   National Archives E101/6/30 nr 6.
23   National Archives E101/7/2 nr 37.
24   National Archives SC8/43/21 nr 11.
25   Ibid.
26   See the discussion by Prestwich, *Edward I*, 482–483.
27   *Calendar of Patent Rolls 1292–1301*, 475.
28   National Archives E101/8/19.
29   *Calendar of Patent Rolls 1292–1301*, 578 and 583; and *Calendar of Close Rolls 1296–1302*.

some 300 metric tons of grain.[30] At the same time, Peter was given the task of expediting the mobilization of ships from the coastal towns of Essex, Norfolk, and Suffolk that were to travel to Berwick on Tweed.[31] Peter had well-established contacts with many of the eleven towns in these three counties that had been tasked by the royal government to provide ships. In particular, Peter had been responsible for organizing the local defense of at least half a dozen of these ports six years earlier, in 1295, including Yarmouth, Ipswich, Orford, Bawdsey, and Lynn, which were to provide fourteen of the nineteen ships demanded by the crown for service in Scotland.[32]

Peter's purveyance of grain and his mobilization of ships in Essex, Suffolk, and Norfolk were closely related. The food supplies were intended for the English army in Scotland. The ships were ordered to go to Berwick on Tweed, which was the main royal supply base for the army in Scotland. Consequently, it is almost certainly the case that Peter was given the two-fold task of obtaining food supplies and transportation for these supplies at the same time. Given his considerable familiarity with the counties of Essex, Suffolk, and Norfolk, the decision to put both of these responsibilities into Peter's hands clearly made considerable sense to the royal government.

In addition to his duties in these three counties the spring of 1301, Peter also was assigned the task of mobilizing and dispatching a further thirteen ships from the counties of Lincolnshire, Northumberland, and Yorkshire, located along England's northeast coast, to Berwick.[33] Peter's fellow commissioner in carrying out this duty was a man named John Thorpe. John also was a royal clerk, who ultimately was raised to the office of royal chamberlain during the final six weeks of Edward I's reign in 1307.[34]

In 1302, Peter was again deeply involved in the mobilization of fleets for Edward's current campaign in Scotland. A large number of seaports in the south-west and south of England in the counties of Cornwall, Devonshire, Somerset, Dorset, Hampshire, Sussex, and the Isle of Wight had reneged on their promises to provide ships for the spring campaign.[35] Chief among these culprits was the city of Bristol. In August 1302, Peter was given broad authority by the king to ensure that these towns either fulfilled their obligations to provide ships and well-armed crews, or paid fines to the crown commensurate with the damage that their failures had done to the royal campaign effort.[36] By September, Peter had completed his

---

30 *Calendar of Patent Rolls 1292–1301*, 589; and C47/22/4 nr 42.
31 National Archives E156/28/106.
32 Ibid.
33 Ibid.
34 Prestwich, *Edward I*, 146. John Thorpe's career also would repay careful examination.
35 *Calendar of Patent Rolls Preserved in the Public Record Office: 1301–1307* (London, 1898), 52–53, 89.
36 National Archives E101/10/21 nr 2 and nr 7. Also see *Calendar of Patent Rolls 1301–1307*, 54 and 61.

task to the satisfaction of Edward I, who instructed the royal clerk to attend him at the royal court in Westminster.[37]

Several months later, in November 1302, Peter was back in the southwest where he visited, in person, a total of thirty-three seaports, and made arrangements for the towns to provide ships and crews for the 1303 campaign season.[38] In an effort to avoid the difficulties that had taken place in the spring of 1302, King Edward dispatched Peter back to the southwest in March 1303 to ensure that the towns fulfilled the promises for ships and men that they had made the previous autumn.[39] In order to facilitate Peter's work in this regard, the king issued orders to the sheriffs, who held office in the southwest, to provide the royal clerk with all of the assistance that he required.[40] Evidently, Peter was successful in obtaining the promised ships and crews as King Edward did not dispatch commissioners to punish the general run of southwestern seaports in 1303 as he had done in 1302. Nevertheless, there was still one group of holdouts, and in May 1303 Peter of Dunwich sent a letter to William Greenfield, the royal chancellor, asking him to compel the bailiffs of a number of towns in Cornwall to contribute ships for the king's service.[41]

In February 1304, Peter was again sent to Scotland, on this occasion to purvey grain in the county of Fife, located between the Firth of Forth to the south and the Furth of Tay to the north.[42] By early April 1304, however, Peter was back in southern England, where he was given the task of helping to mobilize a fleet of twenty large ships, each with a very strong crew, from the Cinque Ports as well as the south coast of England.[43] These ships were to participate in an attack on Flanders pursuant to the recently concluded treaty between Edward and King Philip IV of France.[44] Peter, himself, initially was designated to serve in the English embassy to King Philip's court, but ultimately did not participate.[45]

It would appear that Peter received a leave from royal service in 1305, while he was engaged in several legal actions (more on this to follow). In late spring 1306, however, Peter was once again in Scotland. One of his main responsibilities was to supervise the organization of ships and crews in the regions between the Furth of Tay and Berwick in conjunction with a man named Edward Charles, whom King Edward had appointed as captain and admiral of the northern fleet.[46]

---

37 *Calendar of Charter Rolls Preserved in the Public Record Office* (London, 1908), 27.
38 National Archives E101/10/21 nr 11; and also see *Calendar of Patent Rolls 1301–1307*, 75.
39 National Archives E101/10/21 nr 10; and also see *Calendar of Close Rolls Preserved in the Public Record Office 1302–1307* (London, 1906), 76, 78–79.
40 *Calendar of Patent Rolls 1301–1307*, 128.
41 National Archives SC1/28/59.
42 National Archives E101/10/21 nr 9.
43 National Archives E101/10/21 nr 8. Also see *Calendar of Close Rolls 1302–1307*, 205; and *Calendar of Patent Rolls 1301–1307*, 219.
44 *Calendar of Patent Rolls 1301–1307*, 237.
45 Ibid.
46 National Archives E101/10/21 nr 4.

I have not been able to identify Peter in the royal service after the spring of 1306, although it is clear that he certainly was still alive in the autumn of this year, and retained the affection of the king, who wrote on Peter's behalf to the cathedral chapter in Glasgow.[47]

Who was Peter of Dunwich?

As this brief survey of Peter of Dunwich's career illustrates, he successfully undertook a wide range of crucial military administrative tasks in the king's service. But the question remains: who was this man? It would appear that Peter came from a land-owning family in Suffolk, and had at least one brother whose name was John, and whose family were Peter's heirs.[48] The Dunwich family's possession of a manor in Suffolk likely explains the connection between Peter and the entourage of Roger Bigod, whose earldom included both Suffolk and Norfolk.[49] Similarly, the decision by senior royal officials to utilize Peter to organize coastal defenses in Suffolk, as well as neighboring counties of Norfolk and Essex, in 1295 likely also resulted from the clerk's personal knowledge of the region, connections with the local gentry, and also, perhaps most importantly, his connection with Earl Roger Bigod. Peter's redeployment in this same region in 1301 to mobilize both supplies and ships for the war in Scotland can be understood in the same manner.

Other surviving records indicate that Peter was a cleric as well as a clerk. In January 1304, the king issued a letter to Archbishop Robert Winchelsey of Canterbury (1294–1313), instructing him not to harass Peter of Dunwich in any way because the latter was away in royal service. The crux of the matter was that Peter held a benefice in the archbishopric, and the archbishop wished to contest his possession of it.[50] Just two months later, in March 1304, King Edward sent another letter to Archbishop Robert instructing him to offer all possible assistance to Peter of Dunwich as the latter sought to secure a separate benefice in the diocese of Norwich.[51] In April 1304, King Edward sent another letter on behalf

---

47 National Archives SC1/12/132.
48 For the possession by Peter of property in Suffolk, see W. A. Copinger, *The Manors of Suffolk: Notes on their History and Devolution* 6 vols (London, 1905), II: 195, where Peter of Dunwich is noted as possessing the manor of Westleton in the hundred of Blything. In 1316, the manor had passed into the hands of Alexander of Dunwich, the son of John of Dunwich, who likely was Peter's brother (195). See, in this context, *Calendar of the Letter Books of the City of London c. 1291–1309*, ed. Reginald R. Sharpe (London, 1901), folio 86 b, which includes a letter sent on 22 July 1305 by the executors of Richard, son of John of Dunwich, to Sir Peter of Dunwich. Also see *Calendar of Close Rolls 1302–1307*, 351, where Peter admits to owing 40 marks to a man named Henry Tuke, and accepts that the sum will be levied against Peter's property in Suffolk, unless he repays the debt in full.
49 The fact that Peter was in the entourage of Nicholas de Stuteville, and that the latter was in the entourage of Roger Bigod, suggests that Nicholas's estates were concentrated in Suffolk as well.
50 *Calendar of Close Rolls 1302–1307*, 193.
51 National Archives SC1/14/95.

of Peter, this time to Bishop Robert Wishart of Glasgow (1271–1316) ordering the latter to provide a benefice in the church of Old Roxburgh to the royal clerk.[52] The king followed with a letter in September 1306 in which he ordered William Comyn, one of the chief officials in the Glasgow bishopric, to see to it that Peter continued to enjoy the prebend at Old Roxburg without any interference.[53]

Royal patronage certainly provided Peter of Dunwich with opportunities to gain wealth through the collecting of multiple prebends in both England and Scotland. However, King Edward's aggressive efforts to reward his faithful clerk with sinecures in Scotland did face considerable opposition. In particular, Baldred Bisset (c. 1260–1311), a Scottish ecclesiastic and lawyer who played a leading role presenting the case for Scottish independence to Pope Boniface VIII (1294–1303), sought to deprive Peter of his prebend at the church of Kinghorn in Fife, in diocese of St. Andrews.[54] To this end, Baldred sent a letter to Pope Clement V (1305–1314) claiming that Peter held the prebend unjustly, and should be ejected.[55]

Conclusion

In considering Peter of Dunwich's career, several points should be highlighted. First, it is clear that he was a talented administrator, who had the ability to transfer managerial skills from one set of tasks to another over a period of more than a decade. In addition to establishing a coherent coastal defensive system from disparate sources of military manpower, including local magnates, towns, and royal officials operating at the county level, Peter oversaw the administration of a major supply base, recruited very large military forces, oversaw the purchasing of thousands of tons of grain, and arranged for the mobilization of scores of ships both to carry supplies, and to conduct military operations. In return for this good and faithful service, Peter was rewarded with a string of church benefices, and royal support in maintaining them.

The career of each royal official was necessarily unique. Nevertheless, the career path of Peter of Dunwich does suggest a number of questions that can be asked about the cadre of men like Peter, who made Edward I's military administration work. Did other royal clerks begin their careers in the households of secular magnates, or was lifelong service in the royal household more usual? Were royal clerks generally recruited from the ranks of the gentry, or were they entirely new men, who owed all of their wealth and property to the king? Was it royal policy to deploy royal clerks to operate in the regions from which they hailed, or

---

52 National Archives C47/22/3/39.
53 National Archives SC1/12/132. William Comyn had the title of keeper of the spiritualities in the period 1296–1306.
54 National Archives C47/22/8 nr 1.
55 Ibid.

was this simply a happy accident of Peter of Dunwich's career? These questions, and likely many more, need to be asked about the scores, and perhaps hundreds of royal officials who played important roles in the conduct of war by Edward I, his predecessors, and his successors. The careers of many of these men can be traced, often in as much detail as set out here for Peter, and in some cases, in even greater detail. It is the task of current and future scholars to make full use of the rich veins of thirteenth- and fourteenth-century source materials in order to give Peter Dunwich and his colleagues their due.

Part 3

MILITARY ORGANIZATION

13

THE ORGANIZATION OF MILITARY RELIGION IN THE ARMIES OF KING EDWARD I OF ENGLAND, 1272–1307

King Edward I of England is widely recognized to have been one of the most successful military leaders of the later thirteenth and early fourteenth centuries. Even as a young man, the Lord Edward, as he was then known, was able to maintain the English military position in Wales, and was the only royalist commander to achieve any military success in the otherwise dismal defeat at hands of the baronial rebels at Lewes.[1] Over the course of his long reign, King Edward successfully imposed and maintained English power in both Wales and Scotland. He also preserved an English presence in Gascony despite the massive effort of King Phillip IV of France (1285–1314) to assert direct control over the region. When Edward died in 1307, he left to his son Edward II a realm that was both larger and stronger than the one which he had inherited in 1272.[2]

Current understanding of King Edward I's military organization has benefited from extensive scholarly attention in such diverse matters as recruitment, training, military building, pay, logistics, and campaign strategy. As a consequence, it has been possible to identify the organization, conduct, size, and even personnel of English royal armies during the later thirteenth and early fourteenth centuries.[3]

---

1   The basic biography of King Edward I is Michael Prestwich, *Edward I*, 2nd edn (Yale, 1997). Lord Edward's military success within the context of the overall royal defeat at the battle of Lewes is dealt with by F. M. Powicke, *King Henry III and the Lord Edward: The Community of the Realm in the Thirteenth Century*, 2 vols (Oxford, 1947), 46; Prestwich, *Edward I*, 45–46; and D. A. Carpenter, *The Reign of Henry III* (London, 1996), 284–285.

2   Concerning Edward's Welsh campaigns, see John Edward Morris, *The Welsh Wars of Edward I: A Contribution to Medieval Military History Based on Original Documents* (1901, repr. New York, 1969), and Michael Prestwich, *War, Politics and Finance under Edward I* (Totowa, NJ, 1972), passim. For an overview of Edward I's Scottish campaigns, see Prestwich, *Edward I*, 469–511, and 381–386 for Edward's defence of Gascony.

3   The most thorough monographic work dealing with Edward I's military organization is Prestwich, *War, Politics and Finance*. Prestwich has refined his views in two subsequent works, *The Three Edwards: War and the State in England 1272–1377* (New York, 1980); and *Armies and Warfare in the Middle Ages: The English Experience* (New Haven, CT, 1996), as well as numerous articles. Edward I's campaign strategy, particularly in Wales, has been discussed in depth by Morris, *The Welsh Wars of Edward I*. Numerous studies shed light on individual aspects of Edward's

However, despite the great attention that has been paid to the organization of Edward's forces, there has been one significant lacuna, namely the manner in which the king provided pastoral care to his soldiers. Therefore, in this study an effort is made to adumbrate the organization of military religion in the armies of Edward I both during war and peacetime.[4]

The majority of the sources used in this study fall into three categories: previously unpublished royal pay and expense records, unpublished royal writs, and unpublished letters of protection issued by the royal government. Calendared accounts of the royal pay and expense records produced by the Public Record Office have provided many scholars with a useful starting point for investigating the administrative practices of the English royal government.[5] However, in this study it has been frequently necessary to examine the original rolls in order to obtain the full text of the pertinent documents, and consequently a sense of the intention of their authors. Generally, calendared versions of royal writs and letters of protection provide a schematic overview of the contents of these documents while omitting a considerable body of information pertinent to the examination of English military organisation. In addition to these unpublished texts, this study makes use of a wealth of published documents. Many of these records relate directly to the organization and conduct of the royal household and include Wardrobe accounts, papal bulls, royal and episcopal letters, and chronicles. In addition, episcopal legislation dealing with matters of importance to the entire English church also has proved useful in understanding the organization of pastoral care for soldiers in the English royal armies.

An investigation of King Edward's military organization requires this wide range of documents because the forces available to the English royal government were controlled through a wide variety of written instruments. Throughout his reign, the basic elements of English military organisation were the royal military household, royal garrison forces, shire levies, and military tenants with their

---

military organization, including Alvin Z. Freeman, "Wall-Breakers and River-Bridgers: Military Engineers in the Scottish Wars of Edward I," *Journal of British Studies* 10 (1971), 1–16; Joseph Strayer, "The Costs and Profits of War: The Anglo-French Conflict of 1294-1303", in *The Medieval City*, ed. Harry A. Miskimin, David Herlihy, and A. L. Udovitch (New Haven, CT, 1977), 269–291; and Thomas Avril, "Interconnections Between the Lands of Edward I: A Welsh-English Mercenary Force in Ireland 1285-1304", *Bulletin of the Board of Celtic Studies* 40 (1993), 135–147.

4 Religion has always served an important function in Western warfare. See the monographic treatment by David S. Bachrach, *Religion and the Conduct of War c. 300–c. 1215* (Woodbridge, 2003), and the literature cited there.

5 Many of the financial documents dealing with King Edward I's military organization are calendared in the *Calendar of Chancery Rolls AD 1277–1326* (London, 1912), hereafter *Chancery Rolls*; *Calendar of Close Rolls 1272–1307* (London, 1900–1908), hereafter *CCR*; and *Calendar of Patent Rolls* (London, 1893–1901), hereafter *CPR*.

contingents.[6] The soldiers in these various units served for different periods of time, had different traditions, and different training. Consequently, the various departments of the royal government, including the Chancery, the Wardrobe, and the royal household, and the local administration of sheriffs and bailiffs, as well as individual military commanders were forced to develop written procedures that were specific to each kind of military unit. This was as true of the provision of pastoral care as of many other aspects of military life.

The royal household

The royal household formed the standing core of the royal military organization in England both in peacetime and in war. It should be emphasized that members of both the household and garrison forces were conceptualized and treated as soldiers even when not engaged in hostilities.[7] These men, who earned their living by bearing arms, were drawn from diverse regions and backgrounds, with the result that many of the men lived apart from the parish priests and other local clergy upon whom laymen normally relied to provide the sacraments of confession, communion, and last rites. This situation had the potential to cause significant problems for the spiritual health of these soldiers. Canon twenty-one of the Fourth Lateran Council issued in 1215 had mandated that each adult confess his sins to his own parish priest at least once a year. This canon had been widely interpreted to mean that the parish priest had exclusive control over the spiritual well-being of his parishioners unless some higher authority established an alternative.[8]

---

6   Regarding the military household, see C. Warren Hollister, *The Military Organization of Norman England* (Oxford, 1965), 171–176; and J. O. Prestwich, "The military household of the Norman King", in *Anglo-Norman Warfare*, ed. Matthew Strickland (Woodbridge, 1992), 93–128. Prestwich, *War, Politics and Finance*, 41–66, discusses the importance of the royal military household as an elite unit during Edward's reign. Concerning the military household in combat, see Norman Lewis, "The English Forces in Flanders, August–November 1297", *Studies in Medieval History Presented to Frederick Maurice Powicke*, ed. R. W. Hunt, W. A. Pantin, and R. W. Southern (Oxford, 1948), 310–318. Concerning the regular service of garrison troops in the armies of King Edward I, see Prestwich, *War, Politics and Finance*, 111–112. The military obligation of free men to serve in militia forces is dealt with in ibid., 92–113. Concerning the service of soldiers holding military tenures, see John E. Morris, *The Welsh Wars of Edward I*, 74–79; and Prestwich, *War, Politics and Finance*, 61–66.

7   Here I follow the argument put forth by Prestwich, "The Military Household", passim, who indicates clearly that the fighting men of the royal household were thought of and treated as soldiers even during peacetime throughout the Anglo-Norman period. This point is made for the later period by Prestwich, *War, Politics and Finance*, 42–45.

8   *Conciliorum oecumenicorum decreta*, 3rd edn (Bologna, 1973), 245, "*omnia sua solus peccata confiteatur fideliter, saltem semel in anno proprio sacerdoti ... nisi forte de consilio proprii sacerdotis ob aliquam rationabilem causam ad tempus ad eius perceptione duxerit abstindendum ... Si quis autem alieno sacerdoti voluerit iusta de causa sua confiteri peccata, licentiam prius postulet et obtineat a proprio sacerdote, cum aliter ille ipsum non possit solvere vel ligare*". Even before the Fourth Lateran Council, Archbishop Stephen Langton of Canterbury issued statutes prohibit-

In theory, soldiers serving in the royal military household could have avoided violating canon twenty-one of the Lateran Council by going to their home parishes just before Easter, and confessing their sins to the local priest. However, this solution had the obvious drawback of depriving the king of his personal guard and the core of his army for as long as it took the men to travel home and back to court. Thus, for obvious reasons, the general dispersal of the royal military household in the period before and after Easter was never practised. Instead, soldiers had two options when seeking pastoral care. They could confess their sins to one of the many chaplains who served in the royal household on a full-time basis. One such cleric was Robert of St. Quentin, whose service as one of the king's chaplains (*capellanus regis*) was noted in the royal Wardrobe accounts for 1287 in the context of his receipt of 4 s. 4 d. for his clothing allowance.[9] Chaplains such as Robert traveled everywhere with the king, and consequently were available to provide pastoral care to the soldiers attached to the king's person. For example, a document issued by Wardrobe officials on 6 July 1289 records a payment of 17 s. 6 d. that was made to John Wach for transporting the king's chaplains (*capellani regis*), in the company of the entire royal household, by river boat from Amiens to a place called Cloun.[10]

The second option was made possible by the complex structure of the royal military household. Some soldiers serving in the king's household were under the immediate command of secular officials attached to the royal *familia*, and many of these important men had their own personal chaplains. The soldiers within these smaller units, therefore, presumably had an opportunity to confess to these clerics rather than to the priests employed directly by the king. For example, the Wardrobe accounts note that in December 1286 the wages paid to John St. John banneret and his men were actually received by John's chaplain (*per manus domini Johannis capellano*) [*sic*].[11] This text indicates that John the chaplain was frequently enough in the company of his master to provide pastoral care to his lord's men.

For soldiers, as for all of the other members of the royal court to use one of these two options it was necessary to obtain exemptions from the legislation

---

ing parish priests from hearing the confessions of strangers to their parish without the permission of that person's parish priest, except under conditions of necessity. On this point, see *Councils and Synods with Other Documents Relating to the English Church AD 1205–1313*, 2 vols, ed. F. M. Powicke and C. R. Cheney (Oxford, 1964), I: 30, "*prohibemus quoque ne quis sacerdos sine mandato superioris aut eius qui in parochia curam animarum habet, confessiones recipiat, omissis propriis sacerdotibus vel contemptis, nisi in articulo necessitatis*".

9 *Records of the Wardrobe and Household 1286–1289*, ed. Benjamin F. Byerly and Catherine Ridder Byerly (London, 1986), 61.

10 Ibid., 198.

11 Ibid., 121. It is possible, of course, that John St. John summoned his chaplain from elsewhere rather than sending one of the men already with him in order to collect the money owed for the military service by John's men. But, even if this were the case, the chaplain would still have had to deliver the money to his lord.

issued by the Fourth Lateran Council that granted exclusive oversight over the spiritual well-being of Christian laypeople to their own parish priests. Because the Lateran Council had been summoned and authorized by Pope Innocent III, it followed that exemptions from its legislative acts could be sought from the papal see. It is, therefore, not surprising that King Edward worked diligently to secure papal privileges that permitted his household troops, as well as the other members of his household, to confess their sins, and receive communion when living outside of their own home parishes. For example, after negotiations with Boniface VIII, the pope responded in March 1301 to King Edward's requests by granting permission to the members of the English household to confess their sins to a royal chaplain.[12] This was, of course, of obvious benefit to the soldiers serving in the royal household as well. However, the papal government clearly recognized that at least some of the officers in Edward's military household had their own personal chaplains to whom the men under their command might confess their sins. Therefore, the papal bull noted that this privilege permitted *familiares et servientes* to confess to chaplains actually serving in the royal chapel in those cases when they did not have sufficient priests of their own (*quando non possunt habere copiam proprii sacerdotis*).[13] The papal bull went on to define the privilege accorded to the king and his household by emphasizing that having heard confessions (*audita confessione eorum*) the royal chaplains were permitted to assign penances (*poenitentiam impendant*) for the sake of their salvation (*pro ... salutorem*).[14]

Requests at this time by the king of England for papal privileges could be seen as having the potential to weaken royal power, particularly with regard to control over the English church. The papal government exacted a price for its cooperation not only financially but also in terms of moral prestige. When Edward asked permission for members of his household to confess their sins to royal chaplains, he implicitly recognized that the pope had the power to intervene in matters vital to the well-being of the royal household, and could even reject the king's request. Edward's decision to seek papal sanction for the members of his household to receive pastoral care at court was a significant concession by the king because his government was actively engaged during the later thirteenth and early fourteenth centuries in efforts to limit the ability of the pope to interfere in the governance of

---

12 Edward's original letter to the pope does not survive. However, Boniface's response clearly indicates that the English king was asking for some way to provide pastoral care both to his *familiares* and his *servientes*. As is well known, *servientes* can mean either "serving man" or "sergeant" in the military sense of the term. In this case, it should probably be understood to mean both. Thomas Rymer, *Foedera, conventiones, litere, et cuiuscunque generis acta publica, inter Reges Anglie et alios quosvia imperatores, reges, pontifices, principes, vel communitates* 20 vols (London, 1726–1735), II, 860, "*tui servientes et familiares ... tuis obsequiis familiariter insistentes possunt ... eorum confiteri peccata capellano tuo*". The more recent edition by Adam Clarke, Frederick Holbrooke, and John Caley (London, 1900), sheds no new light on this point.

13 Rymer, *Foedera*, II, 860.

14 Ibid.

the English church.[15] These privileges, therefore, are an indication of how important Edward thought it was to ensure the adequate and legal provision of pastoral care to the soldiers as well as the other members of his royal household.[16]

In order to make effective use of these privileges during military campaigns, the royal government also found it necessary to make the royal chapel mobile through the purchase of the appropriate equipment, including portable altars. However, here too, in his desire to provide the necessary pastoral care to his men while the household was traveling, King Edward had to take cognizance of the increasing tendency of the papal government to define the use of portable altars as a matter to be regulated by the pope.[17] As early as 1255, members of King Henry III's household had obtained papal privileges to utilize portable altars. In that year, Henry de Winham, a subdeacon serving in the royal household, received a

15 Concerning royal efforts to maintain rights of provision against both papal and episcopal challenges, see Ann Deeley, "Papal Provision and Royal Rights of Patronage in the Early Fourteenth Century", *English Historical Review* 43 (1928), 497–527; Geoffrey Barraclough, *Papal Provisions: Aspects of Church History, Constitutional, Legal and Administrative in the Later Middle Ages* (Oxford, 1935); and J. H. Denton, *English Royal Free Chapels 1100–1300: A Constitutional Study* (Manchester, 1970). For King Edward I's relationship with Pope Boniface VIII, see, Prestwich, *Edward I*, 492, 532, and 540.

16 While the suggestion to seek papal permission for household troops to confess their sins to household chaplains may have come from one of Edward's advisors, only the king himself was in a position to authorize an actual request to the pope. Indeed, if any other individual sought to undermine royal initiatives to gain greater control over the English church, he might well have found that Edward was displeased with him.

17 The increasing control of the papal government over the right to possess portable altars is evident from the growing number of requests sent to Rome during the thirteenth and early fourteenth centuries that sought papal permission to have and use them. Among the first papal bulls to address this question was Pope Honorius III's grant on 6 May 1221 to the Dominican order of a license to have and use portable altars. On this point, see *Bullarium Ordinis FF. Praedicatorum*, vol. I, ed. A Bremond (Rome, 1729), 14. Pope Gregory IX issued a similar bull on 10 May 1230 to those Dominicans going to Poland to perform missionary work. See *Bullarium Ordinis FF. Praedicatorum*, I: 32. Pope Innocent IV confirmed the license of the Dominican order to have and to use portable altars while they were engaged in missionary and preaching activities on 5 April 1254. On this point, see Paris, Archives Nationale (AN) L248 n° 252. The papal government also granted licenses to the Franciscan order permitting these friars to use portable altars. However, it appears that the first bull granting this privilege was not issued until 1250. See *Bullarum Franciscanum* vol. 1, ed. J. H. Sbarlea, (Rome, 1759), 537–538. After the mid-thirteenth century, secular rulers also began to seek privileges to have portable altars. See the following for examples from England. In 1302, Pope Boniface VIII issued a bull to Charles, the younger brother of King Philip IV of France, in which he granted him the right to have and use a portable altar. On this point, see AN J723/10. Similarly, Pope Clement V issued to Prince Louis, the second son of King Philip IV, two related privileges on 5 January 1306. First, the pope granted to Louis the right to have his chaplains hear the confessions of all the soldiers serving in his household, to assign them penances and to perform the other sacraments including last rights. Secondly, Clement permitted Prince Louis to have a portable altar when he went on campaign so that his soldiers could participate in the sacrament of communion while in the field. See, AN J692/148 and AN J688/119.

papal privilege to possess and use a portable altar in those areas through which the king traveled but where regular altars were not available.[18]

King Edward followed the precedents established during his father's reign in order to assure the adequate provision of pastoral care to his household, including the troops serving in the *familia regis*. Thus, Edward arranged for the purchase of portable altars and made provision for their transportation with the result that his household troops as well as other members of the household could hear mass and receive communion while on the road. For example, a record from the Wardrobe accounts for 27 June 1286 notes that a payment of 24 s. 4 d. was made to Robert Ayward, a cleric in the royal chapel, for the purchase of one portable altar (*altarus portatilus*), which was bought at the command of the king (*per preceptum regis*).[19] A receipt issued to the same cleric a month earlier shows why the purchase of the portable altar had been necessary. According to the text of the document, Robert was paid for the expenses he incurred while supervising the transportation of the royal chapel that been traveling almost continuously from October until May.[20]

Garrison soldiers

Garrison soldiers, who defended the king's castles and fortresses, may be considered like the royal military household to have been professional soldiers of England's standing army. However, unlike the household troops, the men serving in the garrisons were not attached to the king's person but rather were deployed throughout the realm.[21] When considered logistically, this meant that while the soldiers of the royal household could enjoy the benefits of the royal court including the pastoral care provided by the king's household chaplains, garrison troops could not. In order for garrison soldiers to have satisfactory pastoral care, each unit required either its own chaplain, or access to some other priest who was permitted to hear their confessions, and attend to the other elements of religious life traditionally associated with pastoral care, including the celebration of mass,

---

18 *Calendar of Entries in the Papal Registers Relating to Great Britain and Ireland 1198–1304*, ed. W. H. Bliss (London, 1893), 316. There is absolutely no reason to believe that the soldiers of the royal household were excluded from attendance at masses celebrated on the field on portable altars. As was noted, Pope Boniface VIII explicitly permitted soldiers serving in the royal household to receive pastoral care from the chaplains serving in this body.

19 *Records of the Wardrobe and Household*, 57.

20 Ibid., 31–32, "*pro portagio capelle regis in diversis locis a mense Octobris anno xiiii usque presentem diem computatem et pro altaribus parandis ad diversa loca*".

21 Concerning royal fortress policy, see R. Allen Brown, *English Medieval Castles* (London, 1954); Howard Montagu Colvin, *Building Accounts of King Henry III* (Oxford, 1971); Hilary L. Turner, *Town Defences in England and Wales* (London, 1971); Arnold Taylor, *The Welsh Castles of Edward I* (London, 1986), and Frederick C. Suppe, *Military Institutions on the Welsh Marches: Shropshire* (Rochester, 1994). For the service of garrison soldiers, see Prestwich, *Armies and Warfare*, 206–211.

overseeing the reception of communion, the anointing of the sick, and last rites. This was as true in times of peace as it was in periods of war.

During Edward's reign, the royal government generally contracted with military officers to recruit their own companies to serve as garrisons in particular fortresses.[22] This system allowed commanders considerable flexibility in selecting their men, and removed this responsibility from the local sheriffs, who were already burdened by a multitude of military, financial, and judicial obligations.[23] However, the delegation of recruitment authority by the English royal government to the garrison commanders did not entail a lack of royal interest in the composition of their forces. It was standard military procedure in England at this time that the writ granting command of a fortress to a particular officer included both an indication of the strength of the garrison to be recruited, and the number various skilled workers or support troops necessary for the effective defence of the fortress. For example, on 21 October 1284 Edward commissioned John de Havering to serve as the constable of the new fortress at Caernarvon in Wales, which had been built in the wake of the war fought there from 1282 to 1284.[24] King Edward noted in his writ of appointment that the garrison was to consist of forty men, and that these were to include fifteen crossbowmen, a carpenter, and a mason, as well as one chaplain (*capellanus*).[25] Edward issued similar letters of commission, all of which included the requirement to employ a chaplain, to Walter de Huntercombe, Hugh de Wlonkeslowe, William de Cycun, and William de Leyburn for the garrisons at the Welsh fortresses of Bere, Harlech, Conway, and Criccieth, respectively.[26] Furthermore, when King Edward transferred command of the fortress of Bere from Walter de Huntercombe to Hugh de Turberville on 5 October 1285, the new commander was also informed that the garrison was to include a chaplain.[27]

---

22 Prestwich, *War, Politics and Finance*, 74.
23 Although dated, William Alfred Morris, *The Medieval English Sheriff to 1300* (Manchester, 1927) still provides a good introduction to the subject. Concerning the financial and judicial duties of sheriffs during King Edward's reign, see Prestwich, *Edward I*, 91, 93, and 102–103; and D. A. Carpenter, *The Reign of Henry III* (London, 1996), 151–182, who discusses the decline in political access and power of sheriffs over the course of the thirteenth century just as their administrative responsibilities increased. Carpenter's work on the sheriffs originally appeared as a separate article, "The Decline of the Curial Sheriff in England, 1194–1258", *English Historical Review* 101 (1976), 1–32. Concerning the military responsibilities of the sheriffs, see Prestwich, *War, Politics and Finance*, 84–85, 96, and 99. The division of labor in which fortress commanders were responsible for recruiting garrison troops, and sheriffs were required to select men for the field forces, would appear to have served the purpose of keeping any one individual from acquiring too much power.
24 National Archives C77/5 (*Welsh Roll 1277–1326*).
25 Ibid.
26 National Archives C77/5. All of these fortresses were built in Wales in the wake of the Second Welsh War 1282–1284.
27 National Archives C77/5.

It is of particular interest that each of the constables to whom Edward gave command of one of his Welsh fortresses was required to include a chaplain (*capellanus*) in his garrison despite the fact that these units varied in size. Hugh de Wlonkeslowe, William de Cycun, and William de Leyburn were ordered to recruit garrisons of thirty men while the companies serving under John de Havering, Walter de Huntercombe, and Hugh de Turberville were supposed to consist of forty men each. The insistence by Edward's government that even the comparatively small garrisons at Harlech, Conway, and Criccieth should include a chaplain is an important indication of how important royal officials considered pastoral care to be for the effective maintenance of defences in the newly conquered territories of Wales.

The provision of chaplains to the royal garrisons serving in Wales following the war of 1282–1284 was consistent with traditional English military practice. Throughout the thirteenth century, the English royal government found it prudent to allow its garrison forces access to immediate pastoral care. For example, a report by the Dunstable annalist noted that the garrison of Bedford, which rebelled against King Henry III in 1224, included a chaplain among its number.[28] In his description of the unsuccessful effort by Fawkes de Breauté, the royal commander of Bedford, to revolt against the king, the annalist noted that only the garrison chaplain (*capellanus vero castri*) and three Templars were spared after the fortress was captured by troops loyal to Henry.[29]

Normally, however, narrative accounts from the thirteenth century rarely mention military chaplains. A much more common indication of the service of a priest at a particular fortress is the inclusion of his name and/or office in royal records detailing the funds expended in support of royal garrisons. For example, on 20 March 1266, King Henry III issued letters patent to Henry Sturmy, constable of the garrison at the fortress of Marlborough, instructing him to determine how much money the previous garrison commander, Roger de Clifford, had spent for the maintenance of the men serving there. The new constable's review of the expenses incurred by his predecessor noted the sums spent for the salaries of the garrison including the knights (*milites*), men at arms (*servientes ad arma*), and chaplains (*capellani*).[30]

Such financial records are similarly valuable for identifying the service of the priests who served as garrison chaplains during King Edward's reign. For example, an examination of the pay records for the garrison at Dover makes clear that throughout King Edward's reign there was always a chaplain serving in the fortress, who was responsible for providing pastoral care to the soldiers on garrison duty. For example, on 7 November 1273, before the new king had returned to England from crusade, Edward issued a letter to Joseph de Chauncy, the recently

---

28 *Annals of Dunstable* in *Annales Monastici*, 5 vols, ed. Henry Richards Luard, Rolls Ser. 36 (London, 1864–1869), III: 86–88.
29 Ibid., 88.
30 National Archives C66/84.

installed chancellor of the Exchequer, informing him about the expenses incurred by Stephen de Penecester in carrying out his duties as commander of the fortress at Dover.[31] From the text of Edward's letter, it is clear that Stephen de Penecester had been obliged to borrow money from the royal government in order to pay the wages of the garrison Dover, and Edward wanted this debt to be forgiven immediately. The letter is of particular value to this study because the king described the personnel serving at Dover whom Stephen de Penecester had paid. They included knights (*milites*), men at arms (*servienti equites et pedites*), and a chaplain (*capellanus*).[32]

By 20 June 1280, Stephen de Penecester, who was still commanding the garrison at Dover, had been given authority to utilize the profits from the port there to pay the costs of maintaining his garrison. Edward sent a letter to this effect to the barons of the Exchequer in an effort to eliminate any confusion arising from Stephen's use of the port funds.[33] This document is of value in the present context because, as was the case in 1273, Edward's letter explicitly listed the garrison chaplain as one of the those whom Stephen de Penecester was supposed to pay with the profits from the port at Dover.[34] At least six similar documents survive which explicitly note the service of chaplains in the garrison at Dover between 1273 and 1299.[35]

Moreover, it would appear that Edward himself took a strong personal interest in the spiritual well-being of his soldiers, a view that is suggested by the king's direct involvement in the recruitment of priests to serve as garrison chaplains. Edward's actions with regard to the provision of chaplains to the fortresses of Cornet and Gorey on the island outposts of Guernsey and Jersey in the English Channel provide a particularly good example of the thoroughness with which the king looked after religious care in the army.

The two channel islands of Guernsey and Jersey were significant military assets during Edward's reign, and this was especially true during the four-year conflict against France from 1294 to 1297.[36] During this war, the English government expended considerable human and material resources in the Channel Islands in order to keep them out of the hands of the French, and to deny the French fleet bases closer to Dover. Rather than relying on the loyalty and effectiveness of the local Francophone population, hundreds of English soldiers were sent to serve in the Channel garrisons.[37] However, there was concern that the English troops men

---

31 Stephen de Penecester assumed command of Dover in December 1267. On this point, see *Calendar of Liberate Rolls 1267–1272* (London, 1964), 5.

32 National Archives C54/90. The nature of the chaplain's service is made explicit by the royal description of him as "ministrantus".

33 National Archives C54/97.

34 Ibid.

35 See *Calendar of Fine Rolls 1272–1307* (London, 1911), 33, 415; *CPR 1281–1292*, 83; and *CCR 1279–1288*, 223, 264, and 322.

36 On this point, see J. H. Le Patourel, *The Medieval Administration of the Channel Islands 1199–1399* (London, 1937), 68–69.

37 Ibid.

might not have English-speaking priests available because the indigenous clerics spoke French. A mandate, issued in Edward's name, ordered the king's garrison commanders to bring clerics with them from England to serve as chaplains.[38] It was under this mandate that Henry de Cobham, serving as warden of the islands of Jersey and Guernsey, appointed William de Lespeys, the parson of Winterborne Strickland, to serve as chaplain in the strategically important castle on Guernsey. As the warden emphasized, he took this action because "the chaplain who was there before had been killed by our enemies and our men from England cannot be without a chaplain who speaks their language and can converse on any subject".[39] In addition to William de Lespeys, who served under Henry de Cobham from November 1295 until February 1298,[40] the channel warden also recruited Robert of Cumberwell, a parish priest from Tyberton, who also served with the English troops on the island of Guernsey from November 1296 to July 1297.[41]

Both as his father's lieutenant and as king, Edward earned a reputation as a diligent ruler and military commander. He was concerned for the welfare of his subordinates, and insisted on overseeing personally many of the administrative details that affected those under his command.[42] Consequently, it is hardly surprising that, although he faced the exceptionally difficult challenge of defending his widely separated territories against King Philip IV, Edward also undertook to make specific recommendations to his garrison commanders about priests who might serve as chaplains in the island garrisons. For example, on 6 November 1295, Henry de Cobham received royal orders to fill two vacancies in the chapel of St. Mary in the fortress of Gorey on the island of Jersey.[43] The former chaplains, Robert le Chastelain and Ralph de Marynde, had both died, and King Edward wanted his officer to replace them with Nicholas Evesk, a chaplain, and Nicholas Choffyn, a royal clerk. Nicholas Evesk was already serving on the island of Jersey as a chaplain, presumably attached to one of the military units stationed there. In his letter to the commander of the Channel Islands, Edward noted that Nicholas Evesk had suffered during the recent battle fought between the royal garrison and the French.[44] In recognition of the priest's distinguished service, Edward wanted to reward him with a permanent position as chaplain in the fortress of Jersey

---

38 On this point, see Le Patourel, *Channel Islands*, 72–73.
39 National Archives C47/10/9/2, *"parce ke le chapelain qui estort la avant este ocis de nos anemis et que nostre gent d'englettere non pouvent estre sens chapellain qui lor langue sent entendre et parlar por laquel chose"*. Henry Cobham makes clear in the introduction to this letter that he is acting under the authority granted to him, *"par nostre segnor le roy denglettere"*.
40 National Archives C66/114 and C66/118.
41 National Archives C66/116 and C66/117.
42 Concerning Edward's reputation for paying close attention to detailed administrative matters, see Prestwich, *Edward I*, 92–94.
43 National Archives C54/112.
44 Ibid., *"Nicholum Eveske capellanum occasione dampnae que sustinuit per conflictum nuper factum in praedicta insula de Gereseye inter homines eiusdem insule et quosdam alienigenas inimicos nostros"*.

(*capella Sancti Marie in castro insule de Gereseye*).[45] But the king left open the possibility that Henry de Cobham as commander could choose not to appoint Nicholas Evesk to a permanent position in the garrison. The king indicated that although Nicholas was his first choice, Henry should only accept the priest into the garrison if he considered him to be the man most suited for the position.[46]

Similarly, Edward requested that Nicholas Choffyn be considered to serve as a chaplain in the fortress on Jersey. However, he again added the caveat that the cleric should be offered a place in the garrison only if he were the best suited for the position.[47] Edward added this qualification despite describing Nicholas Choffyn as someone whom he wished to reward for having served the king diligently in many different regions.[48] The inference to be drawn is that the king believed that the officer with direct responsibility for the garrison was best situated to make the final decision regarding the spiritual welfare of his men. Furthermore, it would seem that as an experienced leader, King Edward did not wish to alienate his commander by challenging his judgment in such an important matter.

Indeed, the decisions made by Edward's officers regarding the employment of military chaplains imply both that the king took very seriously the importance of having the best possible man serve in this capacity, and that he trusted the judgment of his commanders. On 29 August 1295, Edward had ordered Henry de Cobham to consider Ranulph Maret for the prebend at St. Heliers church on Jersey "*si idem Ranulphus ad hoc idoneus pro aliis*".[49] However, on 3 February 1297, a year and a half later, Edward noted in a letter to Henry de Cobham that Ranulph had not received the church of St. Heliers, and that this church was once more vacant. Edward, therefore, again asked his garrison commander to consider Ranulph, but only if he were a fitting candidate.[50] Clearly, Henry de Cobham initially had chosen not to appoint Ranulph Maret, thereby demonstrating not only his freedom of action as commander with respect to appointments to chaplaincies, but what would appear to have been his judgment that Ranulph was not the best man for the job at that time.[51]

---

45   Ibid., "*mandamus quod praedicto Nicholo praedictum capellam si vacet et idem Nicholas ad hoc idoneus fuit … aliis comperatis*".

46   National Archives 54/112, "*mandamus quod praedicto nicholo praedictam capellam si vacet et idem nicholas ad hoc idoneus fuit … aliis **comperatis***". (my emphasis). The text of Edward's order, in which he insists that Henry de Cobham, addressed in the second person singular, make a decision about whom to place in the position, demonstrates that the king saw his channel warden as the man with the authority to appoint a chaplain to this office.

47   Ibid.

48   Ibid.

49   National Archives C54/112.

50   National Archives C54/14, "*si idem Ranulphus ad hoc idoneus fuisset*".

51   It is not clear from the surviving texts whether Henry de Cobham held a juridical right of appointment to the various chapels in the castles that he commanded in the Channel Islands. What is clear, however, is that King Edward's letters to Henry treated him as if he did.

We see a very similar royal concern for the spiritual well-being of garrison troops in Scotland during Edward I's wars there. Surviving pay records show the presence of garrison chaplains at Kirkintilloch, Kirkcudbright, Roxburgh, Jedworth, Edinburgh, Struelyn, Lochmaben, Dumfries, and Berwick between 1298 and 1307. In some cases, these men were simply part of the garrison structure, as had been true in Wales and the Channel Islands.[52] In other cases, the chaplains who served the garrisons were members of the military household and his magnates. For example, four royal chaplains named Peter de Shemingdon, John de Dingenton, Gilbert de Grimesby, and Roger de Altbridge appear in the expense accounts of Richard de Bremesgrave serving at Berwick in 1304.[53] Two years earlier, in 1302, Earl Patrick Dunbar's chaplain was also at Berwick, where he was available to provide pastoral care to the troops serving there.[54]

Pay and status of royal castle chaplains

Although much of the responsibility for recruiting garrisons, including military chaplains, was in the hands of local officials, the royal government still determined the pay rates of all the men serving in the standing army, including priests providing pastoral care to soldiers.[55] This practice can be seen in the consistent pay rates paid to garrison chaplains throughout Edward I's reign. For example, sixteen surviving documents recorded in the close rolls over the course of the period 1273–1307 show that the royal government maintained a minimum of two chaplains in the garrison at Windsor during the course of King Edward's reign.[56] During this entire period, the government paid its chaplains a consistent wage of 50 s. per annum at Michaelmas. Surviving records detailing the funds used to support other garrisons in this period, including Marlborough, Northampton, Rochester, Old Sarum, Dover, and Oakham indicate that chaplains serving in these fortresses also received a yearly salary of 50 s.[57]

The apparent standardization of the pay rate of 50 s. per year for chaplains serving in royal garrisons adds to the overall picture of systematic royal policies

---

52 National Archives E101/354/31; E101/8/11, E101/8/25; E39/93/18; E101/8/12 #40 and 53; E101/8/18; E101/8/24; E101/8/27; E101/8/30; E101/9/1; E101/9/9; E101/9/13; E101/9/18; E101/9/25; E101/10/6; E101/11/1 3v.; E101/11/15 2r; E101/12/18 4r; E101/13/16 17r.
53 National Archives E101/10/18 #147.
54 National Archives E101/9/30 #60.
55 Concerning military pay rates in Edward I's armies, see Prestwich, *War, Politics and Finance*, 41–42. However, Prestwich does not address the question of pay for military chaplains.
56 *CCR 1272–1279*, 16, 34, 153; *CCR 1279–1288*, 2, 447; *CCR 1288–1296*, 498; *CCR 1296–1302*, 71, 257, 368, 457, 470; *CCR 1302–1307*, 15, 53, 256, 288, 364, 415.
57 See respectively, *CPR 1258–1266*, 448; *CCR 1272–1279*, 18; *CCR 1272–1279*, 17; *CCR 1272–1279*, 25, 37; and *Calendar of Inquisitions Post Mortem and Other Analogous Documents Preserved in the Public Record Office*, 15 vols (1904–1970, London), III: 461. On this point, also see N. J. G. Pounds, *The Medieval Castle in England and Wales: A Social and Political History* (Cambridge, 1990), 245.

concerning the provision of military pastoral care. However, the efforts of the royal government in this regard may also reflect the influence of the English episcopate on royal policy with respect to the maintenance of adequate pastoral resources in the army. For example, in 1224, Bishop Peter de Roches of Winchester established 60 s. as the appropriate wage for chaplains working in wealthier churches.[58] Over the course of the thirteenth century, many other English bishops including William Raleigh of Winchester (1247), Peter Quinel of Exeter (1287), and Bishop Gilbert of Chichester (1289) maintained 60 s. as the appropriate rate of pay for priests serving in parishes.[59]

At first glance, the wages paid by the royal government would appear to have been lower than those insisted on by the bishops in their statutes. However, if one takes into account the fact that priests serving the royal government as military chaplains also received allowances for clothing and food, it becomes clear that the level of compensation for priests insisted upon by the bishops in their statutes formed a baseline for royal rates of pay. For example, on 13 October 1283, Stephen de Penecester, commander of the fortress at Dover, received funds both to pay the wages of the chaplains serving in the fortress and to supply the clothing allowance of the chaplains.[60] In an even more explicit case, Walter de Pederton, justiciar of West Wales in 1300, noted in his account of the expenditures made at fortress of Llanbadarn (Aberystwyth) that the garrison priest serving there received a 10 s. clothing allowance for half a year's service.[61] When consideration is given to the perquisites available to garrison chaplains, it is clear that royal wage rates were on par with or even superior to those set out in the episcopal statutes.[62]

In addition to the perquisites attached their offices, military chaplains enjoyed the further benefit of relative financial security as compared with the great mass of unbeneficed clergy who found it necessary to seek new employment on a regular basis.[63] In addition, surviving pay records indicate that many of the garrison

---

58 See *Councils and Synods*, I: 129, "*sexaginta solidos statuimus quod cappellani recipiant annuatim*".

59 *Councils and Synods*, I: 406, *Councils and Synods*, II: 1026 and 1084. The stability of wage rates for priests over the course of the thirteenth century, as reflected in episcopal statutes, may help to explain why the wages of chaplains serving in the garrison at Windsor remained stable for thirty years. J. L. Bolton, "Inflation, Economics and Politics in Thirteenth-Century England", *Thirteenth Century England* 4 (1992), 1–14, notes that in the period after 1270, England experienced significant price inflation. It is therefore noteworthy that Edward's government was committed to maintaining stable wages in this inflationary environment.

60 National Archives C66/102.

61 *Ministers' Accounts for West Wales 1277 to 1306*, ed. Myvanwy Rhys (London, 1936), 125.

62 Pounds, *Medieval Castle*, 96, concludes that, in general, chaplains serving in fortress garrisons received a lower rate of pay than the soldiers serving there. However, he points out that the chaplains received room and board so that "their *real* [sic] wage would have been higher".

63 Simon Townley, "Unbeneficed Clergy in the Thirteenth Century: Two English Dioceses", in *Studies in Clergy and Ministry in Medieval England*, ed. David M. Smith (York, 1991), 38–64, emphasizes that there were large numbers of unbeneficed clergy in late-thirteenth-century England, who were forced to take on menial pastoral tasks in order to earn a living.

chaplains enjoyed the additional security of serving in the same fortress for a number of years. For example, William of Hakeburn was appointed as a chaplain in Nottingham Castle on 13 March 1275, and remained in service there until he resigned his position on 29 April 1277.[64] Similarly, Geoffrey Norman was granted a chaplaincy in Rochester Castle on 20 July 1271, and was still serving there in June 1273 when his wage receipts were recorded by the Chancery.[65] In the latter case, the full duration of Geoffrey Norman's term of service cannot be known because of the state of the surviving records.

These extended terms of service entailed distinct advantages both for the government and for the chaplains themselves. Professional soldiers serving long terms of garrison duty had the benefit of priests who understood their concerns, and who were experienced in dealing with the problems specific to a military outpost. The royal government also benefited to the extent that soldiers received the best possible pastoral care. In addition, by retaining priests for long terms of service, the royal government obviated the need to recruit and train new men for the task. The benefits for the chaplains also were significant. They were financially secure. The wages paid to garrison chaplains were competitive with those set forth in episcopal statutes for priests serving in wealthier parishes. In addition, the chaplains received perquisites which substantially increased their 'real' income.

A second, less tangible benefit enjoyed by these garrison priests was the status of being the king's man. They served the royal government, and could depend upon the support of royal agents to protect them from ecclesiastical authorities if certain types of problems arose. The special protection provided to royal chaplains is clear from the efforts of Edward's government to establish exclusive royal control over fortress chapels, and to eliminate all episcopal interference in their operation. Indeed, King Edward consistently opposed the efforts of ecclesiastical authorities to intervene in the administration of military chapels or to investigate military chaplains. For example, on 9 April 1301, the king issued a sealed letter to Stephen Sprot, commander of the garrison at Hastings, in which Edward emphasized his determination that the fortress and particularly its chapel were not to be subject to episcopal control.[66] The king informed Stephen that Archbishop Robert of Canterbury intended to visit the "free" royal chapel in the fortress at Hastings which was entirely immune from the jurisdiction of the prelate, that is *que ab omni jurisdictione ordinari est exempta.* Edward emphasized that Archbishop Richard intended to visit the chapel for the purpose of infringing upon royal rights. In order to avoid this outcome, the king ordered Stephen to deny the archbishop

---

64 *CPR 1272–1281,* 83, 199.
65 *CPR 1266–1272,* 552 and *CCR 1272–1279,* 17.
66 National Archives C54/117. The best treatment of this subject is Denton, *English Royal Free Chapels.*

entrance into the fortress at Hastings, and to prohibit the archbishop and his staff from entering the chapel there.[67]

In this case, the king clearly felt that the commander of the garrison at Hastings, if given sufficient assurance of royal support, could face the challenge posed by an angry archbishop. However, Edward also sought means to sustain control over his fortress chapels and chaplains that did not rely on main force. Following his father's policies, King Edward sought and received papal bulls that excluded his castle chapels from episcopal jurisdiction.[68] In 1275, the king instituted a special office headed by Ralph of Marlowe to oversee the protection of royal rights when they were threatened by episcopal interests.[69]

It appears that Edward ordered Ralph to introduce procedures for dealing with the problems of maintaining the immunity of royal chapels with a particular emphasis upon the use of papal bulls and letters to support royal claims against episcopal opposition. Indeed, shortly after Ralph of Marlowe was recruited, royal officials compiled a dossier of papal documents concerning the immunity of royal chapels.[70] After this dossier was used by Ralph of Marlowe and other royal agents who were concerned with the problems arising from their efforts to maintain royal immunities, it was returned to storage. The receipt for the removal and return of this dossier survives in a memorandum issued on 7 November 1275 to John of St. Denis ordering him to take custody of the collection of papal bulls and letters and to keep them with the other bulls and privileges issued to the king by the pope.[71] Over the course of his reign, Edward was generally successful in his efforts to maintain the liberty of royal chapels from episcopal interference, and this was equally true of royal chapels situated in castles.[72]

Shire levies

King Edward relied heavily on shire levies throughout his reign to provide the numerical preponderance of his military manpower. Royal commissioners working with local officials regularly mobilized many thousands of men to perform

---

67　National Archives C54/117, "*si contingat praefatum Archiepiscopum aut alique alium ex parte sua ad castrum nostrum accedere ad dictum capellam nostram visitandum … nullatenus ingredi permittatis*".

68　Denton, *English Royal Free Chapels*, 95, notes that Henry III received a bull of immunity for royal chapels in 1236 from Pope Gregory IX. In 1250, Henry III worked to expand the immunities enjoyed by fortress chapels by ordering that a bull issued by Innocent IV in 1245 granting limited immunity to the royal chapel at Penkridge henceforth be understood to grant full immunity to all royal chapels.

69　On this point, see Denton, *English Royal Free Chapels*, 103, who considers the question of immunities for chapels in royal fortresses, but does not discuss the military chaplains themselves.

70　See *CCR 1272–1281*, 91 and National Archives C54/92 .

71　Ibid.

72　Denton, *English Royal Free Chapels*, 130–131, has suggested that all of these chapels were exempt from episcopal control.

military service in Wales and Scotland, and even as far away as Gascony, and Flanders.[73] It was not uncommon for ten thousand men of the English shires to be mobilized for a single campaign. Indeed, in 1296 King Edward issued orders for 60,000 infantry to mobilized for a spring campaign into Scotland, although a mobilization on this scale was not actually carried out.[74]

In order to provide military forces of this order of magnitude with a sufficiently large number of chaplains, Edward's government recruited heavily among parish priests. These were the spiritual leaders with whom the English soldiers mustered in the shires were most familiar, and upon whom they relied for their peacetime religious needs. It was, therefore, reasonable for the royal government to turn to these priests to serve as chaplains in the English army. Moreover, there was long precedent for this course of action. As early as 1138, Archbishop Thurstan of York had ordered the parish priests of his archdiocese to provide pastoral care, including hearing the confessions, of shire militiamen who were mobilized to oppose an invasion of northern England launched by King David of Scotland.[75]

The major source of information for the service of parish priests as chaplains in King Edward's armies is provided by a type of document known as a letter of protection. From at least the early thirteenth century, the English royal government had issued such letters to men going on crusade in order to protect them from all types of legal prosecution, and from all debts for a period of time enunciated within the text of the document. Over the course of the thirteenth century, the royal government adapted the form of the letter of protection so that individuals and institutions in royal service would also be immune from prosecution and debt collectors.[76] Letters of protection were particularly valuable for soldiers serving outside their home counties, and large numbers were issued to such men. This practice was so common that many military historians have utilized surviving letters of protection in an effort to identify the military personnel serving in King Edward's armies.[77] However, in addition to soldiers, others in royal service also received letters of protection. These included merchants shipping food to the troops, monasteries and convents supplying grain and wagons for the army, and,

---

73 Concerning King Edward's use of the shire levies in Gascony, see Prestwich, *War, Politics and Finance*, 101. The use of the shire levies in Flanders is discussed by N. B. Lewis, "The English Forces in Flanders", 310–318.

74 Prestwich, *War, Politics and Finance*, 41–48, 92–95, and 470.

75 Richard of Hexham, *De gestis Regis Stephani et de Bello Standardii*, Rolls Series 82, 4 vols, ed. Richard Howlett (London, 1884–1889), III: 161, and Ailred of Rievaulx, *Relatio Venerabilis Aelredi abbatis Rievallensis de Standardo*, Rolls Series 82, 4 vols, ed. Richard Howlett (London, 1886), III: 182. Also see the discussion by Bachrach, *Religion and the Conduct of War*, 153–161.

76 On this point, see Prestwich, *Armies and Warfare*, 109–110.

77 For the use of letters of protection to identify the members of military units, see John E. Morris, *The Welsh Wars of Edward I*, 56–57; Prestwich, *War, Politics and Finance*, 62–65; and Andrew Ayton, *Knights and Warhorses: Military Service and the English Aristocracy under Edward III* (Woodbridge, 1994), 156–169.

of particular importance for the present study, parish priests who were mobilized for service in the army as field chaplains.[78]

In 1277, Edward I invaded Wales and mobilized thousands of men as levies from the shires to serve in the campaign. Among these troops were 1,000 men summoned from the county of Chester.[79] In order to provide pastoral care for these soldiers while they were in the field, the royal government also recruited parish priests from throughout the area to serve with the men. Among these *ad hoc* military chaplains was Gilbert de Mariscis, parson of the church of Cotesmora in the county of Chester. A letter issued to Gilbert by the royal government notes that he is under protection (*protectionem habet*) because he has set out for Wales (*profecturus est in Wallia*) in the king's service (*in obsequio regis*).[80]

Similarly, during Edward's invasion of Wales in 1282, the royal government gave protections to many parish priests to serve as temporary field chaplains for the soldiers of the county levies. For example, John of Merton, the parson of the church of Elmstead in Essex, received a letter of protection on 8 December 1282, which was to last until the next Easter (18 April 1283). He received this letter because of his service in the army campaigning in Wales, that is *occasione instantis exercitus regis Wallia*.[81]

Table 13.1 shows that the length of time for which protections were granted to parish priests during the Second Welsh War of 1282–1284 was short, usually less than a year and sometimes much less. It should be noted in this context that the campaign itself lasted for two years and that considerable military forces remained in Wales after 1284. Thus, in contrast to the long-term military efforts to subdue and then control Wales, the involvement of the parish priests might be comparatively short. These short terms of service by parish priests may indicate that the royal government desired to limit the negative impact of the clerics' absence from their own churches on their own parishioners living at home.[82] Indeed, royal officials issued new letters of protection from April 1282 until June 1283, that is well over a year after the war in Wales had begun. The surviving evidence also indicates that protections were given to parish priests from across much of England, including all of the counties from which the shire levies had been mobilized to fight in Wales.[83] This practice may suggest that the king wanted to utilize parish priests who were familiar with the language and customs of the

---

78 With regard to letters of protections for merchants and ecclesiastical institutions in wartime, see David S. Bachrach, "Military Logistics during the Reign of Edward I of England, 1272–1307", *War in History* 13.4 (2006), 423–440, and in this volume.

79 Morris, *Welsh Wars*, 128.

80 National Archives C66/96.

81 National Archives C77/4.

82 It is clear from the surviving letters of protection that all of these priests were, in fact, the actual parish priests as each is described as a *persona*, that is parson or parish priest.

83 For a list of the counties mobilized to serve in this campaign, see *Chancery Rolls 1277–1326*, 251–252.

Table 13.1 Priests serving as field chaplains during Edward I's invasion of Wales, 1282–1284

Name	Church	County	Term of service
Henry	Ashbury	Berks	23/4/1282–25/12/1282 (Christmas)
John	Thornbury	Gloucester	23/4/1282–unspecified
Richard	Heslerton	York	23/4/1282–29/9/1282 (Michaelmas)
Ralph	Barrow	Chester	28/5/1282–31/10/1282 (All Saints)
John Joye	Idesdale	Shropshire	2/6/1282–unspecified
John	Astbury	Chester	5/6/1282–18/4/1283 (Easter)
Simon	Ainderby	York	10/6/1282–29/9/1282 (Michaelmas)
Robert	Keston	Kent	12/6/1282–29/9/1282 (Michaelmas)
Edmund	Campden	Gloucester	8/8/1282–25/12/1282 (Christmas)
William	Thornton	York	8/8/1282–25/12/1282 (Christmas)
Henry	Ryther	York	16/8/1282–25/12/1282 (Christmas)
William	Canon of St. Chad	Chester	2/9/1282–18/4/1283 (Easter)
Richard	Langeton	Lincoln	3/11/1282–3/11/1283
Richard	Olveston	Gloucester	15/11/1282–29/9/1283 (Michaelmas)
Walter	Bredon	Worcester	15/11/1282–29/9/1283 (Michaelmas)
John	Elmestead	Essex	8/12/1282–18/4/1283 (Easter)
Martin	Stratton	Hereford	8/12/1282–24/7/1283 (Midsummer)
Richard	Cheping Norton	Chester	16/12/1282–24/7/1283 (Midsummer)
Walter	Wotegrave	----------	28/12/1282–24/7/1283 (Midsummer)
Edward	Croxton	Lincoln	28/12/1282–29/9/1283 (Michaelmas)
Richard	Hawksworth	Nottingham	13/3/1283–29/9/1283 (Michaelmas)
Hamo	Rushden	Northampton	25/6/1283–29/9/1283 (Michaelmas)[a]

[a] All of the men listed in the table are identified in the sources as parish priests. The sources for these letters of protection are, respectively, *CPR 1281–1292*, 16; *CPR 1281–1292*, 17; *CPR 1281–1292*, 16; *Chancery Rolls*, 228; *Chancery Rolls*, 222; *Chancery Rolls*, 223; *Chancery Rolls*, 225; *Chancery Rolls*, 223; *Chancery Rolls*, 234; *Chancery Rolls*, 234; *Chancery Rolls*, 234; National Archives C77/3; *Chancery Rolls*, 245; *Chancery Rolls*, 228, 245; *Chancery Rolls*, 245; National Archives C 77/4; *Chancery Rolls*, 260; *Chancery Rolls*, 260; *Chancery Rolls*, 261; *Chancery Rolls*, 260; National Archives C77/4; and *Chancery Rolls*, 273.

soldiers serving in this campaign, as had been the case in the Channel Islands. The fact that priests came from a very wide area also helped to ensure that no one region was stripped of the priests who were required to serve the pastoral needs of the local civilian population.

However, the use of parish priests as military field chaplains occasionally caused problems in the context of canon law. The primary obligation of parochial clergy was to care for the spiritual well-being of the people in their parishes. The general problem of absenteeism by parish priests was addressed, for example, by Bishop William Bitton of Bath and Wells, who issued statutes in which he strictly forbade priests to leave their parishes without episcopal permission.[84] As was suggested in the previous paragraph, the short terms of service of the parish priests

---

84 See *Councils and Synods*, I: 610, "*statuimus quod rectores qui parochiales ecclesias habent in quibus non sunt vicarii constituti in ipsis personaliter resideant nisi de nostra licentia se absentent*".

serving as military chaplains, as indicated by the dates recorded in their letters of protection, may have been the result of a conscious effort of the English royal government to minimize the impact of the clerics' absences on the spiritual well-being of their home parishes. However, even an absence of three months could prove difficult in some parishes, especially if it coincided with the Easter season or other periods of concentrated religious observance.

It would appear that in some instances, Edward's government may have sought to shift the burden of dealing with these problems in canon law and the provision of pastoral care to civilians onto the ecclesiastical hierarchy by making arrangements directly with bishops to provide parish priests for service. The local prelate would then be responsible for choosing those parish priests whom he could easily replace and thereby offer appropriate pastoral care to the parishioners whether they were serving in the king's army or remained at home. For example, during the mobilization of troops and other personnel for a relief expedition to Gascony in 1295, a letter of protection was issued to Bishop William de Louth of Ely. The government extended protection not only to the property of the bishop himself, but also to those who were to accompany him to Gascony. Among those included in the letter of protection were five parish priests (*persona*) and one vicar (*vicarius*).[85] It should be emphasized here that there is no reason to identify these six clerics, who were going to Gascony with Bishop William, as permanent members of his household. Similarly, when Henry of Newark, dean of the cathedral at York, received letters of protection for service in Gascony, he had in his company two parish priests (*persona*), who were also unlikely to have been permanent members of his household because they served parishes of their own.[86]

When we look to Edward I's wars in Scotland, the primary sources of information regarding the service of chaplains with forces in the field, as contrasted with garrison troops, are the extant pay records that were created by clerks of the Chancery and Exchequer. Notably, all of the information regarding military chaplains with troops in field comes from Welsh forces. For example, a Chancery document, which reports on the wages of Welsh troops serving in Scotland in December and January of 1298, records that the five *centenae* from Snowden, under the command of the *centenarii* Howel ab Madok, Lewelin Wel, Jevan ab Mortik, Tuder Parthla, and Griffin ab Howel, were accompanied by a chaplain named Gervais, titled *dominus*.[87] Similarly, an Exchequer record, which recorded the wages of Welsh troops participating in the siege of Stirling Castle in 1304, noted the ten *centenae* of Welsh troops from Ceredigion, were accompanied by two chaplains. The eight *centenae* from a region identified as Denet, in Wales, also were accompanied by two chaplains. Finally, the five *centenae* from Powys

---

85   National Archives C66/115.
86   National Archives C66/115.
87   National Archives C47/2/20 1r–2v.

likewise were accompanied by two chaplains.[88] Given the desire expressed by royal officials, including Edward I, for troops to have access to chaplains who spoke their own language, it is perhaps not surprising that it is the Welsh forces operating in Scotland, who needed to bring chaplains with them from home.

Military tenants

The major distinction to be drawn between shire levies and military tenants is that the latter owed military obligations beyond those imposed upon all free able-bodied men in Edward I's realm.[89] Military tenants of the king held properties for which they owed both personal military service and a complement of well-armed and trained soldiers.[90] Often, these military tenants employed their own personal priests as chaplains for the men under their command. Indeed, some of the king's military tenants went so far as to secure papal licenses so that their personal chaplains could celebrate mass using portable altars in the field. For example, on 13 February 1306, shortly before the royal army marched into Scotland, Hugh Despenser, earl of Gloucester, received a privilege from Pope Clement V permitting him to use a portable altar. This privilege allowed Hugh's military household to participate in the celebration of mass, and to receive communion after confessing their sins to the officer's own household chaplains.[91]

On occasion, however, lords preferred to recruit priests from outside their own households to provide pastoral care to their soldiers. On 19 June 1300, Earl Henry de Lacy of Lincoln received a license from Archbishop Corbridge of York to employ Franciscan friars as military chaplains for the duration of the approaching campaign to Scotland.[92] The archbishop granted permission for the friars serving with the army to hear confessions, absolve the soldiers of their sins, and assign penances.[93] This permission was important because, as was noted, parishioners were required to confess their sins to their own parish priests unless given a dispensation. Indeed, only seven years earlier, Archbishop Romanus, Corbridge's predecessor, had denounced the idea that laymen could confess to mendicants on a regular basis rather than relying on their own parish priests.[94] Parenthetically,

---

88 National Archives E101/12/17, 2r–9r.
89 Prestwich, *War, Politics and Finance*, 67–70.
90 Ibid., 78–91.
91 Concerning the provision of the papal license, see *Calendar of Entries in the Papal Registers Relating to Great Britain and Ireland AD 1305–1342*, ed. W. H. Bliss (London, 1895), 9. The fact that Hugh Despenser sought a papal privilege at this time to use a portable altar indicates that the practice was new, at least to him.
92 *Historical Papers and Letters from the Northern Registers*, ed. James Raine Rolls Ser. 61 (London, 1873), 143.
93 Ibid., "*auditis conscientiarum suarum reatibus, possint absolvere, ipsisque poenitentias injungere salutares*".
94 Ibid., 102–103. However, Romanus was somewhat out of step with his brother bishops. In 1258, Bishop William Bitton of Bath and Wells gave permission for mendicants to hear confessions

Franciscan friars were useful in the role of chaplain on military campaign because, unlike most other clerics, they as mendicants, largely were free of obligations to a fixed place.

Nevertheless, despite the obvious advantages of employing mendicants, the king's military tenants also followed the example of the royal government by having parish priests serve as chaplains with their men in the field. For example, John Wake, who served as one of King Edward's commanders during the invasion of Scotland in 1296, had at least four parish priests to serve with his forces.[95] Similarly, John of Berwick received a letter of protection in November 1296 for the forces he was in the process of mobilizing to serve in Gascony. The men named in this letter of protection included William of Wasseburn, parish priest at Stanford in Nottinghamshire.[96]

Conclusion

At every level of the King Edward's military organization, royal officials and agents employed priests to provide pastoral care to soldiers. Not surprisingly, the king's household forces and fortress garrisons, as the most permanent and highly organized units of the royal army, benefited from the most systematic pastoral organization as well. Chaplains who provided pastoral care to these units served for long tours of duty, received fixed and high rates of pay and benefits, and were subject to royal oversight. Indeed, if it is possible to describe Edward's household and garrison forces as professional soldiers, at least some of the priests serving with them can justly be called professional military chaplains. This was, to a lesser extent, also true of the military tenants who had maintained standing military households. By contrast, the more *ad hoc* units composed of shire militiamen had less firmly structured arrangements for the provision of pastoral care to the troops. When the royal government took direct action in levying men from the shires, these men were accompanied into the field by parish priests from these same shires. This was also true of Welsh levies during Edward I's Scottish wars. The likely efforts of Edward's officials to recruit these priests as chaplains rather than employing the numerous unbeneficed clergy available in late thirteenth-century England indicates that the government agents saw it as important

---

of lay people who were traveling outside of their parishes. The episcopal statutes of Winchester issued between 1262 and 1265 reiterate this point. See *Councils and Synods*, I: 593 and 706. The statutes of Chichester, issued in 1289, did not specifically name the mendicants but nevertheless allowed those with a papal license to hear confessions to provide pastoral care within the diocese. See *Councils and Synods*, II: 1085, "*Nullus presbiterorum alienum parochianum ad confessionem vel communionem corporis Christi presumat admittere sine licentia proprii sacerdotis, nisi privilegio confessiones audiendi a summo pontifice sit munitus*".

95　National Archives C81/11 (*Chancery Warrants*).

96　National Archives C66/116. Concerning John of Berwick's service in Gascony, see Prestwich, *War, Politics and Finance*, 100.

to provide the soldiers with priests with whom they were familiar. However, aside from those cases where bishops can be seen to have selected priests for service in abroad, it is not clear what procedures royal officials used to select one or another member of the parish clergy for campaign duty. Military tenants would appear to have had a range of options when recruiting priests to serve in the field ranging from their own household chaplains to local parish priests, and even willing mendicants. Despite the rather more *ad hoc* nature of recruitment, however, the evidence demonstrates that the provision of pastoral care played as important a role in the organization of shire levies and military tenants as it did in Edward's professional military units.

14

THE *ECCLESIA ANGLICANA* GOES TO WAR

Prayers, propaganda, and conquest during the reign of Edward I of England, 1272–1307

Introduction

It is widely accepted by scholars that the Hundred Years' War, in general, and the reign of King Edward III of England (1327–1377), in particular, witnessed a crucial stage in the development of state sponsored propaganda efforts to mobilize the nation for war.[1] Edward III's government made particularly skillful use of the church to disseminate the justifications for the king's wars in France and against the Scots. The royal government also required bishops and priests to organize a spectrum of religious rites and ceremonies encompassing the largest possible sections of the English population, including both the laity and clergy, to seek divine intervention on behalf of English troops serving in the field. These religious rites included prayers, penitential and thanksgiving processions, intercessory masses, vigils, almsgiving, and fasting.[2]

The administrative structure that made possible both the dissemination of royal propaganda and the organization of this wide spectrum of religious observances

---

1   See, in this regard, H. J. Hewitt, *The Organization of War under Edward III* (Manchester, 1966), 160–165; W. R. Jones, "The English Church and Royal Propaganda during the Hundred Years' War", *Journal of British Studies* 19 (1979), 18–30; A. K. McHardy, "Liturgy and Propaganda in the Diocese of Lincoln during the Hundred Years' War", *Studies in Church History* 18 (1982), 215–227; and idem, "Religious Ritual and Political Persuasion: The Case of England in the Hundred Years' War", *International Journal of Moral and Social Studies* 3 (1988), 41–52; James A. Doig, "Propaganda, Public Opinion and the Siege of Calais in 1436", in *Crown, Government and People in the Fifteenth Century*, ed. Rowena E. Archer (New York, 1995), 79–107, here 83–85, and a recent summary of the topic by A. K. McHardy, "Some Reflections on Edward III's use of Propaganda", in *The Age of Edward III*, ed. J. S. Bothwell (Woodbridge, 2001), 171–192. For a list of requests for prayers by the English government in the period 1305–1334, see J. Robert Wright, *The Church and the English Crown 1305–1334: A Study Based on the Register of Archbishop Walter Reynolds* (Toronto, 1980), 348–360.

2   Regarding these rites, see the previous note, and especially McHardy, "Some Reflections", 176–183.

was the hierarchical church itself.[3] Edward III's government regularly issued writs to English bishops, especially the archbishops of Canterbury and York, and abbots, as well as the heads of the Dominican and Franciscan orders in England, which provided these church leaders with royally approved accounts of important current events. This information was then passed down the ecclesiastical chain of authority through cathedral deans and archdeacons and from there to the parish priests who were responsible for passing on this information to the English people in the form of sermons and other communications. Royal orders for public religious celebrations, including, on occasion, instructions for specific types of liturgies, prayers, processions, and other rites, traversed the same path from archbishops, to bishops and abbots, on to archdeacons, and then to the most local level of parish priests and vicars. The evidence for the royal government's systematic employment of the English church is to be found in numerous surviving copies of royal writs as well as archiepiscopal orders recorded in bishops' registers throughout Edward III's reign.[4]

Edward III clearly benefited from a well-organized and sophisticated military-religious administration. But was this a fourteenth-century creation? This study argues that, in fact, the origins of Edward III's church based propaganda efforts and his mobilization of religious rites on behalf of the army go back half a century to the reign of his grandfather Edward I (1272–1307).[5] It will be shown here that it was the reign of Edward I and not the reign of Edward III that saw the first fully developed military-religious administration for the mobilization of the English church on behalf of royal government's efforts to wage war.[6]

---

3   McHardy, "Some Reflections", 174, aptly describes the bishops of England as "those obliging, all-purpose workhorses of the realm, who had such a crucial role as the links between the crown and the localities".

4   Hewitt, *Organization of War*, 160–165; and McHardy, "Some Reflections", passim.

5   Scholars investigating the reign of Edward III tend either to ignore or deal only superficially with earlier government efforts. This is certainly the case with Hewitt, *Organization of War*. Jones, "English Church", 24; and McHardy, "Some Reflections", 173, note that Edward I's reign served as a model for his successors in the mobilization of religious rites on behalf of soldiers, if not in the active dissemination of propaganda. Neither, however, discusses these practices during Edward I's reign in any depth. Moreover, both Jones and McHardy treat the Hundred Years' War as a period of new intensity in these royal efforts, without, however, quantifying this new intensity. Finally, none of the studies, discussed here, which consider the dissemination of royal propaganda and the organization of public prayers by the English government, focuses on the administrative system required to assure the implementation of royal policy in the period before Edward III's reign.

6   It does not appear that Henry III, Edward I's father, had such a system in place. In an exhaustive reading of all of the surviving administrative documents from Henry III's reign, including the Pipe Rolls, close rolls, patent rolls, and liberate rolls, and the reams of unpublished documents stored in the Public Record Office, I have found only a few references to public prayers of any sort, and none for the army. This is not surprising, however, given the different military histories of the two reigns. Whereas Edward I undertook major campaigns in which tens of thousands of men were

English church at war under Edward I

King Edward I of England was honored in his own day and by subsequent generations as one of the leading military commanders of Europe for his conquest of Wales and Scotland, and for his defense of Gascony against the French onslaught under King Philip IV (1285–1314).[7] Underpinning these successes was Edward's intelligent mobilization and utilization of the resources of his kingdom for carefully considered and planned campaigns. The purely military side of Edward's wars has been examined in detail by numerous scholars.[8] As indicated, however, the religious elements of Edward's military policy largely have been ignored.[9]

As is true of the mid-to-late fourteenth century and the reign of Edward III, the most important sources for identifying the administrative system that made possible the dissemination of royal propaganda and the organization of religious rites are surviving royal writs and the letters of English archbishops and bishops that were recorded in episcopal registers, and in other ecclesiastical documentary

---

mobilized over several years for service in Wales, Scotland, Gascony, and Flanders, most of Henry III's campaigns were small affairs lasting a few months. As a consequence, it is easy to see that Henry III's government did not see the need to undertake the same type of religious and popular mobilization that seemed so important to Edward I and his advisors.

7 Concerning Edward's Welsh campaigns, see John Edward Morris, *The Welsh Wars of Edward I: A Contribution to Medieval Military History Based on Original Documents* (1901, repr. New York, 1969), and Michael Prestwich, *War, Politics and Finance under Edward I* (Totowa, NJ, 1972). For an overview of Edward I's Scottish campaigns, see Prestwich, *Edward I* (London, 1988, repr. New Haven, CT, 1996), 469–511, and 381–386 for Edward's defense of Gascony. Prestwich has refined his views in *Armies and Warfare in the Middle Ages: The English Experience* (New Haven, CT, 1996).

8 Numerous studies shed light on individual aspects of Edward's military organization, including Alvin Z. Freeman, "Wall-Breakers and River-Bridgers: Military Engineers in the Scottish Wars of Edward I", *Journal of British Studies* 10 (1971), 1–16; Joseph Strayer, "The Costs and Profits of War: The Anglo-French Conflict of 1294–1303", in *The Medieval City*, ed. Harry A. Miskimin, David Herlihy, and A. L. Udovitch (New Haven, CT, 1977), 269–291; and Thomas Avril, "Interconnections between the Lands of Edward I: A Welsh-English Mercenary Force in Ireland 1285–1304", *Bulletin of the Board of Celtic Studies* 40 (1993), 135–147.

9 D. W. Burton, "Requests for Prayers and Royal Propaganda under Edward I", in *Thirteenth Century England* 3 (1989), 25–35, provides a useful introduction to the problem, but does not deal with the spectrum of administrative questions arising from King Edward's efforts to disseminate royal propaganda and mobilize public prayers, as well as other religious rites, which are the focus of this investigation. One other aspect of Edward I's military-religious policy that has attracted some attention is the continuing effort by the royal government to provide pastoral care to the various elements of the royal army, including the king's household, garrison troops, the military households of royal retainers, and the shire levies. See David S. Bachrach, "The Organisation of Military Religion in the Armies of King Edward I of England (1272–1307)", *Journal of Medieval History* 29 (2003), 265–286, and also in this volume.

collections such as collegiate chapter books.[10] Additional administrative evidence can be gleaned from the internal memoranda of the government writing office, that is the Chancery.[11] Finally, some corroborative evidence for the effectiveness of the administrative efforts of the crown and church to disseminate information and organize religious rites is provided by contemporary chroniclers.

During Edward I's reign, the royal government regularly sought to make use of the sophisticated administrative apparatus of the church reaching from the archbishops of York and Canterbury down to the parish level, not excluding either the great monastic houses of England or the Dominican and Franciscan orders, to explain and justify royal military policy to the realm as a whole. The government used two methods to mobilize the administrative resources of the church, both of which relied heavily on the English episcopate. The first and more common method was to order the Chancery to issue a writ to the archbishops of Canterbury and York requiring these two leading prelates of England to issue orders to all of the bishops, monasteries, and other ecclesiastical jurisdictions within their archdioceses to carry out the royal will regarding the dissemination of information, that is royal propaganda, and the organization of religious rites on behalf of soldiers in the field. The second method was to issue this same information and orders to all of the leading ecclesiastical officers of the kingdom in the form of a circular writ, thereby bypassing the archbishops. This study will deal with both of these administrative procedures in turn.

In considering the first and more common method, there is a paradigmatic example in the royal writ issued to Archbishop Robert Winchelsey of Canterbury (1294–1313) in August 1297. This text informed the archbishop that King Philip of France had broken a truce negotiated between the English and French forces in Gascony by the bishops of Albano Laziale and Prenestini, then acting as papal legates.[12] Edward I emphasized that despite his own desire for peace he had been compelled with sadness (*cum dolore*) to take up the fight against one who had "attacked and hostilely assaulted our friends and allies".[13] In order to support this military effort, the king required that, "you pour out devoted prayers to the Highest in your own cathedral and that you have this done in all of the churches that are under your jurisdiction and subject to you".[14] As is typical of these documents, the writ coupled the demand for prayers to be organized throughout the archdiocese with a brief synopsis of the royal position regarding the renewal of

---

10 The entries from episcopal registers and collegiate chapter books are cited individually in this chapter.

11 *Calendar of Chancery Warrants AD 1244–1326* (London, 1927).

12 Thomas Rymer, *Foedera, conventiones, literae, et cujuscunque generis acta publica*, 20 vols (London, 1726–1735), II: 781–782.

13 Ibid., "*amicosque ac confeoderatos nostros invadit hostiliter impugnat*".

14 Ibid., "*Paternitatem vestram affectuose requirimus et rogamus, quatenus preces devotas apud Altissimum efundatis et in vestra cathedrali, ac omnibus aliis eclesiis vestrae jurisdictione subjectis illud idem fieri faciatis*".

hostilities, namely that the war was entirely the fault of the French. As a conse-quence, the request for prayers, which ultimately had to be organized at the parish level, brought with it an explicit defense of King Edward's military policy.

Once the archbishops received writs instructing them to disseminate royal propaganda and to mobilize religious rites to invoke divine aid on behalf of English troops, they relied on the traditional ecclesiastical administrative struc-tures to pass these orders down through the hierarchy. A typical example of how these orders were transmitted can be seen in a surviving document issued by the writing office of Bishop Richard de Gravesend of London (1280–1303) to the dean and chapter of St. Paul's Cathedral in July 1298.[15] This order con-tains a long *fragmentum*, that is a portion of a text imbedded within another, of a letter issued by Archbishop Robert Winchelsey to Bishop Richard on the fifteenth of the same month.[16] This *fragmentum* of the archbishop's letter makes clear that the king had issued a writ to Robert Winchelsey requiring him to organize prayers and other rites (*suffragia*) on behalf of royal troops then fight-ing against the Scots.[17] The archbishop in turn ordered that processions and prayers be organized in all of the dioceses within the archdiocese of Canterbury in order to assure the peace of the kingdom and of the English church (*ecclesia Anglicana*). These prayers were to be devoted specially to seeking divine aid on behalf of the king and his supporters. Archbishop Robert added that his subor-dinate bishops were to see to it that these instructions were observed by their own subordinates.[18]

In addition to demanding that his subordinate bishops organize religious rites on behalf of the king and the royal army, the archbishop's letter also contains a detailed discussion of the royal case for war. The Scots and their supporters are

---

15 *Concilia Magnae Britanniae et Hiberniae*, 4 vols, ed. David Wilkins (London, 1737, repr. Brus-sels, 1964), II: 240–242.

16 The nature of the *fragmentum* is evident from Bishop Robert's comment that he was quoting from a letter sent by the archbishop ("*litteras reverendi patri domini R. Dei gratia Cantuar' quae sequitur continens*"). See *Concilia Magnae Britanniae*, I: 241.

17 Ibid., 241, "Thus, during the aforementioned assembly, the king requested through his messen-gers that prayers and other rites be celebrated for him and his men as they engage in their current expedition which they recently began against the enemies of the king and kingdom" ("*ac etiam dominus rex nuper in ultima congregatione praedicta per nuncios suos rogavit, ut pro eo et suis in expeditione praesenti, quam contra hostes ipsius et regni nuper assumpsit, orationes et suffragia hujusmodi fieri*").

18 Ibid., 242, "Thus, we order and command that you undertake the aforementioned processions, prayers, and rites on behalf of the Holy Land, for the peace of the kingdom, for the English church, and especially for the king and his supporters engaged in the present campaign. Furthermore, you are to see that these rites are carried out throughout your entire diocese every day and in every place, and that information about the excommunication is passed on as well" ("*vobis ut supra mandamus et injungimus quatenus dictas processiones, et orationum suffragia, tam pro statu terrae sanctae et pace regni et ecclesiae Anglicanae, quam etiam pro domino rege et sibi adhae-rantibus in sua expeditione praesenti specialiter; necnon denunciationes excommunicationum praedictas per totam vestram diocesim singulis diebus et locis quibis id expediri videritis*").

characterized as having violently invaded the churches and other ecclesiastical sites in England, stealing church property in their "sacrilegious audacity", and presuming to violate the peace of the kingdom and of the church.[19] The surviving *fragmentum* also emphasizes that the archbishop had publicly excommunicated the Scots, information which could hardly have been unknown to either to Bishop Robert or to the cathedral clergy, and that this excommunication was to be promulgated throughout the dioceses subordinate to Canterbury.[20]

The surviving letter from Bishop Richard of London to the dean and chapter of St. Paul's Cathedral is therefore clear evidence that Archbishop Robert's orders, and ultimately the orders of the king regarding the dissemination of royal propaganda and the organization of religious rites, were carried out. In this context it should be emphasized that Bishop Richard's letter specified that the dean and cathedral canons also were obligated either to organize the requested religious rites personally, or to pass on these orders to their subordinates who actually oversaw the parish churches where these efforts were to be undertaken.[21] Thus, just as the archbishop had done with his bishops, the bishops too used the established ecclesiastical administrative hierarchy to disseminate orders downward.[22]

Moreover, in addition to having carried out his duty to transmit information and orders to his subordinates in the ecclesiastical hierarchy, it should be emphasized that Bishop Robert chose to include a substantial portion of Archbishop Richard's letter within his own text. On a practical, bureaucratic level, this was sound administrative procedure because the repetition of information obtained from the archbishop obviated the need for the busy bishop to compose an entirely new document. Furthermore, by including the original text in his own letter, the bishop provided all of the themes that those lower down the hierarchy would need for their own sermons to the laity, including the justness of the royal cause, the atrocities committed by the Scots, and the fact that the latter had been excommunicated

---

19   Ibid., "Both the Scots and their supporters who presumed and still presume to attack violently the churches of England and other church properties, and to burn and despoil with sacrilegious audacity the property of the church and to infringe upon and disturb the peace of the kingdom and the church" (*"necnon Scotos, et eorum complices, qui ecclesias regni Angliae et loca ecclesiastica violenter invadere, comburere, ac bonis ecclesiasticis ausu sacrilegio spoliare, pacemque regni et ecclesiae patenter infringere ac perturbare praesumpserunt et praesumunt"*).

20   Ibid.,241–242, "We order that these excommunicated men be denounced throughout our province" (*"ut dicitur excommunicantes publice per nostram denunciare provinciam facaeremus"*).

21   Ibid., "[we order that these matters] be publicized by you and by your subordinates in the prebends and churches subject to your jurisdiction" (*"in praebendis et ecclesiis vestrae jurisdictione subjectis ... per vos quam per vestros subditos publicari"*).

22   It is likely, even if the lack of direct evidence requires that we be circumspect, that the bishops used the archidiaconal structure to inform their parish priests about what sermons and religious rites were required. Concerning the organization of the English dioceses into effective archidiaconal districts, see Jean Scammel, "The Rural Chapter in England from the Eleventh to the Fourteenth Century", *English Historical Review* 91 (1971), 1–21.

by the archbishop.[23] This method of providing the content for sermons was well known by this time, as it had been standard practice for the papal government to use bulls, the administrative equivalent of royal writs or archiepiscopal orders, to provide thematic material for mendicant preachers and other ecclesiastical officials since the mid-thirteenth century.[24]

As a postscript to this episode, in September 1298, Archbishop Robert Winchelsey sent another circular letter to his "venerable fellow bishops and all of the suffragens of our province of Canterbury", again beginning the process of organizing wide-scale public prayers and other religious rites, including processions, fasting, and almsgiving, in order to support King Edward's forces in Scotland.[25] The archbishop reported that Edward had recently returned from Flanders in order to take personal command of the military operations being conducted in Scotland. Prince Edward, the king's son, had passed on letters sent by his father which instructed the archbishop to institute, "*laudes et gratias*" to God on behalf of the king at the beginning of his expedition against his opponents. Thus, in turn, Robert Winchelsey ordered his subordinate bishops to pour out prayers and carry out other appropriate rites and to have these religious celebrations carried out diligently throughout, "all of your cities and dioceses".[26]

A very similar pattern of diffusion of information and orders was in effect at York, the other archdiocese of England. On 6 June 1301, Archbishop Thomas Corbridge of York (1299–1304) sent out a circular letter to all of his bishops as well as to the other subordinate ecclesiastical jurisdictions within the archdiocese, many of which enjoyed immunities from the local bishops. Once again, the context of the king's original writ and the archbishop's concomitant circular letter was Edward I's continuing effort to establish English control over Scotland. The archbishop therefore set out the royal case for war and ordered that a spectrum of religious ceremonies be put into motion in order to invoke divine aid on behalf of English troops.[27] Although many scores of letters must originally have been sent in order to fulfill the king's desire and the archbishop's obligation to have prayers

---

23 It does not seem unreasonable to suggest that the archbishop's own letter may have included a *fragmentum* of the original royal writ, now lost, in which the king demanded that religious rites, including sermons, be organized on behalf of the troops. The writ sent by the king in August of 1297 to Archbishop Robert Winchelsey, noted earlier, certainly contained many of the same themes that we see in the *fragmentum* of the archbishop's letter, as it survives in the letter sent by Bishop Richard of London to the chapter and dean of St. Paul's Cathedral.

24 Christoph T. Maier, *Preaching the Crusades: Mendicant Friars and the Cross in the Thirteenth Century* (Cambridge, 1994, repr. 1998), 117.

25 *Concilia Magnae Britanniae*, II: 242–243.

26 Ibid., 243, "*illud per omnes civitates vestras et diocesas diligentius fieri facientes*".

27 *Historical Papers and Letters from the Northern Registers*, ed. James Raine Rolls Series 61 (London, 1873), 149–150. See also *The Register of Thomas Corbridge 1300–1304, part I* (London, 1925), 6. The question of immune ecclesiastical jurisdictions is discussed below.

organized throughout the archdiocese, I have found only one surviving copy, the letter issued to cathedral chapter at York.[28]

Thomas Corbridge began his circular letter by stressing that the king's campaign in Scotland was a just war. He emphasized, just as Archbishop Robert Winchelsey of Canterbury had done in his own letters, that the king was fighting for the peace and safety of his kingdom and in order to hold in check the unjustified attacks made against the English by the Scots.[29] As would appear to have become routine, the Scots were characterized as oath breakers who burned holy places, stole property from the church, and were now under the ban of excommunication.[30] The archbishop then stressed his own view that the king's efforts in Scotland would be aided if they were supported by the devoted prayers of the faithful.[31] Thus, "placing our firm hope in God's aid", Thomas ordered that "a special remembrance for the lord king, for all of his men, and for his illustrious son Lord Edward, be held in our cathedral and in all of the churches of our city, dioceses, and province, including both the exempt and non-exempt churches, whether collegial or parish, every day when masses are celebrated either for the living or for the dead".[32] This was an explicit command for regular intercessory prayers during the celebration of mass throughout the province that set aside the traditional administrative prerogatives of the "exempt" churches. Furthermore, these intercessory prayers said during mass were to be supplemented every Wednesday and Friday by processions of both clerics and lay people during which the participants were to sing litanies

---

28 *Historical Papers and Letters*, 149–150.

29 Ibid. The king acted, "with his army for the peace and security of the kingdom of England to suppress the attacks and rabid presumption of the Scots" (*"cum suo exercitu pro tranquilitate et securitate regni Angliae, ad compescendum impetum ac praesumptsuosam rabiem Scottorum"*). Once again, it seems likely that the themes enunciated by the archbishop were either a paraphrase or a direct quotation from the original royal writ issued to him.

30 *Historical Papers and Letters*, 149–150, "who, unmindful of their own salvation, after their oath of loyalty to our lord king, given as to their prince and lord, cruelly attacked the churches and sacred places of the kingdom of England and not without considerable killing. They burned and stole church property and carried it off, setting aside their fear of God. As a result, they have incurred a sentence of excommunication" (*"qui, post fidelitatis juramentum eidem domino nostro regi, ut principi suo et domino ... salutis suae immemores, ecclesias et loca sacra regni Angliae non sine multiplici homicidio crudeliter invaserunt, combusserunt et bona ecclesiastica rapiendo, Dei timore postposito, asportarunt, propter quod in excommunicationis sententiam inciderunt"*).

31 *Historical Papers and Letters*, 149–150, "so that the vigorous prince might direct his path to Scotland, and since we believe that his actions will greatly prosper if they are supported by the devoted prayers of the faithful" (*"ut princeps strenuus ad partes Scotiae jam dirigat gressus suos, cujus actus et opera magis credimus prosperari, si orationibus devotis fidelium infulciatur, nos in Dei adjutorio"*).

32 Ibid, 149–150, *"spem firmam ponentes, vobis mandamus quatenus in nostra cathedrali et omnibus aliis ecclesiis nostrae civitatis et dioecesis et provinciae, exemptis et non exemptis, tam collegiatis quam parochialibus, omni die in missis presbyterorum, sive pro defunctis sive pro vivis celebrantium, ipsius domini regis, et omnium ipsum et illustrem filium suum dominum Edwardum comitantium, memoriam fieri specialem"*.

on behalf of the king and his army.[33] The archbishop of York emphasized that the purpose of these religious demonstrations was to convince God through the piety of the people to protect the king and his army from harm.[34]

In 1303, Archbishop Thomas Corbridge again set in motion a massive effort to mobilize prayers on behalf of the English king and his soldiers fighting in Scotland. One of the series of letters issued by the archiepiscopal Chancery in April of this year has been preserved in the chapter book of the canons of St. John of Beverley.[35] Using a formula similar to that employed two years earlier, the archbishop emphasized his expectation that the cause of the English king in maintaining peace and security in both England and Scotland would be furthered through the prayers of the faithful. Thomas added that he "placed his faith firmly in God who wishes to be sought out by the tearful prayers of the devout".[36] Therefore, just as he had done in 1301, the archbishop issued orders that prayers be said on behalf of the king, his son, and their companions, that is soldiers, at the church of St. John of Beverley and in other parish and collegiate churches throughout his archdiocese irrespective of their exempt status. Moreover, these prayers were to be said both during mass and during processions.[37] These intercessory masses, processions, and prayers were to be celebrated on the approaching Easter Sunday, every other Sunday, as well as on feast days. In addition to these obligations, the archbishop repeated verbatim from the letter of 1301, noted here, his call for biweekly processions by lay people on Wednesdays and Fridays.[38] The archbishop concluded this list of obligations by stressing that these rites and ceremonies would cause God to defend the royal army in battle, bring honor and salvation to the kingdom, and bring benefit to the English church (*ecclesia Anglicana*).[39]

This first method of disseminating royal propaganda and orders for the mobilization of religious rites on behalf of the English army, namely the issuing of royal writs to the archbishops of Canterbury and York would appear, on the basis of surviving evidence in episcopal registers, to have been the primary mode used by

---

33 Ibid., 150.
34 Ibid., "so that our Lord, who rules everything, might guide and direct his steps and acts through his own piety and thus protect and defend the king and his army from their enemies" ("*ut Dominus noster, rerum omnium dispositer providus, pro sua pietate gressus suos et actus dirigat et disponat, ipsumque regem cum exercitu ab adversis protegat et defendat*").
35 *Memorials of Beverley Minster: The Chapter Act Book of the Collegiate Church of St. John of Beverley AD 1286–1347*, 2 vols, ed. Arthur Francis Leach (Durham, 1898–1303), I: 10–11.
36 Ibid., "*Nos in Deo [necnon eo], qui lacrimosis devotorum precibus vult pulsari, spem firmam ponentes*".
37 Ibid.
38 Ibid.
39 Ibid., 11, "May he protect and defend the king and his army from their enemies, restore the tranquility of desired peace, and grant victory over his enemies, for his own honor, for the salvation of the kingdom, and for the sake of the English church" ("*ipsumque Regem cum exercitu ab adversis protegat et defendat, necnon pacis optatae tranquilitatem et de inimicis triumphum habere concedet, ad ipsius honorem, regni salvationem, et totius utilitatem Ecclesiae Anglicanae*").

the royal government.[40] This system had the advantage of using already existing ecclesiastical administrative structures and also the not inconsiderable benefit of transferring the costs of writing and sending countless letters away from the royal Chancery and onto the writing offices of archbishops, bishops, and other ecclesiastical office holders. Despite these advantages, however, the royal government did occasionally bypass the archbishops when seeking to spread propaganda and seek prayers. For example, at the outbreak of war in 1294 against King Philip of France for control of Gascony, the royal government issued a circular writ to the leaders of the English church, namely the bishops, abbots, and heads of the Dominican and Franciscan orders.[41]

Here, King Edward set out the reasons why he had gone to war and sought prayers on behalf of his forces in Gascony. In this context, the king emphasized his belief that man was inherently weak and therefore required the hand of God to sustain him.[42] Edward insisted that if the proper religious rites were performed on behalf of his army, he would then be able to pursue his rights and expose his body in combat without fear. In this case, God would give glory, honor, and praise not only to the king but to the church and the kingdom as well.[43] Thus, just as was noted previously with regard to the royal writs issued directly to the archbishops of Canterbury and York, this circular writ provided the themes that were to be covered in the intercessory prayers for the king and his army. One particularly noteworthy aspect of the writ issued by the royal Chancery is 1294 was the fact that it was commented on by the author of the *Annals of Worcester* who reiterated the basic themes enunciated by King Edward.[44] Indeed, the annalist would appear to have quoted directly from the circular writ that had been sent to the leading ecclesiastical officials of England, presumably copying from the text issued to the abbot of Worcester, which likely was still extant in the monastic archives when

40 This method of transmitting royal orders to the church as a whole remained the primary mode during the reign of Edward III. On this point, see McHardy, "Religious Rituals", 48.

41 Rymer, *Foedera*, II: 639.

42 Ibid., "There is no aid in man, but rather weakness and defects. Because of this, it is fitting that the hand of the divine support our weakness with its strength, so we ask and affectionately command your pious affection so that your hearts rise up to the Lord and you pray devotedly to Him" ("*Cumque in homine not sit auxilium sed infirmitas et defectus, et propter hoc oporteat imbecilitatem nostram Divinae manus sustentari praesidiis, pias affectiones vestras a affectuose requirimus et rogamus, quatenus corda vestra sursum habentes ad Dominum devotis apud Eum supplicantibus insistatis*").

43 Rymer, *Foedera*, II: 639, "In this manner, we will be able to take up this business and defend our just cause without fearing for our body since God has granted glorious triumph and praise to us and to you" ("*ita possumus assumptum negotium prosequi, et justitiam nostram defendere pro qua corpus nostrum exponere non timemus quod Deo cedat ad gloriam nobis et vobis ad triumphum et laudem*").

44 *Annales Prioratus de Wigornia*, ed. Henry R. Luard, *Annales Monastici* IV, Rolls Series 36.4 (London, 1869), 516. For a discussion of the Worcester chronicle and the corpus of "monastic chronicles" in general, see Antonia Gransden, *Historical Writing in England c. 550 to c. 1307* (Ithaca, 1974), 318–320, and 333.

the annalist wrote. The annalist was therefore able to observe that King Edward sent letters throughout the kingdom asking for prayers because he knew that victory derived from heaven.[45]

In 1296, the royal government again issued a circular writ, this time in preparation for a campaign that was intended to recover lands lost in Gascony to the French in the previous two years. The writ, issued to all of the English bishops, the provincial prior of the Dominicans, the minister general of the Franciscans, as well as seventeen abbots, is preserved in a copy included in the register of Bishop John de Halton of Carlisle (1292–1324). As was true in 1294, the royal government again used this document to make the case for the just and defensive nature of the war now underway, stressing that the war was intended to seek the recovery (*recuperatio*) and defense (*defensio*) of royal lands in Gascony.[46]

The final example discussed here offers a glimpse of the royal administration from a different angle. In this case, rather than a surviving writ, there is a calendared entry that records the original royal order, issued on 7 June 1301, that authorized the Chancery to compose and issue writs to all of the bishops and other ecclesiastical leaders in England, instructing them to organize wide-scale public prayers on behalf of the royal army then operating in Scotland.[47] Aside from the fact that this is an example of the mechanics of royal administration at work, this writ would not be of great importance except for the curious fact that it would seem to have been redundant. As noted, a royal writ intended to disseminate royal views on the war in Scotland and to organize public religious rites on behalf of the troops had already been issued to and acted upon by the archbishop of York prior to 7 June 1301. In fact, Thomas Corbridge's letter to his subordinates in which he set out the royal case for war in Scotland and demanded the mobilization of public prayers was issued on 6 June 1301, one day before the issue of the order for the drafting of the circular writ, and thus even longer before these writs actually were written out and reached their destinations. In this case, therefore, it would appear that the circular from the king was intended to reinforce Archbishop Corbridge's orders to his subordinate church officials. At present, however, it must remain an open question why this bureaucratic redundancy took place.

---

45 *Wigornia*, 516, "The king of England, knowing that victory is derived from heaven, sought through letters to have everyone pray so that the King of kings would take up this business and God would grant glory and fitting honor to the kingdom of England" ("*Rex Angliae sciens quod victoria de caelo est, per literas petiit quatinus ab ommibus sic oretur, ut Regis regum dextera assumptum negotium sic disponat, quatinus Deo cedat ad gloriam, et ad regni Angliae commodum et honorem*").

46 *Historical Papers and Letters*, 120.

47 *Calendar of Chancery Warrants*, 127. No copies of this writ have yet been identified, and so the exact words used by the royal clerks must at present remain unknown.

Lay participation in military-religious rites

The surviving royal writs and archiepiscopal/episcopal orders, discussed already, indicate that at least at the administrative level, the royal government was able to disseminate throughout the ecclesiastical hierarchy both propaganda and demands for religious rites on behalf of soldiers in the field. This view would seem to be supported by the fact that writers, such as the author of the *Annals of Worcester*, were able not only to comment on the content of these royal commands, but even to quote from them. But letting clerics know what was required of them was one matter; actually getting the desired information to the laity and then having lay people participate in the desired religious observances was quite another. The remainder of this study will consider these two problems.

The first question that must be addressed concerns the means that church offi-cials, but particularly parish priests and mendicant preachers who had the most direct contact with the English laity, had available to persuade people to listen to royal propaganda and to participate in the desired religious observances on behalf of English troops in the field. In the first instance, parish priests had natural audi-ences at Sunday mass, as well as regular daily and intercessory masses, while mendicants drew crowds on their preaching tours. Thus, if the themes of royal propaganda used to justify war were disseminated to them, there can be little doubt that they were in position to include such themes in their sermons. But does this mean that they did? William de Rishanger (born c. 1250) certainly wanted his audience to believe that this was the case.[48] In discussing the preparations for the royal campaign to Scotland in 1298, William emphasized not only that royal writs defending the war were disseminated throughout the churches of England, but that as a result, "the entire population willingly and with great joy prayed for the king".[49]

The archbishops of England, however, were not content to rely simply on the joyful good will of the laity to assure their attendance at sermons and participation in religious rites, particularly those that required more than simply saying prayers in church. Instead, the archbishops of Canterbury and York turned to an incentive long used by the papacy to mobilize prayers, processions, fasts, and almsgiving

---

48 William de Rishanger, *Chronica et Annales*, ed. Henry Thomas Riley, Rolls Series 28.2 (London, 1865), 193–194. William, who wrote at the monastery of St Albans, would appear to have been something of a specialist in military history. One of his major works was an account of the mid-thirteenth century Barons' War, or baronial revolt against King Henry III. William was therefore likely to have been even more sensitive than the average educated observer to the important role that religion played in the mobilization of public support for war. Indeed, it is not unlikely that his interest in military history led him to discuss matters such as the organization of public prayers by the king, a topic that largely was ignored by his fellow writers. Concerning William's career, see Antonia Gransden, *Historical Writing in England II c. 1307 to the Early Sixteenth Century* (Ithaca, NY, 1982), 4–5.

49 William de Rishanger, *Chronica et Annales*, 194, "*omnis populus sponte et cum gaudio pro Rege fecit orationes*".

on behalf of crusading armies, that is to indulgences.[50] For example, in order to give his subordinates aid in mobilizing the lay population to participate in religious rites on behalf of English troops in Scotland in 1301, Thomas Corbridge authorized the promulgation of an indulgence in the same circular letter in which he set out the royal case for war and demanded the celebration of intercessory rites. The archbishop offered to relax forty days of previously imposed and accumulated penances for any person who prayed devotedly for the army in the manner detailed earlier in his letter, noted here.[51] Thomas then instructed his priests to publicize this promised indulgence widely, but also solemnly, in order to excite the people about the prospect of praying for the king and his troops.[52] Similarly, in 1303, Archbishop Corbridge again ordered his subordinates to offer an indulgence of forty days from penance due for sins committed by lay people who had confessed their sins with a contrite heart and then prayed devotedly for the army. The archbishop once more instructed, "we desire that news of this indulgence be publicized openly and solemnly in order to inspire the devotion of the faithful".[53]

Indulgences of this type were also offered in the archdiocese of Canterbury. Thus, for example, in 1295 Robert Winchelsey authorized the bishop of Bangor to offer indulgences ranging from ten to forty days to the lay people of his diocese. Those who marched in intercessory processions were to receive the greatest spiritual benefits, while those who only recited penitential psalms or offered up prayers were to obtain lesser indulgences. As his fellow archbishop was do some years later, Robert Winchelsey emphasized that the purpose of these indulgences was "to excite favorably the devotion of the faithful", on behalf of the king.[54] Given the paucity of surviving sources dealing with lay religious activity in this period, it is difficult to know whether these indulgences had the desired effect. Nevertheless, the continued utilization of this technique, up through the end of Edward I's reign, to mobilize public participation in prayers would seem to indicate that the archbishops of Canterbury and York, at the very least, had some confidence in them.

---

50 The basic work on the use of indulgences by the papacy remains James A. Brundage, *Medieval Canon Law and the Crusader* (Madison, 1969).

51 *Historical Letters and Papers*, 149, "And so that they might pray devotedly for the army, as is noted above, we mercifully rescind 40 days of penances assigned to them to propitiate God" ("*et suo exercitu devote oraverint, ut superius est expressum, xl. dies de injuncta sibi penitentia Deo propitio misericorditer relaxamus*").

52 Ibid., "*quam indulgentiam aperte et sollemniter ad excitandam devotionem fidelium per vos volumus publicari*".

53 *Memorials of Beverley Minster*, 11.

54 *Concilia Magnae Britanniae*, II: 213, "*ad devotionem fidelium excitandum favorabiliter*".

Conclusion

There can be little doubt that King Edward III made skillful use of the church to disseminate royal propaganda and to organize public religious as well as political support for military action abroad, particularly in France and against the Scots. What is at issue is the origin of the administrative practices that were crucial to gaining public support for these military operations. This study makes clear that it is to the thirteenth rather than the fourteenth century, to the wars of Edward I rather than the wars of Edward III, that historians should turn their attention when considering the first full development of the religio-military administration that facilitated the conduct of overseas wars by the kings of England. Edward I's government made repeated and extensive use of the ecclesiastical administrative system to make his case for war to the English people. Furthermore, Edward I's government made regular use of this same system when mobilizing large-scale public religious rites that were intended to invoke divine aid on behalf of English armies in the field. Thus, at least in this area, the Hundred Years' War must be understood as a continuation of long-standing administrative policies and procedures, rather than as the dawn of a new administrative age or a military revolution.

15

URBAN MILITARY FORCES OF ENGLAND AND GERMANY, C. 1240–C. 1315, A COMPARISON

Scholars long have recognized the important roles played by urban fighting forces in the military conflicts of the High Middle Ages from the eleventh through the early fourteenth century. Such forces pushed the Christian frontiers of Iberia ever southward in this period, and the numerous surviving city ordinances, the *fueros*, record the obligations and rights of the townsmen who fought.[1] Urban militias provided the greater part of the manpower for the internecine wars among the cities of northern Italy for centuries.[2] In addition, these same urban militias, combined into the Lombard League, eventually overcame the might of the imperial armies commanded by Emperor Frederick Barbarossa (1153–1190) at Legnano in 1176. The militias of Paris, Mieux, Orléans, Rheims, and numerous other cities provided a large part of the army available to Philip Augustus at the battle of Bouvines in 1214, and for Louis IX's campaign at Beauvais in 1235.[3] At Courtrai, in 1302, the urban militias of Flanders inflicted a devastating defeat on King Philip IV's mounted forces.[4] However, despite the widespread understanding of the importance of urban militias, and despite the valiant efforts of a few scholars, including several gathered at Swansea University in July 2005, the contributions of these forces to the

---

1 For a valuable overview of the development of urban fighting forces in Iberia and their contribution to the conquest of frontier territories from the Muslims, see James F. Powers, *A Society Organized for War: The Iberian Municipal Militias in the Central Middle Ages, 1000–1284* (Berkeley, CA, 1988).

2 See in this regard William M. Bowsky, *A Medieval Italian Commune: Siena under the Nine 1287–1355* (Berkeley, CA, 1981), 128–150; Daniel Waley, *The Italian City-Republics* 3rd edn (New York, 1988), 53; idem, *Siena and the Sienese in the Thirteenth Century* (Cambridge, 1991), passim; and Aldo A. Settia, "Infantry and Cavalry in Lombardy (11th–12th Centuries)", trans. Valerie Eads, *Journal of Medieval Military History* 6 (2008), 58–78.

3 Léon Louis Borrelli de Serres, *Recherches sur divers services publics du XIIIe au XVIIe Siècle* (Paris, 1895), 465–527; Edouard Audouin, *Essai sur l'armée au temps de Philippe Auguste* (Paris, 1913), 4–32; John W. Baldwin, *The Government of Philip Augustus: Foundations of Royal Power in the Middle Ages* (Berkeley, CA, 1986), 165–175.

4 See the discussion of the battle of Courtrai by Kelly DeVries, *Infantry Warfare in the Early Fourteenth Century: Discipline, Tactics, and Technology* (Woodbridge, 1996).

military efforts of the kingdoms of England and Germany in the High Middle Ages have not received their due attention when compared with Spain, Italy, and France. During the nineteenth and early twentieth centuries, German historians, although driven by a strong romantic-nationalist *parti pris* focused on the nobility, were very productive in writing military history. During the Nazi period, including the Second World War, however, military history often was put at the service of the government's propaganda machine to demonstrate Germany's innate superiority over other nations. Following Germany's defeat and humiliation, the process of de-Nazification led German historians largely to abandon military history except as it related to noble or knightly mentality. All in all, contemporary German historiography of medieval warfare does not take account of the advances achieved in military history writing over the past six decades.[5]

Unlike specialists in medieval German history, scholars working on medieval England have devoted very considerable attention to military history, focusing their research, particularly in the post-conquest period, on the exceptionally rich narrative sources. By contrast, scholars have tended not to take advantage of administrative documents, particularly unpublished administrative documents with which England is even more richly endowed during the same period. As a consequence of this focus on narrative texts, at the expense if not to the exclusion of government records, the presentation of English warfare by scholars has tended to reflect the biases of contemporary authors more interested in pleasing their noble patrons than in providing detailed information about the actual conduct of war.[6] Despite individual scholarly contributions of great merit, therefore,

---

5   Concerning the lack of attention by scholars to the central questions of medieval German military history, see Hans-Henning Kortüm, "Der Krieg im Mittelalter als Gegenstand der historischen Kultur-Wissenschaften: Einer Annäherung", in *Krieg im Mittelalter*, ed. idem (Berlin, 2001), 13–43. With respect to the noble and particularly knight-centered nature of German medieval military historiography in the period before the Second World War see, for example, Hans Fehr, "Das Waffenrecht der Bauern im Mittelalter", *Zeitschrift der Savigny Stiftung für Rechtsgeschichte, germanistische Abteilung* 35 91914), 111–211, especially 118, which despite its title, is focused on the superiority and greater importance of mounted warriors as contrasted with foot soldiers in medieval German warfare. Hans Delbrück, *Medieval Warfare: History of the Art of War III*, trans. W. J. Renfroe (Lincoln, 1982), 365–375, originally published under the title *Geschichte der Kriegskunst im Rahmen der politischen Geschichte* 2nd edn (Berlin, 1923); and Paul Schmitthenner, "Lehnskriegwesen und Söldnertum im abendländischen Imperium des Mittelalters", *Historische Zeitschrift* 150 (1934), 229–267. For the period after the Second World War, see Leopold Auer, "Zum Kriegswesen unter den früheren Babenbergern", *Jahrbuch für Landeskunde von Niederösterreich* 42 (1976), 9–25, especially 16–19; idem "Formen des Krieges im abendländischen Mittelalter", in *Formen des Krieges*, ed. Manfried Rauchensteiner and Erwin A. Schmidl (Graz, 1991), 17–43, especially 19–23; and Malte Prietzl, *Kriegführung im Mittelalter: Handlungen, Erinnerungen, Bedeutungen* (Paderborn, 2006).

6   With respect to the *parti pris* of English chroniclers regarding the importance of mounted troops in general and of the nobility in particular, see Matthew Bennet, "The Myth of the Military Supremacy of Knightly Cavalry", in *Armies, Chivalry and Warfare in Medieval Britain and France*, ed. Matthew Strickland (Stamford, CT, 1998), 304–316.

the discussion of medieval English military history is still dominated by romance, chivalry, and the earthly manifestation of these platonic forms—the mounted knight—who is still treated by many scholars as the most important element in the armies of England.[7]

The modern neglect of medieval urban military forces in Germany and England is perplexing because the sources for both kingdoms are very extensive. The archaeological evidence for Germany is immense.[8] In addition, historians have available a substantial number of narrative works, many of which provide good coverage of urban history. Indeed, some of these texts were written by lay-men living in the very cities about which they were writing.[9] For England, as mentioned, the sources are even richer. Nevertheless, the great wealth of administrative documents has not been used intensively to explore the relative importance of the numerous urban elements that served in English fighting forces. The reason for this is two-fold. First, a selective reading of narrative sources without sufficient regard for their aristocratic *parti pris* has promoted an historically inaccurate focus on the supposed chivalric warrior elite. Secondly, the neglect, except by a small handful of scholars, of the vast body of surviving administrative documents, particularly those that have not been published, has obscured the enormous importance placed by the royal government on all types of "non-knightly" fighting forces, including urban militias.

The burden of this chapter is to highlight the essential features of urban military forces in England and Germany with the intention of drawing some comparisons and contrasts. These two kingdoms, of course, were organized on very different political and constitutional foundations, which had a substantial influence on the organization of urban fighting forces. This study, therefore, concludes with some observations concerning the differences as well as the similarities in the urban militias that were mobilized in England and Germany. Because of the

---

7   For a clear statement of the perceived poor quality and limited importance of non-noble elements in the English armies of the thirteenth century by a leading specialist in thirteenth-century English warfare, see Michael Prestwich, *War, Politics and Finance under Edward I* (Totowa, NJ, 1972), 92–113; restated in idem, *Armies and Warfare in the Middle Ages: The English Experience* (Yale, 1996), passim. With respect to the continuing scholarly efforts to justify the relevance of chivalry in the context of medieval military historiography, see Maurice Keen, "Introduction", *Medieval Warfare: A History*, ed. idem (Oxford, 1999), 1–9.

8   See, for example, Carlrichard Brühl, *Palatium und Civitas: Studien zur Profantopographie spätantiker Civitates vom 3. bis 13. Jahrhundert* 2 vols (Cologne, 1975 and 1990).

9   A large number of these urban chronicles are published in the *Scriptores* series by the Monumenta Germaniae Historica. The two chronicles that are the focus of the discussion of the military resources of the city of Worms were reedited from the original MGH edition and published by Heinrich Boos, *Quellen zur Geschichte der Stadt Worms III: Annalen und Chroniken* (Berlin, 1893), 143–199; and are now available in an English translation in David S. Bachrach, *The Histories of a Medieval German City, Worms c. 1000–c. 1300: Translation and Commentary* (Aldershot, 2014). For an overview of city chronicles, see Elisabeth M. C. Van Houts, *Local and Regional Chronicles* (Turnhout, 1995), particularly 15.

limitations of space, this present work is focused on the period extending from the mid-thirteenth to the early fourteenth century. It also focuses on military matters *stricto sensu* leaving aside paramilitary and extra-legal activities such as policing duties and piracy.

England

Perhaps the best known, and certainly most studied, urban military force in the territories subject to the kings of England consisted of the naval and human resources of the Cinque Ports. This union of ports originally included Hastings, Dover, Sandwich, Rolney, and Hythe but subsequently expanded, under royal charter, to embrace several dozen other towns and cities, including most promi-nently Winchelsea and Rye.[10] Less well studied are the scores of other coastal towns and cities, which also provided considerable naval and human resources to the royal government. Throughout the reigns of Henry III (1216–1272) and Edward I (1272–1307), the crown mobilized enormous numbers of ships and men from the Cinque Ports and most other coastal towns and cities in England, as well as in Ireland. The contributions from these urban centers made it possible for the royal government to conduct large-scale military operations involving the ship-ment of huge quantities of food and materiél in Wales, Flanders, Gascony, and Scotland.

There are many thousands of surviving administrative documents from the mid-thirteenth to the early fourteenth century detailing the deployment of thousands of ships and tens of thousands of men from coastal towns for service carrying supplies, harrying enemy forces, and defending the coast, as well as transporting troops and horses. In 1242, for example, Henry III mobilized naval forces from numerous towns for his campaign against Louis IX of France in the Poitou. In June of that year, Henry III issued orders to the Cinque Port towns to harry the coasts of Brittany and Normandy, and the northern channel port of Boulogne.[11] In August of the same year, Henry III ordered the mobilization of hundreds of additional ships and thousands of men, including twenty-five well-equipped ves-sels and contingents of marines armed with crossbows from Dunwich, Yarmouth, Ipswich, Orford, and Blakeney, to rendezvous at the port of Dover and place

---

10 Regarding the Cinque Ports, see K. M. E. Murray, *The Constitutional History of the Cinque Ports* (Manchester 1935); idem, "Dengmarsh and the Cinque Ports", *The English Historical Review* 54.216 (1939), 664–673; Derek F. Renn, "The Castles of Rye and Winchelsea", *The Archaeo-logical Journal* 136 (1979), 193–202; E. W. Parkin, "The Ancient Cinque Port of Sandwich", *Arhcaeologia Cantiana* 101 (1984), 189–216; N. A. M. Rodger, "The Naval Service of the Cinque Ports", *The English Historical Review* 111.442 (1996), 636–651; David R. Oliver, *Late Medieval Thanet and the Cinque Ports* (Broadstairs, Kent, 1997); and Craig L. Lambert, "The Contribution of the Cinque Ports to the Wars of Edward II and Edward III: New Methodologies and Estimates", in *Roles of the Sea in Medieval England*, ed. Richard Gorski (Woodbridge, 2012), 59–78.

11 *Close Rolls of the Reign of Henry III 1216–1272* (London, 1902-1938), here *CR 1237–1242*, 482.

themselves under the command of the royal constable there.[12] A similar example of the large-scale mobilization of ships by Henry III took place in March 1258, when he sent orders to the Cinque Ports to mobilize 200 horse transports to support his military operations in Wales. These ships were of two types, with 100 capable of carrying sixteen horses each, and the other 100 ships capable of carrying twenty-four horses each. In total, the Cinque Ports were tasked with transporting 4,000 mounts for the king's army in Wales.[13]

During the reign of Edward I, both the number and the scale of military operations were much greater than those during the reign of his father, with concomitantly greater need to draw upon the naval resources of English towns and cities. In April 1282, for example, Edward I followed the model of his father and mobilized an exceptionally large fleet from the Cinque Ports in support of his military operations in Wales.[14] In August 1295, Edward commanded the towns of Great Yarmouth, Colchester, Ipswich, Dunwich, Blakeney, Lynn, and Little Yarmouth to deploy their ships to deter an expected attack by King Philip IV of France against the coast of England.[15] While preparing for a renewed offensive in Scotland in March 1303, Edward I issued letters to all royal officers with jurisdictions along the coast from Southampton to Cornwall to have all of the cities and towns in this region provide ships, men, and matériel for that summer's operations in Scotland.[16]

The increasingly large deployments of ships and crews for military operations by Edward I imposed correspondingly heavy burdens on coastal cities and towns, as well as on individual citizens. In order to alleviate the economic hardship that these urban populations endured when deploying large numbers of ships and armed men for the king's campaigns, Edward I made a practice of broadening the taxable base of the individual cities. In 1295, for example, the king issued orders to the bailiffs of Great Yarmouth to ensure that all men who owed money to support the city's ships paid their fair share.[17] In the body of the royal order, the king's clerk referred to the government's grant to Great Yarmouth of the right to levy fleet taxes on all persons possessing or owning lands and rents in the town who did not, themselves, live there.[18]

However, it was not only as sailors and marines that urban fighting men served the kings of England. Contingents of city militia forces were deployed by the

---

12   Ibid., 456.
13   *CR 1256–1259*, 297.
14   *Welsh Rolls in the Calendar of Various Chancery Rolls AD 1277–1326* (London, 1912), 247.
15   *Calendar of Close Rolls 1272–1307* (London, 1900–1908), here *CCR 1288–1296*, 456.
16   Ibid., 128. Also see the discussion in David S. Bachrach, "King Edward I's Military Bureaucracy: The Case of Peter of Dunwich", in *The Medieval Way of War: Studies in Medieval Military History in Honor of Bernard S. Bachrach*, ed. Gregory Halfond (Aldershot, 2015), 273–281, and in this volume.
17   *CCR 1288–1296*, 460.
18   Ibid.

royal government on campaigns in the field, in defense of royal fortifications, as well as in defense of their own home cities. In 1242, for example, the sheriffs of London were ordered to send a contingent of 120 crossbowmen drawn from the city militia to join the royal army at Dover and participate in the impending invasion of France.[19] In July 1264, a unit of militiamen from Greenwich accompanied by a contingent of forty-eight militiamen from London, under the command of the sheriff of Kent, were deployed to help defend the Thames and Medway estuaries from a potential French invasion.[20] In 1287–1288, several units of militiamen from London, as well as contingents from Bristol, were mobilized to serve in Wales.[21] During the Welsh war of 1294–1295, a contingent of fifty crossbowmen from Bristol was deployed to support the forces holding Lampeter Castle.[22] In 1295, two separate groups of "picked militiamen" from London served in the garrison of the Isle of Wight.[23] Moreover, the use of urban militiamen to serve as part of royal garrisons was continued into the reign of Edward II (1307–1327). In 1315, a continent of city militia from York traveled to Berwick to serve in the garrison there. Each man in this unit was equipped with a crossbow, a gambeson, and a good helmet.[24]

The largest number of urban militiamen in England, however, served in defense of their own towns and cities rather than on campaign. This was particularly true in the dangerous border regions, and in newly conquered territories in Wales and Scotland, where the English government not only built massive fortifications but established towns as well whose populations provided the largest part of the manpower to defend the walls of the fortified royal centers. This process is particularly well documented in Wales where the number of weapons stored in royal strongholds such as Harlech, Conway, and Caernarvon far outstripped the rather small number of professional soldiers deployed in garrisons there.[25] The deployment of up to 300 crossbows and many tens of thousands of quarrels to the royal castle-towns with professional garrisons of fifteen to twenty men makes clear that the burden of defense rested largely on the urban population.[26]

In brief, the urban military forces in the territories ruled by the kings of England within the British Isles were both substantial in their own right and crucial to the conduct of the royal government's military operations. The naval resources

---

19 *CR 1237–1242*, 456.

20 *CR 1261–1264*, 392.

21 National Archives E372/132 1v and 22r; E372/133 18r; C62/65 4r.

22 National Archives E101/5/19.

23 National Archives E101/5/27.

24 National Archives E101/14/33.

25 Concerning the use of the population around fortresses as militia forces, see Ifor Rowlands, "The Edwardian Conquest and its Military Consolidation", in *Edward I and Wales*, ed. Trevor Herbert and Gareth Elwyn Jones (Cardiff, 1988), 41–72, here 52–53; and Frederick C. Suppe, *Military Institutions on the Welsh Marches: Shropshire AD 1066–1300* (Woodbridge, 1994), 17.

26 Concerning the deployment of 300 crossbows at Caernarvon Castle in June 1290, see National Archives C62/66 4r.

including both blue-water and riverine assets, as well as the trained sailors and the marines of coastal cities and towns were essential to the transport and supply of the king's armies. These naval forces also protected the English coast and harried the coasts of the king's enemies. Well-armed and equipped contingents of city militiamen served in the king's campaigns in the field and in royal garrisons throughout England's frontiers, as well as in Wales and Scotland. In terms of both the numbers of men involved and the costs incurred by the royal government in deploying them, the urban fighting forces dwarfed mounted troops of all types, and even more so the "knightly" contingents that filled the accounts of contemporary chroniclers and affect the focus of modern scholars who do not give due attention to unpublished administrative documents.

Germany

In contrast to contemporary English narrative sources, many of which were written for the upper strata of secular and ecclesiastical society, many of the chronicles from thirteenth-and early fourteenth-century Germany were written for, and sometimes by, city dwellers. Moreover, many of the authors of these narrative sources made extensive use of urban administrative documents, most no longer extant, as the basis of their texts.[27] As a result, these accounts frequently discuss the deployment of urban military forces of German cities, and provide extensive details regarding the cost, duration, and conditions of their deployment in a manner consistent with administrative documents produced by the English royal government. Particularly enlightening in this regard are the thirteenth-century chronicles of the city of Worms, which as an urban center was on par with Bristol or Dover, but considerably smaller than London.[28]

---

27 This is particularly clear, for example, in the *Annales Wormatienses* and the *Chronicon Wormatiensis*. A comparison of the extant charters for Worms with the texts of these two narrative sources makes clear that the authors of the latter copied administrative documents verbatim into their texts. See, in this context, Johannes Fried, "Ladenburg am Neckar und der rheinische Bund von 1254/1256", *Zeitschrift für die Geschichte des Oberrheins* 120 (1972), 457–467, here 466; and David S. Bachrach, "The Rhetoric of Historical Writing: Documentary Sources in Histories of Worms c. 1300", *Journal of the History of Ideas* 68 (2007), 187–206.

28 The population of London in 1300 may have been as large as 80,000 people. In this regard see John Schofield, "When London Became a European Capital", *British Archaeology* 45 (1999), 12–13. Scholars have not yet established a population range for the city of Worms during the thirteenth century; however, it is clear that during the middle of this century the city of Worms doubled the size of its walls to 5,300 meters. See Brühl, *Palatium und Civitas* II: 120 and 126. A wall of this size required approximately 4,200 defenders. See the discussion regarding the number of defenders required for walls of specific sizes by Bernard S. Bachrach and Rutherford Aris, "Military Technology and Garrison Organization: Some Observations on Anglo-Saxon Military Thinking in Light of the Burghal Hidage", *Technology and Culture* 3 (1990), 1–17; and reprinted with the same pagination in Bernard S. Bachrach, *Warfare and Military Organization in Pre-Crusade Europe* (Aldershot, 2002). In addition to requiring a very substantial military force to defend its walls, the city of Worms, as will be seen here, had an expeditionary levy of approximately 4,000

A close reading of the chronicles of Worms as well as the surviving charters for the city make clear that this Rhenish port possessed extensive military resources, including a fleet, a large expeditionary levy, and even an artillery train. In the summer of 1242, for example, at the same time that Henry III of England was preparing for his invasion of the Poitou, the city of Worms deployed substantial naval assets in two separate campaigns. In the early summer, the city council of Worms sent a fleet of warships (*naves bellicae*) as well as a large contingent of troops to the aid of the royal city of Kastel, located on the right bank of the Rhine, opposite from Mainz. There, they faced the military forces of Archbishop Siegfried of Mainz (1230–1249), who was in rebellion against the royal government because of the great struggle between the empire and the papacy. However, when Archbishop Siegfried was made aware of the size and strength of the forces from Worms, he withdrew from the siege so quickly that he did not even have time to dismantle his siege engines. Instead, he burned them so that they would not fall into the hands of the Worms city militia. Following this bloodless victory and the raising of the siege of Kastel, the city council of Worms authorized the deployment of a contingent of archers to serve at Kastel to help reinforce the garrison there.[29] About two months later, King Conrad IV of Germany (1245–1254) arrived in person in the Middle Rhine region to deal with Archbishop Siegfried's rebellion. In support of the military operations undertaken by the king, the city of Worms again deployed a substantial fleet of warships as well as a contingent of 200 well-equipped fighting men, who served with Conrad IV for six week.[30] The very next year, in 1243, the city of Worms again deployed a fleet on behalf of the king, along with an additional force of armored fighting men (*armigeri*) and archers.[31] In all three cases, the city chronicles of Worms emphasize that the costs of the operations were borne by the citizens of Worms, themselves.

In addition to having operational control over a considerable section of the Rhine River and the territories along its banks, the city of Worms also deployed large land-based forces to campaign throughout the middle Rhine region. In 1250, Worms mobilized 2,000 city militiamen as well as a specially trained contingent of 100 crossbowmen (*balistarii*) to serve with King Conrad's army as the latter campaigned against the anti-king William of Holland. The forces from Worms

---

men. Under normal circumstances in a pre-modern healthy environment, approximately one-third of the population was comprised of males between the ages of fifteen and forty-four. See Ansley Coale and Paul Demeny, *Regional Model Life Tables and Stable Populations* (Princeton, NJ, 1966). Under a scenario in which the city of Worms had to deploy 4,000 men on campaign and keep approximately 4,000 men in defense of its walls, the overall population of the city would have been a minimum of 25,000 people. Even if this minimum were increased by 50 percent, the population of Worms would still have amounted to less than half of the population of London at that time.

29 Boos, *Annales Wormatienses*, 149. Also see the discussion by David S. Bachrach, "Making Peace and War in the 'City-State' of Worms, 1235–1273", *German History* 24 (2006), 505–525.

30 Boos, *Annales Wormatienses*, 149.

31 Ibid., 150.

played an integral part during this campaign in capturing rebel strongholds, and devastating the territories of Conrad's opponents in the district. In 1260, during the so-called interregnum period, Worms committed even larger military forces to the field. During the siege of the fortress city of Alzey, Worms deployed 4,000 fighting men. Of particular interest in this context is the fact that the city of Worms also deployed numerous siege engines (*machinae et instrumenta*), many of which were purpose-built for this campaign.[32]

The city of Worms was by no means unique in its deployment of substantial military forces for offensive campaigns. The major Rhenish metropolitan sees of Cologne, Mainz, and Trier regularly mobilized large contingents of troops for offensive campaigns. Cologne's urban militia most famously fought triumphantly at the battle of Worringen in 1288 against Archbishop Siegfried of Cologne (1275–1297).[33] However, earlier in the century, the Cologne city militia had fought on behalf of their archbishop. In 1239, the citizens mobilized a fleet of warships (*naves armatae*) to aid Archbishop Conrad (1238–1261) against the count of Seyn.[34] The citizens of Mainz also played important military roles during the thirteenth century. In 1254, the city of Mainz was one of the leaders of the Rhenish league of cities (1254–1256), and its militia took part in several major military operations. In 1254, for example, Mainz led an alliance of cities against the territorial lord Werner of Bolanden. In the course of this campaign, the urban militias captured Werner's fortress at Ingelheim and tore it to the ground.[35] Two years later, in 1256, Mainz led another alliance of cities against Count Diether of Katzenelnbogen, attacking and then rendering indefensible his fortress at Rheinfels.[36] Trier, for its part, had a force of 1,500 mounted and armored troops (*equi phalerati*), who served in the army of the German king Adolf of Nassau (1292–1298) at the beginning of his reign in 1292.[37]

Smaller German cities also deployed quite large and well-equipped military forces. In 1242, for example, the citizens of Aachen held fast to the cause of the Staufen Emperor Frederick II (1212–1250) and King Conrad IV, and provided substantial military aid to help maintain royal control in the lower Rhineland. *Milites* and *cives* from Aachen served in the army of Count William IV of Jülich (1225–1278), the leader of the Staufen party in this region.[38] In 1269, the citizens

32 Ibid.
33 The most recent overview of the battle of Worringen and its political implications for the lower Rhineland is Ulrich Lehnart, *Die Schlacht von Worringen 1288: Kriegführung im Mittelalter* (Frankfurt am Main, 1993), but also see J. F. Verbruggen, *The Art of Warfare in Western Europe during the Middle Ages. From the Eighth Century to 1340*, trans. S. Willard and R. W. Southern (Woodbridge, 1997), 260–275.
34 *Annales Sancti Pantaleonis*, ed. H. Cardouns MGH SS 22 (Hanover, 1872, repr. Stuttgart, 1963), 531.
35 Boos, *Annales Wormatienses*, 154.
36 Ibid., 155.
37 *Chronicon Colmariense*, ed. Ph. Jaffé MGH SS 17 (Berlin, 1861, repr. Stuttgart, 1963), 257.
38 *Annales Sancti Pantaleonis*, 536.

of Colmar joined forces with Rudolf of Habsburg, the future German king (1273–1291), and captured the fortress of Reichenstein, located near modern Riequewihr in Alsace.[39] In 1274, the year after Rudolf became king, the citizens of Strasbourg provided him with 1,500 well-armed fighting men (*milites armati*) to help in his siege of the fortress city of Bern.[40] In 1287, the *consules*, that is the ruling council, of Strasbourg ordered their fellow citizens to prepare a force of 2,000 men to serve in Rudolf's army.[41]

The citizens of Strasbourg were accustomed to working with Rudolf because, before his accession as king in 1273, the Habsburg count had served as the commander (*dux*) of the city militia.[42] Indeed, the relationship of the city of Strasbourg with Rudolf went back to 1259 when its citizens gained independence from their bishop. In this year, the citizens mobilized a large army of both mounted and foot soldiers, which the city chronicler stated comprised half of the military forces of Strasbourg, in order to capture the episcopal stronghold of Mundolesheim located about 10 kilometers away. In addition to these troops, the good people of Strasbourg also deployed a siege train that included stone-throwing artillery (*lapidicidiae*) as well as other engines (*operarii*).[43]

Conclusion

In both Germany and England, cities deployed considerable military forces and played a major role in the conduct of war during the thirteenth and early fourteenth century. There were, however, several significant differences between the urban fighting forces of the two kingdoms. In England, urban militias operated legally only under royal authority. The militia forces of London, Bristol, and York, for example, did not undertake military campaigns against local earls or bishops. Even the raiding activities of coast cities against the ships of foreign powers were highly regulated by the crown. By contrast, cities such as Worms, Cologne, Mainz, and Strasbourg regularly undertook military action on their own initiative and in their own interests. They functioned much in the same manner as city states in northern Italy.

The size of the military forces deployed by individual cities is also significantly different in the two kingdoms. In aggregate, the military forces available from England's cities and towns, particularly naval forces, may well have been roughly equivalent to those in Germany. However, no individual English town or city deployed more than a fraction of the infantry forces of the mid- and large-sized German urban centers. London, for example, had a much larger population

39   *Annales Basilenses*, ed. Ph. Jaffé MGH SS 17, 193.
40   *Ellenhardi Chronicon*, ed. Ph. Jaffé MGH SS 17, 123.
41   *Annales Colmarienses Maiores*, ed. Ph. Jaffé MGH 17, 214.
42   *Ellenhardi Chronicon*, 123.
43   *Bellum Walterium*, ed. G. H. Pertz MGH 17, 109.

than Worms, perhaps three or four times greater, but the city generally was not called upon by the royal government to deploy 4,000 or even 2,000 men for single campaign in this period.[44]

A third distinction between English and German urban centers was the control over artillery. In England, the royal government maintained tight control over the possession and construction of siege engines, and there is no evidence that individual English cities or towns possessed their own heavy siege equipment. By contrast, German cities such as Worms and Strasbourg possessed and, indeed, built their own siege engines. These cities evidently employed their own military engineers and craftsmen. By contrast, in England such specialists were in the pay and under the control of the royal government. Finally, in the context of a conference that is focused on mercenaries and paid men, it is noteworthy that the English kings routinely paid the soldiers of urban militias, particularly during the reign of Edward I. By contrast, the cities of Germany usually paid for their own military operations, even when these were conducted on behalf of the king.

---

44 The only occasion on which the city militia of London was mobilized in substantial part for a military campaign on land was during the baronial war of 1264–1265. In 1264, Simon de Montfort brought the city of militia of London with him to Lewes, where the Londoners comprised about one-third of the army. According to William de Rishanger, the total baronial force at Lewes amounted to 15,000 men. See William de Rishanger, *The Chronicle of the Barons War*, ed. James Orchard Halliwell (London, 1840, repr. London, 1968), 27. Now also see the discussion of the war and this campaign by Adrian Jobson, *The First English Revolution: Simon de Montfort, Henry III and the Barons War* (London, 2012).

16

EDWARD I'S "CENTURIONS"

Professional soldiers in an era of militia armies

Introduction

In the thirteenth and early fourteenth century, a wide range of occupations in England were characterized by a high degree of professionalization.[1] In the military sphere, this type of professionalization has received considerable attention with regard to engineers, and particularly those employed in the construction of siege engines of various types.[2] Similarly, the men who constructed the king's crossbows and fabricated his crossbow quarrels have garnered significant attention from scholars.[3] With respect to military personnel, professional army

---

1 Regarding the details of professionalization in the building trades, including wage rates, and ranks within the professions see L. F. Salzman, *Building in England Down to 1540: A Documentary History* revised edn (Oxford, 1967); D. Knoop and G. P. Jones, *The Medieval Mason*, 3rd edn (Manchester, 1967); *Building Accounts of King Henry III*, ed. Howard M. Colvin (Oxford, 1971); M. de Boüard, *Manuel d'archéologie médiévale de la fouille à l'histoire* (Paris, 1975); and Paul Latimer, "Wages in Late Twelfth-and Early Thirteenth-Century England", *Haskins Society Journal* 9 (1997), 185–205.

2 See in this regard, A. Z. Freeman, "Wall-Breakers and River-Bridgers: Military Engineers in the Scottish Wars of Edward I", *Journal of British Studies* 10 (1971), 1–16; A. J. Taylor, "Master Bertram, Ingeniator Regis", *Studies in Medieval History Presented to R. Allen Brown* (Woodbridge,1989), 289–315; David S. Bachrach, "The Military Administration of England (1216–1272): The Royal Artillery", *Journal of Military History* 68 (2004), 1083–1104; idem, "The Royal Arms Makers of England 1199–1216: A Prosopographical Survey", *Medieval Prosopography* 25 (2004, appearing 2008), 49–75; and idem, "English Artillery 1189–1307: The Implications of Terminology", *English Historical Review* 121 (2006), 1408–1430.

3 Concerning the professionals who built crossbows and made crossbow bolts, see Alf Webb, "John Malemort—King's Quarreler: The King's Great Arsenal, St. Briavels and the Royal Forest of Dean", *Society of Archer Antiquaries* 31 (1988), 40–46; as well as David S. Bachrach, "The Crossbow Makers of England, 1204–1272", *Nottingham Medieval Studies* 47 (2003), 168–197; idem, "The Origins of the English Crossbow Industry", *Journal of Medieval Military History* 2 (2003), 73–87; idem, "Crossbows for the King: Some Observations on the Development of the Crossbow during the Reigns of King John and Henry III of England, 1204–1272", *Technology and Culture* 45 (2004), 102–119; and idem, "Crossbows for the King Part Two: The Crossbow during the Reign of Edward I of England (1272–1307)", *Technology and Culture* 47 (2006), 81–90, which also are included in this volume.

chaplains have been identified as serving in considerable numbers in the armies of Edward I.[4] Members of the military households of English kings also have been recognized by scholars to have developed noteworthy professional expertise in a wide array of military affairs, including logistics, recruitment, and commanding mounted forces in the field.[5]

Absent from discussions of professionalization up this point, however, have been lower ranking officers, particularly those who commanded units of foot soldiers. The burden of this paper, therefore, is to shed light on the large number of men who commanded infantry forces in Edward I's wars in Wales and in Scotland. In this context, I use the term professional to designate men whose primary occupation over a significant period of time was as soldiers.

In setting about to address this problem, the student of Edward I's reign is blessed with a vast corpus of administrative records that shed light on foot soldiers who served in royal armies, and on the officers who led them. These records include memoranda detailing the transfer of supplies, garrison rolls, horse valuation lists, memoranda for the replacement of horses, and, most important of all, pay records. The clerks who drew up these records, whether serving in garrisons or in the field with the troops, or in the more leisurely setting of the Chancery, Exchequer, or Wardrobe, tended to use standardized terminology to describe military matters, including particular types of equipment as well as types of fighting men.[6]

This habit of standardization and, indeed, of terminological precision is important as it allows the modern scholar to identify when new military classifications appear in the records, as well as to differentiate among the various classifications used by royal clerks to describe fighting men in the king's service. The current study relies on my investigation of a corpus of about 2,000 documents dealing with Edward's campaigns, principally in Scotland during the last decade of his reign. Many times this number of documents remain to be read and analyzed, so that the conclusions reached here must be considered tentative, but likely to be borne out by further research, at least for the ten years that are the focus of this study.

---

4   David S. Bachrach, "The Organisation of Military Religion in the Armies of Edward I of England (1272–1307)", *Journal of Medieval History* 29 (2003), 265–286.
5   Regarding the military household, see Norman Lewis, 'The English Forces in Flanders, August–November 1297', *Studies in Medieval History Presented to Frederick Maurice Powicke*, ed. R. W. Hunt, W. A. Pantin and R. W. Southern (Oxford, 1948), 310–318; C. Warren Hollister, *The Military Organization of Norman England* (Oxford, 1965), 171–76; J. O. Prestwich, "The Military Household of the Norman Kings", *Anglo-Norman Warfare*, ed. Matthew Strickland (Woodbridge, 1992), 93–128; and Michael Prestwich, *War, Politics and Finance under Edward I* (Totowa, NJ, 1972), 41–66
6   Regarding this tendency toward standardization and precision in administrative vocabulary, see Bachrach, "English Artillery 1189–1307", 1408–1430; and idem, "Crossbows for the King Part Two", 81–90.

Professional officers

Welsh troops in royal service, men of the shire levies, and men mobilized directly by their lords served, as is well known, in groups of twenty commanded by *vintenarii*. Generally, five such units were then organized in groups of 100 men commanded by *centenarii*, also denoted in royal administrative records by the synonym *constabularii*.[7] English *centenarii* serving in Edward's Scottish wars, who are the primary focus of this study, usually were equipped with an armored war horse, that is their mounts were *cooperti*. In a handful of cases, however, English *centenarii* can be identified as being equipped with non-armored horses, that is their mounts were *discooperti*.[8] Those *centenarii* who possessed an armored horse received a pay rate of 1 s. per day. Officers who had an unarmored horse received just half this rate, that is 6 d. per day.

Given the considerable expense involved in owning a warhorse, it is likely that the majority of the men who served as *centenarii* were of that economic stratum, below the knightly class, to whom King Edward appealed quite frequently to provide the bulk of his heavy cavalry, on the basis of long-established requirements for military service.[9] Many of the 1,200 *centenarii* whom I have identified by name, appear only a single time in the pay records, which I have examined thus far, as leading infantry companies in a single campaign during Edward I's reign. However, a considerable number of these *centenarii* can be identified leading infantry companies year after year, and in some cases for more than a decade.[10] These men clearly chose a military career, and can be identified as professional soldiers. A few examples will serve to illustrate the careers of these officers.

Professional *centenarii*

It would appear that there were, in fact, several career paths open to men who wished to serve as professional infantry officers in Edward I's armies. The first of these is illuminated by the service of a man named Nicholas de Preston, whom I

---

7 Prestwich, *War, Politics*, 106; and the earlier observation on this point J. E. Morris, *The Welsh Wars of Edward I* (Oxford, 1901), 95–96.

8 See, for example, National Archives E372/132 for Robert Dalton who is a *centenarius discoopertus* from Derbyshire.

9 See, for example National Archives E101/6/30 and E101/6/31 for the mobilization orders for 1,270 men with *equi cooperti* from York, Surrey, Norfolk, Suffolk, Gloucestershire, Hertfordshire, Essex, and Herefordshire in 1298. For a discussion of the mobilization of mounted forces in 1298, see Prestwich, *War, Politics*, 68–70. With my collaborator Oliver Stoutner, I subsequently tested this theory with respect to *centenarii* from Yorkshire and Northumberland, and found that many of these men do not appear in the tax rolls for these counties, and likely were below the economic level suggested in the text. See David S. Bachrach and Oliver Stoutner, "Military Entrepreneurs in the Armies of Edward I of England (1272–1307)", *Haskins Society Journal* 27 (2015, published 2016), 179–193.

10 These men are listed in Appendix 1 at the end of the chapter.

have first identified on campaign in early March 1298. He was present at the relief of the fortress of Berwick on Tweed with his company of Lancashire foot archers, with along with more than 2,600 men from that shire.[11] It is not clear whether Nicholas served in Scotland in 1299, but he was certainly back again through the summer and autumn of 1300 as a *centenarius* from Lancashire.[12] For at least part of this period, the Lancashire men were in the garrison at Berwick, which remained a major English magazine and fortress throughout Edward's Scottish wars.[13]

Nicholas was certainly back in royal service no later than 1303, once more in command of foot soldiers as a *centenarius*. However, rather than commanding men from Lancashire, he was listed by Richard de Bremesgrave, the royal receiver at Berwick, among sixteen *centenarii*, who collectively commanded 1,210 foot soldiers *de diversibus comitibus*.[14] As will be discussed in more detail later in this chapter, the designation of foot soldiers as coming *de diversibus comitibus*, rather than from a specific county, was the way in which royal clerks designated men, who had volunteered for service over the winter months or for extended garrison duty, and served together in mixed units of men from all over England. Nicholas was still at Berwick in 1304, again leading a *centena* of foot archers *de diversis comitibus*.[15] However, by June of this year, Nicholas, who was still at Berwick, was now again in command of a *centena* of foot archers from Lancashire. He had assumed command of 101 Lancashire men who had been detached from the *centenae* commanded by two other Lancashire *centenarii* named Walter de Hoton and Adam Chernoke.[16] It is possible, and perhaps even likely, that the men in charge of the Lancashire forces at Berwick turned to Nicholas because of his previous role as a *centenarius* from this county when Walter and Adam departed the army. It appears that Nicholas departed from Berwick later in the summer of 1304, as the garrison roll for August notes that seventy-seven men from his *centena* were seconded for service with another *centenarius* named Thomas de Berwick.[17] There is no record of Nicholas in either 1305 or 1306, but he again went on campaign in 1307. He commanded one of seven *centenae* of foot archers from Lancashire mustered by John de Segrave, one of Edward's chief lieutenants in Scotland.[18] At the beginning of the campaign Nicholas led 100 foot archers but this number was reduced substantially to just sixty men after the troops arrived in Scotland.[19]

---

11 National Archives E101/7/2 9r.
12 National Archives E101/612/25.
13 On 3 August, Nicholas commanded some sixty-five foot archers in the garrison at Berwick. See National Archives E101/8/20.
14 National Archives E101/10/28.
15 National Archives E101/12/17.
16 National Archives E101/11/15.
17 National Archives E101/11/15.
18 National Archives E39/4/3.
19 National Archives E101/612/2.

In sum, Nicholas de Preston led troops from Lancashire in at least four campaigns in Scotland over a period of nine years, and also led a group of men from several counties in the permanent garrison at Berwick for at least a year as well. The number of years in which Nicholas served may well be higher, as there are still many thousands of documents pertaining to these campaigns that I have not yet read. Nicholas' lengthy tours of duty over many years clearly indicate that he had taken on a career as a military officer who specialized in the command of foot soldiers.

A second career path that can be identified among Edward's professional infantry officers saw these men pass back and forth between leading infantry companies and serving as *soldarii*. The term *soldarius*, which had been used since at least the mid-twelfth century by the authors of narrative sources to designate paid fighting men, appears to have been introduced into official use in England by royal clerks in the context of Edward's campaign to Flanders in 1297.[20] This term was used to designate men who volunteered to serve as heavy cavalry in Edward's army, but who were not obligated to do so either because their income level was too low, or because the gentry from their shire had not been mobilized for service in a particular campaign.[21]

A useful example of this type of transition between *centenarius* and *soldarius* is provided by one of the most splendidly named of all of Edward's *centenarii*, John Bagepus. He first appears in royal pay records on 22 May 1295 leading a contingent of ninety-six Cheshire foot archers in Wales, as part of a force of eighteen infantry *centenae* from that shire.[22] The next piece of information that I have identified, thus far, regarding John's service comes from the administrative accounts produced in the course of the large-scale mobilization of English troops in late 1297 to put down a major Scottish rebellion, led by, among others, William Wallace.[23] It was in the context of this campaign that Nicholas de Preston, discussed earlier, also first appears in the royal pay records.

John Bagepus commanded a *centena* of foot archers from Cheshire at Newcastle on Tyne in mid-December 1297 as part of a force of 1,800 men led by the earl of Surrey.[24] John's company took part in the relief of the fortress at Roxburgh in

---

20 The first use of this term that I have identified in English government records is in BL MS 7965, which was edited by Bryce and Mary Lyon, *The Wardrobe Book of 1296–1297: A Financial and Logistical Record of Edward I's 1297 Autumn Campaign in Flanders Against Philip IV of France* (Brussels, 2004), 97. It should be noted that some of the *centenarii* who remained in service in Scotland after the departure of their troops for home were denoted as *valletti* rather than as *soldarii*. On this point, see *Liber quotidianus contrarotulatoris garderobae*, ed. John Topham (London, 1799), 256.

21 I plan a focused study on the *soldarii* in the near future. Now see Bachrach and Stoutner, "Military Entrepreneurs", passim.

22 National Archives E101/5/18 17r.

23 Regarding the campaign of 1297–1298 in Scotland, see the discussion by Prestwich, *Edward I* (Yale, CT, 1997), 476–483.

24 National Archives E101/7/2 2v.

February 1298, and then briefly remained in the garrison there.[25] Sometime before the earl of Surrey's troops arrived at Roxburgh, however, John received promotion to the rank of *millenarius*, perhaps as a result of earlier campaign experience in Wales.[26] The rank of *millenarius*, that is the commander of 1,000 men, appears to have been a brevet rather than a permanent rank.

John Bagepus was one of thirteen *millenarii* present at Roxburgh from 2–14 February, who led 146 *centenae* comprising 14,845 foot archers.[27] By no later than 3 March 1298, John, still holding the rank of *millenarius*, and his *centena* of foot archers had arrived at Berwick.[28] John remained there with his men throughout March and the remainder of the spring, as is indicated by a list of payments issued on 10 June to officers of foot, including Bagepus, by Richard de Bremesgrave, the chief logistics officer at Berwick.[29]

John Bagepus also likely continued to serve in the garrison at Berwick throughout the remainder of 1298 and the first half of 1299.[30] At some point, however, his unit was demobilized and sent back to Cheshire. From late July 1299, at the latest, John Bagepus served at Berwick as a *soldarius* rather than as an infantry officer. Among the other forty-eight *soldarii* in the garrison at Berwick in the summer of 1299 was a man named John le Balancer, who had also held the rank of *millenarius* alongside John Bagepus in March 1298.[31] John Bagepus continued to serve for the next five years, apparently continuously, as a *soldarius* up through the spring of 1304, in the garrisons at both Berwick and Edinburgh.[32] However, at some point in 1304, John again assumed command of a *centena* of infantry, and is identified as a *centenarius* in a 1304 pay roll for troops in Scotland.[33]

In considering John Bagepus' career, we see a man commanding infantry units in at least three separate campaigns over a period of nine years. He was sufficiently respected by his superiors that he was elevated to the brevet rank of *millenarius* during the 1298 campaign in Scotland. Whether John's service as *soldarius* in the period 1299–1304 also included periods in command of infantry *centenae* must await further research. Other officers, however, certainly did pass back and forth between service as *soldarii* and *centenarii*.

One man who followed this path was John de Herle, who first appears serving in Scotland in 1300 as a *centenarius* leading a unit of foot archers from Northumberland.[34] In that same year, John appears in the garrison roll at the fort

---

25 Ibid.
26 National Archives E101/7/2 7v.
27 Ibid.
28 Ibid., 10r.
29 Ibid., 12 v and C47/2/17 nr 4
30 National Archives E1101/7/8 1v.
31 National Archives E101/7/2 10r.
32 National Archives E101/13/34, E101/9/16, E101/10/5, and E101/11/1.
33 National Archives E101/11/29 2r.
34 National Archives E101/13/34.

of Dumfries as a *soldarius*, alongside two other men who also had served as Northumberland *centenarii* named John de Luken and Robert de Herle. The latter was perhaps the brother of John de Herle.[35] In 1301, John de Herle was again serving as an infantry officer leading 130 foot archers from Northumberland.[36] Once more he appears alongside Robert de Herle who also was in command of a *centena* of Northumberland foot archers.[37] John was still serving in Scotland as a *centenarius* in February 1302, although his command had now been reduced to just thirty-three men.[38] But in September 1302, John appeared in the garrison roll for Bothwell as a *soldarius*.[39] He continued as a *soldarius* in 1303, serving at Linlithgow, and in April 1304, he received just under £10, that is approximately 200 days of wages in arrears, for his service as a *soldarius* at this same fort.[40] John de Herle was back in command of a *centena* of foot archers from Northumberland when he received pay in August 1304.[41] In 1305, John de Herle was back in the garrison at Linlithgow, again serving as a *soldarius*.[42]

This regular back and forth between service as a *soldarius* in various Scottish garrisons and as commander of infantry *centenae* from Northumberland gave John de Herle considerable experience leading shire troops. However, just as importantly, by staying in Scotland on an almost permanent basis, John was able to keep well informed, through personal experience, about the state of political and military affairs in the regions in which he led his men. Obviously, both of these types of experience were valuable to John's commanders in the field, and may well have given them confidence that officers such as John could effectively lead even semi-trained levies from the shires. Just as importantly, John de Herle's career is clearly indicative of his status as a professional officer.

Officers following a third career path, like Nicholas de Preston discussed earlier, also began by leading troops from the shire levies, but then took command of units of what appear to have been contract companies of professional foot archers, recruited *de diversis comitibus*.[43] One officer with a similar command experience as Nicholas de Preston, named Richard le Ronet, is described in a royal pay account from 1307 as commanding "foot soldiers from various parts of England, who have been retained for wages at the order of the king".[44] These contract companies of foot archers can be seen to parallel the contract companies of mounted

---

35   Ibid.
36   MS ADD 7966A 108v.
37   Ibid.
38   National Archives E101/7/13.
39   National Archives E101/10/5.
40   National Archives E101/11/1 and E101/11/16.
41   National Archives E101/12/16.
42   National Archives E101/12/38.
43   Prestwich, *War, Politics*, 106.
44   National Archives E101/373/15 13v, "*pedites diversarum partium Anglie retentum ad vadi iuxta ordinacionem Regis*".

troops raised by numerous magnates at the direction and pay of the royal government during Edward I's reign.[45]

Another officer of this type named Gilbert Modi led a company of Northumberland foot archers in Scotland from December 1297 until March 1298, and took part in the relief of Roxburgh.[46] Gilbert was back in Scotland in command of Northumberland troops in 1300, remaining there for at least four months.[47] The next year, however, Gilbert took on command of a *centena de diversis comitibus*, which served at Berwick from July through October 1301.[48] By the end of the year, Gilbert had given up command of this *centena* and joined the garrison at Kirkintilloch as a *soldarius*, mirroring the transition between service as a *centenarius* and *soldarius* seen in the case of John Bagepus and John de Herle, mentioned earlier.[49]

By February 1302, Gilbert was back in command of a unit of foot archers when he received supplies of grain for his seventy-five men from Peter de Chichester, one of the Edward I's household clerks, who was given responsibility for delivering provisions to troops stationed in Scotland.[50] No later than August, Gilbert had again given up command of his *centena* and reentered the garrison at Kirkintilloch, where he served as a *soldarius* until December 1302.[51] In June 1303, Gilbert was at the fortress of Linlithgow. He was still at Linlithgow in July, but by August 1303, he was at Edinburgh, where he is recorded receiving one half-ton of grain on behalf of three other men named Maurice the Welshman, William Spucky, and William the Hobelar.[52] He received approximately three-eighths of a ton of grain that had been distributed from the stores at Berwick, suggesting that he was again in command of a unit of foot soldiers. We again see Gilbert in May 1304, when he was in command of a contract *centena de diversis comitibus* numbering ninety-three men.[53] In August of that year, Gilbert's company had grown to 156 foot archers.[54] Whether Gilbert served in Scotland in 1305 remains unclear, but he

---

45 A considerable number of military contracts survive from the Scottish campaigns. See, for example, National Archives E101/9/15 for a contract with William of Durham for ten heavy cavalry. Also see E101/681/1 for a list of military retainer agreements with Aymer de Valence, earl of Pembroke; Thomas de Berkeley; and Robert Hastang. On the practice of writing up military contracts with magnates for the purpose of obtaining units of mounted forces, see Prestwich, *War, Politics*, 61–64.

46 National Archives C47/2/20.

47 For the command of Northumberland troops see National Archives E101/13/34. For his receipt of just over £6.5 for his service to date, see E101/684/46. At a shilling per day, this amounts to 130 days of service.

48 MS ADD 7966A 109r, 110 v, 111v, 113v, and 114r; and National Archives E101/8/28.

49 National Archives E101/9/16.

50 National Archives E101/7/13. Regarding Peter de Chichester's service under King Edward, see Prestwich, *Edward I*, 158.

51 National Archives E101/10/5, E101/10/14 and E101/11/1.

52 National Archives E101/10/28, nr 28, 30, 31.

53 National Archives E101/12/17.

54 National Archives E101/12/16.

was back for at least five months in 1306, from May to September, again in command of a *centena* of foot archers numbering ninety-five men.[55]

As was true of the other officers noted earlier, Gilbert Modi gained enormous experience leading troops in Scotland, serving there during at least six years between 1298 and 1306. Whether in garrison or in the field, this type of experience was invaluable for maintaining discipline and tactical control over troops, including both men of the shire levies, and those soldiers who volunteered to serve in one of the contract companies. Moreover, as is true of the other officers discussed thus far, Gilbert Modi's career is clearly that of a professional officer.

The three career paths considered, thus far, concern the command of companies of foot archers. The final group of professional officers, by contrast, commanded crossbowmen (*balistarii*). For the most part, crossbowmen served in units of just twenty soldiers, and their officers, correspondingly, were *vintenarii* rather than *centenarii*. Moreover, the officers of crossbow units tended not be mounted and earned only half as much as their mounted contemporaries, that is 6 d. a day rather than 1 s. Another important difference is that virtually all of the crossbowmen whom they commanded, particularly in Edward's Scottish wars, were professionals rather than men of the shire levies.[56]

Robert Lankerdaunce, for example, appears to have begun his military career during Edward I's campaign in Wales in 1295, leading a small unit of just nine *balistarii* in May and June of that year.[57] The pay records indicate that at this early date, Robert's men all came from Cheshire since they are listed alongside the *centenae* of foot archers from that shire rather than separately under the rubric of *balistarii*. During the Scottish wars, royal clerks separated out crossbowmen from other foot soldiers and listed them under the rubric of *balistarii* in both pay records and garrisons rolls.[58]

In 1298, Robert joined the garrison at Berwick as a *vintenarius* in command of nineteen *balistarii*.[59] Robert remained in Scotland, more or less continuously, up through May 1301, commanding his unit of crossbowmen at both Berwick Castle and at the *castrum* of Lochmaben.[60] I have not yet found information regarding Robert's service in 1302, but in 1303 he was in command of a unit of

---

55 National Archives E101/13/16.
56 I have found no information regarding the mobilization of crossbowmen from the shire levies for the wars in Scotland. By contrast, at least one summons of troops from Hampshire, Dorsetshire, and Wiltshire in 1295, called for both foot archers and crossbowmen to serve in Gascony. See *Calendar of Patent Rolls Edward I AD 1292–1301* (London, 1895, repr. 1971), 151.
57 National Archives E101/5/16 and E101/5/18.
58 For administrative purposes, the separation of crossbowmen from foot archers was useful because the men were paid different wages, and required different types of supplies.
59 National Archives E101/7/8; and C47/2/17, which records Robert's receipt of a barrel of wine for his men.
60 National Archives E101/7/20; E101/684/46; E101/13/34; and MS ADD 7966A 64v.

crossbowmen at Lochmaben.[61] By August 1304, Robert was back in the garrison at Berwick again commanding a unit of crossbowmen as their *vintenarius*.[62]

William de Gascony, another *vintenarius* of crossbowman, had a similar career in Scotland. He first appears in 1300, receiving supplies of grain and wine for his nineteen men at Perth on the River Tay in central Scotland.[63] It is not clear whether William served in Scotland in 1301, but in 1302 and 1303, he commanded his unit of crossbowmen in the garrison at Berwick before being transferred to Roxburgh.[64] In 1304, William's unit was back at Berwick.[65] I have not found information regarding William's service in 1305, but he was in command of a unit of crossbowmen at the fortress at Tibbers (Tokborhull?) no later than February 1306.[66]

As is clear from this brief account, Robert and William gave their superiors the benefit of years of experience of service in Scotland, in much the same manner as the *centenarii*, discussed earlier, who commanded *centenae* of foot archers. It should be emphasized, however, that unlike the officers of foot archers, the *vintenarii* of the crossbow units appear to have served almost exclusively in garrisons rather than in the field.[67]

Professional soldiers

The luxury of having large number of officers with years of command experience may well have been one of the reasons King Edward chose year after year to mobilize many thousands of men from the shire levies for military service, both in Wales and in Scotland. But he might also have been influenced in this decision by his knowledge that these shire levies would benefit from the presence of substantial numbers of professional soldiers both in garrison and in the field. The "stiffening" effect of a core of professional soldiers had long been recognized in the medieval West from Charlemagne onward. To cite but one example, Harold Godwinson's housecarls appear to have done an admirable job of maintaining the resolve of the militia forces at Senlac until Harold's unfortunate meeting with a Norman arrow. I alluded, earlier, to two categories of professional foot soldiers in

---

61 National Archives E101/11/19 4v.

62 National Archives E101/11/15.

63 National Archives E101/13/36 nr 219.

64 For Berwick see National Archives E101/9/14; E101/11/1; and 101/9/4. For Roxburgh see E101/10/26.

65 National Archives E101/11/15 and E101/11/16 nr 38, 43, 60, and 61.

66 National Archives E101/13/16 17v.

67 There are very good tactical reasons for deploying crossbowmen in fortifications. The most important of these is that crossbows could be aimed at individual targets while the crossbowman took cover in the defenses offered by the fortifications that Edward garrisoned throughout Scotland and Wales. In addition, a major liability of the crossbow is the considerable length of time required to load the weapon. Crossbowmen deployed in the field require more protection from the enemy while they are loading their weapons than is the case with archers equipped with self-bows.

Edward's armies—the crossbowmen and the foot archers *de diversis comitibus*. I will now describe these in greater depth.

In both 1277 and 1287, King Edward deployed urban militia units equipped with crossbows for his invasions of Wales. In 1277, for example, ninety-eight London crossbowmen under two officers (*constabularii*) reported to Chester in July 1277 for service in Wales.[68] Similarly, a unit of crossbowmen from the Oxford militia served in Chester in this year.[69] Units of London crossbowmen and Bristol crossbowmen also were mobilized for service in Wales in 1287.[70] The practice of deploying urban militiamen armed with crossbows continued in a limited way even during the latter part of Edward's reign. In 1296, for example, a unit of London crossbowmen was dispatched to help guard the Isle of Wight.[71] Edward II also made use of urban militia forces, deploying a unit of crossbowmen from York to serve at Berwick in 1315.[72]

Early in his reign, Edward supplemented these militia units of crossbowmen with large numbers of professional *balistarii* from Gascony, particularly during the Second Welsh War of 1282–1284.[73] During the final third of his reign, however, Edward appears to have relied on domestic companies of professional crossbowmen. These domestic contract companies may have numbered, in aggregate, as many as 1,000 soldiers, particularly during periods of substantial mobilization. In this context, I have been able to identify by name more than seventy *vintenarii* of crossbowmen who served in Scotland between 1298 and 1307.[74] Of these officers, at least twenty led companies in 1304. In July of this year more than 450 crossbowmen served together in the garrison at Berwick, alone.[75]

The detailed pay records for the Scottish wars, and especially documents that recorded payments of wages in arrears, make clear that the individual crossbowmen in these contract companies also served for long periods of time, often stretching on for years. On 12 May 1304, for example, a *balistarius* named Roger de Sutton from the unit of Jordan of Oxford received his back pay at Berwick.[76] The memorandum noted that Roger had spent the entire year in 1303 and the first four

---

68 National Archives E101/3/11 and C62/56 9r.
69 National Archives E372/121 11v.
70 National Archives E101/4/20; E372/132 22r; C62/64 4r; and E372/133 29r. For an examination of the deployment of urban militias by both Henry III and Edward I, see David S. Bachrach, "Urban Military Forces of England and Germany c. 1240–c. 1315, A Comparison", in *Mercenaries and Paid Fighting Men: The Mercenary Identity in the Middle Ages*, ed. John France (Turnhout, 2008), 231–242 and in this volume.
71 National Archives E101/5/27.
72 National Archives E101/14/33.
73 See National Archives E101/3/27 for a total of eighty-five mounted and 876 foot crossbowmen from Gascony serving in Wales. Also see the discussion by Prestwich *War, Politics*, 108, who identifies a total of 210 mounted crossbowmen and 1,313 Gascon crossbowmen serving on foot.
74 See Appendix 2 for the list of crossbow officers whom I have identified thus far.
75 National Archives E101/12/17 and E101/13/16.
76 National Archives E101/11/16 nr 45.

and half months of 1304 in service at Berwick under Jordan's command. Other *balistarii* stationed in Scotland for long terms of service were seconded from unit to unit. A crossbowman named John le Archer, for example, served under the *vintenarius* John Dansard at Berwick for part of 1303.[77] He then transferred to Jordan of Oxford later in the year and remained with his new commander well into 1304.[78] It is not yet clear at whether the individual crossbowmen were free to join a new company when their contracted period of service ended, or if the decision about seconding men from unit to unit rested with the officers, themselves.

The substantial numbers of crossbowmen on what appears to have been long-term service in Scotland led Edward's government to station specialists in crossbow production and repair in many of the fortresses there, including Berwick, Jedburgh, Lochmaben, Dumfries, Edinburgh, Linlithgow, and Kirkintilloch.[79] In addition, specially trained artisans employed by the royal government produced enormous quantities of crossbow quarrels for use in Scotland. Production and repair facilities for quarrels were organized at Newcastle on Tyne, Berwick, Roxburgh, and Dumfries.[80] In addition, the government purchased considerable quantities of crossbow ammunition, including an order for 104,000 crossbow bolts in 1298.[81] All in all, Edward's government devoted considerable resources to ensure that a sizeable contingent of professional crossbowmen were deployed in Scotland on a regular basis. However, this effort was dwarfed by the costs associated with maintaining large numbers of professional foot archers there throughout the period 1298–1307. It is to this group that I now turn.

As Michael Prestwich has noted, royal clerks generally grouped together all foot soldiers in the pay records and garrison rolls according to the shire from which they came.[82] The two major exceptions to this practice, especially in the context of Edward's Scottish wars, were the *balistarii*, noted earlier, and the *centenae de diversis comitibus*. Early in Edward's reign, royal clerks used the phrase *de diversis comitibus* to denote that a particular paymaster was conducting units of infantry from several shires, e.g. ten *centenae* of foot soldiers from Cheshire and eight *centenae* of foot soldiers from Shropshire.[83] By 1295, however, royal clerks had altered their practice so that the phrase *de diversis comitibus* now meant that the men in a particular *centena* were drawn from a several shires. A memorandum regarding soldiers' wages in Wales in May 1295, for example, identifies infantry companies from Lancashire, Cheshire, Shropshire, and also *de diversis comiti-*

---

77 National Archives E101/10/26.
78 National Archives E101/10/26 and E101/11/20.
79 National Archives E101/7/10; C47/22/9 nr 71; E39/93/18; E101/9/9; E101/10/6; E101/11/1; E101/12/10; E101/68/1; E101/8/27; E101/12/18.
80 National Archives C62/74 5r; E101/8/24; E101/9/30 nr 25; and E101/14/1.
81 National Archives C62/74 6r.
82 Prestwich, *War, Politics*, 106.
83 National Archives E101/3/11 for the use of the phrase in this manner in 1277; and E101/3/30 for the use of the phrase in this manner in 1282.

bus.[84] Royal clerks continued to draw this distinction between men of the shire levies and men serving in the companies *de diversis comitibus* through the entire period 1297–1307.[85]

It remains unclear precisely how these units were recruited. However, it seems likely that the men in these *centenae* were drawn from the pool of soldiers who had previous experience serving in the levies, particularly those from the northern shires. Many of the commanders of these companies originally hailed from the north, including men such as Henry Benteley of Northumberland, Henry de Manefeld of Cumberland, John Bristol of York, Philip de Montgomery from York, and Richard de Ludlowe from Northumberland.[86] All of these officers had led units of foot archers from their home shires and thereby had a large number of contacts on which to draw when recruiting men to serve in their professional companies on a long-term basis. The *centenae de diversis comitibus* in aggregate numbered many thousands of men, and they played a substantial role in several campaigns. During the course of 1304, for example, no fewer than forty-nine *centenae de diversis comitibus* served in Scotland.[87] In July of that year, forty-three *centenarii* commanding units *de diversis comitibus*, had a total of 3,923 foot archers under their command.[88]

In order to ensure that the men of the contract companies, and perhaps some of the shire units as well, were equipped for military operations, the royal government devoted considerable resources to stockpiling arrows in Scottish fortresses. The substantial efforts to supply the army at the siege of Stirling in 1304 with both arrows and bows are well known.[89] However, it should also be noted that every garrison in Scotland had on staff both a smith and a carpenter, usually with an assistant.[90] These craftsmen could turn out arrow shafts, and potentially, arrow heads if the smiths had received training in this skill. In addition, at least four garrisons at Newcastle on Tyne, Berwick, Roxburgh, and Dumfries had fletchers on staff.[91] The royal government regularly obtained supplies of glue and feathers for

---

84   National Archives E101/5/16.
85   See, for example, National Archives E101/7/8; E101/13/36; E101/13/34; MS ADD 7966A; E101/7/13; E101/11/1; E101/12/17; and E101/373/15.
86   For Henry Benteley see MS ADD 7966A; E101/8/20; E101/13/34; E101/9/16; E101/9/9; and E101/12/16. For Henry de Manefeld see E101/8/18; E101/3/9; E101/13/36; E101/13/34; E101/7/13; E101/11/1; E101/11/15; and E101/11/29. For John Bristol see E101/8/20; E101/13/34; MS ADD 7966A; E101/7/13; E101/12/16; and E101/12/17. For Philip de Montgomery see E101/11/15; E101/11/29; and E101/13/34. For Richard de Ludlowe see E101/13/34; MS ADD 7966A; E101/7/13; and E101/12/16.
87   National Archives E101/11/15; E101/11/29; E101/12/16; and E101/12/17.
88   National Archives E101/12/17.
89   National Archives E101/12/12. Prestwich, *War, Politics*, discusses the supply of bows and arrows to the besiegers at Stirling, but does not identify the efforts of the royal government to supply these arms on other occasions.
90   See, for example, the list of garrisons in E101/13/34.
91   National Archives C62/74 5r; E101/8/24; E101/9/30 nr 25; and E101/14/1.

the use of these fletchers to make arrows as well as for the fletchers who attached feathers to crossbow bolts.[92]

Conclusion

The bulk of Edward I's troops in the period 1296–1307 were militiamen from the shire levies. It seems, in addition, that many and perhaps a majority of the officers who led them also should be classified as militia. Nevertheless, noteworthy numbers of *centenarii* who commanded units of foot archers, and virtually all of the *vintenarii* who commanded crossbowmen in Scotland were professionals. This cadre of officers provided the king with a wealth of leadership experience and tactical knowledge regarding the peculiar realities of warfare in Scotland. In addition, the thousands of soldiers serving in contract units of foot archers and crossbowmen had the potential to impart an important element of continuity and esprit de corps, as well as practical experience to their more numerous but less well-trained comrades in arms from the shire levies.

Appendix 1: *Centenarii* who can be identified serving in three or more campaigns. These men are organized alphabetically by shire.

Cheshire:

John Bagepus E101/5/18 (1295) C47/2/17 (1297–1298) E101/6/35 E101/6/39 (1298) (1298) E101/7/2 (1298) E101/7/8 (1298–1299) E101/13/34 (1300) E101/9/9 (1301) E101/9/13 (1301) E101/9/16 (1301) E101/9/30 (1302) E101/10/5 (1302) E101/10/12 (1302) E101/11/1 (1302–1303) E101/612/8 (1303) E101/11/15 (1303–1304) E101/12/18 (1303–1304) E101/11/29 (1304)

Cumberland:

Adam Talon E101/13/34 (1300) E101/11/15 (1303–1304) E101/11/29 (1304)

Henry de Manefeld E101/8/18 (1300) E101/13/34 (1300) E101/13/36 (1300) E101/7/13 (1302) E101/11/15 (1303–1304) E101/11/29 (1304) E101/3/9 (1306)

Hugh de Norton MS ADD 7966A (1300–1301) E101/7/13 (1302) E101/11/1 (1302–1303) E101/11/1 (1302–1303) E101/11/15 (1303–1304) E101/12/16 (1304)

Jordan Kendale E101/8/20 (1300) E101/13/34 (1300) MS ADD 7966A (1300–1301) E101/11/15 (1303–1304)

Richard le Bret E101/612/25 (1300) E101/8/20 (1300) E101/11/15 (1303–1304) E101/11/29 (1304)

---

92 National Archives C47/22/4; E 372/139 6r; E372/145 19v; C62/74 5r; and C62/76 2r.

Gloucestershire:

Nicholas le Lung MS ADD 7966A (1300–1301) E101/9/17 (1301) E101/12/16 (1304)

Richard de London MS ADD 7966A (1300–1301) E101/9/17 (1301) E101/12/16 (1304)

Herefordshire:

Dominus Milo Pichard E101/13/34 (1300) MS ADD 7966A (1300–1301) E101/12/16 (1304)

Thomas Pichard E101/13/34 (1300) MS ADD 7966A (1300–1301) E101/12/16 (1304)

William Deverois C47/2/17 (1297–1298) E101/13/34 (1300) E101/9/17 (1301) MS ADD 7966A (1300–1301) E101/12/16 (1304)

William Warin E101/13/34 (1300) E101/9/17 (1301) MS ADD 7966A (1300–1301) E101/12/16 (1304)

Lancashire:

Adam Clou E101/6/1 (1296–1297) E101/8/20 (1300) E101/12/17 (1304)

John de Noteshaw E101/5/16 (1295) E101/7/2 (1298) E101/12/17 (1304)

Nicholas de Preston E101/7/2 (1298) E101/13/34 (1300) E101/612/25 (1300) E101/8/20 (1300) E101/10/28 (1303) E101/11/15 (1303–1304) E101/12/17 (1304) E39/4/3 (1307) E101/612/2 (1307)

Peter le Taillour de Preston E101/612/25 (1300) E101/12/17 (1304) E39/4/3 (1307)

Robert Whetele E101/13/34 (1300) E101/7/13 (1302) E101/11/15 (1303–1304) E101/11/29 (1304) E101/11/15 (1303–1304)

William de Worthington E101/8/20 (1300) E101/9/14 (1300–1303) E101/11/1 (1302–1303)

Northumberland:

Gilbert Modi C47/2/20 (1298) E101/13/34 (1300) E101/684/46 (1300) MS ADD 7966A (1300–1301) E101/9/16 (1301) E101/8/28 (1301) E101/7/13 (1302) E101/10/5 (1302) E101/10/14 (1302) E101/10/28 (1302) E101/11/1 (1302–1303) E101/11/15 (1303–1304) E101/12/16 (1304) E101/12/17 (1304) E101/13/16 (1305–1307)

Henry Benteley E101/8/20 (1300) E101/13/34 (1300) MS ADD 7966A (1300–1301) E101/9/16 (1301) E101/9/9 (1301) E101/7/13 (1302) E101/10/5 (1302) E101/11/1 (1302–1303) E101/12/16 (1304)

John de Herle E101/13/34 (1300) MS ADD 7966A (1300–1301) E101/7/13 (1302) E101/10/5 (1302) E101/11/1 (1303) E101/116 (1304) E101/12/16 (1304) E101/12/38 (1305)

Richard de Bilton E101/8/20 (1300) E101/13/34 (1300) E101/684/52 (1300) MS
    ADD 7966A (1300–1301) E101/9/16 (1301) E101/10/5 (1302) E101/11/1
    (1302–1303) E101/11/15 (1303–1304)
Richard de Ludlowe E101/13/34 (1300) MS ADD 7966A (1300–1301) E101/7/13
    (1302)
Robert de Bilton E101/9/16 (1301) E101/10/5 (1302) E101/11/15 (1303–1304)
Robert de Herle E101/13/34 (1300) MS ADD 7966A (1300–1301) E101/7/13
    (1302) E101/11/16 (1303–1304) E101/12/16 (1304) E101/373/15 (1306)
William de Aspele E101/13/34 (1300) MS ADD 7966A (1300–1301) E101/12/16
    (1304)
William de Dalton E101/684/52 (1300) E101/10/5 (1302) E101/11/1 (1302–1303)
    E101/11/15 (1303–1304)
William le Grant E101/8/20 (1300) E101/13/34 (1300) MS ADD 7966A (1300–
    1301) E101/12/16 (1304)
William de Hedon MS ADD 7966A (1300–1301) E101/7/13 (1302) E101/12/16
    (1304)

Nottinghamshire:

Adam Carbonel E101/13/34 (1300) E101/13/36 (1300) E101/8/20 (1300)
    E101/10/5 (1302) E101/11/15 (1303–1304) E101/11/29 (1304) E101/12/17
    (1304)
Hugh de Clover E101/13/34 (1300) MS ADD 7966A (1300–1301) E101/11/15
    (1303–1304)
Hugh de Oconner E101/8/20 (1300) E101/13/34 (1300) E101/13/36 (1300) MS
    ADD 7966A (1300–1301) E101/7/13 (1302) E101/11/15 (1303–1304)

Shropshire and Staffordshire:

Clement de Casterton E101/13/34 (1300) MS ADD 7966A (1300–1301) E101/7/13
    (1302) E101/11/15 (1303–1304) E101/11/29 (1304) E101/12/16 (1304)
Egidius de Staundon E101/13/34 (1300) MS ADD 7966A (1300–1301) E101/7/13
    (1302) E101/12/16 (1304)
John de Charleton C47/2/17 (1297–1298) C47/2/20 (1298) E101/13/34 (1300)
    MS ADD 7966A (1300–1301) E101/12/16 (1304)
John Langele E101/13/34 (1300) MS ADD 7966A (1300–1301) E101/12/16
    (1304)
John de Spreham E101/13/34 (1300) MS ADD 7966A (1300–1301) E101/12/16
    (1304) E101/12/17 (1304)
John de Stirchester C47/2/20 (1298) E101/8/20 (1300) E101/12/17 (1304)
Robert Dalton E101/7/2 (1298) E101/684/52 (1300) E101/684/46 (1300)
    E101/13/34 (1300) MS ADD 7966A (1300–1301) E101/9/16 (1301)
    E101/10/5 (1302) E101/11/1 (1302–1303) E101/11/15 (1303–1304)
    E101/12/18 (1303–1304) E101/11/29 (1304

Stephen de Acton E101/5/16 (1295) E101/5/18 (1295) E101/13/34 (1300) MS ADD 7966A (1300–1301) E101/7/13 (1302) E101/12/16 (1304)

Dominus Theobald miles de Neyville E101/13/34 (1300) MS ADD 7966A (1300–1301) E101/12/16 (1304)

William de Brideshale E101/5/16 (1295) E101/5/18 (1295) E101/7/2 (1298) E101/12/17 (1304)

William Griffin E101/13/34 (1300) MS ADD 7966A (1300–1301) E101/12/16 (1304) E101/12/17 (1304)

Yorkshire:

Henry de Manefeld E101/612/25 (1300) E101/8/20 (1300) MS ADD 7966A (1300–1301) E101/12/16 (1304)

Hugh de Baskerville E101/13/34 (1300) MS ADD 7966A (1300–1301) E101/7/13 (1302) E101/12/16 (1304)

John de Bristol E101/8/20 (1300) E101/13/34 (1300) MS ADD 7966A (1300–1301) E101/7/13 (1302) E101/12/16 (1304) E101/12/17 (1304)

John de Langton E101/13/34 (1300) E101/684/52 (1300) E101/9/16 (1301) E101/10/5 (1302) E101/11/1 (1302–1303) E101/11/15 (1303–1304) E101/11/29 (1304)

John de Upsale E101/13/34 (1300) MS ADD 7966A (1300–1301) E101/7/13 (1302) E101/11/1 (1302–1303) E101/11/15 (1303–1304) E101/11/16 (1303–1304) E101/12/16 (1304)

Paul Ketell E101/612/25 (1300) E101/8/20 (1300) E101/13/34 (1300) E101/11/15 (1303–1304) E101/13/16 (1305–1307)

Richard de Middelham E101/13/34 (1300) MS ADD 7966A (1300–1301) E101/12/16 (1304)

Richard filius Henry de Wakefield E101/612/25 (1300) E101/8/20 (1300) MS ADD 7966A (1300–1301) E101/12/16 (1304)

Robert Pothou E101/13/34 (1300) MS ADD 7966A (1300–1301) E101/12/16 (1304)

Thomas de Arches E101/13/34 (1300) MS ADD 7966A (1300–1301) E101/7/13 (1302)

William de Alta Ripa E101/13/34 (1300) MS ADD 7966A (1300–1301) E101/11/15 (1303–1304) E101/12/16 (1304)

William de Bateley E101/8/20 (1300) E101/13/34 (1300) MS ADD 7966A (1300–1301) E101/11/15 (1303–1304) E101/12/16 (1304)

William de Den E101/13/34 (1300) MS ADD 7966A (1300–1301) E101/12/16 (1304)

Westmoreland:

Henry de Burgo E101/8/20 (1300) E101/11/1 (1302–1303) E101/11/15 (1303–1304)

Shire not yet identified:

Adam Prendergast E101/7/8 (1298–1299) E101/13/34 (1300) E101/11/1 (1302–1303) E101/12/17 (1304)

Henry Normant E101/13/34 (1300) MS ADD 7966A (1300–1301) E101/12/16 (1304)

Ingeram Scrope C47/2/17 (1297–1298) E101/7/8 (1298–1299) E101/12/17 (1304)

John de Hibernia MS ADD 7966A C47/2/20 (1298) E101/13/34 (1300) E101/7/13 (1302) E101/11/1 (1302–1303) E101/12/28 (1303) E101/12/18 (1303–1304) E101/11/16 (1303–1304) E101/12/20 (1304) E101/12/16 (1304)

John de Pimberton E101/684/52 (1300) E101/13/34 (1300) E101/11/1 (1302–1303) E101/11/15 (1303–1304)

John de Shropham E101/13/34 (1300) E101/11/1 (1302–1303) E101/12/18 (1303–1304)

John Uthank E101/9/16 (1301) E101/10/5 (1302) E101/12/18 (1303–1304)

John Vigrous E101/11/1 (1302–1303) E101/11/20 (1303) E101/12/18 (1303–1304)

Madoc le Waleys E101/684/46 (1300) E101/13/34 (1300) E101/13/34 (1300) E101/7/13 (1302) E101/10/5 (1302) E101/11/1 (1302–1303) E101/11/15 (1303–1304)

Marmaduke de Bilton E101/9/16 (1301) E101/10/5 (1302) E101/11/1 (1302–1303)

Meredith Waleys E101/9/16 (1301) E101/10/5 (1302) E101/11/1 (1302–1303)

Nicholas de Arderne E101/10/5 (1302) E101/11/1 (1302–1303) E101/12/18 (1303–1304)

Nicholas de Denlaco E101/10/5 (1302) E101/11/1 (1302–1303) E101/12/18 (1303–1304)

Patrick le Sauser E101/10/5 (1302) E101/11/1 (1302–1303) E101/12/18 (1303–1304) E101/11/16 (1303–1304)

Peter de Leyberton E101/9/16 (1301) E101/10/5 (1302) E101/11/1 (1302–1303)

Philip Morteyn E101/10/5 (1302) E101/11/1 (1302–1303) E101/12/18 (1303–1304)

Philip Northbridge E101/7/8 (1298–1299) E101/9/16 (1301) E101/10/5 (1302) E101/11/1 (1302–1303) E101/11/15 (1303–1304) E101/11/16 (1303–1304)

Ralph de Benton E101/10/5 (1302) E101/11/1 (1302–1303) E101/11/16 (1303–1304) E101/12/18 (1303–1304)

Richard de Dalton E101/13/34 (1300) E101/11/1 (1302–1303) E101/373/15 (1306)

Richard Galoun E101/9/16 (1301) E101/10/5 (1302) E101/11/1 (1302–1303) E101/12/18 (1303–1304)

Robert Jolif E101/684/52 (1300) E101/10/5 (1302) E101/11/1 (1302–1303) E101/11/1 (1302–1303)

Robert de Wallingsford E101/9/16 (1301) E101/11/1 (1302–1303) E101/12/18 (1303–1304)

Roger de Ravensdale E101/7/8 (1298–1299) MS ADD 7966A (1300–1301)
  Ee101/9/16 (1301) E101/10/5 (1302) E101/11/1 (1302–1303) E101/11/15
  (1303–1304) E101/11/29 (1304) E101/13/16 (1305–1307)
Roger de Sutton E101/9/16 (1301) E101/10/5 (1302) E101/11/1 (1302–1303)
  E101/12/18 (1303–1304)
Sevan de Mare E101/9/16 (1301) E101/10/5 (1302) E101/11/1 (1302–1303)
  E101/11/15 (1303–1304) E101/12/18 (1303–1304)
Simon de Middenhale E101/684/52 (1300) E101/13/34 (1300) E101/684/46
  (1300) E101/11/1 (1302–1303) E101/11/15 (1303–1304)
Stephen de Walton E101/7/8 (1298–1299) E101/13/34 (1300) E101/9/16 (1301)
  E101/10/5 (1302) E101/11/1 (1302–1303)
Thomas de Bradford E101/684/52 (1300) E101/13/34 (1300) E101/9/16 (1301)
  E101/10/5 (1302) E101/11/1 (1302–1303) E101/11/15 (1303–1304)
Thomas de Langton E101/684/46 (1300) E101/11/15 (1303–1304) E101/11/29
  (1304)
Thomas Ramsey E101/13/34 (1300) E101/9/16 (1301) E101/10/5 (1302)
  E101/11/1 (1302–1303) E101/11/15 (1303–1304) E101/12/18 (1303–1304)
  E101/12/38 (1305)
Thomas de Ravensdale E101/8/20 (1300) E101/13/34 (1300) E101/9/16 (1301)
  E101/7/13 (1302) E101/10/5 (1302) E101/11/1 (1302–1303) E101/11/15
  (1303–1304) E101/12/18 (1303–1304)
Walter Aynhou C47/2/20 (1298) E101/9/16 (1301) E101/10/5 (1302) E101/11/1
  (1302–1303) E101/12/18 (1303–1304)
Walter de Chiltone E101/9/16 (1301) E101/10/5 (1302) E101/11/1 (1302–1303)
) E101/12/18 (1303–1304)
Walter de Greneford E101/9/16 (1301) E101/10/5 (1302) E101/11/1 (1302–1303)
  E101/12/18 (1303–1304)
William de Batel E101/13/34 (1300) E101/7/13 (1302) E101/11/15 (1303–1304)
William de Corbridge E101/9/16 (1301) E101/10/5 (1302) E101/11/1 (1302–
  1303) E101/12/18 (1303–1304)
William de la Mare E101/13/34 (1300) E101/11/1 (1302–1303) E101/11/15
  (1303–1304) E101/11/29 (1304)
William Menant E101/684/52 (1300) E101/13/34 (1300) E101/10/5 (1302)
  E101/11/1 (1302–1303) E101/11/15 (1303–1304)
William de Northbridge E101/9/16 (1301) E101/10/5 (1302) E101/11/1
  (1302–1303)
William de Skyeburn E101/684/52 (1300) E101/10/5 (1302) E101/11/1 (1302–
  1303) E101/11/16 (1303–1304)
William de Strother E101/7/2 (1298) E101/9/16 (1301) E101/10/5 (1302)
  E101/11/1 (1302–1303) E101/11/15 (1303–1304) E101/12/18 (1303–1304)
William Usher E101/684/52 (1300) E101/9/16 (1301) E101/10/5 (1302)
William de Weston E101/7/8 (1298–1299) E101/684/52 (1300) E101/10/5 (1302)
  E101/11/1 (1302–1303) E101/12/17 (1304)

Appendix 2: Crossbow officers organized alphabetically

Adam de Dimolin C47/2/3 (1282)
Adam Warin E101/12/17 (1304)
Alex Malton E101/684/52 (1300)
Galfrid de Sherewind E101/13/16 (1305–1307)
Henry de Cherlton E101/13/34 (1300) E101/11/15 (1303–1304)
Henry de Greneford E101/5/10 (1295)
Henry le Taverner E101/13/34 (1300) E101/11/15 (1303–1304) E101/11/16 (1303–1304)
Hugh de Norton E101/7/8 (1298–1299) C47/2/17 (1297–1298)
Hugh Scarlet E101/7/2 (1298) E101/12/17 (1304)
Ingeram de Oxford E101/13/34 (1300)
John de Alta Ripa E101/13/34 (1300) E101/11/1 (1302–1303) E101/11/16 (1303–1304) E101/12/18 (1303–1304)
John Bachelor E101/13/34 (1300) E101/11/1 (1302–1303)
John Ballamer E101/7/2 (1298)
John de Cama E101/7/2 (1298)
John de Crandon E101/13/16 (1305–1307)
John Dansard E101/10/26 (1303)
John de Kenilworth C47/2/3 (1282)
John Latilletur MS ADD 7966A (1300–1301)
John de March E101/13/34 (1300) MS ADD 7966A (1300–1301)
John de Oxford E101/13/34 (1300) E101/10/26 (1303)
John Pragin C47/2/20 (1298)
John Scarlet E101/10/26 (1303)
John Shubode E101/13/16 (1305–1307)
John Tamour E101/13/16 (1305–1307)
John de Thornhull E101/7/2 (1298)
John Wymandeslan E101/13/16 (1305–1307)
Jordan Oxford E101/684/53 (1300) E101/9/9 (1301) E101/11/1 (1302–1303) E101/11/20 (1303) E101/10/26 (1303) E101/11/15 (1303–1304) E101/11/16 (1303–1304) E101/12/18 (1303–1304)
Meredith E101/9/9 (1301)
Nicholas Mewe E101/7/8 (1298–1299) E101/12/17 (1304)
Nicholas de Leyster C47/2/3 (1282)
Peter de Leicester E101/11/15 (1303–1304)
Peter de Malding E101/7/8 (1298–1299)
Peter le Porter E101/11/15 (1303–1304)
Richard de Clavering E101/7/8 (1298–1299) C47/2/17 (1297–1298
Richard de Farnham E101/12/17 (1304)
Richard le Port E101/9/9 (1301)
Richard le Tailleur E101/11/15 (1303–1304)
Richard Wyghton MS ADD 7966A (1300–1301) E101/11/15 (1303–1304)

Robert Cole E101/7/2 (1298)

Robert Darkdamme E101/13/34 (1300)

Robert Fanlin E101/7/8 (1298–1299) E101/9/9 (1301)

Robert de Heketon E101/12/17 (1304)

Robert Lankedaunce E101/7/8 (1298–1299) C47/2/17 (1297–1298) E101/7/20 (1299) E101/684/46 (1300) E101/13/34 (1300) MS ADD 7966A (1300–1301) E101/11/19 4v (1303) E101/11/15 (1303–1304)

Robert Lanerky E101/10/26 (1303)

Roger de Arwe C47/2/17 (1297–1298) E101/7/8 (1298–1299)

Roger de Lam E101/11/1 (1302–1303) E101/12/18 (1303–1304) E101/13/16 (1305–1307)

Roger Lanham E101/13/34 (1300) E101/11/20 (1303) E101/11/16 (1303–1304)

Simon de London E101/12/17 (1304)

Simon le Tanner de London E101/7/2 (1298)

Thomas Foreys E101/13/16 (1305–1307)

Thomas Tegan E101/684/52 (1300) E101/13/34 (1300) E101/11/15 (1303–1304) E101/12/38 (1305) E101/13/16 (1305–1307)

Thomas de la Valeye C47/2/3 (1282)

Walter Baret E101/7/2 (1298)

Walter Brom E101/12/17 (1304)

Walter Kanesham MS ADD 7966A (1300–1301)

William Aurifaber E101/11/1 (1302–1303)

William de Bere E101/7/8 (1298–1299)

William de Boston E101/9/9 (1301)

William de Corham E101/7/8 (1298–1299)

William de Cornbrill E101/11/15 (1303–1304)

William de Dorking C47/2/3 (1282)

William of Gascony E101/13/36 (1300) E101/9/14 (1300–1303) E101/11/1 (1302–1303) E101/9/4 (1303) E101/10/26 (1303) E101/11/15 (1303–1304) E101/11/16 (1303–1304) E101/13/16 (1305–1307)

William de Maltone E101/11/1 (1302–1303)

William Newerk E101/11/1 (1302–1303)

William de Northampton E101/11/1 (1302–1303)

William Panetir E101/9/9 (1301) E101/9/18 (1301)

William Porter E101/13/34 (1300) E101/11/15 (1303–1304)

William Roleston E101/13/16 (1305–1307)

William de Selkirk E101/11/1 (1302–1303)

William de Stenwyk E101/10/26 (1303)

William le Tenturer E101/7/2 (1298)

William de Wakefield E101/7/8 (1298–1299) C47/2/17 (1297–1298)

INDEX

Tables are indicated by page numbers in **bold**.